The Economic Decline of
Modern Britain

Also by David Coates

Teachers Unions and Interest Group Politics
(Cambridge University Press, 1972)
Social Stratification and Trade Unionism (with George Bain and Valerie Ellis) (Heinemann, 1973)
The Labour Party and the Struggle for Socialism
(Cambridge University Press, 1975, 1981)
Labour in Power? A Study of the Labour Government 1974–79
(Longman, 1980)
A Socialist Primer. Vol. 1: Socialist Arguments (ed. with Gordon Johnston) (Martin Robertson, 1983)
A Socialist Primer. Vol. 2: Socialist Strategies (ed. with Gordon Johnston) (Martin Robertson, 1983)
A Socialist Primer. Vol. 3: A Socialist Anatomy of Britain (ed. with Gordon Johnston and Ray Bush) (Polity Press, 1985)
The Context of British Politics (Hutchinson, 1984)

Also by John Hillard

Political and Legal Environments, An Introduction
(Open University Press, 1976)
Institutions and Political and Legal Environments
(Open University Press, 1976)
Political and Legal Factors and Regulation
(Open University Press, 1976)

The Economic Decline of Modern Britain

The Debate between Left and Right

Edited by

David Coates
Senior Lecturer
University of Leeds

John Hillard
Lecturer
University of Leeds

HARVESTER WHEATSHEAF
London   New York   Toronto   Sydney   Tokyo   Singapore

First published 1986 by
Wheatsheaf Books Ltd
Reprinted by
Harvester Wheatsheaf
66 Wood Lane End, Hemel Hempstead,
Hertfordshire, HP2 4RG

A division of
Simon & Schuster International Group

Printed and bound in Great Britain by
BPCC Wheatons Ltd, Exeter

British Library Cataloguing in Publication Data

The Economic decline of modern Britain: the debate
    between left and right
    1. Great Britain—Economic conditions—1945–
    I. Coates, David   II. Hillard, John
    330.941'0858   HC256.6
    ISBN 0–7450–0107–6
    ISBN 0–7450–0145–9 Pbk

3 4 5   93 92 91 90

Contents

Contents

Introduction

There are fashions in problems no less than in dress. Intellectual output follows fashion in much the same way as the chain-store imitates the fashion house. In such a process, an original conception is amplified and distorted until its presence is all pervasive and sense of originality gone. The decline of Britain has been an intellectual topic long in fashion, dating back to at least the end of the nineteenth century. The so-called 'British disease' now permeates virtually every aspect of contemporary social experience. The problem of decline has spawned a literature of ever-growing size and sophistication, but the debate tends to surface in strange places and in a multiplicity of guises. In consequence, much occurs in places which are simply unknown or inaccessible to the general reader or average student. It tends to appear in dusty reviews, obscure journals, pamphlets and easily forgotten volumes.

Naturally, political and ideological divisions run deep in this literature and it is immediately apparent that each viewpoint is consolidated only by reading its own. So doing, a particular corpus of thought ploughs backwards and forwards along the same furrow in relative ignorance of parallel arguments elsewhere. The overall debate comprises a literature which is united in its awareness of a problem but hopelessly divided in its sources and footnotes. The Right cite the Right, the Left the Left, in a dialogue of the deaf where the specification of the problem and its remedies are rarely sharpened by a systematic confrontation between opposites. The orthodoxies of Right and Left tend only to come together on the hustings and then necessarily in a truncated and simplified form.

Our main objective in assembling a comprehensive collection of writings on the subject of the British decline is to deepen understanding by putting the different orthodoxies alongside each other. At the very least, such an exercise can help to overcome difficulties that readers experience in gaining access to the full range of material, and do so in ways which can collate the range of issues in the debate, isolate the areas of conflict within it and examine the wide range of diagnoses and prescriptions. We hope the collection will also identify those areas where assertion has replaced evidence and beliefs have taken precedence over facts. Moreover, by bringing together arguments derived from different vantage points, an anthology such as this can begin to break down the areas of silence and ignorance between political traditions and can illustrate the closeness of the relationship between political position and social analysis. Finally, the book may help the genuinely uncertain and open-minded to move towards an independent assessment of the nature of Britain's decline, by enabling them to survey quickly the arguments and opinions of others. In sum, what follows is a survey of the key recent statements against which policy options have to be set and political choices justified.

The readings share a broadly similar concern, but the political specification of the problem changes along a spectrum from Radical Right to Revolutionary Left. Although there are marked differences in focus, the arguments gathered here at least share a common concern with aspects of *material* life and a preoccupation with real variables. Some analysts may be tempted to concentrate on such themes as moral decay, falling personal standards, and a lack of respect for law and authority. But such dimensions of Britain's decline—if that is what they are—enter here only at the margin; and arguments of an overtly racist kind will not surface at all. There are levels beneath which arguments are too evil to be reproduced and this consideration has dictated the bottom line in the selection. In similar fashion, the causal factors singled out by moving along the political spectrum tend to be both more prosaic and more tangible than those hypotheses based on broad cultural shifts which are cited with equal facility by Born-again Christians and critical theorists. Broad cultural shifts *are* significant, as many of the readings will suggest if you read between the lines, but the primary task here is to locate factors specific to the British state to which such broad and general processes can, at best, constitute only a contextual backdrop.

There are two main themes upon which there exists a consensus amongst all participants in the debate. First, all sense that there is a *problem*, that things in some very real sense are going badly in Britain and need to be changed. Secondly, there is near unanimity on the *cumulative* nature of British decline. All recognise that the causative network is complex and interactive and that the process of decline, once established, seems to be self-sustaining. You will discover that the ways in which the process is described are markedly different, but that the underlying syndrome is constant. There are various patterns of causation but the direction of change always points downwards. There is the *low investment–low investment* pattern in which low investment yields low productivity and competitiveness, low productivity and competitiveness yield low profits and poor business confidence, and low profits and poor business confidence produce low investment. Or there is the *high interest rate–high interest rate* pattern, in which high rates of interest deflate home demand and investment, low home demand and investment produce low production runs, low productivity and poor competitiveness, and low productivity and poor competitiveness necessitate high interest rates to assuage the confidence of speculative capital in view of the resulting balance of payments shortfall. Or there is the *low wage–low wage* pattern, in which low wages produce low demand, and sluggish home markets set up patterns of investment and productivity which keep wages down. And since parallel patterns of 'virtuous' cumulative causation are operating in more favoured nations abroad, the gap between weak and strong opens up steadily, to lock the weak economies (including the British) into the syndrome of cumulative decline from which every government, of whatever political persuasion, is so determined to break.

Where basic disagreements arise initially is in the choice of the elements which are regarded as indicative of the problem. For some it is the recent growth of unemployment and its apparent intractability. For others, it is the longer established propensity of the national economy to suffer productive neglect and relatively poor economic growth. For another section, decline in economic terms is best illustrated by the relegation of the national economy in the league table of international performance on the share of world trade, on foreign penetration of domestic markets and on overall standard of living. For yet others, the problem lies deeper still, and is indicated by the industrial disintegration of the national economy through the phasing-out of local manufacturing activity and the emergence of a decayed economy sustained internationally by the earning power of oil revenue, international investment and banking operations.

Where disagreement in the literature occurs most strongly is over the social forces and institutions which are accorded primary blame for the instigation and sustenance of the process of cumulative decline. Once more, there is a surprising degree of consensus: this time, on what the key institutions actually are and on the need to situate those institutions in the social structure and history from which they have emerged. Accordingly, some weight is invariably attached to the factors of class position and experience, to group practices and cultural norms, and to the impact of the processes of industrialisation, political democratisation and imperial degeneration. The fundamental conflict within the literature arises over how these elements are interconnected and to whom primary responsibility is to be accorded, and this conflict can be mapped along a conventional Left/Right spectrum.

Arguments from the centre of that spectrum tend to throw in the kitchen sink: from trade union restrictive practices on the one side, through managerial incompetence and government interference to socially-exclusive selection processes and rigid establishment norms on the other. As you will see, movement from this centre then follows conventional political lines. Moving to the Right highlights the working class, trade unions and state crisis; Moving to the Left focuses on the ruling class, finance capital and state crisis. Yet this is not to imply that the analyses offered by the Left and Right are really so very different. Indeed, in many ways, their *analyses* (as distinct from their *solutions*) coincide to a strikingly large degree, so that in moving towards the outer limits of the spectrum, the respective viewpoints seem separated only by a fine line. In particular, both the Radical Right and the Revolutionary Left are acutely aware that the genesis of British decline derives from contradictions within the class structure: between public welfare and private accumulation; between the power of organised labour and managerial control; between market processes and democratic social-ism. Also, the extremes of Left and Right will both persuade you that the Centre will no longer hold, that Keynesian corporatism consolidated a balance of class forces which slowed the rate of capital accumulation without creating the political force capable of generating alternative non-market sources of capital and productivity. Britain indeed became a prime case of capitalism in an oxygen-tent. They will both agree that British decline will be halted only by social change of a fundamental kind: back towards a reliance on market forces (according to the Right), or on democratic socialist lines (to the Left). But what each will deny, of course, is the viability of the solution offered by the other. For the Right and the Left there is only one solution (or range of solutions) and their imposition requires a political struggle, of which Thatcherism is but an opening and (even from the Right) inadequate blow.

The readings collected here attempt to enliven the debate between Left, Right and Centre. Part I contains papers which clarify the problem and to which other sections are a response. Then, sequentially, representative views across the political spectrum are reproduced. Part V comprises general statements which identify and survey the broad positions. Finally, a conclusion and suggestions for further reading follow. We have tried our best to bring together all the major contributions to the debate, but we are conscious that on such a wide topic some material may have slipped through unnoticed, and that new material may well be inspired in reaction to the collection here. It would be good to think that, if this is the case, these ommissions could be rectified in later editions of this collection. We will be pleased to hear from readers with material they think appropriate for inclusion in editions to come. We can be contacted at the Department of Politics or School of Economic Studies, University of Leeds, Leeds LS2 9JT.

PART I:
The Deindustrialisation of Britain

Nigel Harris is keen, in the first paper in this section, to establish deindustrialisation as a process which is common to all advanced capitalist economies—certainly to Berlgium, France, Holland, Sweden and the USA, and even latterly to West Germany and Italy. He explains the fall in manufacturing employment in all these countries as the consequence of four processes: the changing relationship between 'productive' and ancillary labour; the effects of the world slump after 1973–74; the relative obsolescence of existing core industries in the context of a new international division of labour; and the centralisation of control within the system as a whole. He argues too that the differential impact of these processes on different economies reflects the intensity with which a competitive struggle is being waged on a world scale, between centralised economic units, and singles out Britain as particularly vulnerable to that competition.

This is a theme which surfaces, differently expressed, in a widely-cited article by *Ajit Singh*. This article is clear on the conceptual problems associated with the notion of deindustrialisation, and cautions against any automatic assumption that the loss of manufacturing employment is either abnormal or a problem. Singh argues that it is in the British case because manufacturing industry has so important a role to play in the balance of payments and in stimulating economic growth. Even this becomes a problem only because, and to the degree that, the enhanced productivity of the shrunken manufacturing sector is insufficient to satisfy consumer needs at home whilst selling enough abroad to meet necessary imports at socially acceptable levels of output, employment and exchange rates. The British problem arises, Singh argues, because locally-based manufacturing is becoming increasingly unable to do that, as evidenced in the deterioration of its trade performance since 1971. There is a basic weakness in the UK manufacturing sector which, when

3

taken with the fall in employment in manufacturing, makes deindustrialisation a matter of serious concern and a source of cumulative economic decline.

John Hughes then documents the speed and severity of that decline in the 1970s, and the stagnation of manufacturing output by the end of that decade. When that is set against the 30 per cent growth of output in the 1960s, the scale and recent intensification of Britain's manufacturing decline becomes obvious. Associated with it too, in Hughes' view, are significant falls in the rate of growth of productivity, employment in manufacturing industry, trade performance, investment in plant and equipment, and manufacturing's contribution to GDP. Hughes argues that these weaknesses are particularly evident in vehicle building and metal manufacture, construction and mechanical engineering, and have been made worse by what he sees as Thatcherite mismanagement of the economy.

Hughes' final remarks on Thatcherism open the debate on causation, and Part I ends with a characteristically economist's survey of what those causes might in the first instance be. *Leslie Manison* examines in turn factors accounting for the low rate of capital formation—the capacity to invest, the willingness to do so, and the resulting productivity of any investment made. He draws attention to the UK's low domestic savings ratio, to a falling rate of return on investment, to high labour costs, to low rates of growth of labour productivity, and to the cost of financing new investment. He explores why the productivity of gross investment in the UK should be so low, examining the rate of growth of the capital stock, its obsolescent industrial distribution, the weakness of the export sector, the impact of domestic deflation on rates of capital utilisation, restrictive labour practices in the context of rising unemployment, and the shortage of technical manpower and managerial talent. The result, as he observes, has been a low rate of return on new capital formation in the manufacturing sector, as the cumulative consequence of this interconnected set of economic weaknesses. It is to the root of those weaknesses that the rest of the volume is then addressed.

1. Deindustrialisation*

Nigel Harris

A spectre is haunting the Treasuries of the advanced capitalist countries. It is not yet, regretably, the spectre of proletarian revolution, but of the obsolescence of capitalism itself, or rather of its great productive engine, industry. In Britain, the trend is known as 'deindustrialisation'. Elsewhere, less alarmed commentators speak glibly of the advent of 'post-industrial society'; but the scale of the problem is revealed in some of the recent figures:

Table 1.1 *Percentage change of the labour force employed in industry*

	(1961)	1974	1978
Belgium		41.2	36.7
Holland		35.6	32.5
France		39.6	37.1
Britain	(47.5)	42.3	39.7
West Germany		47.3	45.1
Italy		39.4	38.3

In West Germany's case, the full decline in these four years is concealed by the fact that the total German labour force was simultaneously declining—by 600,000—so that the absolute loss of jobs in industry is a full 913,000, larger than any other Common Market country. In sum, the European Economic Community has lost 2.5 million jobs in industry, and gained 3 million in services (since the labour force has been increasing faster than the small increase in jobs in most of these countries, there has been a simultaneous increase in unemployment).

*This is an extract from an article which first appeared in *International Socialism*, quarterly journal of the Socialist Workers Party, available from 1S Journal, PO Box 82, London EC.

Changes taking place in four years of world slump would not necessarily indicate a structural decline in industry. For that, we would need a longer period of time. Comparing the past record for the major capitalist powers with 1975–76, what is the picture?

Three countries expanded the size of the manufacturing labour force:

(a) *Japan*. Manufacturing workers in Japan reached a total of 8.5 million in 1957 (or roughly the same as the peak in Britain, 8.6 million in 1961), 10.1 million in 1961 and 13.5 million in 1975. As a proportion of the Japanese labour force, these three years recorded: 19.8 per cent, 22.5 per cent and 25.8 per cent (that is, still *below* the British proportion of 1976: 30 per cent).

(b) *West Germany* reached 8.4 million in 1958, 9 million in 1961, and then declined very slightly to 8.9 million in 1975. As a proportion of the German labour force in these three years, the figures are: 33.4 per cent, 34.7 per cent and 35.9 per cent (these figures are for *manufacturing* employment; earlier ones were for industrial employment, so the two are not comparable).

(c) *Italy*, a late-starter in the advanced capitalist league, increased its manufacturing labour force from 5.5 million in 1961 to 6.1 million in 1975; the proportions were respectively, 27.7 and 32.6 per cent.

Of the rest of the advanced capitalist countries, most experienced decline:

(a) *Belgium*'s peak manufacturing employment—1.2 million—came in 1965, and from there it declined slightly to 1.1 million in 1975. The proportion declined more sharply, from 33.9 to 30.1 per cent.

(b) *France* peaked at 5.9 million in 1974, and then began a slow decline; as a proportion, from 28.1 to 27.9 per cent.

(c) *Holland* reached its target manufacturing employment in 1965, at 1.2 million, and then declined slightly to 1.1 million in 1975; from 28.2 to 24 per cent.

(d) *Sweden*'s highpoint, 1.2 million, came in 1965, followed by a slight decline to 1975, 1.1 million; from 32.4 to 28 per cent.

(e) The *United States*' manufacturing jobs increased from 22 million in 1961 to 26.7 million in 1973, thereafter tending to decline—from 32.5 per cent to 31.6 per cent and in 1975, 29 per cent.

On the latest figures, it seems that West Germany and Italy have also joined the downward trend.

Rising labour productivity, however, can ensure that while manufacturing employment declines both absolutely and relatively, the value of manufacturing output is frequently increasing. For example, the value of manufacturing output as a proportion of GDP increased in Belgium from 31.4 per cent (1965) to 34.5 per cent (1975); in Holland in the same period, from 39.1 to 41.8 per cent. In the United States, by contrast, the proportion fell from between 27 and 29 per cent in much of the 1960s to 26 per cent in 1975.

What are the reasons for the decline? It is difficult to separate the effects of at least four processes taking place: changes in the relationship between 'productive' and ancillary labour; the effects of world slump from 1973–74, with particularly severe effects on heavy industry (steel, coal, shipbuilding, heavy engineering, etc.); the relative obsolescence of existing core industries, and the relocation of manufacturing areas geographically; the increasing centralisation of the system. To take these elements in turn:

The relative decline of productive employment—while labour productivity increases—has massive implications for agitational work against the system, but none for the system as a whole in economic terms. Much of what is called 'unproductive labour' is vital in making possible 'productive labour', and much of productive labour produces waste. The relationship between the two fluctuates constantly, and a relative decline throughout the world system in and of itself has no particular significance, it constitutes a redistribution of activities within the working class, part of efforts to increase the rate of exploitation, and, for us, a hint of the promise of the mastery of labour in the system.

The world slump has had the most dramatic effects on old heavy industry. Increased competition for a stagnating market has threatened all marginal producers, kept alive where they have survived by protection and subsidies from the local State on a purely temporary basis. The devastation of the western steel industry is well known, from the closures in Alsace Lorraine, the threats in Benelux, Sweden, in Britain and the Indiana–Ohio area of the States; the same is also familiar in the massive destruction of shipbuilding. The job losses in 'manufacturing' have been most marked in this area. The key geographical regions present a similar picture. Take for example the old heartland of German capitalism, the Ruhr. Since 1966, 400,000 jobs have been lost in the region, 330,000 people have left the region, and still the regional unemployment rate is double the national average.

Capitalism is a system that, in its process of change, affects areas very differently. Thus, the transition from the industrial core of the late nineteenth century (textiles, iron and steel, coal, shipbuilding, etc.) to that of the period after the second world war (vehicles, light engineering, petrochemicals) was also a shift in location. In Britain, it involved a shift from the old industrial centres in the North-East, the

North-West, Scotland and Northern Ireland, to the West Midlands and the South-East. The system follows the same principles as that involved in open-cast mining or a plague of locusts—the devastation of an area takes place for a given period, then industry moves on. Now, it is said, the post-war core of industry is increasingly obsolete. Those areas dependent upon this set of industries will increasingly decline: this is the death sentence for the old West Midlands, based upon vehicles and engineering. The process in Britain is complicated by the decline of light manufacturing in the urban areas, producing another phenomenon, the 'inner-city crisis'.

New areas, it is proposed, will generate the next core of industries to push the system forward. In the United States, the decline in the north-east (and now also in the north) is contrasted to the developments in California in the west, and the explosive growth in the south, Texas and Georgia among others. The core industries proposed are already well known: electronic products, petrochemical products, marine biology products, etc. It is not usually mentioned in this connection that the last major transition of the system, from 1914 to 1945, involved mass unemployment, Nazism in Germany, two world wars and various other 'transitional factors'.

Most of the last three factors are presented frequently by commentators on the question. There is however another element that gives meaning to all three, the differential effects of slump and structural change on the leading competitors. The different degrees of 'deindustrialisation' on different countries reflects the savagery with which the world competitive struggle is now being fought. Implicit in deindustrialisation is an increased centralisation of the system, increased dominance and control by a smaller and smaller group of powers. The hysteria arises, not from some common process, but because of the unequal distribution of the process between countries, so that some advanced capitalist countries are being shoved out of the competition.

Changes in the share of exports of the twelve leading manufacturing exporters—not the most accurate guide—gives us some crude index of this centralisation process. Three countries—the United States, Japan and West Germany—had a combined share of these exports of about 38 per cent in 1952; by 1970, they held 50 per cent and on average, 52 per cent between 1972 and 1977. The United States is one of the countries in relative decline in manufacturing terms, and this is partly reflected in the export figures. West Germany's share of the exports of the twelve leading manufacturing countries increased from 15 per cent in the early 1960s to over 20 per cent in the mid 1970s. Japan expanded from 9 per cent to over 15 per cent, while the United States declined from 22 to 16 per cent (Britain, incidentally, with a share very close to the United States in 1950, 26 per cent, declined to 16 per cent in 1960 and between 8 and 9 per cent in the mid 1970s). While there is much talk of some backward countries securing the part of world manufacturing, in this, the top league, there is no room for them to compete except on the margins . . .

Britain shows a much more exaggerated form of the general trend of deindustrialisation, and it is this which underlies the sporadic hysteria of the British ruling class—the *relative* decline in the capacity to compete in this bit of the world system. In this sense, the terrors of deindustrialisation are not at all new, but link to the growing obsession with survival that has dominated the British ruling class since the mid-1950s. For much of this period, the immediate preoccupation has been with the balance of payments, but for essentially the same reasons.

British manufacturing employment fell from 8.6 million in 1961 (36 per cent of total employment) to 7.4 million in 1976 (or 30.1 per cent). Manufacturing was not at all the sole loser. If we compare average employment figures between 1961 and 1966 (to eliminate short-term variations) with those for 1976, the breakdown of declining job sectors was as follows:

Table 1.2 Job losses (1961–66 compared to 1976)

1. Agriculture, forestry, fishing	384,000	(or 40%)
2. Mining and quarrying	327,000	(or 48.4%)
3. Manufacturing	1,199,000	(or 14%)
4. Construction	5,000	(or 0.3%)
5. Gas, electricity, water	51,000	(or 12.7%)
6. Transport and communications	164,000	(or 9.6%)
7. Distributive trades	202,000	(or 6.0%)
Total loss	2,332,000	(of which, manufacturing provided 51.4%)

Thus, while the proportionate decline in manufacturing was not at all the worst—that position is held by the mines, followed by agriculture—its absolute size is more than half of the total job loss. At the same time, other sectors generated a larger number of jobs. The net addition of jobs was 104,000, far too small to take up the expansion of the labour force, even if we could assume that 60-year-old miners or toolmakers could convert to being social security clerical staff.

Simplifying the figures, we can see a net shift between manufacturing and professional and scientific: between 1961 and 1976, the first declined by 1.3 million, the second increased by 1.5 million; between

Table 1.3 Job gains

8. Insurance, banking, finance	403,000	(or 51.8%)
9. Professional and scientific	1,377,000	(or 55.8%)
10. Miscellaneous services	381,000	(or 17%)
11. Public administration and defence	275,000	(or 20%)
Total gain	2,436,000	(of which, professional and scientific provided 56.5%)

1971 and 1976, to put it another way, 'production industries' lost just over half a million jobs, and 'other industries' put on just under 2 million. The changes reflect an overall tendency for British capitalism to become converted to a servicing centre in the world system . . .

2. UK Industry and the World Economy: A Case of Deindustrialisation?*

Ajit Singh

The notion of deindustrialisation as applied to an advanced industrial economy immediately raises a host of conceptual difficulties. First, there is the simple, but by no means entirely trivial, question: What is so special about industry that one should be concerned about 'deindustrialisation'? There has also been a considerable loss of employment from agriculture, but not much has been said, at least by economists, about 'deruralisation'. Second, it may well be that deindustrialisation (particularly in the sense of loss of employment from the industrial sector) is a long-run structural feature of all advanced industrial countries; beyond a certain level of economic development or 'industrial maturity', it may not be possible to increase the proportion of the labour force employed in industry and Britain, for historical reasons, may have attained such a level of maturity earlier than some other advanced countries. Third, and much more important, in an *open* economy, the so-called phenomenon of deindustrialisation may be no more than a normal adjustment to changing domestic and world market conditions. In fact an important purpose of this paper will be to argue that, in an open economy, the question whether deindustrialisation can in any sense be regarded as implying 'structural maladjustment' cannot be properly considered in terms of the characteristics of the domestic economy alone. Such a proposition has a sensible meaning only in the context of the interactions of the economy with the rest of the world, i.e. in terms of its overall trading and payments position in the world economy . . .

However, before considering these questions there is a logically prior issue which must be discussed; namely, why should one be so concerned with the fate of the manufacturing sector, while neglecting other sectors,

*Reproduced with permission from the *Cambridge Journal of Economics*, vol. 1, 1977, pp. 113–36. Copyright 1977, by Academic Press Inc. (London) Limited.

for example, services? This is a particularly relevant question in the case of the UK economy, since it has been argued that its comparative advantage is now in services, rather than in manufacturing.

The answer seems to me to lie chiefly in two major factors: (a) the relative contributions of manufacturing and services to UK exports and the balance of payments; and (b) structural characteristics of the manufacturing sector and its potential for technical progress and productivity growth. We shall briefly examine each of these in turn.

As far as (a) is concerned, it is, indeed, true that invisibles have traditionally made an important contribution to the UK balance on current account: the account usually consists of a positive balance of invisibles and a negative one on visible trade. However, since, for historical reasons, UK firms and citizens have been major investors abroad, net credit on interest, profits and dividends (IPD) usually form a fairly large part of the surplus on invisibles. Now, quite apart from the fact that a significant proportion of the IPD credits are regularly reinvested abroad, if the economy is in disequilibrium and an improvement in the balance of payments is sought, one cannot normally rely on a greater contribution from this source. An increased capital outflow will usually be required to generate greater dividends, profits and interest payments in the future, but this will *inter alia* worsen the balance of payments in the short and the medium term. For this reason, as well as the issue of comparative advantage mentioned above, the relevant comparison is really between trade in manufactures and that in private services (tourism, sea transport and civil aviation, city and financial services, etc). Table 2.1 compares the relative importance, and very roughly the relative performance, of trade in these two sectors of the economy. The first thing to notice is that the value of manufactured exports usually runs at twice the level of gross credit from services and that this ratio has remained much the same over the last decade. Secondly, although a proper examination of the question of compara- tive advantage would take us too far away from the main subject of this paper, we note that in recent years the UK does appear to have performed relatively better in its trade in services than in manufactures. The trade ratio (which is used here as a rough indicator of trade performance) for services has remained more or less constant since 1968, while that for manufactures has fallen sharply since 1971. This phenomenon is particularly striking in view of the fact that during the last decade the government has accorded much more generous tax and subsidy treatment to manufacturers relative to services than before.

Can one then conclude that there is no need for concern about deindustrialisation in the UK economy, and that more resources should

Table 2.1 The relative performance of manufacturing and services:[a] UK 1966–75

	Ratio of exports of manufacturers to those of private services (currant values)	Trade ratio for manufactures[b]	Trade ratio for private services[b]
1966	2.37	0.31	0.08
1967	2.04	0.24	0.10
1968	2.10	0.21	0.13
1969	2.19	0.24	0.12
1970	1.98	0.23	0.12
1971	1.95	0.25	0.12
1972	1.87	0.16	0.12
1973	1.91	0.11	0.11
1974	2.04	0.09	0.13
1975	2.14	0.14	0.13

[a] 'Exports' and 'imports' of private services are defined so as to include credits and debits in invisible trade on account of sea transport, civil aviation, travel and 'other services'. Other services include commissions, etc on imports and exports, telecommunications and postal services; film and television royalties received and paid; services rendered by and to UK enterprises; construction work overseas and financial and allied services such as banking, insurance and merchanting. Interest received by UK banks and other financial institutions and profits of their overseas branches, subsidiaries, etc are not included, nor are interest paid to foreign banks, financial institutions and profits to their UK subsidiaries, branches etc.
[b] The trade ratio is defined as (exports—imports)/(exports+imports). Its maximum value is +1 (indicating complete trade advantage) and its minimum −1 (indicating complete disadvantage). *Ceteris paribus*, a reduction in this ratio over time denotes a loss of competitiveness.

in fact be allocated to the expansion of private services? Considering the balance of payments position alone, there are strong grounds for thinking that the latter course would at best produce no more than a minor improvement. The main reason for this becomes clear when trade in 'services' is examined at a more disaggregated level; it turns out that almost the whole of the surplus on these services is contributed by a category known as 'other services' (which includes the City's financial services, royalties etc). The credits on sea transport, civil aviation and tourism are roughly matched by equivalent debits in each case, and there has been relatively little improvement in this situation over the last decade. On the other hand, there has been an enormous growth in the credits from the City's financial services (a sevenfold increase during the last decade), but their total gross value (about £700 million) in 1975 amounted to only a tenth of total service exports and to less than 5 per cent of exports of manufactures. So, although there may be scope for further expansion of financial and possibly some other services (such as tourism), this is unlikely, on the basis of past trends, to have more than a small impact on the overall trade balance. The continuing importance of the manufacturing sector for the balance of payments can therefore hardly be overstated. This is particularly so since any modest improvement in the balance, brought about either by the allocation of more resources to services or their more efficient utilisation, could easily be more than offset if the trading performance of the manufacturing sector were to continue to deteriorate.

The other major reason for giving special attention to the manufacturing sector is its significance from the point of view of the structure of the economy. Many people would accept that it is a dynamic sector with increasing returns and a high growth of productivity, especially compared with the service sector, where both the level and the rate of growth of productivity tend to be much lower. Although, on the basis of the evidence produced to show the validity of Verdoon's law, there may be some dispute about whether manufacturing is subject to 'dynamic economies of scale' in Kaldor's sense, (see Kaldor, 1966; Rowthorn, 1975) there is a great deal more solidly—based relevant evidence concerning the dynamic role of the manufacturing sector in economic growth. For instance, Cripps and Tarling, 1973, in their analysis of the growth process in advanced industrial countries during 1959–70, have confirmed Kaldor's hypothesis that there is a close relationship between the rate of growth of a country's GDP and the growth of its manufacturing sector. This relationship is much closer than would be expected (since manufacturing is quite a large component of GDP) on purely statistical grounds; it is also closer than that observed between the growth of GDP and of other sectors of the economy. Therefore, from the point of view of the future growth potential of the economy, a shrinkage in its manufacturing sector is clearly a cause for legitimate concern.

We turn now to the nature and extent of the decline in UK manufacturing industry in recent years. It will be useful first to examine this phenomenon in a historical perspective, i.e. in terms of long-run structural changes in the economy. Figure 2.1 shows the proportion of the labour force employed in manufacturing over the last 100 years, as well as the proportion of GDP contributed by this sector since 1907.

Although such long-run comparisons inevitably involve statistical problems, Figure 2.1 demonstrates how difficult it is to sustain the thesis of 'deindustrialisation' for a mature industrial economy like that of the

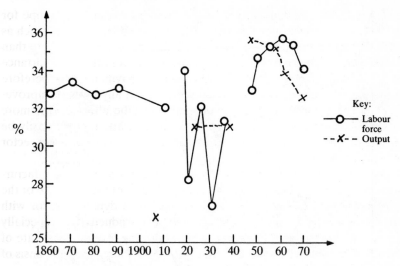

Figure 2.1. Share of manufacturing in the UK economy: labour force 1861–1970 and output (in current prices) 1907–70

UK, when one considers changes over a period of a century. Indeed, the proportion of the labour force engaged in manufacturing activity was just about the same in 1970 as it was in 1871. This proportion certainly did not remain constant throughout, but if we abstract from cyclical fluctuations, its general level was much the same (perhaps slightly lower) in the interwar period as in the 50 years before the first world war. There was, however, a trend increase in manufacturing's share in the labour force (of about 4 percentage points) between the mid-1930s and the early 1960s; it has since been slowly declining.

As far as the proportion of output contributed by manufacturing is concerned, the picture is slightly different. Even when the share of manufacturing in net output is measured in current prices, there was some trend increase between the period before the first world war and the interwar period. There was a relatively larger increase between the middle 1930s and the middle 1950s, but since then there has been a decline.

In order to examine in greater detail the more recent trends in the share of manufacturing in output and employment, Figure 2.2 shows the period 1955–75. It also includes a series for overall unemployment as an indicator of cyclical fluctuations in the economy. The chart clearly shows that there has been a trend decline in the proportion of the labour force employed in manufacturing since the early 1960s, which accelerated in the late 1960s. Thus there was. a large fall in the proportion

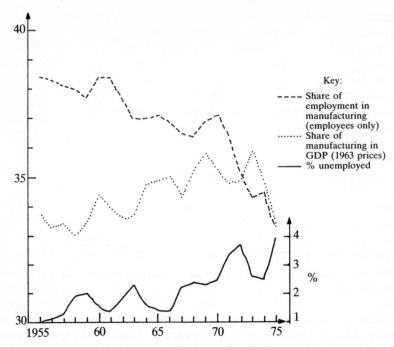

Figure 2.2. The share of manufacturing in the UK economy (employment and output) and the percentage of the labour force unemployed 1955–75

employed in manufacturing between the recession year 1972 and 1975 (i.e. the year before the cyclical trough was reached) than between the recession years 1968 and 1972. The latest figures show that, in absolute terms, the numbers employed in manufacturing have decreased by nearly 1 million between 1968 and 1976; by 1976 the proportion employed in manufacturing had fallen to 32 per cent.

However, if we consider the share of manufacturing in output at *constant* 1963 prices, the picture is rather different. We find a very slow secular increase in share until the latest downturn in the economy in 1973, since when it has fallen much more sharply than in previous recessions. On the other hand, if the contribution of manufacturing is measured in current prices (not shown in the figure), there is clear evidence of a trend decline since the middle 1950s.

Next we consider the important hypothesis that deindustrialisation in the sense discussed above (i.e. a trend reduction in the share of manufacturing at least in the labour force, if not in output) is not simply a feature peculiar to the UK economy, but is a long-run structural feature of all industrial economies. The argument is simply that all advanced economies, owing to increasing similarities in their patterns of demand, may be subject to similar structural changes. These may result in the transfer of labour from manufacturing to other sectors of the economy, and the behaviour of the UK manufacturing sector may therefore be no different from that of the rest. Evidence bearing on this hypothesis is set out in Tables 2.2 and 2.3, which compare the UK and a group of other industrial countries over the last two decades in terms of their growth rates of output and employment, as well as the proportions of the labour force employed in manufacturing and the shares of manufacturing in GDP (at constant prices).

Table 2.2A tells the familiar story of a UK growth rate in manufacturing lower than that of most other countries in every period. Table 2.2B is, however, much more interesting. First, it shows that, although during the most recent period employment fell more in the UK than anywhere else, the UK was not the only country to suffer a reduction—the majority of countries did so. This was a notable break with experience up to the mid-1960s, when growth of output in manufacturing in every country was associated with rising employment. One plausible explanation is that, as a consequence of the liberalisation of world trade and increased international competition, as well as the worldwide merger movement, a considerable amount of rationalisation took place within the manufacturing sector. This enabled both output

Table 2.2A. Growth rates of manufacturing output between cyclical peaks:[a] the UK and other industrial countries (% per annum at 1963 prices)

	Early to mid-1950s	Mid-1950s to early 1960s	Early to mid-1960s	Mid to late 1960s	Last peak to 1973[b]
Belgium	3.64	5.77	—[c]	4.89	8.34
France	4.88	4.40	6.87	5.86	6.55
Germany	11.30	7.99	6.12	5.53	3.82
Italy	7.57	6.61	9.59	6.81	5.07
Japan	13.81	14.59	11.46	13.14	7.26
Netherlands	6.24	5.94	5.63	7.06	5.56
Sweden	3.05	3.35	8.29	4.36	3.28
UK	3.76	2.81	3.28	2.78	2.95
USA	2.86	2.40	7.39	3.36	4.66

[a]Cycles do not necessarily coincide for al countries.
[b]Except in case of Japan, where 1972 is the end-year.
[c]The cycle for Belgium runs from 1957 to 1964, so the figure in the previous column runs from mid-1950s to mid-1960s

Table 2.2B. Growth rates of employment* in manufacturing between cyclical peaks:ᵃ The UK and other industrial countries (% per annum)

	Early to mid-1950s	Mid-1950s to early 1960s	Early to mid-1960s	Mid to late 1960s	Last peak to 1973[b]
Belgium	0.42	0.82	—[c]	0.16	−0.08
France	0.51	0.37	2.19	0.44	1.21
Germany	5.82	2.93	1.75	0.65	−0.58
Italy	1.62	1.52	5.28	1.18	0.21
Japan	6.27	5.63	4.19	2.74	1.76
Netherlands	1.92	1.29	1.69	−0.13	−2.45
Sweden	0.93	0.21	5.96	−1.24	0.32
UK	1.17	0.73	0.49	−0.46	−2.78
USA	1.01	0.28	1.74	1.62	−0.43

*Employment refers to wage and salary earners only.
[a,b,c]See notes to Table 2.2A.

and productivity to grow, despite the fall in employment. It is a moot question whether this was a once-and-for-all fall, so that a further reduction in the manufacturing labour force could lead to a fall in manufacturing output. Secondly, Table 2.2B shows that, apart from the Netherlands, the UK was the only country for which employment in manufacturing fell between both the last two cycles. Also, relative to other countries, manufacturing employment in the UK fell further during the last period, as well as over the last two periods taken together.

Table 2.3A shows that, as far as the share of manufacturing in GDP is concerned, UK experience during the last decade has not been very different from that of other countries. This could, however, be misleading, since a lower manufacturing growth rate in the UK probably meant a relatively lower growth rate overall. Nevertheless, Table 2.3B indicates that between 1970 and 1973 the proportion of the UK labour force employed in manufacturing fell appreciably faster, although it still remained larger, than in many other countries. The relatively larger proportion of labour force in manufacturing has traditionally been an important characteristic of the UK economic structure; it derives from the fact that historically this country has had a much smaller agricultural sector relative to other countries.

To sum up, the empirical evidence indicates that, since the late 1960s, Britain's manufacturing labour force has decline faster, both compared with its own experience over the previous two decades, and relative to

Table 2.3A. Share of manufacturing in GDP (at 1963 prices), at cyclical peaks from 1950 to 1970 and for years 1970 to 1973: the UK and other industrial countries[a]

	Early 1950s	Mid-1950s	Early 1960s	Mid-1960s	Late 1960s	1970	1971	1972	1973
Belgium	n.a.	27.8	–	31.3	33.5	33.5	33.4	33.8	34.1
France	33.6	34.7	35.0	36.4	37.3	n.a.	n.a.	n.a.	n.a.
Germany	32.1	37.4	40.6	42.3	44.8	44.8	44.4	44.3	45.0
Italy	20.4	22.6	24.0	27.6	31.2	31.2	30.7	31.2	32.0
Japan	18.5	23.5	27.6	29.2	33.6	n.a.	n.a.	n.a.	n.a.
Netherlands	28.3	28.9	29.9	30.8	32.9	3.29	33.2	33:2	33.8
Sweden	26.4	25.6	25.4	30.6	31.6	31.6	31.7	32.6	32.7
UK	32.4	33.8	34.4	34.8	35.9	35.6	34.9	37.2	35.7
USA	28.7	28.5	27.7	29.7	29.9	28.3	28.1	29.2	30.7

[a]See notes to Table 2.2A.

Table 2.3B. Share of total labour force[a] in manufacturing, at cyclical peaks from 1950 to 1970 and for years 1970 to 1973: the UK and other industrial countries[a]

	Early 1950s	Mid-1950s	Early 1960s	Mid-1960s	Late 1960s	1970	1971	1972	1973
Belgium	35.1	35.2	—	35.4	34.1	34.1	33.7	33.2	33.4
France	n.a.	27.8	27.2	28.1	27.6	27.8	28.0	28.0	28.1
Germany	34.1	34.2	38.5	39.3	40.5	40.5	40.2	39.7	39.8
Italy	n.a.	22.8	26.3	29.2	31.7	31.7	32.0	32.1	32.2
Japan	n.a.	19.8	22.5	24.3	26.7	27.0	27.0	26.9	27.4
Netherlands	30.8	30.8	28.2	28.2	26.2	26.2	25.7	24.9	24.5
Sweden	n.a.	n.a.	n.a.	32.4	27.6	27.6	27.3	27.1	27.5
UK	39.3	40.1	37.5	36.5	36.3	36.4	34.0	32.8	32.3
USA	n.a.	26.2	26.6	27.7	27.2	26.1	25.1	24.9	25.3

[a]Labour force refers to total civilian employment; see also notes to Table 2.2A.

that of other countries. With respect to the growth of real output in manufacturing, there is a small trend reduction when compared with the past UK experience, but not when compared with previous performance in relation to other countries.

Finally, to complete the picture, we shall briefly examine the implied movements in the growth of productivity in the UK and in other industrial countries. Although the rate of growth of manufacturing output in the UK during the last decade was lower than in the previous ten years, a fall in manufacturing employment has meant that there has been no reduction in the rate of growth of productivity. Output per man hour in manufacturing during 1965–75 grew, if anything, at a slightly higher rate (about 3.5 per cent a year) than during the period 1955–65 (about 3 per cent per annum). However, since 1973 there have been signs of stagnation in productivity growth. This is in contrast to the previous recessions (since the mid-1960s), when a 'shake-out' of labour led to improved productivity performance. Relative to other countries, the UK's productivity growth was still low, but there appears to have been a slight narrowing of the gap in recent years.

The question now arises as to how we should assess the above evidence from the point of view of the structure of the economy. Loss of employment in the manufacturing sector (or, for that matter, in any sector) is clearly undesirable and socially and economically wasteful, if it leads not to redeployment elsewhere, but only to increased overall unemployment. However, as far as the efficiency and growth potential of the manufacturing sector are concerned, it could be argued that the loss of manpower was in fact a positive feature, in that it reduced previous overmanning without adversely affecting productivity performance. Thus, unless the evidence of loss of employment is supplemented by other data, and, more importantly, unless there is a clear notion of what constitutes an 'efficient' economic structure, one cannot conclude that the recent deindustrialisation of the UK economy implies any structural maladjustment of the economy, actual or potential.

The debate about 'deindustrialisation' reflects more than a concern with the general problem of unemployment . . . The crucial issue here is what does one mean by an 'efficient' manufacturing sector in an open economy such as the UK? We saw above that the manufacturing sector is the major source of foreign exchange earnings on current account. More importantly, we have seen that it is potentially the main means through which an improvement in the balance of payments could be sought sufficient to correct the existing disequilibrium. Therefore, given the normal levels of the other components of the balance of payments, we may define an efficient manufacturing sector as one which (currently as well as potentially) not only satisfies the demands of consumers at home, but is also able to sell enough of its products abroad to pay for the nation's import requirements. This is, however, subject to the important restriction that an 'efficient' manufacturing sector must be able to achieve these objectives at socially acceptable levels of output, employment and the exchange rate. These qualifications are essential, since otherwise, at a low enough level of real income or employment, almost any manufacturing sector might be able to meet such criteria of efficiency.

In operational terms, a structural problem can arise in this sense, if the manufacturing sector, without losing price or cost competitiveness, is unable to export enough to pay for the full-employment level of imports. Some evidence of this phenomenon in the UK is found in Table 2.4. The table (columns 3 and 4) shows that since the middle 1960s the UK has had an increasing price advantage relative to its main competitors (owing to progressive devaluations of the currency). This is true whether such advantage is measured in terms of relative changes in the export prices of manufactures, or in terms of the more appropriate variable of 'efficiency wages', i.e. relative movements in the indices of unit labour costs measured in a common currency (dollars). In spite of this, there appears to have been a trend deterioration in the underlying current balance, which is reflected in the fact that even in 1975 there was a large deficit on current account, when nearly 4 per cent of the labour force was unemployed. By contrast, in 1970–71 there were sizeable surpluses, which were achieved at a lower rate of unemployment and

Table 2.4. UK current balance, unemployment and indices of price and cost competitiveness, 1963–75

	Current balance (£000 millions, 1975)	% of labour force unemployed	Index of price competitiveness[a] (1970 = 100)	Index of cost competiveness[b] (1970 = 100)
1963	0.34	2.30	101.3	⎫
1964	−0.89	1.65	101.9	⎪
1965	−0.06	1.43	105.2	⎬ (average 1963–67)
1966	0.23	1.46	106.6	⎪ 109.0
1967	−0.67	2.31	105.8	⎭
1968	−0.59	2.41	99.7	
1969	0.93	2.42	98.7	
1970	1.39	2.56	100.0	100.0
1971	1.18	3.35	100.9	
1972	0.20	3.68	99.3	
1973	−1.22	2.58	92.2	
1974	−4.53	2.53	90.5	87.6
1975	−1.71	3.94	n.a.	87.0

[a]The index of price competitiveness is the ratio of UK to weighted average export ($) prices for major competitors in respect of manufactured goods.
[b]Index of relative unit labour costs: UK to weighted competitors' ratio ($) 1970 = 100.

with less favourable relative prices. The Cambridge Economic Policy Group, on the basis of their model of the British economy, estimate that at full employment the current amount deficit in 1975 would have been of the order of £4000 million.

The UK therefore seems to be becoming increasingly unable to pay for its current import requirements by means of exports of goods and services and property income from abroad. Earlier we saw that there has been little, if any, deterioration in the trading position of services over the past decade. Furthermore, as far as net income from interest, profits and dividends from abroad is concerned, there has been an increase in the contribution from this source during the last three years. The disequilibrium in the current account is, therefore, basically due to a market deterioration in the visible trade account since 1971.

A disaggregated analysis of visible trade shows that there have been two major factors responsible for this situation. First, after having remained more or less constant for a number of years, the terms of trade have moved sharply against the UK since 1972, and especially since the oil price rise in 1973. This has led to a much higher import bill for food, raw materials and fuel (in spite of lower volumes of these imports as a consequence of the recession in the last two years). Secondly, and quite independently . . . instead of compensating for this rise by an improvement, the trading performance of the manufacturing sector has greatly deteriorated since 1971. An analysis of the commodity and area pattern of the trade in manufactures . . . shows that the main reason for the poor trading performance of this sector is the large and continuing decline in recent years in the UK's manufacturing trade balance with the advanced industrial countries. At constant 1970 prices, the trade balance in manufactures with these countries moved from a positive figure of more than £950 million in 1970 to a negative figure of £251 million in 1975. (During the same period, the corresponding balance with the rest of the world—including the oil-exporting countries— increased from £1956 million to £2794 million) . . .

The important question is why, for example, the income elasticity of demand for manufactured imports in the UK is higher than in other countries. The first point to note here is that it would be difficult to attribute this phenomenon to peculiar features of the structure of UK demand. This is because, for well-known reasons, there is a growing uniformity in the patterns of demand in all advanced countries. Futhermore, to the extent that both the level and the rate of growth of income have been lower in the UK than in a number of competitor countries, it is also unlikely that there have been more rapid *changes* in the pattern of demand in the UK than elsewhere.

The UK's higher income elasticity of demand for imports (as well as the low income elasticity of world demand for UK exports) stems from deficiencies on the supply side—a manufacturing sector which clearly responds rather ineffectively to changes in domestic and foreign demand. However, it is significant that such deficiencies are not revealed by a conventional comparative analysis of the structure of UK industry. Recent studies . . . show, for instance, that the structure of manufacturing industry in the UK is not much different from that of West Germany—measured in terms of the sectoral distribution of outputs and factor inputs. Over the period 1954–72, the lower rate of growth of UK industry relative to that of West Germany is attributable almost entirely to poorer UK performance (in every sector), rather than to differences in industrial structure between the two countries. Similarly, it does not appear to be the case that the overall pressure of demand on resources has been generally higher in the UK than in other countries. It could be argued that if an economy is normally run too close to the margin of resources, this will diminish its ability to respond rapidly to changes in domestic and foreign demand, and hence result in unfavourable income elasticities for imports and exports. Panić (1975) however, points out that throughout the period 1957–72 the margin of spare resources (as measured by the ratio of potential to actual GDP) was lower in West Germany and France than in the UK.

The basic weakness of the UK manufacturing sector is shown by an analysis of the dynamic factors in the production system. The evidence of a number of surveys of individual industries undertaken by the National Economic Development Office suggests that the main reason for the UK's high income elasticity of demand for imports (as well as the unfavourable export elasticity) is to be found in the lower quality, design and general performance of its products relative to other countries. . . . These non-price factors are most likely to be related above all to the lower rate of growth of UK industry. The faster growing, more dynamic economies are in a position to achieve greater technical progress and make product improvements in all the above-mentioned directions, and are therefore able to respond more effectively to changing patterns of demand as consumer incomes rise. If this line of argument is correct, an increase in the rate of growth of UK industry is required in order to correct the underlying trade disequilibrium. This in turn depends on two factors: (a) the rate of manufacturing investment, and (b) how effectively investment is utilised.

But, whatever index is used, the UK's investment record in recent years has been disappointing. On the basis of a detailed analysis of the manufacturing sector, Woodward (1976) shows that, whereas between

1954–56 and 1963–65 manufacturing investment at constant prices grew by 39 per cent, between 1963–65 and 1972–74 it grew only by 19 per cent. More recent statistics show that during 1970–75 net investment in manufacturing at constant prices was running at about four-fifths of the levels reached in the previous five years. Further, over the period 1964–72, manufacturing investment as a proportion of GDP was on average lower in the UK than in most competitor countries (the US being a notable exception). There is also some indirect evidence that, relative to large firms elsewhere, large UK manufacturing firms may be investing more abroad than at home. According to UN data, the value of production abroad by UK multinationals in 1973 was more than twice the value of their exports from the UK; for the Japanese and West German multinationals, the corresponding proportions were 0.38 and 0.37, respectively.

As far as the effectiveness of investment is concerned, there is conflicting statistical evidence on the relative efficiency of the utilisation of investment in the UK, as compared with other countries. However, casual observation suggests that, owing to the nature of worker-management relations in this country, the UK's relative performance in this respect also may well be poor. Nevertheless, it could be argued that, if there *were* a faster rate of growth and higher employment, it would lead to great cooperation between the two sides of industry and hence better utilisation of resources.

To sum up, the evidence outlined here suggests that there are serious weaknesses on the supply side in UK manufacturing, which make it increasingly difficult for it to meet foreign competition in either home or overseas markets. It is these facts, when considered in conjunction with the reduction in the labour force in manufacturing, which make 'deindustrialisation' a matter of serious concern. In view of the sluggish rate of investment, low growth and high unemployment, it is difficult to see how such deficiencies, which pertain to the dynamic factors in the production system, can be remedied. The evidence suggests that, left to itself, the situation may continue to deteriorate in the manner postulated by Myrdal's theory. The relative absence of these dynamic factors (which manifests itself in slower technical progress, product innovation and ability to respond to demand changes as compared with competitors) may continue to lead to growing inroads by competitive imports, poor export performance and hence balance of payments difficulties and low growth.

Finally, it is important to recall that the whole of the discussion of this section has assumed 'normal' levels of other components of the balance of payments. But there is at least one component of visible trade (minerals, fuels, etc.) which may be expected to show an enormous improvement over the next few years, as a consequence of the development of North Sea oil. Depending on the size of the surplus, the country could in principle then have a balance of payments equilibrium at full employment, and at desired levels of real income and exchange rate, even if the trading position of the manufacturing sector continued to decline. This is, however, not a sustainable position in the long run, since, unless the manufacturing sector improves and becomes more dynamic, it may not be able to pay for the full employment level of imports at a later stage, when the oil flow runs out. The situation in this respect could become somewhat like that in the period before the First World War. As Lewis (1967) points out, during 1870–1914 the balance of payments surplus (owing at that time to remittances from abroad) saved Britain from having to make the changes in its productive structure necessary to meet the growing foreign competition in manufactures. But after the war, the flow of property income from abroad dropped sharply, and the UK then had to face the necessity of 'earning a living through successful competition in manufacturing, both in her home market and abroad; and this problem she has not solved after 40 years of grappling with it'.

It has been argued in this paper that liberalisation of trade and free capital movements are not always necessarily beneficial for a country. Because of the uneven development of the world economy and of the productive potential of different regions, there may be many periods when participation in the international economy under such arrangements can lead to disequilibrium and be seriously harmful to a country's economy. The detrimental effects can work in a number of ways—most importantly, through the level and structure of demand and through investment. Once the economy is in long-run disequilibrium, for whatever reason, continued participation in international economic relations on the same terms as before may produce a vicious circle of causation. As a consequence, a country in a weak competitive position may have balance of payments difficulties, which lead the government to have a lower level of demand, which leads to lower investment and hence lower growth of productivity and continuing balance of payments difficulties. There may be no automatic market mechanism to correct the disequilibrium.

The deindustrialisation of the UK economy which has occurred in recent years has been only in the sense of loss of employment from the manufacturing sector. This loss has been greater than in other industrial countries, and also as compared with the trend rate of decline in the UK itself during the last two decades. Between the recession years of 1968 and 1976, employment in manufacturing fell by nearly 1 million workers; the proportion employed in manufacturing decreased from 36 to 32 per cent. There has, however, been no reduction in manufacturing output, although there was a slowdown in its rate of growth. Because of falling employment, the rate of growth of productivity has, if anything improved during the last decade as a whole; however, there is evidence of stagnation since 1973. It has been argued here that the observed loss of manufacturing employment, as well as these other features of the relative performance of the manufacturing sector, cannot, by themselves, be regarded as an indication of structural maladjustment of the economy or an 'inefficient' manufacturing sector.

I have suggested that the concept of an 'efficient' manufacturing sector in an open economy must be considered in broader terms. To the extent that manufacturing may constitute the major source of foreign exchange earnings for a country, an 'efficient' manufacturing sector must also be able to provide (currently and potentially) sufficient net exports to meet the country's overall import requirements at socially acceptable levels of output, employment and exchange rate. It is in this important sense that, in spite of the growth in productivity, there is evidence that the UK manufacturing sector is becoming increasingly inefficient. The evidence suggests a structural disequilibrium, whereby the trading position of the manufacturing sector in the world economy continued to deteriorate, in spite of increasing cost and price competitiveness. Deindustrialisation is a symptom or a consequence of this 'inefficiency' or of disequilibrium, rather than its cause; this disequilibrium needs to be corrected if the manufacturing sector is not to decline further.

The main policy implication of the above analysis is that a faster rate of growth and concomitant dynamic changes in the system of UK manufacturing production are required in order for it to be able to compete successfully in world markets and in its own home market. The question as to what is the best, or even the most feasible, way of bringing about such a transformation raises extremely complex issues. . . . All that one can say in general is that the structural disequilibrium may be so deep seated, and the economic and political environment may be such, that in spite of the benefits of North Sea oil, it may not be possible to bring about the required modifications in the production system without fundamental institutional changes. More specifically, it may well require, perhaps for a considerable period, an abandonment of the regime of free trade and free convertibility of currency.

3. Deindustrialisation Gathers Pace: the 1970s*

John Hughes

So, to start with, we pass in review the major indicators that—taken together—show the serious and many-sided character of deindustrialisation as it developed in the 1970s . . .

(I) MANUFACTURING OUTPUT FROM GROWTH TREND TO DECLINE

We have to avoid the possibility that periods of decline within a trade-cycle are pointed to as signs of decay. The best way of identifying the longer-term trends that are emerging is to measure from trade-cycle to trade-cycle, using the four- (or sometimes five) year cycle familiar in post-war years.

Our first figures measure average output of manufacturing in successive cycles over the last 20 years, and the broad measure of the percentage change in output from one cycle to the next.

Table 3.1: Manufacturing output from cycle to cycle (trough to pre-trough year)

Years	Average output index (1975=100)	% change, cycle to cycle
1958–61	69.8	
1962–66	81.3	+16
1967–70	94.4	+16
1971–74	103.1	+ 9
1975–80	101.3	− 2

*Reproduced from J. Hughes, *Britain in Crisis: Deindustrialisation and how to fight it* (Nottingham, Spokesman Books, 1981) pp. 10–26.

Table 3.1 presents us with the astonishing spectacle of the long period expansion of manufacturing moving down from around 16 per cent over a typical trade-cycle, to less than 10 per cent in the early 1970s, and to something worse than zero growth in the latter half of the 1970s. But is this the chance effect of measuring cyclical troughs? Table 3.2 measures from cyclical peaks, and projects into the early 1980s.

Table 3.2: Manufacturing output from cycle to cycle (peak to pre-peak year)

Years	Average output index (1975=100)	% change, cycle to cycle
1960–63	74.3	
1964–67	86.0	+16%
1968–72	97.4	+13%
1973–78	103.9	+ 6½%
1979–82 (est.)	96.0 (est.)	− 7½% (est.)

When output from cycle to cycle is measured in this way (grouping into each cycle the years starting from a 'peak') the same basic trends emerge—if anything even more ominously. Table 3.2 shows clearly the long period deterioration in performance as measured in output growth, first of all leading to sharply lower growth rates and then—in the current cycle (and with a slight degree of estimation)—into absolute decline.

Indeed, what is now occurring is something unique in British industrial history since the industrial revolution. Thus, comparing *decades*, manufacturing output had risen over 30 per cent over the two trade-cycles largely located in the decade of the 1960s; but over the decade from the early 1970s to the opening of the 1980s, there has been *no growth at all*, indeed the official statistics indicate a small decline over the decade. The 1960s with their growth rate of over 30 per cent were not unusual; all the decades from the 1930s to the 1960s had shown similar rates of growth in manufacturing in the UK. A decade without any overall growth is unprecedented.

Within earlier post-war trade-cycles we became familiar with the sequence labelled 'stop–go', that is with a period of almost static output followed by relatively rapid growth. On the trends signalled over the previous and the present trade-cycle we now have to cope with a cycle of 'stop–decline'. That is, in manufacturing the most favourable years in the cycle look like the 'stop' (or very slow growth years of earlier cycles), but these are succeeded by years with major falls in output. Thus in the 'growth' years after 1975, the annual increase in manufacturing output never exceeded 1½ per cent, and by 1979 had only advanced 4 per cent above the output level of the 1975 recession year. By contrast, the falls in output as cyclical depression develops (after 1973, and after 1979) have been much more severe.

(II) THE CURB TO MANUFACTURING PRODUCTIVITY

The unprecedented curtailment of output growth has been accompanied by an unusually marked reduction in the long-term improvement in labour productivity (output per person employed) in manufacturing. This marked reduction in productivity can be directly connected with the major loss of market share, reduction of output, and undercapacity working of substantial sectors of British manufacturing industry. (This strongly-marked decline of particular sectors is commented on subsequently.) But, in turn, the weak performance of productivity affects costs per unit of output and feeds back into possible loss of competitive strength. In part, again, this links to relatively high levels of industrial disputes in certain industries, affecting output and overall productivity. Besides this, most economists would expect weak productivity performance to connect with a relatively weak thrust in investment in new productive capital equipment. So the deterioration in labour productivity in manufacturing cannot be isolated from a number of other dimensions and measures of weak industrial performance and deindustrialisation.

But productivity is important to the total argument *if* there has been a considerable weakening of earlier trends of improvement and *if* this deterioration is more apparent in the UK than with other industrial countries.

Between the 1968 cyclical peak and the 1973 cyclical peak labour productivity (output per person employed) in UK manufacturing had risen by 21 per cent; measured per hour the improvement was slightly more, some 23 per cent. There was nothing unusual in this: in the previous cycle, the productivity gain had been over 20 per cent in five years.

But from 1973 to 1979, again comparing a cyclical peaks, labour productivity in UK manufacturing rose by only 5 per cent. In other words by less than an average of 1 per cent per annum over the six years concerned. In terms of output per person per hour the performance looks slightly better, but still hourly productivity rose by less than 9 per cent over the six years.

British manufacturing was alone among the major manufacturing powers in this extreme curtailment of its productivity advance. Hourly labour productivity in manufacturing in USA and in Italy rose around 20 per cent from 1973 to 1979. For Japan, France and Germany, the advance was close to 30 per cent.

Nor can it be argued that the slump of the 1980–81 period is 'correcting' this poor productivity performance. Labour productivity generally deteriorates as cyclical depression sets in (particularly due to the unavoidable wastes involved in serious undercapacity operation). This has been true of the period after the 1979 peak (so far as it can currently be measured) as it was true after the 1973 peak. Despite the massive reductions in the labour force in manufacturing in 1980, and a fall in average hours worked, the evidence is that the fall in output per hour worked is somewhat greater than in the previous recession.

(III) THE FALL IN MANUFACTURING EMPLOYMENT

Even with the slower growth in productivity in the most recent trade-cycle the downward shift in the trend of output has led to major falls in employment. Employment in manufacturing has been falling through each trade-cycle since the late 1960s. Major falls in the recession phase of each cycle have been followed not by growth of employment but by a plateau of employment (as between 1972 and 1974) or a slight decline (as between 1976 and 1979).

Employment in manufacturing through the 1960s was relatively stable; the peak year for employment was 1966 with 8.4 million workers in British manufacturing. The 1970s opened with around 8.15 million workers employed. The figure for the middle of 1980 was no more than 6.66 million, a fall of 1½ *million in a decade*. And this had occurred despite a fall of around 10 per cent in the average weekly hours worked per 'operative' in manufacturing.

Employment in manufacturing over the trade-cycle from the late 1960s to the employment peak in 1973/74 fell by nearly 500,000. Most of this was concentrated in the recession years (employment figures tend to lag slightly behind changes in output); between 1970 and 1972 employment fell by more than half a million (or by around 7 per cent).

From the peak years of 1973/74 to the weakly-marked peak of the late 1970s employment in British manufacturing fell nearly 700,000. Employment by mid-1979 was only slightly over 7 million compared with 7.7 million in 1974. The employment fall that was concentrated in the recession years from 1974 to 1976 was one of 8 per cent, around 600,000 workers . . .

There are a number of reasons why such an employment fall may have quite shattering social and economic implications for Britain. One is that manufacturing industries are disproportionately important in the economy as employers of *manual* labour; around 70 per cent of manufacturing employment even in the late 1970s consisted of manual workers. *Most* of the fall in manufacturing employment represents a decline in manual jobs—and this is not compensated for elsewhere in the economy. Indeed, official data show the total 'input' of *manual* working hours in British manufacturing by late 1980 as only *60 per cent of the level in the mid-1960s* before the long period decline began. A 40 per cent fall in total manual working hours in manufacturing in a decade and a half. Besides this, such employment had represented a massive concentration of work skills of many kinds. Moreover, the impact of decline has been concentrated particularly in regions of the country where this emphasis on manual work in manufacturing had been most marked. The residual problem of human and social waste is now enormous and still rapidly growing.

Back in the late 1960s manufacturing employment accounted for about 36 per cent of the total number of employees. By 1980 the proportion had fallen to around 27½ per cent. By 1981 to 1982 it will have fallen further. In particular, no equivalent source of employment for male manual workers has opened up. In the first half of the 1970s there was substantial increase in public service employment (particularly of women) to offset some of the manufacturing decline, but that offsetting process has been brought to a halt by public expenditure constraints. Thus the decline in the proportion of employees who are in manufacturing employment is being increasingly reflected *not* by employment elsewhere but by a growing army of unemployed; unemployment has risen from 2 per cent of total employers in the late 1960s to 6 per cent in the late 1970s, and to much higher ratios in the early 1980s.

(IV) THE WEAKENING OF MANUFACTURING'S NET EXPORTS

An unprecedented, and from the point of view of the national economy appallingly serious, deterioration in the net export balance of UK manufacturing developed in the 1970s. (By net exports is meant the balance of manufacturing exports minus manufacturing imports.) Any interpretation of the decline in net exports of the manufacturing sector in the 1970s has to take into account the impact of successive stages of trade-cycles on the balance of trade. Thus, an extremely serious deterioration of the manufacturing balance of trade had occurred by 1973, at the culmination of the Heath government's ill-balanced dash for growth.

Nevertheless, the simple picture of the deterioration over the entire decade is close enough to the main trend, and striking enough for its message to be unmistakeable:

> In 1970 (on a 'balance of payments' basis) manufacturing exports exceeded manufacturing imports in value by 59 per cent. By 1979 manufacturing exports were only 10 per cent higher in value than imports.

The worsening of the balance of *finished* manufacturers was even more strikingly bad than the overall manufacturing figures just quoted. In 1970 the value of manufactured exports of finished goods was *over twice* that of finished manufactured imports. By 1979 exports of finished manufactures were *a mere 12 per cent higher* in value than finished imports.

In the course of the 1970s that pattern of decline was one of an extreme deterioration to 1973 (by which time the value of manufacturing exports was only 18 per cent higher than that of imports); a recovery to 1977 (bringing the value of exports back to 30 per cent more than that of imports); and then a further dramatic decline to 1979.

But if we more directly compare 1973 and 1979, since both these years represent cyclical 'peaks' of UK economic activity, the worsening of the country's manufacturing trade performance is only too evident. Thus, between 1973 and 1979 manufactured export volume rose by 20 per cent (finished manufacturers rising by 19½ per cent); by contrast the volume of imported manufactures rose by 55 per cent (that of finished manufactures by 66 per cent). That not only indicates the increasing 'openness' of the UK economy that developed over the last trade-cycle, but also the extreme disproportion that was evident in the movements in trading volume.

It should be emphasised, however, how staggering a deterioration opened up simply between 1977 and 1979. Between these years the volume of manufactured exports ceased to grow (and finished manufactures fell by 2 per cent); the volume of manufactured imports rose by 29 per cent (finished manufactured imports by 39 per cent).

Within these overall figures for manufacturing it is important to recognise some quite shattering and unprecedented examples of decline in major commodity groups. That in passenger motor cars has been most widely recognised; the actual figures still should have the capacity to shock. Measuring, again so as not to exaggerate, from the cyclical 'peak' of 1973 to that of 1979, the volume of exports of passenger cars fell by 18 per cent while the volume of imports rose by 94 per cent. But the performance in *capital goods* must be regarded as at least as disturbing a phenomenon—potentially an even more serious one. The volume of capital goods exports has declined slightly since the mid-1970s, while the volume of imports has risen nearly 60 per cent between 1975 and 1979.

The accelerated pace of the deterioration in net exports after 1977 can be attributed in considerable part to declining competitiveness linked to rising *relative* unit labour costs. Between 1975 and late 1976 devaluation of sterling and the operation of the 'Social Contract' had improved competitiveness (a major fall of some 14 per cent in comparative unit labour costs) with the beneficial effects to trading performance that have already been noted. But from then to the second half of 1979 relative unit labour costs rose by nearly 40 per cent. With the continued rise in the exchange rate of sterling in 1980, and high rates of UK inflation, the rise in relative unit costs has continued steeply. We have yet to see the cumulative effects on the manufacturing trade balance of a quite unprecedented scale and pace of comparative cost deterioration.

The manufacturing sector, then, has increasingly failed to secure an adequate surplus of exports over imports; it has less and less assisted the management of a reasonable overseas payments balance at or near full employment. Even with rapidly increasing export revenues from North Sea oil there was a major swing back to a current account deficit in 1979, in an economy well short of full employment in most regions. The balance of trade in goods other than oil directly deteriorated by £3 billion between 1978 and 1979; over £2.2 billion of this was on manufacturing trade account.

(V) DECLINE IN MANUFACTURING'S SHARE IN GROSS DOMESTIC PRODUCT

One element in the argument about 'deindustrialisation' has been that if the main manufacturing industries contribute a declining share to the total domestic product of the country it could enhance the problems involved in financing an adequate level of public services. Here, as with the balance of payments, it is true that there is—for some time to come—a contribution available from the increased output of the oil and energy sector of the economy. However, the relative decline of manufacturing in this sense must involve increasingly difficult problems of managing, for instance, the transfers required to finance the public services.

The adverse impact on public finance has been twofold. First, the massive decline in manufacturing employment that has previously been discussed has reduced the tax base of employees in employment (more particularly, as argued earlier, because employment elsewhere has not risen to compensate for the manufacturing employment decline). The outcome is one of substantially fewer workers, especially male manual workers, in full-time employment, and a long-term growth in unemployment. Thus revenue to the Exchequer has been curtailed and social benefit payments necessarily increased.

Secondly, the state has been moved to protect to a considerable extent the post-tax profitability of industrial companies, and to increase direct grants and other forms of aid to them (for instance, to encourage higher rates of investment than would otherwise have occurred). The Bank of England in an article in its *Quarterly Bulletin* in June 1980 produced some interesting estimates as to the scale of the reductions in taxation involved. Whereas in the late 1960s and early 1970s the estimated annual taxation on industrial and commercial companies was equivalent to around 4 per cent to 5 per cent of the real value of their trading assets, by the late 1970s taxation had fallen to around 1½ per cent of the value of such assets (in 1977 and 1978) or even less (in 1979). As far as can be judged from the Bank's article, the fall in taxation on industrial and commercial companies (this is wider than manufacturing, but much of the fall would have been concentrated on manufacturing companies) comparing the late 1960s with the late 1970s was as much as 3 per cent of the entire national income. This fall in taxation largely shielded the post-tax income of such companies (says the Bank, real rates of return have remained 'relatively stable') but massively depleted the revenue accruing to the public finances. The 'real tax burden' according to the Bank 'fell sharply' in the 1970s partly because of the extension of 100 per cent initial depreciation allowances on plant and machinery to the whole country in 1972, and partly due to Healey's introduction of tax relief on companies' stocks late in 1974. Grants and other expenditure support, on the other hand, were built up from many directions, including regional grants, and selective investment assistance; these amounted to around £2000 million a year in the late 1970s, not including labour market services such as industrial training, and most of this was directed at manufacturing industries.

One way, then, of viewing the decline in the manufacturing sector is to measure the fall in its share of the total national income produced each year, and to notice also its diminishing scale as compared with the fabric of public sector non-commercial services.

The decline in manufacturing's share of GDP (national income) is marked, and appears persistent whether it is peak years of manufacturing activity that are measured or troughs:—

Table 3.3: Manufacturing: Share of gross domestic product (factor cost)

1969	33.0%	
1971	31.8%	(trough)
1973	30.9%	(peak)
1975	28.6%	(trough)
1979	27.8%	(peak)

Source: National Income and Expenditure, 1980, edn., Table 1:9.

In the course of no more than ten years the share of manufacturing in the national income has shrunk from 33 per cent to under 28 per cent. Roughly its share was diminishing by ½ per cent each year. And this was substantially before North Sea oil added a major new component to national output.

At the same time, the relative scale—within the total national product—of manufacturing and of the public services was changing substantially. We take as the public services the combined range of public administration, defence, public health and educational services. In 1969 the scale of these services (as measured in the total of the country's GDP) was altogether only 36 per cent of that of the manufacturing sector. By 1973 the figure was 43 per cent. By 1979 these public services in scale totalled 50 per cent of the manufacturing sector's contribution to GDP. This does not legitimate the extent and nature of public services' expenditure cuts in the later 1970s. But it does signal the increasing difficulty in managing a balanced economy with adequate public services in face of the deindustrialisation of Britain's manufacturing industries.

(VI) THE DECLINE IN MANUFACTURING INVESTMENT

In earlier post-war years there were many critics of the comparatively low rate of investment (i.e. of real investment in plant, machinery, buildings) made by UK manufacturing industry. Nevertheless, the general picture could be set down as (a) a fairly strongly marked cycle of such fixed investment activity in each trade cycle, but (b) a substantial real advance in total investment expenditure from one trade-cycle to the next.

For instance, the manufacturing fixed investment peak in the year 1970 was in real terms 25 per cent higher than the earlier trade-cycle peak year of 1961. Through the 1950s and 1960s the rhythm had been one of considerable real advance. After 1970 that came to an end.

Indeed, the 1970 level of manufacturing capital expenditure was never reached subsequently (measuring in real terms). Taking 1970 as 100 the development of capital spending in the 1970s looks as follows:—

Table 3.4: Manufacturing: Gross fixed capital formation
(Constant 1975 prices) 1970 = 100

Peaks		Troughs	
1970	100	1972	81
1974	91	1976	80
1979	93		

Source: National Income and Expenditure, 1980 edn.

This was all there was to show for the increased emphasis placed from the 1975 recession onwards on selective and other aid to maintain manufacturing investment, and the increased importance of investment directed into publicly-owned manufacturing corporations.

But such figures, serious as they are (given the weight of new investment by trade rivals), may still not give an adequate view of the contribution to deindustrialisation coming from a flagging process of new investment. For these figures are for *gross* spending. A substantial part of that spending would be needed simply to cover depreciation and replacement needs. What was happening to *net*, to estimated *additional*, capital expenditure?

Government statistics provide an estimate of this based on assumed lives of plant and equipment, and on the cost of replacing existing equipment. Any such measure can only be seen as a broad guide to the trends that were developing, but what such figures do point to is exceptionally disturbing.

On this basis we find *net* capital spending falling at the 1974 peak to no more than two-thirds of the level in 1970. The 1979 peak was once again lower. In the cyclical troughs net capital expenditure falls away even more steeply, typically to little more than half the level of the previous peak.

The sheer inadequacy of recent levels of net capital spending by UK

Table 3.5: Manufacturing: net* fixed capital expenditure in the 1970s
(1975 constant prices)

Year	£ million	Index (1970=100)	As % of net domestic product
1970 (peak)	2101	100	2.5
1972 (trough)	1143	54	1.3
1974 (peak)	1418	67	1.5
1976 (trough)	841	40	0.9
1979 (peak)	1207	57	1.2

Source: National Income and Expenditure, 1980 edn.
*Gross fixed capital expenditure *minus* capital consumption.

manufacturing emerges starkly in the final column of Table 3.5. Even in 1972 net capital spending accounted for no more than 2½ per cent of the (net) domestic product of the country—this in a period of rapid technological change and displacement and intensifying international competition. By the cycle of the latter half of the 1970s, manufacturing industry's net capital expenditure is fluctuating around no more than 1 per cent of the total national product. The main engine of manufacturing growth and future competitiveness must necessarily be a technologically relevant process of new capital expenditure. But this was what investment spending had been reduced to in the 1970s—and even before the onset of the slump.

(VII) SECTORS IN MAJOR DECLINE: A DANGER OF CUMULATIVE COLLAPSE?

The unevenness of the 'deindustrialisation' process was emphasised earlier. Another way of putting this is to say that particular sectors have shown major declines in output and loss of market share. Given the nature of modern industrial economics, the disadvantages of enterprises operating substantially below planned capacity, the loss of dynamic economies of larger-scale operation, the greater difficulty in managing processes of major technological innovation, all this could create conditions for cumulative decline. 'Sectoral retreat' did not save the British motor-cycle industry. Moreover, market and supply links (input–output relationships) may widen the area of such longer run depressive contraction over a number of industries, and concentrate the displacement effects in particular regions.

The general point is well put in the recent symposium on 'Deindustrialisation':

> on the supply side there is a vicious circle of declining market share, declining profits and investment and declining competitive power, which must aggravate the weakness of British industry in the absence of resolute government action. In some versions great emphasis is laid on dynamic economies of scale and the advantages enjoyed by other countries supplying expanding markets, able to invest more and innovate more rapidly, reinforcing their competitive position and so establishing themselves in an ever-widening range of markets. A picture is painted of a relentless cumulative process working in favour of the strong and against the weak. De-industrialisation on this showing is the lot of the weak unless they assert themselves against the strong. (Blackaby, 1979, p. 11)

This looks uncomfortably close to the industrial groups in which decline has been concentrated. But it may have significance too for the erstwhile rapidly expanding sectors of output whose rate of advance has slowed down very noticeably over the last trade cycle. Such loss of momentum may be a warning sign. Thus both the chemicals sector and electrical engineering increased output by over 20 per cent in the cycle that peaked (for these industries) in 1974. By 1978 they had managed to increase output by only around 4 per cent above the 1974 peak.

Two manufacturing sectors, vehicles and metal manufacture, stand out as having ceased to show output growth in the earlier trade cycle; output in the 1973 peak was no higher than that achieved in the late 1960s. In each case they show steep declines since the 1973 peak. In the case of ferrous metal manufacture the 1979 level of output was about 20 per cent below the 1973 peak and fresh decline is in prospect. In the latest cycles steel production has fallen considerably more than consumption, indicating loss of market share.

By 1978–79 crude steel output had fallen back to the levels of output of the late 1950s; but most recently closure plans and estimates of falling demand indicate a further major contraction (to output levels of the

Table 3.6: Changes in steel output and consumption

Trade cycles (trough to trough)	Crude steel output	Finished steel consumption
1962–67	+17%	+14%
1967–71	Zero	+ 6%
1971–75	−18%	− 8%
1975–80 (est.)	−40%	−20%

early 1950s, over 40 per cent below the peak at the beginning of the 1970s).

Output of the vehicle sector as a whole had fallen about 16 per cent from the 1973 peak by 1979. The incidence of strikes in this sector had risen from an already high level, and contributed to the adverse output performance in 1978 and 1979, years of high demand. Perhaps the most dramatic indication of rapidly deteriorating performance is provided by passenger car output. The best measure of this is the ratio of total output of passenger cars to home registrations (the difference representing reasonably well net export or import).

Table 3.7: UK passenger car production as % of new registration

1970	152
1972	117
1974	121
1976	104
1978	77
1979	64

Thus, in the course of the decade the output of cars has moved from a net export surplus of around half the total UK market to an import surplus of over one-third of that market. The extreme impact on overseas trade has already been noted; merely measuring from 1975 the adverse swing to net imports (for the category of all types of 'road vehicles') was at current prices the equivalent of about £2½ billion a year, by 1979.

Other important sectors with falls in output from the 1973 peak to 1979 (which we are taking as representing a cyclical peak before the recession of 1980/81) can be briefly indicated. In face of a fall in output in construction of about 14 per cent from the 1973 peak (a fall which owes much to disproportionate capital cuts in public spending) the output of 'bricks, cements, etc.' has fallen over 20 per cent below the 1973 peak. This influence must also have been felt in 'timber, furniture, etc.', which shows output falls of approximately 14 per cent from 1973 to a 1979 peak. Mechanical engineering peaked in 1974. Output in 1978 and 1979 has been running at around 8 per cent below the 1974 level. It is more difficult to describe the performance of the 'textile' industries; there was a feeble peak in 1976, some 14 per cent below the 1973 peak, and since then output has fallen further. Import/export ratios for mechanical engineering and for textiles have been worsening in recent years. Finally, shipbuilding also shows a falling trend within which it is difficult to discern anything that might be called a cyclical peak.

It seems helpful to bring together all these sectors that show a clear decline in output between the 1973 peak and the 1979 peak and indicate their performance (see Table 3.8). Through Table 3.8 we are looking at the industries that so far have been most evidently trapped in the processes of decline and deindustrialisation. Despite the fact that the slump of 1980–81 has not yet reached its trough, it seems helpful too to indicate how far the same industries' output had fallen *below the 1975 recession trough* by the autumn of 1980. The official data is shown in the table.

It must be emphasised that these industries are a very substantial part of total UK manufacturing. At the 1973 peak they employed around 3½ million workers. Their combined 'weight' (proportion of base year production) in the official production index for manufacturing is *nearly half the total* (48 per cent of the total).

Table 3.8: UK manufacturing output: Slump added to long period decline

(Sectors with major falls in output comparing 1973 and 1979)
(1975 output as 100)

Sectors	Previous cycle			Current cycle	% Decline	
	Peak 1973	Trough 1975	Peak 1979	(near trough) last 3 mths Aug–Oct. 1980	Peak to peak (73–79)	1975 to latest 3 mths
Coal & petroleum products	120.6	100.0	105.3	90.7	−13	− 9
Ferrous metals	129.5	100.0	104.4	64.8	−19	−35
Non-ferrous metals	117.1	100.0	105.5	86.6	−10	−13
Mech. engineering	97.1	100.0	91.4	(81)*	− 6	(−19)
Shipbuilding	95.4	100.0	78.1	66.6	−18	−33
Motor vehicles	118.8	100.0	99.3	73.4	−16	−27
Metal goods n.e.s.	110.4	100.0	98.5	74.2	−11	−26
Textiles	117.1	100.0	96.7	71.9	−17	−28
Leather, leather goods	107.1	100.0	91.8	64	−14	−36
Bricks, cement	120.7	100.0	94.6	76.5	−22	−23
Timber, furniture	120.2	100.0	103.0	81.1	−14	−19

Source: Data from *Index of Indsutrial Production.*
*September to November, 1980.

Yet these industries embracing nearly half of the manufacturing total (on the 1975 index base):

At the 1979 cyclical peak had output around 15 per cent *less* than at the 1973 peak;
By autumn 1980 were operating at output levels about 25 per cent *below* the 1975 trough.

These then are some of the dimensions by which the deindustrialisation of the British economy may be measured; the overall change from long-term growth to decline; the curb to productivity, the fall in employment in manufacturing; the weakening of manufacturing net exports; the decline in manufacturing's share of GDP; the decline in investment; the extensive sectors in serious (and potentially cumulative) decline. If all these are brought together they signal the most profound structural crisis for the British economy. But all of that has been made far worse by a grossly mismanaged recession, which in the hands of the Thatcher government has turned into a devastating slump.

4. Factors Influencing Growth*

Leslie Manison

The poor growth performance of the UK economy, which was the subject of much discussion in the 1960s, (Kaldor, 1966; Henderson, 1966) has continued in the 1970s. . . .

There has been much debate as to what have been the major factors explaining the United Kingdom's disappointing economic growth performance. While some writers have emphasised the slow rate of accumulation of factor inputs, particularly of physical capital in industry, (Bacon and Eltis, 1975) as a major factor hindering the growth of British production, others have stressed the inefficient use or allocation of existing productive capacity as being important in explaining the UK's relatively slow rate of economic growth. (Cripps and Tarling, 1973) In what follows, an attempt is made to identify some of the factors causing the UK's slow rate of economic growth, especially since the early 1960s, taking cognisance of the ideas put forward in recent literature on the subject.

I. FACTORS ACCOUNTING FOR THE UNITED KINGDOM'S LOW RATE OF CAPITAL FORMATION

Capacity to Invest

In broad terms, an economy's rate of capital formation will be determined by the economy's capacity to invest in the form of the resources available to finance investment and/or by the willingness to invest. The resources available for investment will in turn be determined

*Reproduced from L. Manison, 'Some factors influencing the UK's economic growth performance', *IMF Staff Papers*, International Monetary Fund, Washington D.C., vol, 25, December 1978, pp. 705–38.

by the economy's domestic savings performance and its ability to attract capital from overseas. Detailed savings data in a comparable form for some major industrial countries are available only for the years 1963 to 1975 (Table 4.1). These data indicate that the rate of net domestic savings in the United Kingdom over this period was considerably lower than in all other major industrial countries except the United States.

Table 4.1: Selected major industrial countries: saving ratios and labour income share, 1963–75

| | | Net domestic saving, of which | | |
| | | Households | Corporate and quasi-corporate | Compensation of employees as % of |
	Total	(as % GDP)	enterprises	national income
UK	9.1	4.4	1.9	66.1
West Germany	15.6	8.4	2.5	58.3
Japan	24.9	15.3	3.6	53.7
Canada	11.3	4.5	3.8	62.2
USA	7.5	5.4	1.8	64.0

Sources: OECD, National Accounts of OECD Countries, 1974, vol. 2, and 1975, vol. 2 (Paris).

One needs next to account for the factors contributing to the UK's relatively low domestic saving ratio, especially of that in the household sector. It has been argued in the economic literature that wage and salary earners tend to have a lower propensity to save than do profit earners and that a change in the factor distribution of income will tend to affect the overall saving ratio. While there is much intuitive support for this proposition, it has not been subject to any rigorous empirical testing for UK data. One can note, however, that over the period 1963 to 1975 labour income in the UK represented a higher proportion of national income than in other major industrial countries (Table 4.1). The countries with the lowest domestic saving ratios—namely, the United Kingdom, the United States and Canada—were also the only economies where compensation of employees as a percentage of national income exceeded 60 per cent. On the other hand, the fall in the share of profits in domestic incomes in recent years in the UK has been accompanied by substantial rises in the personal saving ratio. Notwithstanding, most commentators have attributed the rise in the personal saving ratio to such factors as the need to reconstitute real cash balances following their erosion by inflation and the uncertainty generated by higher rates of unemployment and inflation, and to increased contractual savings (mainly contributions to pension funds and life assurance premiums) induced in part by the British tax system, rather than to the change in the factor distribution of income.

It has been contended that the UK authorities have conducted their short-term demand management policies in such a way as to produce a bias toward consumption as against investment. Lord Kahn and Michael Posner, in a memorandum submitted to the Expenditure Committee of the House of Commons in July 1974, noted that when moving from a 'stop' to a 'go' policy, the UK authorities have mainly used fiscal expansion in the form of reductions of taxation, but have relied largely on monetary and credit restrictions when moving back from the 'go' to the 'stop' policy phase. On the basis of this, they argue that 'fiscal expansion [cutting rates of taxation] operates, on the whole, by benefitting consumption; while the restriction of the availability of credit operates, on the whole, by discouraging investment. Thus investment is constantly restrained in booms and consumption encouraged in slumps. The economy has been the victim of a highly perverse ratchet effect.' In this connection, the most recent attempts to arrest the rapid growth of monetary aggregates and to reduce the public sector borrowing requirement (for example, in the latter months of 1976) were centred on restrictive monetary measures and cuts in public sector capital expenditure, while subsequent efforts to reflate the economy have encompassed mainly reductions in income taxes.

A number of writers in attempting to explain the high personal saving ratio in Japan in the post-war period have emphasised that the Japanese economy seemed to benefit from a 'virtuous circle' in which a high growth rate of income contributed to a high saving ratio, which in turn facilitated a high growth rate of output (Mizoguchi, 1968). This explanation is consistent with theories about consumer behaviour that hypothesise that consumption habits of previous years strongly influence consumption in the current year. By the same token, the inference could be drawn that the UK has been locked in a low growth rate/low saving rate circle, which has severely hampered the capacity to invest.

Limited data also indicate that the relatively poor savings performance of the corporate sector in the UK has contributed to the relatively low rate of domestic savings. The contribution of the corporate sector in the United Kingdom to the domestic savings effort, as elsewhere, has fallen quite sharply since the early 1960s, a development that appears to have been associated with the falling rate of return on capital employed in this sector. Savings of companies fell from 44.7 per cent of total domestic savings in the period 1963–66 to 19.0 per cent in 1967–70 and further to 13.1 per cent in 1971–75. The fall in the internally-generated funds of corporations has led to greater reliance on external funds to finance investment. This has been reflected in a fall in the ratio of funds raised through rights issues to debt capital from an average of 69.3 per cent in the period 1966 to 1970 to 25.1 per cent in the following six years. Some of the factors accounting for the erosion of corporate profits are discussed in the following sub-section.

It can be argued that even if a country's domestic savings performance is poor, resources for investment in an open economy, like that in the UK, can be easily obtained by borrowing from abroad. That is, the real constraint to investment will be the willingness to invest. This appears to have been true in the UK up to about 1973, where despite the poor domestic savings performance and an array of controls on external capital outflows only a small percentage of funds was obtained from external sources. In the three years 1974–76, however, with domestic savings falling in the face of higher gross capital formation, external borrowing rose sharply. The latter development contributed to a weakening of the external payments position and to higher nominal interest rates, which in turn eventually had detrimental effects on the rate of private investment (Bacon and Eltis, 1976). It is in this sense that the domestic savings effort can indirectly constrain investment. It is noteworthy that Japan and the major industrial countries of Europe, which achieved high rates of capital formation over the period 1962–75, had relatively strong domestic savings performances and were net lenders to the rest of the world.

Willingness to Invest

Within the constraints set by the availability of investible resources, the actual rate of capital formation will be determined by the willingness of entrepreneurs and other entities making investment decisions to deploy the investible surplus in actual capital formation. The desire to invest will in turn be determined by a multitude of factors. Keynes, in *The General Theory of Employment, Interest and Money*, postulated that the inducement to invest will be determined by the relationship between the marginal efficiency of capital (the expected rate of profit on a contemplated new investment) and the rate of interest, with the rate of investment being pushed to the point on the investment-demand schedule where the marginal efficiency of capital in general is equal to the market rate of interest. More recent studies have refined this relationship and have related investment demand to the valuation ratio, which is defined as the ratio between the rate of return on capital employed and the cost of capital. In these studies, the actual rate of return on existing capital assets is used as a surrogate for the expected rate of profit on a prospective investment, since it is argued that if current rates of profit are changing, enterprises not only will have more or less internally-generated funds to invest but also are likely to have more or less incentive to undertake further investments, given the cost of capital.

There is considerable evidence suggesting that the rate of return on capital employed in UK industry has been falling, especially since the mid-1960s. The pre-tax rate of return, which averaged 10.8 per cent in the 1960s, fell to an average of 8.2 per cent over the next four years, decline sharply to 4.6 per cent in 1974, and further to 3.5 per cent in both 1975 and 1976 (Table 4.2). The post-tax rate of return recorded a similar decline and would have fallen to zero by 1974 but for tax relief on profits derived from increases in the value of stocks. The fall in company profitability in the United Kingdom is indicated also by the decline in the share of gross trading profits of companies net of stock appreciation as a proportion of domestic income from an average of 13.8 per cent in the 1960s to an average of 11.1 per cent over the next four years, and further to an average of 6.4 per cent in the three years 1974 to 1976.

Whether the rate of return on investments in the UK has been lower than in other countries, and has been a factor causing the relatively slower rate of capital formation in that country, is worth exploring. Given the caveat that one should exercise considerable caution in comparing data on company profitability across countries, there is evidence suggesting that the rate of return on corporate capital in the United Kingdom has averaged a lower level and declined more sharply than in other major industrial countries . . .

A major factor contributing to the relatively low level of company profitability in the UK appears to have been the relatively high proportion of value added of companies taken by labour costs in the United Kingdom. Comparable data are not available for the corporate sector as a whole on the share of labour costs in value added for major industrial countries. Figures for the manufacturing sector, however, indicate that the share of company income going to labour in the UK is high compared with most other industrial countries. During the period 1960–75, compensation of labour employed in the manufacturing sector as a proportion of domestic product originating in that sector averaged more than 70 per cent, and by 1975 it had increased to 75 per cent. In the United States, labour's share in the output of the manufacturing sector also averaged more than 70 per cent, while in Italy the share was 67 per cent and had risen to about 74 per cent by 1975. In the other major industrial countries, however, the share of manufacturing output

Table 4.2: *United Kingdom: Rates of return, cost of capital, and profit shares in industrial and commercial companies, 1960–76 (%)*

	Rates of return on capital employed in industrial and commercial companies after deducting stock appreciation[1]		Post-tax real cost of capital[3]	Gross trading profits of companies net of stock appreciation as a proportion of domestic income
	Pre-tax	Post-tax[2]		
1960	13.2	9.7	8.8	15.9
1961	11.4	8.1	8.3	14.5
1962	10.4	7.6	6.3	13.7
1963	11.3	9.2	5.8	14.7
1964	11.7	9.3	6.5	14.7
1965	11.2	6.6	5.3	14.2
1966	9.8	5.5	5.7	12.9
1967	10.2	5.9	5.0	13.0
1968	10.0	5.3	3.9	12.7
1969	8.8	4.1	4.0	11.7
1970	7.8	3.4	4.4	10.7
1971	8.3	4.3	4.6	11.6
1972	8.8	4.3	5.1	11.6
1973	7.8	4.5	6.1	10.5
1974	4.6	2.2[4]	6.6	6.8
1975	3.5	3.3[4]	5.9	6.0
1976[5]	3.5	2.9[4]	6.8	6.5

Sources: Bank of England, *Quarterly Bulletin* (June 1977); UK Central Statistical Office, *Economic Trends* (various issues).

[1]Ration of earnings (gross trading profits *plus* rent received *less* depreciation and profits owing to stock appreciation) to the average capital stock in the period. Capital stock and allowances for capital consumption are valued at the current replacement cost.

[2]After deduction from profits of taxes on interest and dividends in the hand of recipients, as well as direct company taxes. Only current investment incentives are taken account of, and the impact of past investment incentives on the companies' actual tax bill has not been allowed for, since the computations of the actual rate of return are intended to be 'forward looking'.

[3]The real cost of capital is defined as the rate at which the companies' future earnings are discounted by the capital market in valuing the securities on which those earnings will accrue, whether in the form of interest, dividends or retentions. In the Bank of England, *Quarterly Bulletin* (June 1977), it is estimated by dividing 'forward looking' post-tax profits (after allowance for stock relief) by the financial valuation of the capital stock.

[4]Adjusts for tax relief on stocks.

[5]Provisional estimates.

absorbed by labour was lower, especially in France, West Germany and Japan.

In accounting for the decline in the profitability of British industry, one cannot attribute it to the growth in real average labour earnings outstripping that of labour productivity in the manufacturing sector. In this sector, the annual average growth rate in output per person employed was 3.2 per cent over the period 1963–75, while that of the real product wage was 2.9 per cent. The divergence between the growth of real average earnings and of labour productivity appears to have been the reverse for industrial and commercial companies outside the manufacturing sector, because increases in earnings were only a little below, or in line with, those in the manufacturing sector, while productivity growth was appreciably less. The latter development was particularly pronounced in the 1970s when the growth of the labour productivity in the non-manufacturing sector was less than one-third of that in the manufacturing sector.

In the UK manufacturing sector, the sharpest fall in company profitability appears to have taken place since 1973, when prices of inputs of fuels and materials to industrial companies rose much faster than the prices of manufacturing output at a time of decelerating sales turnover. While wholesale prices of materials and fuel purchased by the manufacturing industry rose by 119.5 per cent over the three years from the second quarter of 1973, wholesale prices for the home sales of manufactured output and of the unit value of manufactured exports increased by 78.5 per cent and 89.2 per cent, respectively. The inability of British manufacturers fully to pass on cost increases in higher output prices in recent years can be ascribed in part to the increasing price competition in world trade in manufactures and to uncertainties about prospective demand, domestic price controls and other restrictive regulations, which have effectively limited freedom in price-setting.

Even though the growth of real average labour earnings in the manufacturing sector has not risen appreciably more rapidly than labour productivity, it could still be said that the failure of real wages to adjust to the 1973–75 upheaval in material and input costs contributed to the sharp decline in company profitability from 1973 onward. That is, the brunt of the adjustment to the rise in commodity prices and fuel costs was borne by profits. In this context, the shape of gross property income in corporate value added in the UK fell by 5.4 percentage points between 1973 and 1975, whereas in the other major industrial countries the change in the gross profit share over the same period ranged from a fall of 3.1 percentage points in Italy to an increase of 1.2 percentage points in Japan. It was only from the last quarter of 1975 to the third quarter of 1977 that there was a significant reduction in real wages, which helped to alleviate pressure on profit margins; over this period, real wages fell by about 8 per cent.

The rate of growth of labour productivity in the manufacturing sector in the UK has been well below that of all other major industrial countries except the United States. The relatively slow growth of labour productivity in British industry coupled with the slow growth in installed capacity has meant that manufacturers have experienced difficulties in supplying orders, especially in periods of buoyant demand. In each of the business upswings since 1960, the annual increase in labour productivity in the manufacturing sector reached a peak of just under 8 per cent and then fell back sharply. The marked deceleration in the growth of labour productivity following each cyclical upswing was due partly to supply constraints, such as shortages of component parts and technical manpower impinging upon the growth of manufacturing output. Consequently, British manufacturers in general have not been able to lower their average unit costs to the same extent as rival overseas producers through having longer production runs. Furthermore, the fragmented structure of British industry, caused in part by government support of ailing plants, has resulted in a duplication of capital capacity in many sectors of industry and has contributed to higher overhead costs per unit.

The fall in the profitability of investment appears also to have been associated with an underlying decline in the marginal physical productivity of capital. Although the capital stock has tended to become increasingly under-utilised with each cyclical trough, there appears to have been a secular decline in output per unit of capital since the mid-1960s for both the whole economy and the manufacturing sector. The sharper fall in capital productivity in the 1970s in the UK than in other major industrial countries appears to be another factor explaining the steeper decline in profits in the UK. A discussion of the factors accounting for this decline and the low incremental output/capital ratio in the UK is presented in section II.

While the low and declining rate of profitability of UK corporations may have contributed to the relatively low rate of capital formation, especially in the manufacturing sector, the incentive to invest has also been influenced by the cost to companies of the finance needed to acquire or to form physical capital. In a Bank of England article, it was estimated that the real cost of capital for industrial and commercial companies in the United Kingdom (Bank of England, 1976) declined appreciably in the 1960s, the fall being in line with the post-tax rate of return on capital. Thereafter, it rose quite sharply, and in the three years 1974–76 it was considerably above the post-tax rate of return on capital.

It appears that the fall in the rate of return on capital employed and developments in the cost of capital go some way toward explaining the low rate of fixed industrial investment in the United Kingdom . . .

In summing up this section, it could be said that the slow rate of capital accumulation in the UK, relative to that in other major industrial countries, has been due to both a low and declining capacity and a lack of willingness to invest. The low ability to invest has reflected a poor domestic savings performance over most of the post-war period. Rapid increases in labour costs per unit of output have reduced the flow of internally-generated funds in the corporate sector and have increased the flow of income to the less thrifty or less investment-prone segments of the population. In this connection, the diminution of profits, arising from the growth of real wages outstripping that of labour productivity, appears to have been most pronounced for enterprises outside the manufacturing sector. With labour and capital costs—and more recently, material and fuel costs—rising rapidly in the face of limited capacity to raise output prices and to expand company turnover because of domestic price controls and strong international competition, profits have been squeezed and the incentive to invest consequently has diminished. In addition, the fall in corporate profit rate seems to have been associated with an underlying decline in the marginal physical productivity.

II. FACTORS CONTRIBUTING TO THE LOW APPARENT PRODUCTIVITY OF GROSS INVESTMENT

An economy's rate of economic growth will depend not only on the rate of capital formation but also on the output return on that capital formation. The gross incremental output/capital ratio is used in this paper to measure the apparent productivity of new capital formation. This ratio in the UK has consistently been below that in other major industrial economies over the last 20 years. Only in West Germany since 1960 has the apparent productivity of gross investment fallen to a level comparable with that in the UK.

An examination of the growth of the capital stock in the various types of manufacturing industry for the UK over the period 1962–75 reveals that the capital stock in so-called heavy (basic metals and metal products) industries grew at a considerably slower rate than that in other manufacturing industries. The gross capital stock at replacement cost in the 'iron and steel' and 'other metals, engineering, and allied' industries increased at annual average rates of 2.6 per cent and 2.7 per cent, respectively, over the period 1962–75, while the capital stock in other manufacturing industries rose at an annual average rate of 3.4 per cent. In fact, it was in the food, drink, tobacco and chemical sectors that the capital stock grew most rapidly. Similar data on capital formation within the manufacturing sector do not seem to be available for other major industrial countries; however, data on changes in the composition of output in the manufacturing sector of certain industrial countries suggest that capital resources have been allocated to the metals, metal fabrication, machinery and transport-equipment industries at a more rapid rate than in other manufacturing industries. Only in the UK, and perhaps in Italy, was the growth rate of production in so-called heavy industries below that of the manufacturing sector as a whole.

It is in the heavy and chemical industries that the scope of obtaining high output returns on new capital formation would seem to be greatest, since such industries have been the most technologically dynamic and have given the greatest opportunities for achieving economies of scale. The products of these industries have also experienced the most rapid growth in world trade over the post-war period.

The UK's lack of capital capacity in rapidly growing world industries has been most conspicuous at times of cyclical upswings in the world economy, when the UK manufacturing sector has been unable to satisfy fully the large increases in demand for certain finished manufactured goods. This was most evident in the boom of 1973 when UK manufacturers could not meet the demand for such vital products as steel, castings, electric motors, specialist machine tools and diesel engines. Panić has in fact argued that this lack of supply capacity has led also to the UK having a higher income elasticity of demand for imports of manufactures than that of other major industrial countries, especially for finished goods (Panić, 1975). He estimates that the income elasticity of demand for imports of manufactures was 3.09 for the United Kingdom over the period 1957–72, compared with 2.14 for West Germany, and 2.19 for France. Panić and Rajan in an earlier study found that the UK trade performance deteriorated relatively faster in the commodity groups, for which world demand was growing rapidly, than in those in which it was growing slowly (Panić and Rajan, 1971). And the OECD in its 1978 economic survey of the United Kingdom states 'there is indeed some very impressionistic evidence which suggests that it is precisely in those industries in which investment efforts have been relatively low since the beginning of the decade that foreign penetration has advanced most rapidly' (OECD, 1978). Consistent with this line of argument is the hypothesis of Bacon and Eltis (1975) that boom periods in the British economy since 1965 have tended to become shorter because of the slower growth of productive potential resulting from the slowdown in industrial investment. With each successive boom, the limits to supply have been approached more quickly. This has led to an upsurge in imports and an administered halt in the boom because of the need to correct a widening balance of payments deficit. Bacon and Eltis pointed out that 40 per cent of Britain's machine-tool requirements were supplied from abroad in 1974, compared with 20 per cent in 1955. Thus, it seems that low capital expenditure in potentially dynamic areas of the manufacturing sector has contributed indirectly to truncating periods of rapid economic expansion, and consequently has reduced the overall rate of economic growth over longer periods of time.

Not only has UK industry been a relative disadvantage during periods of peak demand but also the low rate of capital formation in technologically advanced industries in the UK manufacturing sector has both prevented the rapid diffusion of new technologies into the productive process via so-called embodied technical progress and contributed to the decline in the ability of British industry to compete internationally in markets for more sophisticated products at times of slacker demand. The UK's lack of investment in the development of sophisticated products appears to be indicated by data collected by the National Economic Development Office that show that unit values of UK exports within most product groups tend to be lower than those in West Germany and France, especially in the engineering sector, while the reverse appeared to be true for unit values of imports (NEDO, 1977). Relative to other major industrial countries, the UK seems to be slipping downstream in the product cycle, producing cheaper and less sophisticated goods with a lower rate of return. The same goods, like textiles, which the UK exported to former British colonies, are now often produced by these countries and other developing economies in the first stages of their industrialisation. Thus, it appears that the UK with its low value-added industries has been more vulnerable to low-cost competition.

In the post-war period with world trade in manufacturing expanding at a more rapid rate than world output of manufacturers, all major industrial countries other than the UK and the USA seem to have taken advantage of this situation through expanding their exports of manufactures at a faster rate than that of output, especially through increasing the heavy industry composition of such exports. Once manufacturers in countries such as Japan, Italy and France have penetrated foreign markets with their products, they have been able to spread their fixed costs over higher outputs and, thus, have reinforced their competitive edge in world markets. The inability of UK manufacturers to penetrate export markets is indicated by the fact that in the period 1960–76 the UK share in the volume of the manufacturing exports of the eleven largest OECD countries decline from 15.3 per cent to 8.3 per cent. The poor performance of British manufactured exports has been most evident with regard to exports of machinery and transport equipment, which have lagged considerably behind those of world exports in these commodities. The relatively high income elasticity of UK demand for imports and the relatively low elasticity of UK exports with respect to foreign trade suggest also that UK production of manufactures is of goods that are growing relatively slowly in world trade. At the same time, data on import penetration from 1968 to 1976 show that domestic market penetration has been most pronounced in industries producing machinery and transport equipment (*Economic Trends*, 1977).

The question arises as to why a greater amount or proportion of capital formation has not flowed into the more technologically dynamic and more export-oriented manufacturing industries in the UK. One hypothesis sometimes put forward is that UK producers tend to treat exporting as a peripheral activity, a tendency that may be based in part on the past unprofitability of exporting. It is contended that UK enterprises have exhibited a tendency to shift more resources into exports at times of domestic recessions, which have usually been in phase with recessions in the world economy, and to switch them back to the home market when domestic demand recovers. The loss of UK export market shares appears to have been least in periods of slack world demand for manufactures. While there have been fairly marked short-term fluctuations in the relative profitability of exporting and of selling in the domestic market since the mid-1950s, there does not seem to have been any period, with the possible exception of the years 1974–77, in which there has been a sustained improvement in relative export profitability of a magnitude that would induce producers to reorient their activities towards the export market. Moreover, with the decline in the overall profitability of industry since the early 1960s, a large increase in the relative profitability of exports would be required to coax out more capital formation for export-oriented production. It is further contended that with an increase in export profit margins, resulting from a devaluation in the pound sterling, manufacturers have tended to aim at maximising short-run profits through keeping the foreign currency prices of the products unchanged rather than by using their improved price competitiveness to gain market shares and to enhance longer-run export profitability. This behaviour of exporters may be indicative of their belief or experience that improved export profitability arising from devaluations is unlikely to be sustained, partly because of subsequent upward pressures on domestic wages and prices. It has also been argued that investment in export-oriented and import-competing industries has been discouraged because changes in relative costs and prices *vis-à-vis* foreign competitors have not been sufficient to offset non-price competitive factors that have caused other major industrial countries to gain market shares at the expense of UK producers (Fetherston, *et. al*, 1977).

The output return on new capital formation will depend also on the efficiency with which it is combined with and used by other factors of production. Efficient use of plant and equipment may be limited by a shortage of complementary factor inputs. It was fashionable in the mid-1960s to attribute the sluggish growth of British secondary industry to the slow growth of labour supply available for employment in the non-agricultural sector. However, this hypothesis seems to have been abandoned in recent years by its former adherents, especially as the coexistence of high unemployment and the slow growth of secondary industry became more pronounced. For example, Kaldor in 1975 said,

> I was wrong in thinking in 1966 that . . . her [the United Kingdom's] comparatively poor performance was to be explained by inability to recruit sufficient labour to manufacturing industry rather than by poor market performance due to lack of international competitiveness . . . In particular, I would now place more, rather than less, emphasis on the exogenous components of demand, and in particular on the role of exports, in determining the trend rate of productivity growth in the United Kingdom in relation to other industrially advanced countries. (Kaldor, 1975)

In fact, it has been argued that restrictive labour practices in the UK have led to an overmanning of plant and equipment and a consequent depressing of the output return on capital. Recent years have been characterised by organised groups of workers being preoccupied with resisting changes intended to improve productivity because of the fear of unemployment rather than by employers being preoccupied with problems of labour shortages.

While there does not seem to have been any shortage of unskilled labour to man effectively new capital equipment at least in the latter part of the post-war period, a number of writers have argued that there has been a shortage of technical manpower and managerial talent, especially of engineers, in the UK economy (Peck, 1968). In the aforementioned article by Matthews and King on how to regenerate British manufacturing industry, it was stated that 'the real bottlenecks in this country (not necessarily abroad) are in skilled labour and managerial talent'. Studies by NEDO (1977) indicate shortages of mechanical engineers in certain industries. In a detailed but earlier study of 68 factories in the UK electrical engineering industry, however, a group of writers found no convincing evidence to support the conclusion that there is a general shortage of scientists and engineers in British industry, but at the same time warned against generalising the results of their study (Layard, *et. al.*, 1971).

Have British managers been less productive than their overseas counterparts in the management of capital equipment and/or have they been guilty of making poor investment decisions? It is difficult to determine to what degree management and labour are responsible for the poor output return on investment in the United Kingdom. Matthews and King contend that

> 'the evidence suggests that when British managements seek to raise productivity by the use of modern methods and equipment, they find themselves obliged to accept conditions as to manning, operation or pay that cancel out much of the advantage of making changes and are not insisted upon by the employees of their competitors abroad. Managers have also had to devote much more time to dealing with labour disputes at the expense of innovatory tasks of prime importance to economic growth.' (Matthews and King, 1977)

Some writers argue that British management seems to be only slightly less efficient than US management. Although US firms operating in the UK do not achieve levels of productivity equal to those that they attain in USA or in West Germany, their levels of productivity tend to be somewhat higher than the average of locally-owned companies. Pratten contends that the greater independence between managing directors and work operations in British corporations is a factor contributing to management's poorer relative performance (Pratten, 1977). He argues that the managers of most German and Swedish companies are supervised by boards of directors of which the managing director is the only director who is active in the day-to-day management of the company. If the board finds that a managing director is incompetent, he is replaced. On the other hand, in the UK it is difficult to change managing directors, because most work in the business. Furthermore, it is more difficult for them to take a dispassionate view, and factions can develop. It is further contended by Pratten that management's efficiency in the use of capital equipment in the United Kingdom is rendered difficult by restrictive labour practices that often result in the overmanning of machines. However, it is argued by Eric Moonman, Chairman of the All-Party Parliamentary Management Committee, that the relatively poor performance of UK managers in the home market also reflects their relative lack of qualifications and their low level of motivation. He adds that the failure of the best qualified graduates to come into industry reflects very largely the poor image that industry has in Britain. In particular, the production and marketing aspects of business have not attracted the élite. In fact, Sir Henry Phelps Brown argues that the UK educational and class system has done the country a disservice by diverting ability away from industry (Phelps Brown, 1977). The aversity of industry to potential managers and the poor motivation of actual managers probably also reflects the relatively poor pay of British managers. The findings of a Royal Commission on the distribution of income and wealth indicated that the real disposable income of British managers has been declining steadily since 1969 and that they earn considerably less than their counterparts in France and the United States. These findings are supported by data that suggest that there has been an increase in recent years in the emigration of UK managers to overseas corporations.

One also should consider whether the highly publicised labour disputes in UK industry have resulted in capital equipment being less utilised or more idle than in other major industrial countries. However, an international comparison of the number of days lost per 1000 employees as a result of industrial disputes over the period 1965–74 reveals that considerably more days were lost in the United States, Canada, and Italy than in the UK: only Japan, West Germany, and France seemed to be relatively free from industrial disputes. The United Kingdom's reputation of being unusually strike-prone seems to derive from the much publicised record of a few dispute-prone industries (mining, automobile manufacture, shipbuilding, and the servicing of docks) and the tendency for labour disputes to be more disruptive because of the relatively greater vertical integration of UK industry.

It is also possible that the low capital productivity in the UK may have resulted from a relatively high under-utilisation of capital equipment caused by a relatively low level of domestic demand. The pressure of demand, which theoretically can be defined as the difference between potential supply of goods and services, as determined by the productive capacity of the economy, and the actual demand for goods and services is in practice different to measure. To the degree that indices of capacity utilisation are comparable, it does not seem that the average utilisation of capital capacity in the manufacturing sector of the UK has been lower than in other major industrial countries to the extent of being an important factor accounting for the relatively low marginal output/ capital ratio in the UK.

There are, of course, many other factors that will determine the differences in the efficiency with which capital and other factor inputs are used in the UK and other major industrial countries. Some of these factors, such as different attitudes to work and authority and the intensity of work effort, appear to be quite important, but unfortunately they are difficult to quantify. In concluding this paper however, it can be said that an important factor explaining the relatively low incremental output/capital ratio in the UK appears to have been the very low output return obtained on new capital formation within the manufacturing sector. This low return seems to have resulted from an allocation of new capital formation within this sector that was different from that in other major industrial countries. In the UK, there has been a relatively greater flow of capital resources into lagging industrial sectors, such as textiles, food and beverages, and relatively less into the more dynamic export-oriented heavy and science-based industries. Accordingly, UK industry has not been able to take full advantage of the marked upswing in world trade in manufactures over the post-war period. This tendency has manifested itself in a loss of export market shares and rising import penetration, which in turn have led to periodic balance of payments constraints on the growth of output. It is possible that in certain industries the shortage of complementary factor inputs, such as skilled manpower at the technician and engineer levels, together with inefficient management, may have contributed also to depressing output returns on new capital formation.

PART II:
The View from the Right

Margaret Thatcher's answer to her own question—of what has gone wrong—is to argue that we suffer from too much government—that government itself has become over-extended, bureaucratised and remote from the people. In her view the cost of this authoritarianism has been the erosion of personal involvement and participation, when in fact what we need is an extension of that space in which—free from government interference—personal decisions and individual responsibility can hold sway. In economic terms, that means a reduction in the scale and depth of government involvement, and the creation of space for enhanced private initiative. That view is represented here by *Lord Keith*.

For him, the problems of the British economy derive not from failures of industry or the City, but from the activities of successive British governments. The inadequate levels of investment in manufacturing plant and equipment derive in part, in his view, from price and dividend controls, excessive taxation on individuals and companies, barriers to capital transfer and general government antipathy to profit-taking. He argues that companies cannot be expected to invest when inflation is high, and inflation will remain high for as long as governments refuse to control the money supply and refuse to reduce their own expenditure in the unproductive welfare sector. For Lord Keith, the government can swallow too much of the nation's wealth, and when it does so wealth-creation itself becomes the first casualty. This will happen particularly quickly if the cost of investment is inflated by government competition for funds to finance unproductive current expenditure and to support declining and unprofitable industries. It will happen too if the small business sector is burdened by penal rates of taxation, by excessive employee protection, or by wage inflation fuelled by the strong trade unionism of public employees. In sum, then, for Lord Keith, 'ever-spreading legislation and central control is leading to an over-valued currency, to increased administrative costs for both commercial enterprises and the public sector, and to reduced incentives and to inefficiency.' Only a reduction in the empire-building propensities of the state will free private enterprise to flourish again.

This 'crowding-out' thesis—by governments of private wealth creation—is particularly associated with the work of *Robert Bacon and Walter Eltis.* They are quite clear that trade union power is a consequence, and not a cause, of Britain's economic decline, and that it is not enough to draw attention to low rates of labour productivity. What in fact underpins both, in their view, is a great structural shift in employment since 1961, out of manufacturing industry into service employment, particularly in the public sector. This non-industrial employment then places great stress on an already only slowly growing industrial base, consuming its products, taking from it resources which otherwise might have gone into industrial development, adding to tax burdens, and inspiring militant trade unionism to recapture ground lost by slow growth and high taxation. For them, the most burdensome aspect of this non-industrial employment is on investment itself which, by blocking rapid economic growth, leaves the commodity-producing areas of the economy under-capitalised and the whole society disproportionately vulnerable to inflation and unemployment in a recession.

Overmanning and underproduction are also themes in the *Times* editorial, which is included here because it is so representative of the way the arguments of the Right are handled in popular discussion. The editorial draws attention to low productivity, and to the likely annihilation of industries lacking the new technology. Only efficient businesses, it argues, will survive; and they alone can pay the high wages on which affluence depends. In their absence, deindustrialisation will ensue, and the capacity to finance the welfare state will dwindle. Low productivity is the key to the nation's future; and if it has a prime cause, then the editorial team at the *Times* see that to be the use of trade union power to block necessary industrial modernisation.

Trade union power is then the theme picked up by *Sir Keith Joseph* and by *F.A. Hayek.* Inflation will not end, they tell us, until trade unions bargain responsibly; and they won't do that until the general framework surrounding trade union activity is altered. In particular, according to Sir Keith Joseph, we have to move away from the 'bizarre' political and economic beliefs of the British labour movement: that capitalism is bad, that management is the enemy, and that nationalisation is preferable to private ownership. All this encourages class war, resistance to necessary technical change, and antipathy to entrepreneurial initiative, the self-employed and the rights of the consumer. Industrial militancy can only damage companies, lower living standards and slow the creation of new jobs, so that trade union members themselves experience lower wages, longer working hours and less job security than would otherwise be the case. For Sir Keith, only a new set of legal limitations on militant trade unionism, and a break from the myths of labourism, can open the way to national recovery.

To this, Hayek adds that the political power of trade unions is also damaging, because it induces politicians to buy electoral popularity and industrial peace by inflating the money supply, with long-term deleterious consequences for consumers, non-unionised workers and the mass of union members. Legal changes therefore need to be made, for without them recovery will be impossible; and we will never leave behind what *Peter Jay* calls 'Englanditis'—the over-extension of government because of electoral pressures which can be indulged because the political sphere, unlike the economic, is not constrained by the 'invisible hand' of the market. And as *Sir John Hoskyns* makes clear, even the Conservative government under Margaret Thatcher have yet to put their faith fully in market processes. Until and unless they do, he argues, and until they recognise the need to cut welfare spending and constrain the unions, industrial decline in Britain will continue apace.

5. What has Gone Wrong*

Margaret Thatcher

Let us try to analyse what has gone wrong.

I believe that the great mistake of the last few years has been for the government to provide or to legislate for almost everything. Part of this policy has its roots in the plans for reconstruction in the post-war period when governments assumed all kinds of new obligations. The policies may have been warranted at the time but they have gone far further than was intended or is advisable. During our own early and middle period of government we were concerned to set the framework in which people could achieve their own standards for themselves, subject always to a basic standard. But it has often seemed to me that from the early 1960s the emphasis in politics shifted. At about that time 'growth' became the key political word. If resources grew by x per cent per annum this would provide the extra money needed for the government to make further provision. The doctrine found favour at the time and we had a bit of a contest between the parties about the highest possible growth rate: 4 per cent or more. But the result was that for the time being the emphasis in political debate ceased to be about people and became about economics. Plans were made to achieve a 4 per cent growth rate. Then came the present government with a bigger plan and socialist ideas about its implementation, that is to say if people didn't conform to the plan, they had to be compelled to. Hence compulsion on prices and incomes policy and with it the totally unacceptable notion that the government shall have the power to fix which wages and salaries should increase.

We started off with a wish on the part of the people for more government intervention in certain spheres. This was met. But there came a time when the amount of intervention got so great that it could

*Reproduced from a lecture by the Rt Hon. Margaret Thatcher to the Conservative Political Centre, 10 October 1968.

no longer be exercised in practice by government but only by more and more officials or bureaucrats. Now it is difficult if not impossible for people to get at the official making the decision and so paradoxically although the degree of intervention is greater, the government has become more and more *remote* from the people. The present result of the democratic process has therefore been an increasing authoritarianism.

During July [1968] the *Daily Telegraph* published a rather interesting poll which showed how people were reacting against this rule of impersonal authority. The question was

> In your opinion or not do people like yourselves have enough say or not in the way the government runs the country [68 per cent not enough] the services provided by the nationalised industries [67 per cent not enough], the way local authorities handle things [64 per cent not enough—note this rather high figure; people don't like remote local authorities any more than they like remote governments].

[Since then] more and more feature articles have been written and speeches made about involving people more closely with decisions of the government and enabling them to participate in some of those decisions.

But the way to get personal involvement and participation is not for people to take part in more and more government decisions but to make the government reduce the area of decision over which it presides and consequently leave the private citizen to 'participate', if that be the fashionable word, by making more of his own decisions. What we need now is a far greater degree of personal responsibility and decision, far more independence from the government, and a comparative reduction in the role of government.

These beliefs have important implications for policy . . . if we accept the need for increasing responsibility for self and family it means that we must stop approaching things in an atmosphere of restriction. There is nothing wrong in people wanting larger incomes. It would seem a worthy objective for men and women to wish to raise the standard of living for their families and to give them greater opportunities than they themselves had. I wish more people would do it. We should then have fewer saying 'the state must do it.' What is *wrong* is that people should want more without giving anything in return. The condition precedent to high wages and high salaries is hard work. This is a quite different and much more stimulating approach than one of keeping down incomes.

Doubtless there will be accusers that we are only interested in more money. This just is not so. Money is not an end in itself. It enables one to live the kind of life of one's own choosing. Some will prefer to put a large amount to raising material standards, others will pursue music, the arts, the cultures, others will use their money to help those here and overseas about whose need they feel strongly and do not let us underestimate the amount of hard earned cash that this nation gives voluntarily to worthy causes. The point is that even the Good Samaritan had to have the money to help, otherwise he too would have had to pass on the other side.

In choice of way of life J.S. Mill's views are as relevant as ever.

> The only freedom which deserves the name is that of pursuing our own good in our own way so long as we do not deprive others of theirs, or impede their efforts to obtain it . . . Mankind are greater gainers by suffering each other to live as seems good to themselves than by compelling each to live as seems good to the rest.

These policies have one further important implication. Together they succeed at the same time in giving people a measure of *independence from the state*—and who wants a people dependent on the state and turning to the state for their every need?—also they succeed in drawing power away from governments and diffusing it more widely among people and non-governmental institutions.

6. Industry, the City of London and Our Economic Future*

Lord Keith

I want in this article to discuss some of the issues which, over the last few years, have been put forward as being largely responsible for our economic failures. Much of what I have to say will echo Lord Seebohm's comments in the lecture which he gave in 1975. He too saw the dangers that the actions of the state and the spread of its bureaucratic tentacles have caused us. I share his view that it is not industry and the City, but the government and its intervention in the detail of our economic affairs that are responsible for our troubles and for undermining what used to be a sound and effective system.

The charges made against industry and the City by the interventionist school of detailed planners, whether they come from Westminster or Whitehall, from Transport House or Congress House are:

(1) there has been a failure to invest in productive industry;
(2) finance for industrial investment has either not been available at all, or available only in unsuitable forms;
(3) small businesses have failed to develop and so to add to employment and to the creation of wealth;
(4) the competitiveness of industry in international and domestic markets has steadily declined.

Let us look a little at each of these four main charges and try to seek out the truth.

INVESTMENT

Admittedly, the level of new investment is, and has been for some time,

*Reproduced from the Ernest Sykes Memorial Lecture, Bristol, 1977.

low. Why is this? The main reason in my view is that the expectation of earning a satisfactory return on new investment is not high enough to justify, in the eyes of businessmen and those who lend them money, the use and cost of resources to finance it. This is due to:

(a) the high cost of finance;
(b) the poor use that industry can make of resources when financed;
(c) price controls;
(d) dividend control, which makes the return to the shareholder unattractive by comparison with other uses of his savings, having regard to the risk he runs.

This adds up to an absence of incentive both to the large established business and to the individual entrepreneur. The individual is also afflicted by high taxation on close companies, and by the impossibility of thinking for more than one generation at a time, which capital transfer tax has created.

When an opportunity does arise which appears to offer a satisfactory return on investment, industry has not been slow to invest (e.g. North Sea oil, despite the fact that the government changed the rules after the game had begun). Companies have also been willing to invest large amounts in countries overseas where the climate is more favourable. The cost of investment has been enormously increased through the effects of inflation, the responsibility for which cannot be laid at the door of either industry or the City. The failure to allow depreciation at replacement cost, which can lead in effect to tax being paid from capital, has deprived companies of funds which should properly have been retained for future investment. The cure for inflation, which lies in cutting public sector expenditure and in firm control of the growth of money supply, has led to cuts in consumption and high unemployment, both of which affect market prospects adversely and act as a further damper on investment. Growth in the public sector, most of which is essentially unproductive, in the sense that it creates no new wealth, has diverted resources which could otherwise have been used for creating this new wealth. Events have indeed shown that the welfare state which we have built during the past 30 years is like a house with no foundations; while we were building it we failed to create the resources that were needed to provide it with a sound economic base and to finance the extensions that we have made to it more or less continuously since the end of the war.

The lesson that the public sector cannot absorb more than a certain proportion of the nation's resources without harming the economy as a whole seems at last to have been learnt—though there are still pressures to restore the cuts that have been made and even to add new items of expenditure. Even so, the government has concentrated its cuts on capital spending, while leaving current spending relatively unscathed. This action has certainly added to the depth of recession, as spending on capital has the effect of increasing total employment by a multiple of the primary employment provided by the investment itself; whereas this is not true of current expenditure, which does not even contribute to current production. The result has been the combination of high inflation and high unemployment—what is known as stagflation—that we have seen in recent times. Public expenditure should certainly be reduced, but within the lower total more should go on capital and less on current expenditure. It is no use saying that we cannot cut the social wage; investment means doing just that. And it is clear that if a choice has to be made between the personal and the social wage, the preference of the individual is always to preserve his personal income.

Another cause of low investment has been the public attitude to profit. Profit produces not only a modest return to the man who puts up the money—very modest indeed when one compares the downward trend of dividends with the upward trend of wages and costs—but also the wherewithal to finance new investment. Profitable business consists in taking a collection of assets—labour, capital and raw materials—and turning them into finished products, with a greater value to the community than the individual assets have by themselves. This added value is profit, and is in fact the wealth upon whose creation our general prosperity and the financing of the welfare state depend. We need also to remember that upon the earning of satisfactory profits depends the ability of pension funds to maintain the value of the pensions paid to their members. Though the investments are made by the pension funds, who are thought of as faceless institutions, the benefit of their activities goes to millions of individuals. It is these individuals who are the dominant force in today's stock market, and it is against their interests rather than those of the shrinking band of private investors that policies of dividend control are directed.

So, to sum up, we can hardly expect investment to increase unless the real return to the investor, whoever he may be, is improved; and we should cease to delude ourselves that it is out of spite or lack of patriotic feeling that industrialists hold back from investment.

FINANCE FOR INVESTMENT

The second charge is that even when industrialists are disposed to put money into new buildings, plant and equipment, the City (to use that much abused generic term) either cannot provide them with the necessary funds or can do so only on terms or in ways that cause them serious difficulty. In considering this charge, let me start by quoting the evidence of the Accepting Houses Committee to that august body known as the Wilson Committee, or to give it its proper title, the Committee to Review the Functioning of Financial Institutions—to my mind a somewhat otiose task.

The Accepting Houses said:

> There are no hard arguments to justify the political contention that the financial institutions have contributed to the relatively poor industrial performance of the UK in the past 20 years through a failure to provide or procure funds for investment. Such criticisms prove on examination to rest on ill-informed or unsubstantiated assertions rather than on hard arguments.

I have already mentioned the development of North Sea oil. Here the necessary financing has been made available, despite the vastness of the sums required, with only the unavoidable minimum of difficulty. Where there have been problems they have had to do either with the inherent risks of some of the more marginal fields or because of doubts over the intentions of the government or its creature the British National Oil Corporation. I accept that much of the finance provided has been essentially short-term; but given the method of operation of the petroleum revenue tax and the consequent rapid payback period, this was understandable and inevitable. The high interest rates of the time the funds were needed and the high probability that rates would fall underlined the advantages of short-term finance for this rather special situation.

When considering finance for investment, the role of government is no less important than it is in influencing policy on investment. This is particularly true when government is actively seeking to control the growth of the money supply. In these circumstances the supply of money is limited while the propensity of the general public to consume is unlikely to change significantly. Again, to quote the Accepting Houses Committee:

> The Public Sector Borrowing Requirement was inescapable. In competing for the available funds, it was never a question of whether the public sector or the private sector would 'win' in meeting its requirements. The private sector was bound to lose. The only element of doubt was the level at which the cost of finance would cause the private sector to cease to compete.

To put it another way: through its monetary and fiscal policies, the government determines both the price and the quantity of money. It has no external disciplines comparable to those which bear upon the private sector, except for the political unpopularity it may incur because of the inflation and unemployment which flow from its actions. The risk is therefore that the government will pre-empt finance for unproductive current expenditure or to support declining or unprofitable industries, with the result that only the specially profitable areas of the private sector such as North Sea oil are able to survive.

We also have to take into account the present overhang of public debt. There must be a given long-term level of debt that an industrialised society can sustain without damage. Historical analysis shows that when this level is exceeded for any long period of time, compensating economic forces within the system tend to bring the debt level back into equilibrium by causing the real value of the debt to decline through a fall in the value of money. We ought perhaps to be asking ourselves whether our own economy is not showing symptoms the cause of which may be a disproportionately high level of debt. It may be sound policy to run a budget deficit when there is a good deal of slack in the economy; but when output recovers ought we not to aim for a budget surplus? The United Kingdom has a heavy burden of internal and external debt, and we should be asking whether repayment of some of this might not be a better use of North Sea oil revenues rather than other politically more attractive uses. Were central government borrowings thus reduced, this could, through a decline in the cost of long-term funds, give a powerful boost to private investment and restore the long-term capital market in London which has for several years been perforce completely inactive.

There has also been a notable change in the pattern of investment. For some years now, individuals have tended to avoid direct involvement in securities markets, and have preferred to entrust their savings to professional fund managers. To a large extent this is due to the effects of taxation, but it has also been affected by governmental action to control the money supply. This has acted on interest rates and altered the supply/demand relationship in the securities markets. The exercise of control has caused higher volatility in securities markets and has led to the concentration of funds in professional hands. This, in turn, has led to even greater volatility in the market as fund managers, spurred on by the emphasis on short-term performance, have increasingly moved in the same direction, concentrating their investment in the same sorts of securities. This higher volatility increases risk, and the consequence of this has been a rise in the cost of funds for loan to, or investment in, industry. There has also been a concentration on the shares of larger companies which has had the effect of making smaller companies less attractive.

The flow of savings through the various institutions, such as pension funds, insurance companies, unit trusts and investment trusts, is influenced by government legislation and by concealed direction, and by their taxation status. Thus the insurance companies' investments are limited by the various Insurance Acts and influenced by the close supervisory interest now shown by the Department of Trade. Unit trusts must comply with various regulations as to marketability and type of investment. The status of investment trusts depends upon their meeting regulatory requirements in the conduct of their affairs. Pension funds are bound to invest in capital equipment, directly or indirectly, if the production of goods is to be sufficient to pay real pensions. All of these institutions must, of course, match the nature of their assets to that of their liabilities to the investing and saving public, and for this reason managers of the funds are rarely as free as is sometimes supposed.

Inflation causes major problems for the banks, as its effect on their balance sheets is a brake upon the expansion of their business. In order to keep their capital and reserves at least constant in real terms they ought to maintain large margins between borrowing and lending interest rates; but this may not always be commercially practicable for extended periods—nor, one suspects, would it be politically acceptable.

For those with higher incomes, the taxation system discriminates against income and in favour of capital gains. This can lead to such a concentration on capital gains and such reluctance to invest for longer-term income objectives that it can encourage speculation rather than lending or productive investment. This tendency is reinforced by the fact that for investors, at least, there is no taxation relief equivalent to that which companies get on stock appreciation. This can and does mean that investors are taxed on paper rather than real gains, so that they are forced to move towards higher-risk investments aiming at capital gains. It is this sort of environment which can cause funds to move into non-productive ventures, and can encourage excesses such as the ill-fated property boom of the early seventies.

Coming back to the main charge that the City does not provide enough finance for industry, there is one last question which must be asked. It is: 'Where does the money go?' If it is not lent or invested, what happens to it? Do individuals, institutions, or the banks really find it so attractive to keep it without earning any return at all? Of course not. It is all mobilised towards those who are prepared to pay most for it. If a fund manager doesn't invest, and leaves his money in the bank, then the bank lends it on, and in the ultimate that money is borrowed either by the government, industry or the general public. In recent times, the government, by paying such high rates on gilts, has been pre-empting much of it.

THE DISCOURAGEMENT OF SMALL COMPANIES

There are many problems facing the small man with a business that has good prospects of growth and thus of providing new opportunities for employment. Most of them can be traced back to government influence. I have already said that the tax system discourages risk-taking because owners and managers do not see the point of paying even higher tax rates on their increased income. On top of this, many of our best managers and technicians have been driven abroad by the lack of financial incentive caused by high taxation, capital transfer tax, and penal taxation of close companies—now mercifully relieved to some extent. Once they go, there is no inducement—indeed every discouragement—to return. For someone trying to create a small business there is the difficulty of building up and keeping enough capital to give a worthwhile stake and attracting suitable outside finance while still keeping control. Should it be a family business, capital transfer tax is there as an obstacle in the path. Value added tax imposes a heavy administrative burden, and the increasing mass of new legislation, especially the Employment Protection Act, adds further to the strain. It is surprising that any new enterprises at all come into being in a system which has so many inbuilt obstacles. Even in Russia the differential in remuneration between managers and labourers is greater than it is in the UK. Penal taxation on incomes at the higher level makes it impossible to build a fortune from work without reliance on capital profits. This must discourage businessmen from taking the long-term steps which would lead to a more competitive Britain.

Furthermore, the figures show that employees in the public sector— central and local government and the nationalised industries—gained a pay advantage over their private sector counterparts in the early 1970s, and have held it ever since, setting the trend in virtually every year up to 1977. Again this year it seems likely that it will be in the public sector that the more extravagant claims will be made. Employees in the public sector are well organised and not subject to the same extent to the discipline of market forces. Their employers cannot be made bankrupt and so far the taxpayer has always been forced to bail them out, thus diverting resources that could be put to much better use. We need to find some new and more effective way of running our affairs in the public sector.

OUR COMPETITIVENESS

Our lack of competitiveness against the rest of the industrialised world is glaringly obvious. Some of the causes I have already touched on. The price of labour has been forced up by the public sector. Other measures such as pension legislation, equal pay for women and protection for the lower paid, although no doubt politically and socially desirable, have increased costs substantially in a period when industrial output has actually declined, as is shown by *Economic Trends*, 1973–77.

Industry is prevented from abusing monopoly power by the operation of the monopolies and restrictive practices legislation, but there are no similar controls over union power. In an industrial partnership between labour and capital, similar rules should apply to both partners, if it is to remain workable. But the greatest cause of our failure to compete is our abysmally low productivity by comparison with that of our chief competitors. We have all read the figures for the automobile industry, but the same is true for steel, for coal, and for many other of our major industries. Until we tackle this problem we have little chance of recovering and of creating the wealth we need to finance the welfare services we should all like to see. North Sea oil may give us a respite, but we must use the time to cure this basic illness of our economy.

On another aspect of our lack of competitiveness, I should like to say a word about the effect of the exchange rate. For much of the post-war period sterling was over-valued, and was kept so by fixed exchange rates and controls over the export of capital. This had the effect of damaging our export competitiveness just when the rest of the world was experiencing vigorous growth. The result was that we failed to share in the growth, so that our relative position in world trade declined steadily.

After several devaluations and finally a move to 'controlled' floating rates, our export industries began, at long last, to make worthwhile headway, only to find that all of this was once again threatened by the prospect of an over-valued currency.

Rates of exchange should ensure parity of purchasing power between nations, allowing for relative prospective rates of change of price levels. Currently, however, sterling is moving towards a position which is over-valued on these criteria for four main reasons. These are the renewed confidence following the adoption of commendable monetary policies by the government, the euphoric reception of the initial effects of North Sea oil flows, official reluctance to countenance lower long-term interest rates and the distorting effects of the continuing exchange control regulations preventing capital export from the UK.

Whilst greater international confidence in sterling is to be welcomed, reflecting as it does our fundamentally improving prospects, our exporters are being penalised by the government's unwillingness to let interest rates fall and by the restrictive control regulations, both of which push sterling to artificially high levels.

The Treasury no doubt believes that it is right to make sure that long-term interest rates are high enough to enable it to carry out the sizeable funding which will be required over the next 18 months if it is to keep monetary expansion within desired levels. This reasoning is to my mind rather short-sighted, because while rates are high foreign inflows make the funding problem worse, and increase the cost of servicing debt which, to the extent that it involves a transfer of income to foreigners, is a real drain on our economy. The funds attracted from abroad are being left in the reserves without productive employment, and this cannot be sensible. It is the equivalent of an individual taking on an expensive overdraft only to hoard the money with no useful return.

The exchange control regulations preventing export of capital can no longer be justified on any rational grounds. They impair efficiency, restrict both personal and industrial freedom, and create an artificial overvaluation of sterling as well as keeping our currency reserves higher than is necessary for our needs or good for world trade. The current controls are also contrary to the spirit and letter of the Treaty of Rome. There seems no valid reason why exchange controls over export of capital outflows should not now be liberalised and indeed we may be injuring our own best interests by maintaining them in their present severity. The recent relaxations are too trivial to have any material effect.

CONCLUSION

I said at the outset that I should be attempting to show that most of the present deficiencies in our economy spring from ill-considered intervention in detail by the state, and by the excessive growth of the public sector, which now consumes well over half of everything produced in this country, mostly on activities which themselves consume wealth with no countervailing production.

Deliberate economic handicaps have been imposed upon private sector service industries, which despite them have created substantial foreign earnings. We should be building on their successes and dismantling these handicaps now that we can afford to do so. In doing this we would be recognising that as the Third World moves further towards industrialisation we must move on to other areas of endeavour if we are to compete and to make room for the Third World in international trade.

All the evidence suggests that if there have been any shortages of finance they have occurred only where the government has pre-empted the available funds by pricing industry out. The remedy is clear. The government must drastically reduce its borrowing requirement, and preferably start repaying some of its debt. If this requires elimination of its fiscal deficit so much the better. It could also do much to stimulate the economy, when this is required, by moving from current to capital expenditure.

The flow of revenue from North Sea oil gives us a breathing space and affords us some flexibility, but it is no cure for UK's structural economic problems; indeed, it brings problems of its own with it, particularly on the monetary and exchange rate fronts.

Ever-spreading legislation and central control is leading to an over-valued currency, to increasing administrative costs for both commercial enterprises and the public sector, to reduced incentives and to inefficiency. Our economy and the investment which supports it will prosper if government provides the right environment. Without that environment the bureaucratic smog may stifle productive endeavour, despite the opportunities for it that are now visible.

The right environment is that which reinforces success and provides suitable rewards for it, and does not divert resources into saving the unsaveable. It implies no more controls than are strictly necessary, and requires that political decisions are taken for longer-term objectives than has been the custom over the last two decades.

Both industry and the City are ready and willing to play their full part in a revitalised Britain. The real question is whether the state is willing and ready to relinquish its own domestic empire-building for the sake of a healthier economy.

7. Too Few Producers*

Robert Bacon and Walter Eltis

Those who seek to manage economics or advise on their management are either tinkerers or structuralists. Tinkerers believe that a country's economic ills can be cured by adjusting demand, the exchange rate or the money supply, and by persuading workers to accept periods of wage restraint. Structuralists are concerned with the underlying structure of economies, and believe that tinkering about will not suffice where this is out of line. Treasury civil servants are generally tinkerers, and they usually seek to put things right by adjusting what they actually control. Many politicians are also tinkerers, and indeed in many economies minor adjustments to this and that are all that is needed to produce highly satisfactory results. In these economies—West Germany, Japan and recently France are examples—the underlying structure has been such in the past 15 years that government control of effective demand, the money supply and the exchange rate were really all that was needed to produce an economic environment where businessmen and workers could co-operate to increase wealth and real incomes at very rapid rates.

There are other economies with an inappropriate underlying structure where tinkering is not enough, and it is becoming increasingly recognised that Britain—like many underdeveloped countries—has an economy with serious structural problems. This is now recognised by a growing number of economists, and politicians ranging from Mr Tony Benn on the Left of British politics to Sir Keith Joseph on the Right. Mr Benn has drawn attention to the problems raised by Britain's declining industrial base, while Sir Keith Joseph has been concerned about the continuing fall in the proportion of the economy that is allowed to respond to market forces, and to produce outputs that consumers are actually prepared to pay for. The account of the deterioration in the

*Reproduced from R. Bacon and W. Eltis, *Britain's Economic Problem: Two Few Producers* (London, Macmillan, 1978), pp. 1–33, 110–16.

structure of the British economy which will be given in this [paper] will support those who believe that Britain's industrial base should be strengthened and also those who think that Britain's problems would be easier to solve if a higher fraction of output was marketable. The tinkerers, in contrast, can provide no viable solution. All their remedies, tax reductions, tax increases, devaluations, incomes policies of various kinds, have been tried again and again, and they have failed to arrest the underlying deterioration of the economy that has occurred . . .

The underlying factors that are most commonly blamed for the deplorable situation that has been outlined are either militancy and obstruction to progress by the trade unions, or inadequate industrial productivity. It is a little implausible that trade unions have the power and desire to destroy the British economy when they do nothing of the kind in the successful capitalist economies where communism is actually strong. Those who believe that the trade unions are responsible for Britain's troubles must therefore argue that they are able and willing to disrupt an economy in a society which has, by objective tests, less support for extremists than most others.

What has in fact happened, . . ., is that deductions from pay packets grew so much from 1963 to 1975 that the average living standard in terms of what can actually be bought in shops rose only 1.5 per annum—and since 1973 it has actually fallen. The same has been broadly true for workers and salary earners on average earnings, 1⅓ times average earnings, and ⅔ of average earnings. Compared with 1963, about 14 per cent more of the pay packets of all three groups is now deducted for income tax and social security contributions to pay for the higher 'social wage'. Without this increase in 'deductions' what the average workers' wages could buy would have risen 43 per cent in twelve years instead of the 19 per cent they actually rose. Workers and salary earners with just average earnings now suffer deduction of nearly 30 per cent from their pay packets, which is more than bank managers and university professors had to pay in tax and national insurance contributions in 1963.

It is often argued that workers and salary earners do not notice higher taxation in their wage negotiations, and that they welcome the higher 'social wage' that greater public spending represents. The 'social wage' does not, however, enter into the money wage bargains that trade unions negotiate, and the period 1963 to 1975 when deductions from pay packets increased so sharply was one when there was growing pressure for higher money wages. Some workers have been better organised than others to achieve high increases in money earnings, and these workers with powerful trade unions have managed to increase their living standards in terms of take-home pay by much of the extra amount needed to compensate for higher taxation.

What has happened since 1963 is that all too often those who sought higher living standards, or the mere continuation of car and home ownership (which have risen in cost far more than prices in general) found that they could only obtain these by making full use of their trade union power, with the result that ordinary workers turned to aggressive union leaders to produce results. That a politically moderate population has chosen to be represented by immoderate trade unions is plausibly explained once it is appreciated that this was in many cases a response to a situation where a rising cost of living and rising taxation made the preservation of living standards increasingly difficult. With a halving of the rate of growth of industrial production, less has been available to raise living standards; so workers have had to progress at the expense of other groups rather than by accepting a roughly constant share of a rapidly growing national product. It is consequently possible to argue that the failure to achieve reasonable growth in living standards in recent years has led to the militant and obstructive trade union activity from which Britain has suffered. Hence this has been a consequence of Britain's great economic failures. It has not caused them, and things started to go wrong long before unions became militant. The underlying cause of Britain's troubles must therefore lie elsewhere.

Britain's lamentable productivity record is often seen as the root of the trouble. Certainly Britain's industrial productivity is low by international standards, and it is still falling in relation to productivity elsewhere. However, the evidence that has been outlined shows that Britain's general economic performance deteriorated sharply when the period 1965–75 is compared with the previous decade. What is not often appreciated is that in contrast industrial productivity increased very much more quickly in the second decade. Output per man hour in manufacturing industry increased at an annual rate of only 3.0 per cent from 1955–65, but it increased 4.0 per annum from 1965 to 1974. Thus, if productivity is what matters most as many suppose, things should have gone very much better after 1965 than in the previous decade. Efficiency increased more quickly, which should have meant that all Britain's problems were easier to solve. Certainly Britain's growth rate of industrial productivity was still low by international standards after 1965, but it was not all that low. West Germany, France and Italy achieved growth at an average rate of 6.0 per cent against Britain's 4.0 per cent, but Britain's growth rate was still exceedingly high by historical standards, and it could have led to the 'economic miracle' that so many have expected for so long. That productivity rose faster is compatible with the view that many of the industrial policies of successive governments were beginning to produce results. There may have been contributions here from the tougher approach to restrictive practices from the end of the 1950s onwards, which meant that there were fewer price agreements which sheltered the inefficient. There may also have been contributions from the 'little Neddies' set up in the early 1960s which examined the particular productivity problems of a wide range of industries. There was also a great takeover movement in the early 1960s which was often assisted by the government and led to the absorption of a number of small and sometimes inefficient firms by larger and more favoured ones. There were also great increases in the numbers receiving education in virtually all the relevant age groups. Finally, successive governments gave substantial tax assistance to investment, and this must have led to the replacement of much obsolete plant. Our machine-tool survey showed that by 1971 the service life and average age of British machine tools were almost exactly the same as in the USA over a very wide range of machine tool categories and user industries. These helpful developments which almost certainly resulted from sensible and beneficial government industrial policies could have set the foundation for an acceleration in Britain's growth rate. This would then have provided the extra resources to satisfy the aspirations of workers for higher material living standards, and at the same time increased the capital stock in both the public and the private sectors, provided a sufficient supply of goods for overseas markets to pay for the country's import requirements, and produced in due course the kind of growth in welfare services that successful economies have achieved. In practice, the great improvement in the rate of growth of industrial productivity for which so many worked intensively in government and industry did none of these things. In the event, and only party because of the world recession, industrial production increased less than half as fast as productivity, with the result that more than half the benefits from extra productivity resulted, not in the production of more goods but in the employment of fewer men for shorter hours. Higher productivity meant sackings, and a decline in the availability of overtime. This was not true over all industries, but it was true in the great majority.

A 40 per cent increase in productivity in ten years could have allowed the same number of men to produce 40 per cent more in the same number of hours. In the event more than half the potential increase in output was lost because the number of men employed in industry fell 14 per cent and hours of work also fell substantially. It is from this basic fact that the disastrous course the British economy followed in 1965–75 stems, and this was one result of the real structural maladjustment of the British economy that has occurred in these ten years and is still occurring. If Britain manages to cut overmanning in industry, which many regard as the economy's greatest weakness, productivity will advance still more rapidly than in the recent past, and the reduction in overmanning will produce still faster falls in industrial employment and in hours of work. It must then be emphasised that it is not the rate of growth of productivity that has let Britain down. What has let Britain down is that this has been allowed to produce growing numbers of redundancies instead of the increase in employment, and growth in the availability of real resources that should have resulted. It is this basic fact, and the reasons for it, which needs to be explained, and one of the purposes of this [article] is to show just what went wrong and why.

It is beginning to be appreciated that a very great structural shift in employment has occurred in the British economy since about 1961, and this can be looked at in several ways. Perhaps the most significant is that employment outside industry increased by over 40 per cent relative to employment in industry from 1961 to 1975 and that this increase was most rapid into the public sector. The facts, which are of crucial importance, are set out in Figures 7.1 and 7.2. These also show that the shift in employment from industry to services, and public services in

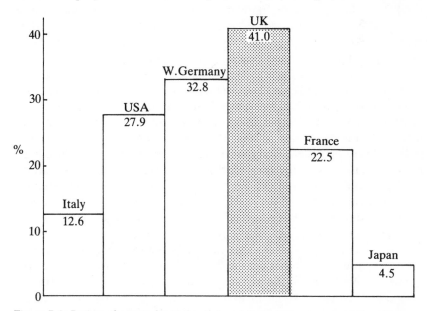

Figure 7.1. Ration of non-industrial to industrial employment: percentage change, 1961–75 (excluding agriculture)

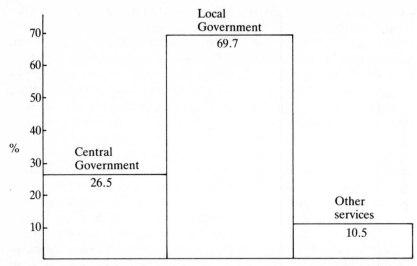

Figure 7.2. Percentage change in service sector employment by category in Great Britain, 1961–75

particular, had no equal in any other large western developed economy. Virtually all modern economies gradually shift workers out of industry and into services as industrial efficiency rises, and aspirations grow for better education and welfare services, as well as for the many services provided in the private sector. They do not, however, have 41 per cent shifts in just 13 years, and cannot without great strain.

In Britain's case the actual strain may not have been quite as great as the crude figures indicate. The employment of women (including many who work only part-time) increased 65 per cent faster in services than in industry, while the employment of men increased only 28 per cent faster. Hence, in so far as men are more important to industry (and women have become a vital part of the labour force in many firms) the strain caused by the structural shift in the labour force was less than the 41 per cent figure would indicate. But even a 28 per cent shift is a very considerable one.

The details of the shift which occurred in Britain are set out in Figures 7.2 and 7.3 which show where the extra workers in British service occupations went. It will be seen that employment by local authorities rose 70 per cent, and that central government employment rose 27 per cent. By contrast, in the remaining services like retail distribution, banking, finance, insurance, entertainment, and so on, employment expanded only 11 per cent on average, so the shift from industry has been most rapid into public-employment. The Oxfordshire County

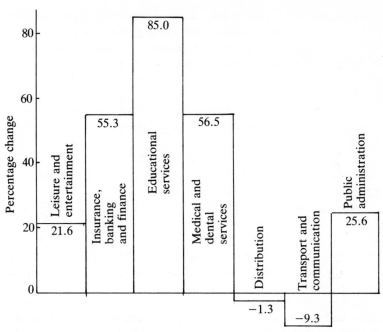

Chart 7.3. Percentage increase in service sector employment by category in Great Britain, 1961–75

Council now employs more workers in Oxfordshire than British Leyland. Within the public sector, employment in education at all levels has risen, and employment in the provision of health and welfare services has risen. All would agree that these are vital to any civilised community, and it is a realisation of this by all political parties that has done so much to bring about these very great structural shifts in the labour force. It must be emphasised that the shift has been as rapid under Conservative as under Labour governments, and employment in education increased more rapidly when Mrs Thatcher was Secretary of State for Education and Science (1970–74) than in 1964–70; and during the same period, when Sir Keith Joseph was Secretary of State for Social Services, employment in the provision of health and welfare services grew 8.2 per cent faster than employment in general. . . .

Much research is needed to discover whether the great increase in public sector service employment that occurred in Britain in 1961–75 produced substantial improvements in public services of a kind that other economies which increased public sector employment less quickly failed to achieve, or whether the improvements to services were peripheral in comparison to the extra costs involved. Whether the social benefits were minor or substantial, the shift had very great consequences for the rest of the economy, and a strong case can be made out that this very great structural change played a significant role in the deterioration in Britain's economic performance that has been recorded.

The deterioration occurred in the following way. Industrial production must supply the entire investment needs of the nation, and a very high fraction of its consumption; for durable consumer goods like cars, television sets and so on, clothing, and even quite a high proportion of what workers nowadays spend on food, have to be provided by British or foreign industry. In addition to this, a country like Britain that needs to import a high fraction of its food and raw material requirements must export more industrial products than it imports. The various private sector service industries make a valuable contribution to the balance of payments, but this has never been sufficient, and it is never likely to be to finance the food and raw materials that Britain must buy from overseas, so a large export surplus of industrial production is always likely to be needed.

Now if non-industrial employment grows by 40 per cent in relation to industrial employment, as happened in Britain after 1961, there will be added pressures on industrial production. With more workers employed outside industry, more industrial production will be required for the consumption of those who have played no direct part in producing it. Similarly, more investment outside industry will be needed, and the capital goods will all have to be taken from the output of the industrial sector itself. It must follow that less industrial production will be available for investment and consumption by those who actually produce it or that all the extra goods the non-industrialists require will have to be imported. All these needs can, of course, be met if industrial production can be increased rapidly, but it has already been pointed out that in Britain the rate of growth of industrial production was exceedingly slow. Hence most of the extra goods for the consumption of the vastly larger numbers of teachers, social workers and civil servants, and the extra buildings to house them (which were particularly needed as a result of local government reorganisation), could only be supplied by building fewer factories in industry itself, by allowing industrial workers to consume a smaller fraction of what they produced, and by exporting less or importing more. . . . In 1961 59 per cent of industrial production was consumed and invested outside industry itself. By 1975 non-industry took 68.5 per cent, leaving just 31.5 per cent for industry and the balance of payments in place of the 41 per cent that was available in 1961. Industrial workers therefore had to consume a smaller proportion of what they produced, and what matters crucially is that the proportion of industrial production that was exported (less imports of manufactures) fell from 15½ per cent to 11 per cent; and the proportion that was invested in industry itself, net of capital consumption, fell by one-fifth from 8.2 per cent to 6.8 per cent of sales of industrial production. The great increase in non-industrial employment and the accompanying increase in non-industrial investment therefore took resources away from the balance of payments and industrial investment, and this is precisely what Britain could not afford to cut if the country was ever to escape from the trap of an industrial sector too small to provide all that was required of it. It is also obvious that the reduction in the fraction of industrial output that industrial workers were themselves allowed to consume was only achieved at a cost of the increase in industrial conflict that has been remarked upon as group after group of workers attempted to ensure that it was not they who suffered reductions in living standards to pay for the increased employment in the public services. . . .tax increases greatly slowed down the growth of real living standards of all but those who got sufficient increases in money wages to compensate for higher taxation. But the wage increases that the more militant obtained squeezed profits and industrial workers paid only 2 per cent of the 9 per cent extra that had to go outside industry. Hence most of the non-industrial sector's extra consumption and investment has grown at the expense of net exports and of investment in industry itself, which the government has sqeezed by making deflationary periods predominate to an increasing extent in the stop-go cycle.

The squeeze on industrial investment is perhaps the most serious effect of all, because it influences the whole future development of the economy. Net industrial investment fell, as a fraction of final sales of industrial production, to 3 per cent in 1972, 3½ per cent in 1973, 6.0 per cent in 1974 and 6.8 per cent in 1975 (about half the increase from 1973 to 1975 was investment for North Sea oil) from levels of 8 per cent to 9 per cent in the mid-1960s. This has had two devastating consequences for the economy. First, the reduction in the share of investment has greatly reduced the rate of growth of industrial capacity. Thus, while Britain was investigating enough to raise industrial production 3 per cent per annum or 35 per cent in a decade until the mid-1960s the rate of growth of industrial capacity is probably only about two-thirds of this today. This means that when demand is expanded as the economy recovers from depressions as in 1972–73, the plant is just not there to meet the country's requirements for goods. Hence articles which are normally produced in Britain have to be imported and the goods are just not available to exploit export opportunities. With a lower share of net investment this has become true over an increasing range of industrial products. In consequence attempts by governments to move towards full employment produce vast balance of payments deficits, which make continued expansion impossible. A prolonged share of net investment of only 3 per cent to 6 per cent in industry will gradually reduce the rate of growth, with the result that the Treasury's expansion plans which used to be based on growth rates of 2.5 per cent to 3.5 per cent will need to be revised downwards extremely drastically. In addition, the deep problem that declining industrial investment is producing is unemployment which is becoming increasingly structural—the unemployment due to insufficient factories from which underdeveloped countries suffer— and this will undermine the whole fabric of society if the trend is allowed to continue. It has been pointed out that output per man-hour has been rising about 4 per cent per annum in manufacturing industry since 1965. If this continues—and it is likely to—and there is only sufficient capacity to raise industrial production 2 per cent per annum, the number of men that firms employ must fall 2 per cent every year or hours of work must fall 2 per cent each year. In practice these have both been falling sharply in recent years.

The fall in industrial employment in relation to non-industrial employment is what has caused Britain's difficulties, and this trend will continue, making the situation worse each year unless investment recovers to its pre-1965 levels . . .

There is therefore a basic explanation of a structural kind of the underlying deterioration in Britain's economic performance and the succession of crises that have become increasingly severe until they threaten to undermine the repute of orthodox political parties and all that can follow from this. The explanation is that successive governments have allowed large numbers of workers to move out of industry and into various service occupations, where they still consume and invest industrial products and produce none themselves; their needs have, therefore, been met at the expense of the balance of payments, the export surplus of manufactures, and investment in industry itself, so the deterioration in the balance of payments and in Britain's rate of growth can be explained. Once the effect of taking away an increasing proportion of what workers produce is recognised, the great acceleration of wage inflation also becomes readily explicable, and the need for tougher and tougher incomes policies (which other major developed economies have not needed) to attempt to contain inflation. In monetarist terms, the unemployment rate that is compatible with stable prices (produced by a money supply that grows at the same rate as production) has risen drastically—in other words, there has been a great increase in what Professor Milton Friedman calls the *natural* rate of unemployment (Friedman, 1968). An economy that will not accept this exceedingly high natural rate of unemployment will have extraordinary inflation or draconian incomes policies instead, like Britain. Hence the whole range of economic options deteriorates sharply and societies in this terrible position must choose between very high unemployment or extra-rapid inflation, which is now undoubtedly the case in Britain, as it is in much of Latin America.

However, this explanation for Britain's decline needs to be refined . . . Instead of dividing economic activities into those that are *industrial* and those that are *non-industrial* they can be divided instead between those that produce *marketed* outputs and those which do not. Almost everything that industry produces is *marketed*, that is, it is sold to someone. The private-sector services are sold, so they are *marketed*. Defence, on the other hand, is not marketed; no one now pays for the use of a regiment or frigate. What the National Health Service provides, and most schools, is also not marketed, and the services provided by policemen and civil servants are not marketed; so they must spend their incomes on the marketed products of the rest of the community.

These cases are clear-cut but others are less so; thus, the Post Office only markets a fraction of its output because it makes substantial losses. If sales revenue covered only half its total costs one could say that half its output was marketed, like that of an industrial company, while the other half would correspond to the non-marketed output of a civil service department. Concorde will cost Britain over £1000 million but it will probably produce marketed outputs of only £100 million, so its effect on the economy will resemble those that would be produced by a second University of Bristol located at Filton (with more money to spend than ten ordinary universities). In short, industrial production is only marketed in so far as it is sold, so all subsidies to any firm whatsoever must be subtracted from industrial production to show what industry's marketed output is. At the same time all the services that are sold contribute to the economy's total of marketed output, which is a total that matters a great deal.

All exports are marketed, so the economy's entire exports of goods and services must be drawn from the economy's total pool of marketed output. All investment is marketed so this must also come from the economy's total marketed output. Finally, all the money that workers, salary earners and pensioners spend must necessarily go to buy marketed output. *Hence the marketed output of industry and services taken together must supply the total private consumption, investment and export needs of the whole nation.*

A difficulty Britain has suffered from since 1961 is that the proportion of the nation's labour force that has been producing marketed output has been falling year by year; at the same time those who have had to rely on others to produce marketed output for them, civil servants, social workers and most teachers and medical workers, have become increasingly numerous, and they have had to satisfy their requirements by consuming goods and services that diminishing numbers of market sector workers are producing. In addition, loss-making firms in the public and private sectors have been taking more out of the economy's pool of marketed output than they have been putting into it. Finally, pensioners and all those who receive money from the government are entitled to consume marketed output and produce none. . . . In 1961 the entitlement to buy marketed output by those who did not produce it directly was 41½ per cent (before tax). By 1975 the entitlement of those who did not produce marketed output had risen to 62 per cent, so on a pre-tax basis 20½ per cent less remained for those who actually produced the economy's entire marketed output. Their own consumption needs and the export requirements of the whole economy and resources for investment in the market-sector of the economy had to come almost entirely from what was left after the non-market sector had taken 20½ per cent more before tax. Put in these terms the argument is clear-cut . . . an economy can in principle suffer from two kinds of problem if the ratio on non-market expenditure is raised significantly. First, if the share of output received by workers and salary earners is reduced to provide the extra resources the government needs, wage inflation may accelerate, or alternatively if the money supply is controlled, more unemployment will be needed to check it. If net-of-tax profits become lower instead of wages, investment will suffer to an extent depending on how near companies are to their borrowing limits, and if investment falls, the economy's rate of growth of productive capacity is likely to fall with the result that technical progress will produce growing redundancies instead of rapid output growth. The only way of avoiding this is to achieve capital-saving technical change—and this will not happen easily.

The increase in non-market expenditure in Britain has produced both kinds of adverse effect. Attempts were made to finance extra non-market spending at the expense of workers' consumption, and deductions from pay packets rose by about the 9 per cent of marketed output needed for this, so the economy could in principle have achieved a transition where workers bore the entire cost. But workers did not acquiesce in this, so wage inflation accelerated, unemployment rose and incomes policies had to be made increasingly strict. Through the extra inflation they caused, workers managed to pass the bulk of extra taxation on to companies, so these ended up having to pay for the larger non-market sector. Companies have responded by investing less (and with its faster productivity growth rate, the country has needed more investment, not less, to maintain employment in the market sector) so the economy has also suffered from declining market sector employment, and this started to decline rapidly long before the onset of the world recession. Britain is therefore suffering from both growing structural unemployment, and a situation where incomes policies have to be tougher or unemployment higher than before to contain inflation. And the adverse trends, if left unchecked, will continue so that structural unemployment will become still higher and workers still more discontented.

That is how Britain's crisis has come about, and it has now been explained more technically than before. The one question that still requires an answer is why the country has failed to achieve the capital-saving technical progress that would have allowed it to grow faster and invest less at the same time. It can be supposed that industrialists base their choice of plant on the relative costs of labour and capital. The cost of employing labour has risen sharply in Britain since 1961. Taxes on employment to finance improved social security benefits have risen greatly, and money wages have also risen considerably relative to product prices. But the cost of capital has risen too, for when firms approach their borrowing limits it is to be expected that they will attach a high notional cost to the use of extra capital. Hence the costs of capital and labour have both risen sharply, but it may well be that the cost of labour has risen more. If it has, firms may have biased their investment in the capital-using and labour-saving direction—thus accentuating the problem.

But the problem would still have been solved if Britain had been able to achieve rapid capital-saving productivity growth. This is the solution of those who see Britain's weaknesses as the result of failures by workers and managements to achieve adequate productivity growth. It will be evident from what has been said that merely to have raised productivity faster would not have solved Britain's problem. Higher labour productivity with *the same capital requirements to produce a unit of output* would have actually increased the investment needed to prevent growing structural unemployment in the market sector, and what was needed was higher productivity and *a fall in the investment required to produce a unit of output* at the same time. . . . the first of these we called curing *overmanning*, and the second curing *under-*

production. Britain suffers from both, given the evidence on machine-tool use and the Think Tank's study of the motor car industry, but *under-production* is the fault that is crucially relevant to the country's problems.

The Think Tank lists several reasons why the British motor car industry obtains less output from the same plant than firms on the continent of Europe, and they cite examples of similarly equipped assembly lines producing 75 per cent and 120 per cent more on the continent. They say that British assembly-lines move more slowly which reduces output per unit of capital. They also suffer more interruptions from stoppages. Of the total production lost from these, manufacturers are said to attribute 40 per cent to shortages of materials due to external disputes, or poor stock control where necessary materials and components are not ordered in time. Finally, British plants lost twice as many hours through mechanical breakdowns even though the British industry employs 80 per cent more workers on maintenance. If these faults apply to many British industries as they probably do—it is unlikely that the car industry is unique—it will be evident that much underproduction is due to failures by management and labour on the shop floor. There is relatively little that governments can do to put such matters right. But there is one aspect of underproduction where governments may be able to give a little assistance. The utilisation of plant can obviously be improved if output grows more rapidly, for this will allow items of equipment in particular firms that are only used for a few hours a week to be used for longer. Moreover with faster growth of demand, workers can raise productivity without losing their jobs. Therefore if Britain could achieve a faster rate of growth by other means, such as investing more and allocating more resources to activities that are directly productive, the output of existing plant should rise where it is not inefficiency due to labour and managements that is holding it back, so there could be a double benefit in some industries. The world's fast-growing economies have the lowest capital costs of growth, which makes their growth easier to sustain. If Britain could once get out of the vicious circle of slow growth, low demand for the output of particular items of plant and an industrial environment where efficiency all too often causes redundancies so that incentives to improve productivity are minimal, much might be achieved. In sum, much progress might be made to cure Britain's problem of underproduction if governments can start to solve some of the economy's other problems.

Governments will therefore need to tackle the profits squeeze, and the investment squeeze that this has caused. Here the Left's position is absolutely clear-cut. It accepts that there has been a profits squeeze and welcomes it. This is what it has always fought for. But it recognises that the consequent squeeze on investment matters. With capitalism unviable as it is in Britain in the middle 1970s, the Left knows that the state will have to ensure that there is enough capital in the country to provide the jobs that are needed, for without profits companies simply cannot ensure this. The Left thus has a wholly consistent approach to this problem. Moreover, many on the Left appreciate that the extra investment that is needed must be financed mainly at the expense of the private sector services. . . . There is no other sector where it would willingly cut consumption and investment to the necessary extent, and it is widely believed that private sector services are consumed more by the better-off than the poor—though many private services export a great deal and are indispensable to productive processes, so what should be squeezed (obviously office building and property development, the Left would say) would require much research and good judgement.

A pro-market sector government, in contrast, must set about reversing the sequence of events which led to the profits and investment squeeze of 1961–75. If the government's requirements fell back from 45 per cent to 36 per cent of marketed output, 9 per cent extra could go to net-of-tax wages or profits, and in all probability both would gain. This should lessen the pressure for money wage increases, and at the same time the temptation to moderate workers to elect militants to represent their interests. In so far as companies benefited from lower taxation, there would be more internal finance for investment and more willingness to borrow; and with rising profits the stock exchange should become more buoyant, enabling fast-growing companies to obtain equity finance on reasonable terms. In addition, with all these favourable trends for profitability, international investment should again be attracted to Britain to supplement the country's domestic resources. . . .

And the British people must decide, either to strengthen the market sector so that it can function effectively, or to support the Left. Once the choice is made, it is crucial that the policies chosen be continued long enough to allow the balance of the economy to be restored.

8. The Sparks are Falling on the Gunpowder*

The Times

The Times Newspapers' stoppage arose out of the management's proposals for a complete range of productivity agreements, and was certainly influenced by the belief that British industry can only survive if there is a change, indeed a revolutionary change, in productivity. In our own affairs we have achieved agreements which do provide for much higher productivity; in general terms productivity per man will be more than 30 per cent higher, we have agreements to introduce advanced electronic equipment, and pay will be at the top end of the Fleet Street scale, but not outside it. The significance of these agreements, and the consequences of not trying to reach such agreements, can be shown by one comparison. By 1981 it will very possibly cost *The Financial Times* at piece rates on the continued use of obsolete equipment, as much to set a news column as it will be costing *The Times* on electronic machines to set a page.

It was of course a year of agony to go through. If at the beginning we had foreseen that the stoppage would last 50 weeks, and then would only be settled within a few hours of a final deadline, it must be doubtful whether we would have gone ahead. Yet the alternative was a miserable one. Without a willingess to press the question home, it would not have been possible to negotiate the new agreements. The evidence for that is that the rest of Fleet Street, which is on average more overmanned than we were—and with the exception of the Mirror Group, does not have any comprehensive introduction of the new technology—has not even tried to negotiate comparable agreements.

*Editorial, 13 November 1979.

92

PROTECTIONISTS

Yet during our absent year it has not been the productivity of Fleet Street, but that of Britain which has become the essential question. Fleet Street does not face foreign competition; it is placed by natural circumstances in the position in which the protectionists want to put the whole of British industry. National newspapers can therefore survive at an even lower level of comparative productivity than the rest of Britain. Yet the Fleet Street disease is only the British disease in a more acute form.

Indeed while we have been away our warnings about the consequences of low British productivity have increasingly been fulfilled. The fight for the survivial of British Leyland continues, and no one could do more than Sir Michael Edwardes to try to save that company. But despite the ballot vote in favour of redundancies, it remains a fight against heavy odds. The crisis of British Leyland stems from low productivity, with output per man a fraction of that achieved by their main international competitors. Low productivity and irregular production have resulted in low investment, and low investment has contributed further to low productivity.

ANNIHILATION

The same threat hangs over shipbuilding and steel. In all three industries, cars, shipbuilding and steel, British output per man is probably no more than a third of the normal international competitive level. Indeed that seems to be the crisis point. Even efficient British firms are usually overmanned by between 50 and 100 per cent; they survive because the British standard of living and therefore of wages is below the average of our competitors. Inefficient British firms are often overmanned by 200 per cent and upwards; they tend to disappear.

In the 1980s this disparity of productivity will probably become much greater. A technological revolution is taking place which substitutes electronic for mechanical systems; in specific cases it can give an increase in productivity per man of several hundred per cent in a single jump. The introduction of these systems is dependent on trade union agreements. Yet if we take British productivity as 100, and American, German or Japanese as 200, and then multiply our competitors' productivity by, say, 5, to allow for the general adoption of electronic methods, we are left with productivity ratios of 10:1. Such ratios are not maintainable, and where they apply, the low productivity mechanical

British industry will be replaced by its high productivity electronic foreign competitors. It is not just the end, it is annihilation.

How could it be otherwise? Customers want good service; they want to be able to buy a good product, with reliable delivery, at a fair price. Even in a period of buoyant world trade, reasonable productivity is necessary if these requirements are to be met. As we are entering a period of recession of world trade, competition becomes more intense. The world-wide shift from mechanical to electronic technology offers opportunities to raise productivity and quality which our competitors take and we reject. Britain is left competing with obsolete equipment and gross overmanning against modern electronic equipment and tight manning standards. That is suicide.

Such is the reality of the matter, and it is the lack of a sense of reality in Britain that is particularly disturbing. This was apparent in *The Times* dispute. Even some journalists, even on occasion journalists with a professional knowledge of industry, seemed to feel a resentment at the idea of higher productivity, rather than welcoming it. It is not for us to criticise the coverage of other newspapers except in one respect. The majority of the comment showed either ignorance or even more astonishingly complacency about the situation they themselves were in. It was like men on a burning ship watching a shipmate swimming ashore through dark currents, and saying, 'Look at the poor fellow—he is liable to be drowned, and he is certainly getting wet.' Beneath their feet the sparks are falling on the gunpowder.

In the end only efficient businesses survive; at any stage it is efficient businesses which pay the highest wages. Efficiency requires that the resources of the business should be used as well as possible; in particular it is wicked to waste people and their work, for work is mankind's chief resource. To achieve efficiency it is necessary to welcome change and new techniques. A manager who wastes labour is letting down not just his shareholders, but the people who work for him, and more broadly the nation; he is unpatriotic. He puts his employees jobs at risk; he makes it impossible for them to earn as high pay as they would otherwise get, or perhaps to earn anything at all.

Yet this is not how the British think. The British view is that jobs are absolutely scarce, which of course in a low productivity industry they soon become. If jobs are scarce, they argue, the best thing to do is to impose them on the employer and to make him employ more people than he needs. New techniques destroy old jobs to build new ones, so we reject new technology.

FINANCIAL BASE

The problem of productivity is normally seen in terms of industry and of competiveness in export markets. The problem extends however into services, and particularly into public service. It is notorious that spending on most public services has risen, both in nominal and in real terms, but that the public find no improvement in benefit: we are not better taught or cared for, though expenditures on education and health have risen greatly. Now the government is trying to stablise public expenditure in real terms, and the public believe, probably correctly, that this will mean a cut in the real quality of the services. That is because productivity is still falling.

If the National Health Service ever does collapse, it will certainly be because productivity has failed. It may be because of the failure of productivity in industry, whose success is the financial base for all our public services. It may be because the productivity of the Service itself falls too low. There are problems of productivity in the operations of the service; a child with a heart murmur will be examined on average more than six times by different doctors before reaching the consultant to whom he is referred. There are still greater problems of low productivity in support services. We are in danger of moving from a hospital service primarily staffed by doctors and nurses to one primarily staffed by porters, cleaners and cooks. This shift of emphasis from principals to support staff can already be seen at the National Theatre or Covent Garden, where it is the low productivity and high pay of sceneshifters which raises the cost of productions, not that of actors or musicians. 'Did you see the Ring? Weren't the sceneshifters magnificent, a most moving performance?'

The danger is therefore a double one. Britain is already an industrial country with such low industrial productivity that we are rapidly becoming disindustrialised; we have a welfare system which has such low productivity that we have the choice between abandoning our welfare priorities or allowing welfare expenditure to consume too much of our national resources. Either way, low productivity is actually threatening our existing standard of living, let alone our capacity to increase it. Low productivity is the central issue of our political life, as it underlies all the others; it is the issue of our national future.

Many factors, including social attitudes and the effects of inflation, help to account for the low productivity of Britain relative to our main competitors, but there is one prime cause, which is the destruction of the free market in labour. Broadly speaking, productivity matches the degree to which men are free to sell their labour in the best market, to obtain the full price they individually are worth. Only if rewards are proportionate to output, can an economy maximise output. In countries where workers are very free, as in the United States or Germany, productivity is at its highest. In what might be termed capitalist closed-shop economies, such as Britain, productivity is only about half as high. In communist countries, productivity is only half of the closed-shop group: there is no doubt that the Sovet Union, with wholly regimented labour, is much less efficient than Britain.

HISTORIC DIVISIONS

It is unfortunately not realistic to hope that higher productivity can come from the unions. Union power depends on restricting the free market in labour; the closed shop or the union dominated shop are natural trade union ambitions. Indeed they add to union power in the same degree that they lower productivity. Yet the inevitable effect of closing the labour market is to make it impossible to raise productivity to its maximum, or even to a level at which our industries can survive. Multiple closed shops operating together, reflecting arbitrary or historic divisions of labour and obsolete craft technologies, make competitive efficiency impossible. The old technologies have a will to live, but from the nation's point of view their survival is not compatible with that of the industries they dominate.

There are three political approaches to a resolution of this problem. The Left want to carry socialism further and complete the structure of a commanding socialist state, allied to dominant trade unions. That is the objective of Mr Benn and the NEC of the Labour Party. The effect on Britain's standard of living could only be catastrophe. The centre, moderate Labour, Liberals and moderate Conservatives, hope to contain the problem, because they believe that it is not possible to confront it. They may be correct in that view, but all they offer is catastrophe in slow motion. Mrs Thatcher and Sir Geoffrey Howe believe in trying to reverse the process, and so far as Treasury measures can help to restore reality—tax cuts, ending exchange control—they have been taken.

The government deserve to be supported for what they are doing, particularly perhaps by those who are moderates, who should recognise that this is not a question of preference, but a matter of national economic survival. The market is the only force powerful enough to have any chance of curing the British disease. The government can perhaps be criticised on two grounds. Mrs Thatcher's administration is better at policy than at persuasion; it is highly motivated without being sufficiently motivating.

IMMUNITY

There is a cause to be taken to the country. If on *The Times* we had been able to rely on an informed public opinion, our agreements would not have required 50 weeks, not 50 days, not 50 minutes. People would have been pressing for higher productivity as the only conceivable way to raise pay and secure jobs. It is the employer who does not instal new technologies against whom reasonable men would strike. There is as yet no such informed opinion.

The government should also face the trade union issue. At present legal protection, to the point of total immunity, is given to trade unions, even when their actions are preventing managers saving dying industries. Of course unions deserve a fair deal, but the unions who—perhaps with the best intentions—have been destroying British Leyland do not deserve legal immunities denied to the men who are trying to save British Leyland. Nor is it in the interest of their members that they should have these immunities. Unfortunately the government propose only secondary changes which will not alter the balance of power, weighted as it is against those who try to raise productivity.

We want the government to plead their case, but we even more want the public, and particularly the broad moderate majority to understand the issue. Low productivity is killing Britain; states more socialist than ours have even lower productivity, there is therefore no safety in socialism; states with free opportunity of employment have far higher productivity, and that is the direction in which to move. It is perhaps easy for a newspaper to write such things, though not all do so; on *The Times* we have at least been willing to live our beliefs, and it is the urgency of the national issue which justifies even that experience. But it has been a sad way to spend our 195th year.

9. Solving the Union Problem is the Key to Britain's Recovery*

Sir Keith Joseph

We see the power of trade unions and the way it is used as one of the major obstacles barring the road to national recovery.

I now seek to outline our thinking, so that the point from which we start the debate is understood. I can best do this by asking five key questions . . . The first is:

SHALL WE EVER CURE INFLATION?

Powerlessness against inflation leaves people angry and frightened. Rational economic behaviour is upset. Everyone seeks the largest possible share of next year's banknotes—the only production which we know will rise.

In such a climate of fear, anger and mistrust, everyone is forced to destructive action. Workers cripple or even bankrupt their firms; savers switch from productive investment; management concentrates on short-term survival instead of long-term growth. In this situation, the members of powerful trade unions appear, on the face of it, to be uniquely fortunate. Collective action seems to give to the individual negotiating strength which he does not possess alone.

Unfortunately, the inevitable response of trade unions and trade unionists to an inflation which they did *not* directly create, makes the cure of inflation more difficult.

Most people now see monetary discipline as a necessary but not sufficient condition for economic growth and stability. Had both parties and the 'Establishment' in general recognised this in the early 1960s, we

*Reproduced from a pamphlet of that title, published by the Centre for Policy Studies, February 1979.

98

might all have been less ready to embark on the road of growth in public spending with its attendant heavy borrowing and currency debasement. [Some people] . . . may say that, if the powerful unions do not moderate their claims, we will claw back the extra they win through extra taxation, as well as tightening monetary control. But—as many people have already pointed out—this would mean that the price of what are seen as excessive wage awards for some will be paid for mainly by those who do not benefit from them. Members of weaker unions, non-union labour and businesses will foot the bill in higher taxes, fewer jobs, more bankruptcies . . .

The central problem . . . is . . . the present ability of trade unions to force the rest of society to pay for the inflation which unions themselves are now making it harder to eliminate. This brings us to the second question:

WHY WON'T THE UNIONS BARGAIN RESPONSIBLY?

The unions can react only to the framework within which they operate. In addition to the monetary framework, which obliges unions to prepare quite rationally to safeguard their members from further inflation, there is the legal framework.

Our unions have been uniquely privileged for several decades . . . The predictable result has been the growing use of strikes and the strike threat. In a trade dispute most things seem permitted for the union side: breaking contracts, inducing others to break contracts, picketing of non-involved companies, secondary boycotts. A trade dispute can be between workers and workers; it can concern matters of discipline, membership, facilities; it may even relate to matters overseas. All this is unique to Britain; there is nothing like it in other countries.

As we would expect, this militants' charter, as Jim Prior has called it, has bred militants and driven moderates underground. Indeed, we are now seeing militants increasingly taking over control from union officials.

Union leaders, having in many cases failed to educate either themselves or their members, while winning for them excessive powers, have lost the ability to control them. National economic failure and the militants' charter have given a supreme opportunity to the left-wing minority whose instincts are destructive, who are bitterly opposed to the free-enterprise economy which most people want. The result is growing confusion. Shop stewards disregard union officials; workers start to distrust shop stewards. Members strike when ordered by their unions to work, and—less often—work when ordered to strike.

We now face an unstable situation; the collapse of socialist expectations; increasingly ruthless efforts by big unions to escape the consequences; inter-union warfare; and the fruits of the militants' charter. Politicians who urge restraint on union leaders, or who criticise their members for greed, ignore the forces at work.

To ask one union to sacrifice its own interests 'for the national good' without guarantee that other unions will do likewise is as unrealistic as it is to urge housewives not to anticipate a bread strike or motorists not to fill up before a petrol strike. The national good can be secured only by changing the framework, the rules of the game and then ensuring that everyone plays fairly by them. This is what Margaret Thatcher has called for.

The answer to the second question is, therefore, 'No, the unions cannot bargain responsibly so long as government provides a framework—monetary, fiscal and legislative—which discourages effort and encourages irresponsibility, and so long as unions have the power to respond to inflation in a way which makes it more difficult to end it.'

So the third question:

IF UNIONS WON'T BARGAIN RESPONSIBLY, WHY CAN'T WE HAVE A STRICT INCOMES POLICY INSTEAD?

The delayed but damaging consequences of formal and institutionalised incomes policies are now well known. We have experimented with different arrangements of more or less rigid control of pay for about 20 years. During that time, inflation has reduced the value of the pound by over 75 per cent. Unemployment has nearly trebled, yet industry reports skilled labour shortages. Our share of world trade has fallen sharply. Business profits as a share of GNP have fallen catastrophically. Real take-home pay has been almost stagnant. Over the same period, virtually every one of our competitors has left us far behind, despite the impact of OPEC price rises and in many cases without our advantages of North Sea gas and oil; and without using pay controls. Almost every year we have produced a smaller share of the world's goods and a larger share of its banknotes. Our problem today is the same as it was 20 years ago, but writ larger: 'We want other countries' goods more than they want ours.'

When we look at the evidence, do we really believe that without all these attempts at government controls, we would have done even worse? I suggest that the reality is much simpler. The reality is that, if we had emulated the more successful economies, in monetary policy, labour relations and the scope given to the workings of the market, we would have done much better.

The difference between Britain and other advanced industrial countries is as much political as it is economic. And this brings us to the fourth question:

WHY MUST BRITAIN BE THE ODD MAN OUT?

The visible signs of Britain's unique course—as it slides from the affluent western world towards the threadbare economies of the communist bloc—are obvious enough.

But why has this happened? Why does our prevailing political economy look increasingly eccentric in the western world?

There are, perhaps, three main differences between Britain and most other countries which may account for our eccentricity. First, there is the virtually unique link—constitutional, financial, ideological—between the Labour Party and most of the large trade unions. There is their joint commitment—airily dismissed as 'not serious', but stubbornly surviving all the same—to complete nationalisation. Secondly, there is an intellectual preference for top-down control rather than the untidy dynamics of free enterprise. This reference survives from early post-war when many intelligent and able people supported Labour's plans from a mixture of idealism—not to be sneered at—and a fundamental confusion of thought. This was the false analogy between war—in which wealth is dissipated under central control for a single national purpose—and peace, in which wealth is created as a result of the dispersed fulfilment of millions of unknown and private purposes.

Thirdly—and this is the heart of the matter—there are the bizarre political and economic beliefs of Britain's 'labour movement'.

THE MYTHOLOGY OF THE LABOUR MOVEMENT

The reason why the 'labour movement' has been such a disaster for the people it professes to serve is that too many of its leaders have presented the movement as a war of liberation, a war between 'good' socialism and 'bad' capitalism. In the mistaken belief that free enterprise is 'the class enemy', they have taught workers to resist efficiency, obstruct management, insist on overmanning, resent profit and ignore consumers. Like other wars, this class war is destructive of what exists, vaguely optimistic about the rewards which will come when peace breaks out. It develops a supporting propaganda which presents the enemy as less than human, oversimplifies the issues, relieves the troops of the burdens of individual conscience. 'I was only obeying orders,' says the troops. 'I can't control the feeling of my members,' say the leaders.

The ancient ideology of the labour movement asserts an economic war between 'us'—which is taken to mean the working population—and 'them', the class enemy. But who is the enemy in labour's eyes? It is all those whose economic functions are incompatible with, or peripheral to, achieving the socialist state as they see it. Thus, self-employed, entrepreneurs, managers, landlords, non-union workers, shareholders and, behind the routine sentimentality, pensioners, schoolchildren, hospital patients, all are 'non-persons'. They are either economic opponents who, by working successfully, make the free-market economy stronger and state socialism less desirable; or they are non-combatants, unavoidable civilian casualties, irrelevant to the battle plans.

You may think that I exaggerate. But how else can we explain decent men closing hospitals, intimidating non-union members, striking when one of their fellows is sacked for stealing, damaging property, disrupting children's education? Normal people can only do such things either because they have been persuaded that the war of economic liberation gives them a moral right to do them, or because they dare not challenge the orders of their union officials, shop stewards of left-wing militants.

Labour mythology presents the worker as the servant of 'them', the bosses. But reality is different. The assets of big companies are largely owned by pension funds and insurance companies, not by the managers. The true employer is, of course, the customer, who pays all wages. The whole enterprise is, in financial terms, very small compared with the real economic purpose it serves, which is to allow people, as both workers and consumers, to employ each other's labour as efficiently as possible. It lives typically on a profit of a new pence in every pound of its total production.

It is important to understand just how heavily the cards are stacked against any enterprise that tries to challenge the militants' charter. The enterprise cannot count on subsidy to help survive the dispute, as strikers can. Its financial haemorrhage starts immediately, as its hard-earned savings bleed away. Other companies may have to pay guaranteed lay-off pay to their workers who are not involved in the strike at all. Secondary picketing may force them to halt operations altogether.

If, after surrender to strike action, the struck-against company has to reduce its workforce, it must add to the cost of the strike and of increased wages, substantial redundancy payments to the workers it has been forced to lay off. The militant's charter looks increasingly like a charter for the systematic destruction of law-abiding, job-creating, free enterprise, in the name of socialism.

LIVING STANDARDS—DREAM AND REALITY

Perhaps the most important element in labour's mythology is the belief that trade unions are responsible for all increases in members' living standards.

In truth, there is no way in which striking itself, going slow, working to rule, overmanning or restrictive practices can do anything but lower the national living standards and obstruct the creation of new, well-paid jobs. Militant action cannot produce goods, build hospitals, save lives, pay for pensions. Economic and social progress comes from doing sensible things, not from refusing to do them. Prosperity comes from new inventions, good equipment, effective management, efficient work practices, higher individual output. There is nowhere else that prosperity can come from. Like governments, trade unions can either assist in this process or else impede it. This is the limit of their positive powers in the economic sphere, as distinct from other important areas, like working conditions and safety.

Because this has not been understood, the bitter reality, now increasingly borne in on us, is that our unions have robbed their members of the only thing they can sell, their own productivity. The net result is that everyone must work longer hours, for less money, in shabbier factories, with older equipment than his counterpart overseas—and draw a much smaller pension when he retires. And the alleged 'inhumanity of the market', against which the labour movement claims to fight for its members gives way to the inhumanity of organised labour, in which decent union members do many things which are not done in the non-unionised sector, or in other spheres of life, and of which they must be privately ashamed.

Perched on this structure of muddled thinking and propaganda sits the *raison d'être* of the trade union, the free collective bargaining process as practised in Britain, the process which is expected, year after year, to produce higher living standards from static productivity. Where are they to come from?

The whole bargaining process is riddled with confusion and contradiction. The link between productivity and real pay is ignored. Everyone demands above-average wages. Everyone wants parity with those above them, differentials from those below.

In Britain, the working man, the pensioner, the sick and the disabled, yes, and the lower-paid too, are just beginning to pay the real price for labour's long years of anti-business propaganda and for its frightening ignorance of the economic and commercial processes which alone can improve their lot.

The answer to the fourth question, therefore, is: 'Britain is the odd man out primarily because the historic link between the Labour Party and the TUC has institutionalised a romantic, outdated and economically illiterate socialism which the people of this country don't want and which the people of most other western countries have firmly rejected.'

So the fifth and final question is:—

HOW DO WE BREAK OUT OF THE TRAP?

The walls of our economic prison are closing in upon us, because all our social and economic problems reinforce each other. We don't have unlimited time, because each year the problem gets harder, the prison cell smaller . . .

There are many big and difficult things we have to do if we are to escape from the trap. We have to hold and then reduce government's share of national spending and abate inflation. Just as important, we have to remove the fears that inflation will soar again. We have to work out a systematic approach to pay determination in the non-market public sector. . . . We have to reduce the present power of the trade unions to damage the economy and at the same time reduce the pressures which encourage them to do so.

Each of these objectives, and there are many others, is an immense task. Each is an exercise in analysis, innovation, persuasion and cooperation. And when they are all achieved, they give us no more than a stable platform on which to build, in place of today's slow disintegration. They give us no more than a few stepping-stones on the way to national recovery.

The first of these stepping-stones must be the replacement of the militants' charter by a moderates' charter. This requires a carefully thought out strategy, cool nerves and clear heads. It is understandable that people feel indignation at what is going on, anger at our sense of national impotence. Indeed, there would be something wrong with the British people if we were no longer capable of strong feeling about such things. But—as Jim Prior has suggested—moral indignation can cloud our judgement. If we are to succeed, we have to think clearly and argue fairly. Only then will firm action be possible.

We say that union power should be reduced, not because we are 'anti-union', nor because we think it is the sole cause of our problems, but because the present imbalance of power bars our way to national recovery.

10. 1980s Unemployment and the Unions*

F.A. Hayek

INFLATION, EMPLOYMENT AND TRADE UNIONS: BRITAIN, 1980s

The problem of inflation, the problem of employment, and the problem of the excessive power of the trade unions have become inseperable in present-day Britain. Although seen as a problem of economic cause and effect, there is no such thing as 'cost–push inflation'. The only effect of an excessive rise of wages (or of the price of anything else) would be that what is offered cannot be sold. *Politically* the problem of trade union power is the primary problem because, so long as government has the control of the money supply, it will be forced to resort to the palliative of inflation which temporarily disguises the effects of a rise of wages on employment but leads to cumulative arrears of omitted adaptations which merely store up later trouble.

Trade unions, in their present form, have become part of the British way of life, and their power has become politically sacrosanct. But economic decline has also become part of the British way of life, and few people are willing to accept that as sacrosanct. Many British people are beginning to see the connection between the two. Yet this insight is in such conflict with what most of them believe the trade unions have achieved for the mass of wage earners that they cannot see a remedy. This dilemma overlooks the unique privileges the unions enjoy in Britain, which have placed them in a position where they are forced to be anti-social, as even one of their friends, Baroness Wootton, has had to admit.

*Reproduced from '1980s Unemployment and the Unions', Institute for Economic Affairs (1984), pp. 19, 22–4, 51–8, 64.

False claims to benefit the population as a whole

Unions have gained the public support they still enjoy by their pretence of benefiting the working population at large. They probably did achieve this aim in their early years when more or less immobile workers sometimes faced a single factory-owner. I do not, of course, deny the trade unions their historical merits or question their right to exist as voluntary organisations. Indeed, I believe that everybody, unless he has voluntarily renounced it, ought to have the right to join a trade union. But neither ought anyone to have the right to force others to do so. I am even prepared to agree that *everybody* ought to have the *right* to strike, so far as he does not thereby break a contract or the law has not conferred a monopoly on the enterprise in which he is engaged. But I am convinced that nobody ought to have the right to *force* others to strike.

Trade Unions' Legal Privileges Obstruct Working-Class Prosperity

Such would be the position if the general principles of law applicable to all other citizens applied also to the trade unions and their members. But in 1906, in a typical act of buying the swing-vote of a minority, the then Liberal government passed the Trades Disputes Act which, as A.V. Dicey justly put it, conferred

> upon a trade union a freedom from civil liability for the commission of even the most heinous wrong by the union or its servant, and in short confer[red] upon every trade union a privilege and protection not possessed by any other person or body of persons, whether corporate or incorporate. . . . [it] makes the trade union a privileged body exempted from the ordinary law of the land. No such privileged body has ever before been created by an English Parliament [and] it stimulates among workmen the fatal illusion that [they] should aim at the attainment not of equality, but of privilege. (*Law and Public Opinion in England*, 1914)

These legalised powers of the unions have become the biggest obstacle to raising the living standards of the working class as a whole. They are the chief cause of the unnecessarily big differences between the best- and worst-paid workers. They are the prime source of unemployment. They are the main reason for the decline of the British economy in general.

TRADE UNION MEMBERS GAIN BY EXPLOITING OTHER WORKERS

The crucial truth, which is not generally understood, is that all the powers employed by individual trade unions to raise the remuneration of their members rest on depriving other workers of opportunities. This truth was apparently understood, in the past, by the more reasonable trade union leaders. Twenty-three years ago, the then chairman of the TUC (Mr Charles, now Lord Geddes) could still say that he did

> not believe that the trade union movement of Great Britain can live for much longer on the basis of compulsion. Must people belong to us or starve, whether they like our policies or not? No. I believe the trade union card is an honour to be conferred, not a badge which signifies that you have got to do something whether you like it or not. We want the right to exclude people from our union if necessary, and we cannot do this on the basis of 'Belong or Starve'.

There has evidently been a complete change. The present ability of any trade union to obtain better terms for its members rests chiefly on its legalised power to *prevent other workers from earning as good an income as they otherwise might*. It is thus maintained, literally, by the exploitation of those not permitted to do work that they would like to do. The élite of the British working class may still profit as a result, although even this has now become doubtful. But they certainly derive their relative advantage by keeping workers who are *worse off* from improving their position. These groups acquire their advantage at the expense of those they prevent from bettering themselves by doing work in which they could earn more—though somewhat less than those who claim a monopoly.

Free society threatened by union curtailment of access to jobs
If a free society is to continue, no monopoly can be allowed to use physical force to maintain its privileged position and to threaten to deprive the public of essential services that other workers are able and willing to render. Yet all the most harmful practices of British trade unions derive from their being allowed forcefully to prevent outsiders from offering their services to the public on their own terms. The chief instances of such legal powers are intimidatory picketing, preventing non-members from doing particular kinds of jobs such as 'demarcation' rules, and the closed shop. Yet all these restrictive practices are prohibited in most of the more prosperous western countries.

Union restrictive practices have hurt the working man

It is more than doubtful, however, whether in the long run these selfish practices have improved the real wages of even those workers whose unions have been most successful in driving up their relative wages— compared with what they would have been in the absence of trade unions. It is certain, and could not be otherwise, that the average level of atainable real wages of British workers as a whole has thereby been substantially lowered. Such practices have substantially reduced the productivity potential of British labour generally. They have turned Britain, which at one time had the highest wages in Europe, into a relatively low-wage economy.

British price structure paralysed by political wage determination

A large economy can be prosperous only if it relies on competitive prices to coordinate individual effort by condensing all the information fed into the market by many thousands of individuals. The effect of the present system of wage determination in Britain is that the country no longer has an internal price structure to guide the economic use of resources. This is almost entirely due to the rigidity of politically determined wages. If it is no longer possible to know the most efficient use of the natural talents of the British people, it is because relative wages no longer reflect the relative scarcity of skills. Even their relative scarcity is no longer determined by objective facts about the real conditions of supply and demand, but by an artificial product of the arbitrary decisions of legally tolerated monopolies.

Impersonal nature of market decisions makes them acceptable

Prices or wages cannot be a matter of 'justice' if the economic system is to function. Whether it is necessary for maintaining or increasing the national income to draw people into tool-making or services, or to discourage entry into entertainment or sociological research, has nothing to do with the 'justice' or the merits of the 'needs' of those affected. In the real world, nobody can know where people are required but the market, which absorbs and digests the myriad bits of information possessed by all who buy or sell in it. And it is precisely because the decision is not the opinion of an identifiable person (like a minister or commissar) or a group fo men (like a cabinet or politbureau) but results from impersonal signals in a process that no individual or group can control, that makes it tolerable. It would be unbearable if it were the decision of some authority which assigned everyone to his job and determined his reward.

British Governments have supported union coercion
I would be prepared to predict that the average worker's income would
rise fastest in a country where relative wages are flexible, and where the
exploitation of workers by monopolistic trade union organisations of
specialised groups of workers are effectively outlawed. Such exploitation is, however, the chief source of power of individual labour unions in
Britain. The result of thus freeing the labour market would inevitably be
a structure of relative wages very different from the traditional one now
preserved by union power. This result will have to come about if the
British economy is to stop decaying.

While a functioning market and trade unions with coercive powers
cannot coexist, yet it is only in the free system of the market that the
unions can survive. Yet the unions are destroying the free market
through their legalised use of coercion. The widespread use of force to
gain at the expense of others has not only been tolerated but also
supported by British governments, on the false pretence that it enhances
justice and benefits the most needy. Not only is the opposite true; the
effect of this tolerance and support of union coercion is to reduce
everybody's potential income—except that of trade union officials.

Trade unions' legal privileges the chief cause of unemployment
Impeding increases in productivity and hence real wage growth is not
the worst effect of current trade union practices. Even more serious is
the extent to which they have become the chief cause of unemployment,
for which the market economy is then blamed.

The volume of employment is not a function of the *general wage level*
but of the structure of *relative wages*. The contrary belief, still widely
held in Britain by economists and politicians, is due to a unique
experience of this country. It arose after Britain returned to the gold
standard in 1925 at the pre-war parity between sterling and gold, when
wages, which had risen considerably during the wartime inflation,
proved generally too high for the country to maintain its exports. It was
in that very special atmosphere that discussion about the relationship
between wages and unemployment started, and the belief came to be
held that the crucial factor was the general level of wages. The writings
of Keynes unfortunately seemed to support this error.

The situation after 1925 was entirely exceptional. The normal cause of
recurrent waves of widespread unemployment is rather a discrepancy
between the way in which demand is distributed between products and
services, and the proportions in which resources are devoted to
producing them. Unemployment is the result of divergent changes in the
direction of demand and the techniques of production. If labour is not

deployed according to demand for products, there is unemployment. But the most common cause is that, because of excessive credit expansion, overinvestment has been encouraged and too many resources have been drawn into the production of capital goods, where they can be employed only so long as the expansion continues or even accelerates. And credit is expanded to appease trade unions that fear their members will lose their jobs, even though it is they themselves who forced wages too high to enable the workers to find jobs at these excessive rates of pay.

FULL EMPLOYMENT REQUIRES CONTINUAL CHANGES IN RELATIVE WAGES

Once such a misdirection of resources has taken place, tolerably full employment can be restored only by redirecting some of them to other uses. This is, of necessity, a slow process, even when wages are flexible. And so long as substantial unemployment prevails in such a large sector of the economy, it is likely to set up a cumulative process of deflation. Even maintaining total final demand cannot provide a cure, because it will not create employment in the overexpanded capital industries. The unemployment there will continue to operate as a persistent drain on the income stream. It cannot be stopped, or lastingly compensated for, by the expenditure of new paper money printed for the purpose or created in other ways. The attempt to cure it by adding to the supply of money must lead to accelerating inflation. Yet this has been the futile policy of recent British governments.

Such unemployment can be effectively cured only by redirecting workers to jobs where they can be lastingly employed. In a free society, this redirection requires a change in relative wages to make prospects less attractive in occupations or industries where labour is in surplus and more attractive where the demand for labour is expanding. This is *the essential mechanism which alone can correct a misdirection of labour* once it has occurred in a society where workers are free to choose their jobs.

Keynes' responsibility for 'the final disaster'

The final disaster we owe mainly to Lord Keynes. His erroneous conception that employment could be directly controlled by regulating aggregate demand through monetary policy shifted responsibility for employment from the trade unions to government. This error relieved trade unions of the responsibility to adjust their wage demands so as to sell as much work as possible, and misrepresented full employment entirely as a function of government monetary policy. For 40 years it has thus made the price mechanism ineffective in the labour market by preventing wages from acting as a signal to workers and employers. As a result there is divided responsibility: the trade unions are allowed to enforce their wage demands without regard to the effect on employment, and government is expected to create the demand at which the available supply of work can be sold at the prevailing (or even higher) wages. Inevitably the consequence is continuous and accelerating inflation.

FUTILITY OF NEGOTIATING REFORM WITH UNION LEADERS UNTIL DEPRIVED OF LEGAL PRIVILEGES

It is an illusion to imagine that the problems Britain now faces can be solved by negotiation with the present trade union leaders. They owe their power precisely to the scope for abusing the privileges which the law has granted them. It is the rank and file of the workers, including many trade union members, who ultimately suffer from this abuse. I believe they could be helped to understand this cause of their suffering. Their support must be obtained if the system that is destroying Britain's wealth and well-being is to be changed.

One of the more recent General Secretaries of the Trade Union Congress, the late George Woodcock, wrote about 'the fear and dislike in which many of our own people seem to hold our own trade unions.' A political party in which trade unions have a major constitutional role cannot strike at the source of their power. If I were responsible for the policy of the Conservative Party, I would rather be defeated at the polls than be charged with policy which lacked a clear mandate to remove the legal sources of excessive trade union power. This a trade union party, of course, can never do. The only hope is that an appeal to a large number of workers over the heads of their present leaders will lead to the demand for a reduction in their powers.

No salvation for Britain until union privileges are revoked

There can be no salvation for Britain until the special privileges granted to the trade unions three-quarters of a century ago are revoked. Average real wages of British workers would undoubtedly be higher, and their chances of finding employment better, if the wages paid in different occupations were again determined by the market and if all limitations on the work an individual is allowed to do were removed.

Britain can improve her position in the world market, and hence the price in work effort at which her population can be fed, only by allowing the market to bring about a restructuring of her whole internal price system. What is ossified in Britain is not the skill of her entrepreneurs or workers, but the price structure and the indispensable discipline it imposes. The present British economic system no longer signals what has to be done and no longer rewards those who do it or penalises those who fail to do it . . .

There is no hope of Great Britain maintaining its position in international trade—and for its people that means no hope of maintaining their already reduced standard of living—unless the unions are deprived of their coercive powers. So long as they possess them, even the wisest union leaders can, as we see every day, be forced by little groups to exercise them. This is killing enterprise after enterprise and causing a continuous dissipation of capital, the full effect of which we have not yet experienced. As a result of a mistake of legislation in the past they have Britain by the throat and cannot understand they are killing the goose which lays the golden eggs.

I am not qualified to judge what is today politically possible. That depends on prevailing opinion. All I can say with conviction is that, so long as general opinion makes it politically impossible to deprive the trade unions of their coercive powers, an economic recovery of Great Britain is also impossible.

It is sufficiently alarming when one watches developments in Britain from the inside. But one is reduced to complete despair when one observes what is happening in the rest of the world while Britain remains paralysed by the consequences of the privileges irresponsibly conceded to the trade unions by law. When one watches how even Japan is now being beaten in ever more fields by South Korea and other newcomers who have discovered the benefits of free markets, one cannot but shudder when one asks how in a few years' time Britain is to get the food to feed her people.

WILL BRITAIN PAY THE PRICE OF THE UNION SACRED COW?

This is not merely a question of whether Britain can do without Japanese or Korean cars or other products. It is a question of how other people can be made to buy British ships, or shoes, or steel, or textiles, or chemicals, when not only Japanese and Korean factories and shipyards produce them more efficiently and cheaply, but more and more other people surpass Britain in an astounding versatility—and when not only British scientists and engineers but increasingly also skilled British workers find that they can do better in countries whose business structure has not been ossified by trade union restrictions.

A drastic change may still provide an outlet, but after another decade, during which nobody dares to touch the sacred cow, it will certainly be too late . . .

11. Englanditis*

Peter Jay

We in Britain are a confused and unhappy people. So are those of our fellows on the Continent of Western Europe who have their wits about them. So too are our many friends in the United States who rightly see in the anguish of the United Kingdom the advanced stages of a disease that has already taken hold throughout Western Europe and this is beginning to show its unmistakeable symptoms in the United States.

There may or may not be anything we can do about the grounds for our unhappiness, which as things stand is thoroughly well founded. But there is no need to be confused. We can try at least to understand the basis of our morbidity, even if this requires some acutely painful reassessments of cherished institutions and values.

We are unhappy because the foundations of our prosperity seem to be eroding faster and faster and because we can neither find nor agree upon any sure remedy for this decay. We are confused because we do not clearly understand why all this is happening to us, whether it is due to the malefactions of subversive groups, the incompetence of governments, defects of national character, the rhythms of history, the luck of the draw, or what.

The search for someone to blame adds to the confusion and the bitterness. Government and governed become more and more alientated from one another. The governors believe the governed to be irretrievably greedy, feckless, idle and recalcitrant, while the governed believe the governors to be stupid, corrupt, power-crazed and unrepresentative. Likewise class is set against class, the middle classes denouncing the rapacity of the workers, while the workers rail at the privileges and the hypocrisy of the better-off.

In Britain region is set against region, and separatism gains steady support in Ulster, in Scotland, in Wales, and, by reaction, in England itself. Only the Labour Party can any longer claim a vestige of nationwide support, and even it could not get even 30 per cent of the potential electorate to support it in 1974; but for London and Bristol, the Labour Party would be virtually unrepresented from the whole of the south of England.

The fissures spread out in all directions like an ice-fall: disintegration in slow motion. Labour unions, business management, and City financiers are locked in a triangle of mutual vituperation and incomprehension. Union leaders point to the lack of investment in productive industry. Industrialists complain that the capital markets and the banks do not support them because the financiers' time horizons are too short and their understanding of industry is negligible. And the investors ask how they can be expected to put up capital when the unions pre-empt all, or more than all, the potential return on new plant and equipment.

Weak labour unions with low-paid members loudly support same-all-round ceilings on pay increases while their stronger brothers, in entrenched industrial positions with higher-paid workers, stoutly defend their 'differentials' and angrily compare their lot with the standards enjoyed by bloated capitalists, whom they still imagine—not always wrongly—to be living like a caricature of a nineteenth-century railway baron. The media critise everyone and everything; and almost everyone blames the media for the lack of national unanimity and commitment.

It is an unedifying spectacle and an unprofitable arrangement. Nor does it touch at any point on the true causes of the problem. These causes are deep-seated and general, embedded in the very organisation of our society. They are also complex and abstract. Therefore they are little perceived; and the analysis of them cannot compete with the more readily intelligible, concrete and enjoyable sport of exposing 'guilty men' and baiting those who are in what is supposed to be 'power'. There are no guilty men, of course, but there are defective institutions.

The political and economic organisation of modern liberal democracies is dedicated, above all, to the satisfaction of individual wants. How are we to establish what individuals want? By asking them. How are we to ensure that they get what they want, at least so far as possible? By letting them make the decisions. How do we arrange that? By letting them elect their governments and by letting them spend their money in a free competitive market-place.

This engagingly simple political philosophy may indeed have been a useful antidote to the depredations practised on mankind by authoritarian and paternalistic regimes in the name of higher values. But, alas, it already has built into it the tension—historicists might say the contradiction—that lies at the root of our present troubles. For, as the great Austrian economist, Joeseph Schumpeter, pointed out, the market-place for votes and the market-place for goods operate according to vastly different and frequently incompatible criteria. When the domains of the economic and political market-place overlap—as they often do—they come into serious conflict.

The political arena is a market-place in votes. Rival teams organise themselves to win a majority or at least a plurality of support so that they can exercise power. The only cost of voting for one team is that you cannot vote for another. The teams naturally and inevitably seek to outbid each other by offering more of whatever they think the voters want. There is no mechanism that requires the bids to be internally consistent or forces voters to balance more of one good against more of another.

The economic arena is—or at least supposedly starts out as—a market-place in money. But here the individual chooses quite different-ly. He makes small decisions all the time instead of one big decision every few years. Each decision is marginal, to spend his next penny on a little more of this rather than a little more of that. He does not have to pledge all of his income for the next few years to one of a short list of comprehensive packages.

Thus, the economic and political market-places offer different incentives to entrepreneurs. The political entrepreneur asks what most people want. The economic entrepreneur must ask himself what people want most. Intensity of wants becomes all-important where the person choosing has to give up something—namely, the opportunity to spend money on something else—each time he chooses.

Second, in the economic case the coin in which the chooser casts his vote—the money he pays for his purchases—is also the resource that the supplier needs to continue and maybe expand the process of supply. In the political case, while votes are the bases of power, they are not the material that power uses. The command over the resources of power comes from the taxing power, which is awarded by a plurality of votes. There is no mechanism for ensuring that a plurality of votes implies a commitment by the voters of the quantum of resources needed to fulfill the programme on which the winning political team has won an election.

The economic market-place requires the citizen to exercise his choice and to commit the resources needed to fulfill it in the single act of purchase whereby he parts with his money. This essential feature of the price mechanism, together with the assumption that individuals will normally seek their own best economic advantage as both consumers and suppliers, is the foundation of liberal economics.

It is the 'invisible hand' that economists since Adam Smith have recognised as the built-in guarantee not only of consistency in economic choices, but also of the optimal matching of available resources to individual wants. Of course, everyone is familiar with a thousand-and-one different ways in which the process does not operate or is prevented from operating in this idealised fashion. Perhaps the most widely quoted of these defects is that purchasing power, post-tax as well as pre-tax, is unequal and must necessarily be so, if the market is to have incentives for serving individual wants.

These imperfections have provided the political pretext, though not the main motive, for intervention by government in the economic domain. It is not necessary here to review the vast literature on the proper scope for the limits of such intervention. Suffice it to say that there is nothing in the operation of the political market-place that requires that those limits be observed.

Indeed, the essence of democratic politics is a gigantic celebration of the fact that you *can* get something for nothing, or at least that *you*—the individual voter—can get something for nothing, even if as the ancients had it, *ex nihilo nihil fit*; for government, with its legalised powers of coercion, can award benefits here while it charges costs there. That indeed is the whole nature of the restribution of wealth and income, an almost universally accepted function of government.

The point here is not to question the legitimacy of this aspect of the political process, but to emphasise that it is a process without any sensitive or automatic regulator. In the very long run, it may be argued, societies will discover that it does not pay them to sacrifice too much of the incentive functions of incomes to the cause of equality or 'fairness'; but any such feedback is problematic and highly uncertain.

The conflict between the different logics of political and economic choice is most clearly manifest in the relationship between unemployment and inflation. Since Keynes, since the war, since the British *Employment Policy* White Paper of 1944, and since the American Employment Act 1946, a pledge of full employment has been an indispensable ingredient in any bid for electoral victory.

After the experiences of the 1930s, almost every voter—or so all politicians have assumed—has regarded the avoidance of mass unemployment as an overriding political objective. After the writings of Keynes and even more after the simplified popularisation of his writings and their endorsement by governments the politicians and the public have also assumed that the means of securing high employment always lay at hand.

Whenever unemployment looked like it was rising to politically embarrassing levels—and the threshold of embarrassment was extremely low by previous historical standards—the response was to put more spending power into people's pockets, whether by cutting taxes, increasing government spending, or easing credit conditions through monetary policy.

It was recognised in theory that one might go too far in this direction, overheat the economy, and cause inflation. But it was not doubted that there was a safe zone in which something approaching full employment could be maintained without running risks of serious inflation. The exact trade-offs within that zone between degrees of full employment and degrees of price stability were thought to be described, by a stable relationship know as the 'Phillips curve'.

The economic realities were unhappily different. The belief that, outside the narrow range of the Phillips curve, the regulation of spending power (known as 'demand management') affected the price level alone or the employment level alone, according to whether the pressure of demand was above or below the full employment zone, was false.

The truth is that in the short term—for the first year or two—demand management mainly affects the real volume of spending, output and therefore employment, while in the longer run it mainly affects the price level. The notion inherent in the popular understanding of Keynes— that an economy could be indefinitely underemployed through deficient demand without prices eventually being forced down sufficiently to clear markets, including the labour market—was a dangerous misunderstanding of the unhappy experiences of the 1930s.

None the less, the belief was almost universal in British economic circles and increasingly predominant in American and Continental European circles that, provided actual overheating of the economy was avoided (and with it 'overfull employment'), budget deficits and the associated expansion of the money supply could be used more or less without limit to head off any incipient rise in unemployment.

At the same time, there were objective reasons why unemployment was likely to rise above the levels regarded as 'full employment', even in the absence of any positively deflationary actions by government and the central bank. These were and are of two kinds, both barely recognised and little understood: the general imperfections of the labour market; and the operation of what is variously known as 'free collective bargaining' and as 'trade union monopoly bargaining'.

Imperfections of the labour market include anything that keeps job-seekers and vacancies from being instantly matched to one another.

As the pattern of demand and the techniques of supply constantly evolve, different kinds of workers are required by different entrepreneurs in different places. It takes time to convert some workers from one role to another. Others can never be converted and have to be replaced by a new and differently-trained generation.

There is a real personal cost to moving, which often makes workers willing to remain unemployed, sometimes indefinitely, rather than take work in a faraway place. People are naturally reluctant to pull up the roots of family, friendship, and all the familiarities of home', and they are further discouraged by British public housing regulations which automatically take away an occupier's title to very low-rent accommodation if he moves to another district.

And there are a thousand-and-one other major and minor frictions that normally result in a degree of mis-match, at any moment in time, between labour force and work opportunities. The mismatch cannot but be reflected in a margin of the workforce being out of work, or at least between jobs, at any one time. The size of that margin, of course, will also depend on the capital endowment of industry and on its rate of change in relation to the rate of change of the skills of the workforce.

This margin may, in Professor Milton Friedman's words, be called the 'natural' rate of unemployment, although this should not be taken to mean that it is established by any law of nature. It is just a catch-all phrase for all the circumstances *other than the manipulation of monetary demand by governments* that influence the level of unemployment.

The role of free collective bargaining may be regarded as a second and separate reason why conventional post-war full employment politicies were incompatible with price stability—or indeed with a stable rate of inflation—or it can be seen as a special case of the first general reason. The latter way of putting it emphasises the monopolistic character of collective bargaining by labour unions. The effect of charging a monopoly price for labour must inevitably be to reduce 'sales', that is, employment, below the market-clearing level. Some people will get paid more than they would under perfect competition in the labour market, but others will not get jobs at all.

The effect, therefore, of a widespread pattern of monopolistic bargaining in the labour market will be to increase the numbers unemployed—in other words, to raise the 'natural' rate of unemployment. This, as has often been pointed out, is in itself a once-and-for-all effect. But like the once-and-for-all effects of other labour market imperfections, it gives rise to an accelerating, eventually explosive rate of inflation when it is combined with a government commitment to maintain by demand management a lower rate of unemployment than this new 'natural level'.

As soon as the level of unemployment begins to approach the higher 'natural' rate, government rushes in with injections of additional spending power, whether by fiscal or monetary means. These monetary or fiscal injections initially increase demand and so check or reverse the rise in unemployment. But this creates an imbalance of supply and demand in the labour market. Either unemployment is now below the natural rate, or it is below the rate that is needed just to inhibit the further exercise of labour unions' monopoly bargaining power.

In consequence, the price of labour rises once again. If final prices are not raised to cover this, businesses close and unemployment rises once again. If prices do go up, consumers' incomes will buy less, the volume of sales falls, output falls, and unemployment rises once again. Whereupon government is forced to intervene again with another injection of extra spending power. Before long, consumers and pay bargainers—indeed, everyone involved in the economy—gets used to continuing inflation. It becomes built into expectations, and so the stimulative effects of any given amount of governmental 'reflation' are eroded. Governments then begin to increase the dose; and there is no end to this process of trying to keep the actual inflation rate permanently ahead of constantly catching-up expectations until the stage of hyperinflation—and breakdown—is reached.

It is not strictly necessary, however, to express the role of free collective bargaining by labour unions as a special case of the natural rate of unemployment hypothesis. More simply, it can be said that in anything short of a total buyers' market for labour—which would imply a level of unemployment many times greater than any post-war government has even contemplated—labour monopolies can progressively force up the price of labour.

Since there is no corresponding increase in the value of output, the extra claims on the available resources have to be neutralised by rising prices, which then become the bases for the next round of pay claims. It may well be that the sum of all the monopoly pay claims, expressed in terms of the real purchasing power demanded, is greater than the national output available to satisfy them. In that case, equilibrium in the short term can only be maintained if inflation continuously runs ahead of the inflationary expectations of the pay bargainers or if the labour monopolies are permitted to price themselves out of their jobs until they are deterred from further exercise of their market power. Since governments are pledged not to let the second happen, they are forced to choose the other horn of the dilemma and to inflate at an accelerating rate.

Surely, it will be said, western democracy is not going to wreck itself on such absurd and obvious nonsense. Unfortunately, it probably will, at least on the eastern side of the Atlantic . . . the operation of free democracy appears to force governments into positions (the commitment to full employment) that prevent them from taking steps (fiscal and monetary restraint) that are necessary to arrest the menace (accelerating inflation) that threatens to undermine the condition (stable prosperity) on which political stability and therefore liberal democracy depend. In other words, democracy has itself by the tail and is eating itself up fast.

12. Mentioning the Unmentionable*

Sir John Hoskyns

Despite an unusually long period of financial stability and gradual recovery, and well before the recent slide in the oil price and the pound, doubts about any kind of economic miracle were already on the increase. Continuing tactical crises, so familiar in the 1960s and 1970s, are now less frequent. But the post-war strategic crisis—the long process of national decline and fall—remains. On present policies it is unlikely to be surmounted.

Labour costs in Britain are again rising while they are static or falling for our main overseas competitors. The financial burden of supporting the retired population, and especially the very old, grows heavier. State pension payments as a proportion of total UK personal income have more than doubled in the past 20 years and the percentage is likely to grow by nearly half again over the next 15 years.

The working population has increased by 1 million since 1970 (400,000 since 1979) and will grow by a further half-million by 1990, and there are no signs of unemployment falling. All-embracing welfare provision appears to undermine the economic process necessary to support it. The hidden economy grows, as people migrate to a non-taxpaying regime.

Any suggestion of radical change runs into opposition from vested interest groups, which, seeing no sign of an economic miracle, cling grimly to what they hold: home-owners, parents, council employees, business interests, trade unions, professions, farmers, and the MPs who represent them.

The preservation of 'today'—and, indeed, yesterday—remains sacrosanct; tomorrow is regarded as expendable. In this deadly negotiation between the present and the future, the first-order problems are

*Reproduced from *The Times*, 11–13 February 1985

scarcely discussed: the £40 billion of social security spending, much of it effectively demand-determined and thus uncontrollable; the economic effects of welfare in all its forms; the growing cost of the health service; the poverty and employment traps which block the escape from unemployment into paid work; the economic costs of collective bargaining and employment protection; the tax burden on the low and average paid; indexation; the right, in practice, to be paid for declining to take available work.

These problems interact. Most of them are consequences of patch-work policy-making by past governments. Many are the results of specific pledges given by politicians under pressure. Together they imprison governments in what appears to be an inevitable historical process of decline. The 'policy box' in which ministers are locked is too small to contain any solutions.

Paradoxically, it is the relative success of Mrs Thatcher and her government since 1979 which brings these problems into our range of vision. Memories are short and people already forget the years when governments lived from crisis budget to crisis mini-budget. Already we take for granted the fall in inflation, the defeat of public sector strikes, the reduction in trade union power, the slimming of the civil service, the huge programme of denationalisation, the removal of all those hopeless controls and regulations—prices, dividends, profit reference levels, exchange controls, pay norms.

All this was done in the wake of the 1979 doubling of oil prices. We forget that in 1976 the government was borrowing today's equivalent of nearly £30 billion and inflation was over 25 per cent.

We forget the days when the growing tax burden on the average worker was sold back to him as 'the social wage', and concern about trade union disruption routinely dismissed as 'scaremongering'. Because previous governments were always fire-fighting, they never confronted the country's central dilemma: our unsustainable post-war political economy.

The present government, despite all its inevitable mistakes, is the first to reach the threshold of the Augean stables. Its predecessors were swept away, exhausted and discredited, before they even got to the stable door. Today we ask whether the government is capable of long-term strategy. We never asked the same question of its predeces-sors because they were burnt out long before the question arose.

Where is Britain trying to go? Where would unchanged policies take us? What are the likely long-term consequences of a cautious strategy of 'consolidation'? Might the political and social tensions arising from further radical change undo the likely benefits? What do we mean by lasting recovery—political and economic stability as a sort of 'second world' economy or a true reversal of 100 years of decline? Is the latter possible, or is decline now programmed into the British character?

It is a matter of risk-analysis. The penalty of overkill—that is, developing a programme which turns out to be more radical than neccessary—may be less than the penalty for 'underkill', the more familiar British tendency to do too little, too late.

If we conclude that settling for a quiet life now may produce unquiet lives for our children, then we have a duty to make policy on worst-case assumptions. If, on the other hand, we conclude that a radical programme is simply not possible, then we had better concentrate our minds on how to preserve political stability with continued relative decline. But this, of course, has been the unspoken establishment posture for most of the post-war period until 1979, and the results are not encouraging.

I believe the government must err on the side of overkill. If other industrialised economies were in a similar state to our own, we could afford complacency. We would all be equal and all relatively poor. But that is not the case. It is true that there are signs of the British malaise in other European economies, and that they too are beginning a painful reappraisal. But we start from a long way behind. Perhaps more important, our cumulative 'policy configuration' may have made our economy inherently unstable, so that the mechanisms by which it adapts to change and external shock threaten to break down under stress.

The present government—radical enough by post-war standards—operates in a hostile intellectual climate, shaped by governments which generally took the line of least resistance. It is a climate which makes rational thought difficult. All actions are judged in terms of conduct today, rather than results tomorrow. Symptoms are treated as causes. Those who propose painful measures are accused of wanting them for their own sake.

It is a world of moving goalposts, with little awareness of causes or consequences, no comparison with the past, or with the experience of other countries. There is a total unawareness of secondary economic effects. The teaching of what Lord Bauer, has called 'priceless economics' has reinforced the widespread belief that 'in today's complicated world, the market no longer works', which has led to policies that have harmed millions.

It requires great courage for ministers to speak the truth in such a climate. Courage requires convictions which are the fruit of intellectual effort, not of blind faith. It is not the job of civil servants to develop such convictions (they must, after all, stand ready, at the limit, to serve a

Marxist government if one is freely elected), while ministers simply do not have the necessary thinking time. So they find themselves describing objectives for which they are unable to devise measures, or committing themselves to measures whose consequences they cannot predict.

We all know that there is an ideological battle between those working for stability and recovery and a minority which, to put it plainly, hates Britain, hates the United States and NATO, supports the Soviet Union and wishes to destablise the democratic system. But there is also an intellectual civil war—perhaps even more dangerous—within the establishment, between those who know that time is running out and who feel the impulse to go back to first principles and think the problem through: and those who prefer the *status quo* or are simply too tired to go on thinking at all. To an alarming extent, those who are prepared to make the effort are outside Whitehall and Westminster.

The businessman is sometimes part of this problem. Like politicians and civil servants, he will have organised himself for coping with the present state of affairs. By the time he is in his mid-40s, he may have looked around and concluded that Britain, however sickly "will see me out". If enough people, in and out of Whitehall think like that, it probably won't.

The Thatcher government's first term concentrated on *financial* stability: the control of inflation, public expenditure and borrowing, public sector pay and the first steps to reduce union power. Now, everyone is beginning to talk about secondary issues of the 'we must' variety; we must increase the number of engineers; we must make education more responsive to industry; we must improve our product design; harness our national research effort more closely to industry; change public attitudes to wealth creation; be more entrepreneurial and so on.

There is nothing wrong with these ideas. But an entire and crucially more important phase is missing; *economic* stabilisation, without which all these worthy ideas are scarcely worth discussing. We still need a quiet revolution in every aspect of our present policies for spending, taxing, earning, working and caring for those who cannot work. This, I believe, is recognised more clearly by outside policy groups than it is in Whitehall and Westminster.

In this wider and intellectually richer world, party-political viewpoints are becoming less relevant. People starting from different political positions are brought closer together by their analysis of Britain's problem.

But it will not be enough for these outsiders to present analysis and prescriptions. They have first to persuade the official and elected policy makers to think in a different way, and to look at an uncomfortably different agenda.

TAMING THE WELFARE STATE

The debate about whether the government should 'cut taxes or reduce unemployment' stems from the belief, widespread even in establishment circles, that economic activity is essentially a zero-sum game; that it is not possible for one group of people to receive an advantage except at the expense of another group. It is not clear whether the Chancellor's critics believe present tax levels to be, by some happy accident, optimal, or too low, so that an increase could yield more revenue for 'infrastructure' spending. If the latter, what upper limit should there be, and why?

There is a similar confusion about whether infrastructure investment should be increased to avoid physical collapse, because it would produce a better economic return than other ways of using the money, or because of its employment effects. Even if increased infrastructure spending were labour-intensive, not subject to planning delays, geographically matched to the worst unemployment areas, and created jobs which survived after the programme was over, the important questions are never asked. Why is it that the economy functions so badly that there are now 2 million people whether by necessity or by choice, between jobs, and why have over 1 million been unemployed for more than a year? What is the actual process by which increased infrastructure spending would cure this systemic malaise?

The attempts by successive governments up to 1979 to make everyone's life appear, as far as possible, free of charge, have led to a growing proportion of gross domestic product being spent by government. In 1955 the government spent less than 34 per cent of a much smaller GDP on goods, services, transfer payments and capital formation. For 1985/86, even after annual GDP growth of between 2 and 3 per cent for three successive years, the figure will be 41 per cent, or £141 billion, including £9 billion of interest on accumulated government borrowing. This figure compares with about 37 per cent in the US. 34 per cent in Japan and 26 per cent in the new industrialising countries of the Far East.

The spending and taxing burden, for a fragile economy like Britain's, has now passed its tolerable limits. The call for lower income tax should not be dismissed by those who are well enough off to do so, as Poujadist self-indulgence. Over 30 years we have become conditioned to very high income tax rates, levied at low income levels. The combination of low growth and increasing taxation (the 'fiscal drag and social wage' regime of the 1960s and 1970s) has made the average British worker the lowest paid and most highly taxed in Europe. We have become accustomed to government taking between a quarter and a half share of every commercial transaction, and to an Inland Revenue which seems to be almost at war with the private citizen.

There is growing evidence that low-tax economies grow fast and high-tax economies grow slowly. And yet for much of the past post-war period governments have seemed not to think that there was any connection between the burden of spending and the performance of the economy.

Lower taxes have their effect at the margin. Tax cuts do not, overnight, make the entire working population 3.75 per cent more diligent or adventurous. They cause unknown individuals and companies to do things they would not otherwise have done—things that will be economically rational because the decisions are taken by the individuals directly involved. That is how economic change takes place.

There is no possibility of any real economic transformation for Britain without *very* large reductions in the tax burden. There is no chance of such reductions without *very* large reductions in spending. So what are the government's spending objectives? They have already changed from 'reducing spending as a proportion of GDP' to 'holding spending constant as a proportion of GDP'. Are we trying to reduce spending, in order to make lasting growth possible, or hoping for growth, in order that spending should, for presentational purposes be a smaller proportion of GDP? At present the mere task of holding public spending constant seems to be virtually impossible. Why is this so?

About £40 billion of the 1985–86 public spending programme of £14 billion represents transfer payments in the form of pensions, unemployment benefits, supplementary benefits, housing benefits and child benefits, not to mention £7 billion of rates rebates and nearly £2 billion of farm payments. Much of this expenditure is indexed against inflation and effectively 'demand determined', that is to say, not limited by government decision.

Once upon a time, demand-determined expenditure was seen as the ideal Keynesian stabliser during a down-swing in the business-cycle. But the scales of benefit, and the numbers receiving them, are now so big that this expenditure is itself destabilising and self-enlarging. The larger these numbers get, the more over-burdened and sluggish the economy becomes, so that the numbers of the dependent population increase yet again. The whole process resembles the control engineer's nightmare—

the thermostat that responds to a rise in temperature by turning on the heating. The hotter it gets, the hotter it gets.

We must add to these large blank-cheque commitments the cash demands of a public sector that faces little or no competition, is heavily unionised, and often lacks the most rudimentary information about costs. The public services (that is the public sector excluding national-ised industries) employ over 5 million people, or about 9 per cent of the population, compared with an estimated 6 per cent in France and West Germany. Their total bill for 1985 comes to a further £40 billion.

The problem of public expenditure reduction is insoluble without major policy and organisational reforms. Government must cash-limit transfer payments, just like other spending. That limit requires a judgement about what the productive economy can stand in terms of tax and what it needs in terms of incentives. There is no reason, in principle, why transfer payments should escape cuts that fall on other spending. Governments cannot indefinitely honour such pledges on the basis that the productive economy must somehow achieve worldwide competitive performance and what is left of the value it adds. In the end, spending can be determined only by supply. The longer that day is delayed, the more abrupt and painful the change will be.

The first step is consistently to uprate benefits by less than inflation. That would also accelerate the fall in inflation itself, with other beneficial side-effects. The second is to remodel Britain's welfare state to reflect more closely the original Beveridge aim: a safety-net for those in need. With the shrinking of an overgrown transfer system would come simultaneously a reduced tax burden on the lower-paid and significant increases in help to those in real need.

The third step is to transfer as much of the public services as possible, including parts of the health service, to the private sector. The more we can do this, the more present waste can be reduced. As has often been pointed out, the rapid growth of spending on the health service is party due to the fact that it is provided free at the point of consumption. Supply is therefore rationed by a combination of waiting-lists and declining service standards.

People might well be ready to pay more, not less, for health care if they were allowed to. Spending on health would then be demand-determined, too, but on the basis of price. This reversal of emphasis, whereby health care becomes demand-determined and social security supply-determined, is fundamental. Free and unlimited welfare pay-ments create their own dependent population, with destablising social and economic consequences. But cash-limited health care penalises people who are *ill*. Putting this right requires a fundamental rethink, on the lines (we hope) of the Fowler reviews.

The welfare state is, at one and the same time, Britain's proudest achievement and biggest man-made disaster. It is astronomically expensive compared with the economy that supports it: incomprehensible to use or administer; open to abuse, and therefore increasingly abused; mean and degrading for those who really need its help. The scale of the problem and its effects on what are regarded as 'normal' values and behaviour are scarcely recognised because they have come about so insidiously, over so many years. The study of Britain's welfare state is now virtually a life's work. It is doubtful whether Whitehall has a real understanding of the present system, let alone the energy and will to design a new one.

Beveridge introduced national assistance as a temporary and transitional measure to relieve poverty, pending full introduction of his comprehensive national insurance system. In 1948 it cost £62 million. By 1982/83 the cost of its successor, supplementary benefit, had risen in real terms to £6,263 million, despite much higher living standards. The post-Beveridge welfare state now costs a total of some £54 billion annually.

By the 1970s, universal benefits such as child benefits had extended the welfare principle to the centre population, rich and poor alike. At the same time, the state earnings-related pension scheme marked a further step forward by the state into personal pension provision. This over-ambitious scheme to index state pensions, and to pass to future generations the cost of an unfunded, pay-as-you-go system, is likely to present nightmare problems as it moves towards maturity in the early decades of the next century.

This unplanned growth has, perversely, obscured the plight of those in greatest need: the chronically sick, the blind and the disabled, for whom society could care with far greater generosity if the total welfare burden were reduced.

Britain's welfare state was based on the impossibility of universal provision. It was allowed to evolve with no clear aims or principles. Its systematic interaction with the real economy was scarcely even considered. Beveridge's national assistance was intended as a safety-net which would reduce in size as national insurance covered the needs of the overwhelming majority of the population, which never really happened. In 1948, national assistance covered 1 in 33 of the population. Today, 1 in every 8—a total of some 7 million people—receive supplementary benefit. Between *20 and 30 million people* are now recipients of social benefits of different kinds.

Provision has never been based on fixed criteria of 'need'. Its growth is thus self-fuelling. 'Poverty' has been redefined upwards in line with living standards, producing an inherent instability in the system. There is no true insurance principle, so that it is uniquely subject to 'moral hazard'. The system's resulting size, incoherence and complexity require almost 80,000 civil servants and a budget of £1.5 billion for its administration alone.

The present system is undesigned. It resembles a tower-block built by simply allowing a few hundred bricklayers to come in and start laying bricks. Is the system meant to eradicate poverty absolutely, measured against fixed needs? Or relatively, against the income of others? How do we measure entitlement? Should entitlement be universal, as for child benefit? Dependent on a contribution record, as for unemployment benefit? Measured against need, as for supplementary benefit? On a fixed scale or discretionary? Paid automatically or against specific application? Should benefits be free-standing or should one benefit give entitlement to another?

The system we have today has all of these mixed up together. Because we do not know whether benefits should be contribution-linked or not, unemployment benefit will come from the Department of Employment, and supplementary benefit from the DHSS. Because we are not sure whether benefits should depend on registration for work, there is no effective means of confining benefits to those genuinely unable to find work. The welfare and tax systems might as well have been developed in different countries, so perverse are their interactions.

What is the first step from the present shambles to a supportable welfare state? As the Institute for Fiscal Studies and others have proposed, a negative or reverse income tax would be the most effective way of providing income support for those in real need. The best—perhaps the only—way to do this would be by integrating the tax and benefit systems. This idea has been postponed as 'too difficult' for the last 15 years. But the impending computerisation of PAYE now makes it possible.

What is more, a computerized tax system provides an automatic way of assessing tax or measuring need; a means test without stigma. Such an arrangement would require a permanent and realistic definition of basic 'need'. Benefits must be in cash, not in kind. This gives the recipient a chance to match his resources to his actual situation, with a great reduction in administrative complexity.

There must be a real inducement to work. In the US a number of states have introduced 'Workfare' to complement welfare. The principle is simple and obvious: it should not be possible for people to receive benefits paid for by others while making no attempt to earn for themselves. This would require the state to provide work of some kind for the recipients. Provision of such work might cost more than its marginal value. The aim would be to provide a mechanism, at the margin, for discouraging abuse and emigration to the black economy.

Make-work schemes cannot directly solve the longer-term unemployment problem but they might reduce the danger of welfare abuse, and thus increase the number of people ready to take lower-paid jobs which are often impossible to fill even with today's high rate of unemployment. The Community Programme could provide the model for such a scheme, though it is not at present linked to a system by which people have to register to work in order to receive benefits.

The new welfare system should be based on privately provided compulsory insurance, with the state paying the premiums of those who cannot afford to provide for themselves. It must be driven by contributions, provided personally or by the state, not by demand at the point of consumption. This is the only basis for any system viable in the long term. The insurance principle was essential to the Beveridge concept, yet state national insurance has become so distorted under political pressures that it is no longer insurance in other than name.

Private insurance health care already provides for a substantial proportion of routine or less than catastrophic needs. If we can lay to rest the old argument that private health care robs the health service (which has long been deteriorating under the corrupting effect of unionisation and the reorganisation of the early 1970s), more people could be encouraged to self-insure by tax relief, partial or complete, so that they do not have to pay twice over—to the state and the private system. The insurance approach is not free from complications, but it could provide the key to [a] permanent redesign of the British welfare state so that it can serve those who really need it, without eventually crippling the economy.

In 1945 Britain committed itself to full employment by demand management, and simultaneously embarked upon wholesale nationalisation and the creation of a welfare state, before rebuilding its productive base. It has not yet recovered—and may never recover—from that strategic error. For much of the subsequent period, policy-makers took the wealth-creating process for granted. Government spending increased, based on economic growth projections that never came true. As the spending increased, so the productive base became increasingly debilitated.

To borrow a phrase, private-sector business—that neglected asset on whose performance all politicians' dreams of social progress ultimately depend—had become locked into a cycle of relative deprivation. We have to go back to first principles and decide what welfare really means, what levels of incentives the working population needs, what tax burden the productive economy can bear, and then start to reshape the processes by which people, savings, skills and inventions come together to create value.

TAMING THE TRADE UNIONS

Today there is growing awareness that a major cause—perhaps *the* major cause—of UK unemployment is the rigidity of the labour market. Rent control, wage councils, employment protection (Labour's legislation of 1975 has been left almost untouched by the Conservatives), health and safety regulations and the burden of PAYE and VAT collection for small businesses all play a part.

But central to unemployment and to the functioning of the economy as a whole has been the role of the trades unions. The unions are not the sole cause of Britain's post-war economic failure, but few still argue that they are not an important part of it. Their role since the war may itself be a reflection of the individual's frustration in a low-growth, high-tax, low-opportunity, inflation-prone economy.

Trades unions began as Friendly Societies in the nineteenth century, before the welfare state existed and when many substantial businesses were owned by proprietors, rather than by financial institutions and private investors. Friendly Societies acted to defend the individual against oppressive or capricious employers.

Today the situation is entirely different. Since 1906 the unions have been free, uniquely, to incite breaches of employment contracts without exposure to civil action. For nearly 40 years we have had a large and elaborate welfare state, employing millions of people, organised by trades unions which have effective monopoly in the various services.

The growth of the welfare state and employee protection legislation should have reduced the need for trades unions. Instead, they grew larger and stronger, and became most concentrated in the welfare state services themselves. It is time to question whether the British economy, already so weak, can afford to carry either of these burdens, let alone both together, in their present forms.

Despite the changes since 1979, there is still widespread nervousness and confusion about facing the union problem head-on. British moderation is always carried to extremes. The ultimate sanction on which all legislation rests—the exposure of trades union funds to civil action—was politically unthinkable right through 1979, 1980 and 1981.

The iniquitous section 17(3) of the 1980 Act, whereby a union can 'black' a company completely uninvolved in a dispute because it happens to be a first customer or first supplier of the struck-against company, still stands. The unstated assumption is that the unions had an historic right to do at least *some* financial violence which was denied to others under the law.

Many will now argue that the government has surely gone far enough. I suggest, however, that it is now time to consider whether the 1906 Trades Disputes Act, which confers on trades unions their unique immunities from actions in tort, should be repealed. Those who argue that there is 'no place for the law in industrial relations' fail to understand that the law of contract is central, not least to protect the employee. If there really was no place for the law in industrial relations, what might an unscrupulous employer do to his employee?

Collective bargaining is an inherently destablising device. Each bargaining group is under competitive pressure to catch up with better-paid groups. Those groups are then under pressure to restore the differentials between them and lower-paid groups. The pressure is always upwards and starts from an assumed base of full indexation for the cost of living. Normally, a free economy tries to adjust to the business cycle by a combination of fluctuating unemployment and fluctuating real wages. By resisting the latter, trades unions help to increase the former, but their impossible aim is to resist both.

It is sometimes argued, in a muddled defence of collective bargaining, that pay negotiations are different from other contract negotiations (for example, the sale of a house or a car) because the two parties *have* to do a deal in the end or their organisation ceases to exist. They cannot 'walk away'. But that is precisely because the bargaining is collective, not individual. A non-unionised company can dismiss the unsatisfactory employee, just as the individual employee can leave the unsatisfactory employer.

With individual and binding contracts, each side would be as well protected as the contract between them provides, and employment protection would have been effectively privatised.

Collective bargaining tends to debase labour because it assumes that workers—'the lads'—are treated as units of production, at best children, rather than individual and responsible human beings. It is thus almost inevitable that union propaganda tries to recreate a world in which the employers can be represented as nineteenth-century ironmasters. For without such a world, what becomes of the old trades union role?

Collective bargaining does nothing for the 'dignity of labour' because it requires pay to be administered rather than earned by individual performance. It is thus the great leveller within the collective group. It will subsidise those who are ineffective and rob those who give good value. It must deal in emotional crowd scenes. It can take little account of individual circumstances. The married man with a mortgage will be forced to strike along with the young revolutionary. The strike may be an exciting diversion for one man, the last straw for another.

Freedom to break contracts or exercise monopoly power is corrupting. It leads quickly to the concept of collective lawbreaking and is the ideal instrument for the political activist. Unions have thus become unfriendly armies for collective offensive action rather than friendly societies for the defence of the individual. Where closed shops exist, they are effectively conscript armies, too. It is not surprising that communist infiltration of British trades unions has been intensive since the early 1920s.

It is truly astonishing that the Advisory, Conciliation and Arbitration Service still has a statutory duty to promote collective bargaining as we approach the twenty-first century. There are four real protections for the individual worker: freedom of association within the law; the rival employer to whom he can transfer; greater financial independence; and the law of contract itself, as the non-striking miners have discovered.

The EETPU, first under Frank Chapple and now under Eric Hammond, clearly recognised many years ago that old-fashioned class-based trade unionism was obsolete. The electricians have pioneered no-strike agreements, in particular with foreign companies like Toshiba setting up in the UK. The EETPU is really saying, 'If we promise not to use the unique privileges granted to British trades unions, will you allow us to be your exclusive union?'

They may well be leading the way towards a new union role—a sort of twenty-first-century Friendly Society, with greater emphasis on training (and perhaps, one day, advice to members over their *individual* employment contracts and the provision of unemployment insurance). But the sunset unions will need pressure to follow them, either from the accelerating decline of the sunset industries themselves or as a consequence of employment contracts being made legally enforceable, as they are for the rest of the working population.

We should also remember that a company is free to withdraw recognition and thus either end collective bargaining or, perhaps as a result of a ballot of its workforce, bargain with a staff association instead of the union.

The British are very good at finding reasons for not doing uncomfortable things. Our desire to do things by halves is very strong. Some will argue that the EETPU is already showing the way, perhaps with the AUEW following, and that there is therefore no need to do anything more. Others will be reluctant to offend responsible trades union leaders who have done much to resist communist infiltration and to prevent the present chaotic arrangements from doing even more damage.

But there is no guarantee that obsolescent institutions will reform themselves. We cannot count on other unions providing farsighted leaders capable of strategic thinking. Indeed, we cannot guarantee that the EETPU will not at some future date fall into communist hands again. The trades unions—from the most responsible and professional to the most politicised and class-obsessed—will fiercely resist any measures designed to weaken their power.

The union question must be seen in perspective. The trades union movement is a privileged minority. Despite the rhetoric of the mid-1970s, it has never 'spoken for the working class of this country'. It now represents 10 million people out of an employed population of 24 million, an electorate of 43 million, and a total of 56 million.

Yet its collective power can still put many organisations—particularly large companies, state industries and public services—under such pressures that more effort is devoted to preserving a *modus vivendi* with the unions than to satisfying customers.

The greater the trade union pressure, the greater the need for a company to achieve a non-competitive, semi-monopolistic situation.

IBM employs 17,000 people in the UK, with no trades union organisation, every employee having an individual contract with the employer, merit payment and an annual performance review, with first-line managers on the shop-floor instead of a mixture of foremen and shop stewards. When people argue that it is not practicable for large organisations to enter into individual contracts with their employers, they should realise that there is no difference, in principle, between a manager in a big company and the proprietor in a small one doing precisely that. Management is, above all, about the leadership and development of *people*. There was never a 'right' to manage, only a duty. That duty has been neglected in Britain at a terrible price over the long years of union dominance. As someone put it: 'The Americans waste money, the British waste people.' It is a waste we can no longer afford.

PART III:
The View from the Centre

As we leave the analyses of the Right to consider those of the Centre, the tone of the literature becomes more measured, the arguments more complex, and the implied solutions more obtuse. For here there is a greater sensitivity to the range of barriers that stand in the way of economic regeneration, and to their origins in an imperial and industrial past. *The Hudson Report* is typical in its sense of national assets being wasted by social inertia and the absence of clearly agreed and pursued objectives. It is typical too in its sensitivity to the legacy of the Victorian era, to the existence of an establishment which was slow to see the need to break with Victorian patterns, and to the way in which—because of that inactivity—opportunities were missed, assets were dissipated and a national style (of compassion, deference, even anti-industrialism) was consolidated which is now in need of reform. This Victorian legacy is a key theme too for *G.C. Allen*: leaving a 'cult of the amateur' to block industrial regeneration through the failure of the education system to produce industrial leaders and civil servants of quality. In arguing this, Professor Allen is close to the views of *Anthony Sampson*, for whom the government's own civil service is a key element of that Victorian legacy, part of an apparatus of power and privilege mesmorised by its own past and antipathetical to reform. Like the Spanish empire before it, the British spawned social forces and institutions which were unable to respond positively to imperial decay. As he puts it, 'Britain achieved the dismantling of the empire with remarkably little political revolt, but found it much harder to change her social structure to ensure her commercial survival.'

If the image of Don Quixote stalks Sampson's analysis, more prosaic concerns attract *Sir Henry Phelps Brown*. By carefully marshalling the appropriate evidence, he is able to discount at least most of the argument that public sector activity has 'crowded out' private initiative

139

through high taxation and borrowing, and the argument that industrial strikes have done much the same thing through their impact on business costs and expectations. He too gives more weight to the past: to the impact of class differences and class practices—particularly in the spheres of industrial relations and technological innovation—and like the Hudson Report, comes to see the need for a new culture and a replacement of old attitudes and practices.

When we ask which attitudes and practices are then to be replaced suggestions again begin to differ. Harold Lever and George Edwards concentrate on the need for change in banking practices. For them, the key to Britain's declining competitiveness in world markets has a lot to do with differential banking involvement in industrial funding. Foreign banks lend their local industries money on a different scale, and on different terms, from those normal in the United Kingdom. Foreign banks lend generously and they lend long. British banks lend little and lend short. For Lever and Edwards, 'such prudence can lead to poverty'; and the road to economic recovery lies through a banking initiative to match those common in West Germany, France and Japan.

The institution *Michael Stewart* thinks is in need of reform is the political system itself. He is aware, like many of the contributors to Part III, that the causes of Britain's decline are many and varied: in his case structural, technical, managerial and political in character. But the weight of Stewart's critique falls on the last of these—the lack of continuity in government policy which derives from a Victorian style of political opposition no longer in keeping with modern times. Government now has too vital a role to play to be at the beck and call of policy differences orchestrated for electoral reasons; and in that Jekyll and Hyde dance, industrial decline proceeds unchecked.

If for Stewart it is the lack of continuity in government policy which is the key, for *Sidney Pollard* and *Stephen Blank* it is just the reverse. Here, economic decline is again to be explained partly by reference to the role of governments, but now the weight of critique falls on the persistence of certain policy directions, no matter which government is in power. For Pollard, the problem lies in the long-established Treasury indifference to the needs of industry, its over-commitment to the symbols of power (not least the exchange rate of sterling) and its neglect of the underlying economic base which alone can give those symbols their substance. Pollard sees this Treasury 'blindness' to economic realities as itself reflective of City influence and of the domination of the Treasury by civil servants still trained in, and geared to, attitudes derived from the Victorian period.

Stephen Blank sees that 'blindness' too, but treats it less as a historical legacy than as a consequence of a set of policy decisions taken by British governments immediately after the war, and sustained thereafter. He is aware of the considerable *internal* barriers to economic growth: what he calls 'a wide range of serious defects of industrial structure, labour organisation and work and management practices'. But he sees the inability to deal with those as deriving from *external* constraints, from the prior commitment of successive British governments to the maintenance of their own world role. For him, it is foreign policy which holds the key to economic failure, through the way in which the strength of sterling became symbolic of an attempt to restore Britain's international position by consolidating a 'special relationship', economically and militarily, with the United States. It was the pursuit of that relationship and that world role which involved 'the restoration of sterling's international transaction and reserve function, fixed exchange rates, overseas investment directed particularly towards the sterling area, government spending and lending to the Commonwealth and sterling area, and the maintenance of a British military and defence presence in these areas.' Blank is keen to stress how bipartisan was the support for all this after 1945, how high a price it came to have for economic regeneration and how, in consequence, the story of British politics—particularly in the late 1940s and late 1960s—must be seen as one of lost opportunities which are now so very difficult to recall.

13. The Wasting of Assets*

The Hudson Report

There is something that must be said at the start. The British crisis is basically an economic crisis—whatever else may lie behind it. It is a failure to grow industrially and economically at the same rate at which other neighbouring countries are growing. But is economic growth so important? Anyone who looks about him at landscapes ruined by heavy industry, or heaped with mine slag, or at poisoned rivers, or who considers the nature of much modern factory and bureaucratic work, or who reflects upon the triviality or ugliness of so much that industry produces, is justified in asking that question. If Britain today, and Britain historically, is a serious nation, this has not come about simply because Britain has been a major industrial producer or, by the standards of the world as a whole, because it has been a rich society. It is because Britain has been an innovative society, a place of ideas and of art, a country which has established a standard of justice.

There thus are those in Britain today who would ignore, or who rationalise, the economic retardation of the country because they believe modern industry and the practical values of industrialism are aesthetically and morally objectionable. Or they say that these issues are irrelevant to what is *really important* in Britain's society and future . . .

At this point we will make only a short response. Those who object to industry and growth must tell us how to be fed and clothed without it. Britain is not a self-sufficient country and its standard of living is in decline. Even if the British people were willing to adopt a radically changed social system and sacrifice many of today's luxuries (and there are no signs that they are), Britain would still find itself faced with how

*Reproduced from The Hudson Report, *The United Kingdom to 1980* (London, 1974), pp. 3, 6, 7, 82, 110–13.

to supply for itself the necessities of life. It must trade simply to have enough food . . .

The present reality is that it is Britain that is the unstable and socially divided nation, economically depressed. Today, the continental states overall have not only a vastly better economic performance but also superior popular standards of living and amenity—and they enjoy, overall, a rather more impressive political condition. Even Italy, supposedly the other 'sick man of Europe', suffers mainly from a political ineptitude that, in its effect upon the society as a whole, is rather less important than ineptitude in Britain's leadership. The Italian state, as such, is in important respects irrelevant to what happens in Italian society. The dynamism of Italian society and of the Italian economy, and in many places of the regional and urban governments of Italy, gives better reason for optimism than is possible to feel when considering Britain today. Italy's problems are those of obsolescent institutions in a vitally developing society; the Italian crisis derives from the bursting of old structures under the power of social change and development, and the vigour of the industrial economy. Britain's problems consist of a decline in both governmental competence and economic performance: a universal loss of dynamism. The distinction is a fundamental one . . .

We hold that Britain's fundamental troubles come from within the society, and from certain economic, social, and institutional forces which are peculiarly British: aspects of British culture and an inheritance of a particular British historical experience . . .

ASSETS THAT HAVE BEEN WASTED

Britain is a nation with formidable assets as well as the troubling liabilities we have already discussed. The strengths of the society are so obvious that one is tempted to ignore them in [an article] such as this. Europeans and Americans have every reason to know and to be grateful for the tenacity of the British and the stability of Britain's political institutions. The country's parliamentary system has been the envy of troubled Europe. The competence, intellectual quality and integrity of Britain's civil service have made it virtually without equal. The level of formal scholarship and the quality of British university research and discussion are also probably without real equivalent abroad. Yet despite these assets, and others, the economic troubles of the country persist and deepen. Even British technology, which has been in the first rank of innovation, and the manifest commercial talents of the country, seem in practice to prove irrelevant to the nation's problems. Somehow they are not deployed properly; there seems to be an inability to make these advantages serve great economic and social purposes. Despite an extraordinary tradition in science and technology, British innovations seem to have to go elsewhere to be exploited, to be applied, and manufactured. Despite having produced the greatest economists of the last two centuries, Britain finds its economy mismanaged. These are persistent failures; and it is difficult not to believe that the sources for these failures lie in part in social and cultural factors exceedingly difficult to cure . . .

The absence of any strong commitment to future change has meant the misuse or even destruction of key elements of Britain's social, intellectual and economic reserves that would under different conditions represent considerable assets. Many of these elements—like the stability of its political system, the innate sense of fairness in public debate and the capacity to compromise—are still the well-polished currency of foreign opinion about Britain. But they are falling under increasing strain as the tensions that economic pressures generate invade the processes of negotiation or setting of priorities that make up the daily round in government and manufacturing. At a less abstract level, the qualities of intellectual strength, of technological competence, and of the economic resilience that traditionally derived from Britain's status as an island—and an island of considerable regional variations— have not been fully exploited. To some degree this resulted from the barriers to change that class or convention erected. These barriers were also the damaging consequences of an inadequate perception of the very direction of change. The two acting together, social inertia and the absence of objectives, could not help but produce a general condition of stagnation and drift.

The Victorian Legacy

Britain in the 1970s is very largely the creation of the mid-Victorian period. This fact, while it carries with it some of the positive legacies of Victorian Britain into the contemporary world, also accounts for the greater part of contemporary Britain's weaknesses. Many of the country's problems are Victorian problems, or stem from attempts to operate Victorian solutions in a society that exists in a late twentieth-century world. In a nutshell, Victorian Britain attempted to come to terms with a crude industrialism; the Britain of the 1970s has refused to look beyond it.

Coming to terms with the social and economic realities of Victorian Britain meant asking questions about the society of that time that are strikingly similar to those raised today. But the solutions that today must be sought cannot borrow from the outmoded norms of the 1880s any more than lessons learnt in the administration of British India can apply to issues of, say, Britain's regional devolution in the 1970s. That modern Britain has not moved further than posing those same questions in over 100 years is moreover a pertinent comment on the stagnation of modern Britain's pace of political change.

In short, the Britain of the 1860s and 1870s was required to ask itself what kind of industrial society it was to have, and how the tensions that such a society would increasingly generate were to be mitigated. It is true that the electoral reforms of 1832 had amended the rules of the political game in favour of certain new classes, and that the Britain of the mid-century held an unrivalled position as a manufacturer and trader (between 1840 and 1870 world trade grew by some 500 per cent, with Britain a major beneficiary) but it was yet to come to terms, for instance, with the urban desolation and complex problems of social reorganisation that rampant industrialisim had brought. It was yet to define its own circumstances. In the event, Victorian Britain defined its new situation by making a compromise between the existing form of social structure and its economic and intellectual potential. The society still lives with that compromise.

The years around 1870 were punctuated with legislative and social innovation, changes that stemmed in part from a resolve to set, from a position of clear economic leadership, a model for the civilised world. The Britain of 1870 was, after all, the most prosperous son of the industrial revolution, and perhaps even felt that it could afford the luxury of altering the social foundations of a traditional structure. The Reform Act 1867 extended the franchise well beyond the limited scope of the 1832 legislation; further broadening came in 1874 and 1884. The higher posts in the civil service were opened to competitive examination for the first time. In 1873 the bewildering mass of convention and legal form that passed for English law was refined and partially codified in a Judicature Act which brought a limited uniformity to an important social mechanism. The Education Act which brought a national system of elementary education came in 1870. A local government board was established. In 1871 a Trade Union Act and a consolidating Factory and Workshops Act appeared. Laws on liquor licensing, the political status of the armed forces and the functioning of the limited liability company were added to a lengthening list of regulatory or innovative instruments without precedent in English parliamentary history.

There was, however, a crucial flaw in this process of adaptation. For, underlying these decisions to modify the operational characteristics of

British society was a generalised belief among members of the political and administrative élite that Britain would continue to be the dominant industrial force in the developed world, a belief that was already, by the 1870s, demonstrably unrealistic. The result was a synthesising of elements of reform with a failing economic vitality, a series of social enactments introduced into a situation of economic decline.

The issues posed in the Britain of a century ago were not, as some contemporary reformers thought, ones of subtle or partial modification of social and political structure—extension of the franchise here, rationalisation of trade union status there. They were issues that arose because of the incipient weaknesses characteristic of British society in an industrial age—weaknesses that were truly to threaten Britain with the permanent position of being 'workshop of the world'—a place of manual tasks and depressing factory life. The issues at stake were those of reorienting British society to fit it for the high industrialism of the twentieth century, and these issues were evaded.

For the Britain of Victoria's day was not at the zenith of its power: it was already well beyond it. Although the introduction of those popular items that have been regarded as the certain sign of a mass-consumption society—the bicycle, the safety match, the advertising hoarding— suggested an economy in full flood, serious questions were being asked in more contemplative quarters about the long-term prospects. A Royal Commission on the Depression in Trade and Industry reported in the mid-1880s that the economy was beginning 'to feel the effect of foreign competition in quarters where our trade formerly enjoyed a practical monopoly'. While British exports of coal mounted dramatically, and were regarded by those in high places as vindication of their faith in the economy's overwhelming strength, it needed only a slight degree of cynicism also that those very exports pointed to the rapid industrialisation of rivals abroad. British investment in her industries lagged behind levels in the United States and Germany and invention after invention slipped out of the hands of British manufacturers to be exploited and refined elsewhere. The Britain of 1870, in fact, was a mirror-image of the Britain of today; as David Landes put it in the *Cambridge Economic History of Europe*: '[in 1870] all the evidence agrees on the technological backwardness of much of British manufacturing industry—on leads lost, opportunities missed, markets relinquished that might not have been.'

The foundations of present-day Britain were therefore laid on the shifting soil of a failing economy, and were so designed that the social disjunctions that were component parts of that inherent weakness were actually buttressed in the name of reform. And there were two important reasons why this was so. First, there was little real incentive for change in an establishment then still believing—erroneously—that it commanded an unassailable economic bastion. The establishment was not prepared to alter the society that guaranteed its own position, especially when it was convinced that the society's strength in fact rested on an organisation and cohesion it had itself fostered over generations. Second, there was no comprehensive view held in political circles of that time about the nature of Britain's future beyond vague insistence that tomorrow could only be a more glorious and more prosperous extension of the imperial present, an insistence that was built into the social fabric itself. As a result the potential strengths available to the society in the economic sphere were dissipated. What might have been assets were progressively rendered inconsequential or simply wasted through mismanagement. In essence, then, we suggest that Britain once-and-for-all break with its Victorian past, and renew in these closing years of the late twentieth century the process of social and psychological evolution that has been in abeyance for nearly a century.

The Needs Of The Present Day

That we say 'in abeyance for nearly a century' may astonish some. Were there not important political reforms on the eve of the first world war? Important social legislation under the aegis of Labour after the second? But we have spoken of 'social and psychological' evolution—and we would say that the fundamental 'feel' of British society has hardly altered in a century. Only the economic decline has gone on, with its characteristic embittering of quasi-Victorian social relationships.

What we call for, then, is both simple and immense—a shift in Britain's national style. Faced with the intellectual and moral dilemmas we have examined (for the dilemmas before Britain are not merely economic ones) the question of what Britain should *do* cannot really be answered with any list of new programmes or of innovations in technique. The popular and professional literature on Britain's plight suffers from no shortage of practical suggestions. Clearly, a hundred reports of investigatory commissions have recommended most of the specific suggestions we shall make in the following pages. What is to be done is not all that difficult to say—nor is there any question that to the problem of Britain's failing economy a whole series of attractive answers exist, depending on whether one prescribes for Britain from the standpoint of Right or Left or Centre.

Certainly no specific remedies will work for Britain if there is not a shift, a deep shift, in psychology, in will—in short, in style. For style in this case is everything. Everything that follows then must be understood as subordinate to this. For style is the habit of action and decision that derives from those assumptions about political and economic reality. We would argue that Britain's present economic difficulties and social difficulties derive ultimately from a kind of archaism of the society and national psychology: a habit of conciliation in social and personal relations for its own sake, a lack of aggression, a deference to what exists, a repeated and characteristic flight into pre-industrial, indeed pre-capitalist, fantasies, a suspicion of efficiency as somehow 'common', a dislike for labour itself—all of course accompanied by a deep inner rage at the frustrations and obfuscations which contemporary Britain demands of its citizens and an equally signifcant envy for the worldly goods that others, Americans, Belgians, Germans, French, have and which the stodgy pattern of a more traditionalist British society and economy cannot provide.

14. The Cult of the Amateur*

G.C. Allen

. . . [T]he deterioration in Britain's economic position in recent years can be attributed in some considerable part to mistakes in government policy. But the country was in trouble long before state intervention in industrial affairs was of significance or the public sector absorbed much of the national income.

EARLY WEAKENING OF BRITAIN'S INDUSTRIAL LEAD

As early as the 1870s there were signs that Britain's industrial supremacy was being challenged and by the end of the century it had lost the lead in several branches of production . . . It was probably inevitable that Britain should lose its predominant position in all the older manufacturers as other countries industrialised, and it was by its failure to secure a large share of the newer trades then coming into being rather than by its loosening its hold on some of the old industries that Britain's weaknesses were becoming most obvious in the years before the first world war. Two industries were to become of outstanding importance. In motor cars Britain by 1914 ranked as a poor second to the United States. In electrical equipment it was surpassed by both the United States and Germany. The same applied to the manufacture of automatic machine-tools . . .

It is significant that many of the entrepreneurs in the newer lines of production at that time did not come from the well-established firms in those industries which might have seemed their most likely parents. Thus, at the beginning of the motor age, the larger engineering firms

*Reproduced from G.C. Allen, *The British Disease*, Hobart Papers 67 (Institute of Economic Affairs, London, 1976), pp. 30–42.

149

were sceptical of the prospects of the motor vehicle and left the development of the industry to pioneers from electrical engineering, cycle-making and repairing, tinplate-ware manufacture and sheep-shearing machinery production. Many of these firms were very small at the outset. Similarly, rayon manufacture was introduced not by any of the major firms in the great textile industries but by a specialist silk weaver who happened at a critical moment to have in his employment an imaginative chemist.

How can we explain this slackening in Britain's industrial growth in this period? The once ample supply of cheap rural labour available for manning industry was drying up but labour, skilled as well as other kinds, was certainly not scarce. Some critics have put the blame on Britain's financial organisation: the preoccupation of the London capital market with overseas investments (so it is claimed) deprived domestic industry of the capital it needed for modernisation. Yet in those days manufacturing firms seldom made public issues. They usually built up their resources from the reinvestment of profits and in the industrial areas there were many other channels through which enterprising manufacturers could obtain capital. Even the British banks, often contrasted unfavourably with the German banks as sources of invest-ment funds for industry, were by no means so aloof as is often made out. In the early 1900s the Managing Director of Midland Bank, having taken the measure of a hitherto unknown supplicant, had little hesitation in advancing a huge sum to put GEC on the road to success. If the London capital market was often less forthcoming, this attitude cannot be ascribed wholly to institutional defects; it may be explained by the generally unimpressive quality of Britain's industrial leaders at that time. The reluctance was probably wholly justified, for the rise in the amount of capital per head invested in industry after 1900 was not accompanied by any increase in productivity.

It was unfortunate that at a time when entrepreneurial initiative in British industry was flagging, the law become more favourable than hitherto towards conspiracies of trades to promote their commercial interests and towards contracts in restraint of trade. This change, which occurred as a result of a series of Court decisions, confirmed by the famous Mogul judgement of 1892, provided firms with additional safeguards against competitive pressure and opened the way to restrictive practices of various kinds. However, as long as the country remained faithful to free trade, the power of such cartels and monopolies as were formed was necessarily weak in the large number of industries exposed to foreign competition in the home market. Indeed, in Germany cartelisation was carried much further than in Britain, and in the British industries that depended mainly on foreign markets a strongly competitive character was preserved. How was it, then, that the competition failed to keep the member firms in these industries up to the mark? The answer may be that, while free competition is highly effective in transforming potential entrepreneurial energy into kinetic energy, its capacity to *create* the potential is limited. This at any rate seems a reasonable inference from the industrial experience of the period.

The unconventional wisdom of Schumpeter may throw light on this problem. In a well-known passage, he declared that the kind of competition that counts is

> the competition from the new commodity, the new technology, the new source of supply, the new type of organisation—competition which commands a decisive cost or quality advantage and which strikes not simply at the margin of the profits and output of existing firms, but at their foundations and their very lives. (Schumpeter, 1943)

What he called 'the gale of creative destruction', which, according to him, was the really powerful agent of change and progress in a dynamic society, not least in Britain between, say, 1760 and 1870, seems to have blown itself out in the industry of this country by the last years of the nineteenth century.

We are thus led back to the proposition that industrial progress depends primarily on the quality of industrial leadership and we have to consider whether that quality had deteriorated since the great days and, if so, for what reasons. Evidence must be sought in many directions, especially in managerial recruitment and training, social attitudes and education.

COMPLACENCY BY DESCENDANTS OF PIONEERS

Complacency after a long period of success was perhaps to be expected. As Arnold Toynbee (1960) said: 'History shows that the group which successfully responds to one challenge is rarely the successful respondent to the next.' The descendants of the pioneers are tempted to take things easy. The institutions created to serve one stage of development may prove to be intractable and frustrating at the next stage, but may survive none the less through the force of tradition and convention. This generalisation seems to describe what happened in Britain, and the development did not pass unremarked by critical contemporaries, especially those aware of what was happening in other countries.

Kipling's bitter rebuke to his fellow countrymen in the poem, *The Islanders* (1902), was intended to stir them from their complacency in defence; it would have been equally well justified if directed against their economic and technical deficiences. Yet the gadflies failed to pierce the thick hide of the Edwardians.

DISDAIN FOR TRADE

Besides the general causes of decadence which, according to Toynbee, are likely to afflict every civilisation in some stage of its development, there were present in Britain some special, and perhaps rather extraordinary, causes that converged to transform so many of the heirs of the great industrial innovators into complacent routineers. In order to analyse these we must make a brief excursion into English social history. In England, unlike some western societies before the French Revolution and many Asian societies, rigid divisions between castes, each with its appropriate functions, did not exist. The Tudors and those that came after them held that a man must do 'his duty in that state of life into which it *shall* please God to call him', and a man of ambition found his fulfillment in ensuring that he was called to a higher class than that into which he was born. In the seventeenth century, after the country was launched on its career as an international trader, those who made money as merchants naturally sought to elevate themselves into the class above them, the landed gentry. This was the path to social esteem and political and administrative power. They purchased country estates and married their daughters to the sons of the squires. Once the merchant families were established in their new class, they did their best to forget their origins. An historian has pointed out that, whereas the Elizabethan and Jacobean monuments in the parish churches record the origin of many a squire's wealth in his prosperity as a mercer or haberdasher, from Queen Anne's time there were few parallels.

> The more commercial England in fact became, the more general was the contempt for trade among the landed gentry who were themselves largely its offspring; . . . it was among the children of these rich, retired tradesmen that there sprang up such a contempt for whatever savoured of the shop or the counting house. (Ashley, 1914)

ANTI-MANUFACTURING SNOBBERY

The tradition of snobbism was transmitted intact to the new wealthy families of industrialists who rose on the tide of Britain's manufacturing supremacy in the nineteenth century. They too delighted 'to play the sedulous ape' to the landed gentry. Their ambition to adopt the habits and manners of their betters provided a splendid opportunity for alert educationalists. Hence the proliferation of the public boarding schools after the time of Thomas Arnold. The schools proved to be an effective instrument for bestowing gentility on the sons of the rough and warty industrial pioneers, and their vitality down to the present time can be attributed to the persistence of the same type of social ambition. Continental Europeans have seized on what is only a half-truth when they explain the existence of these boarding schools by their theory that the English dislike their children. André Maurois showed a more accurate perception in his comment that the schools were a means for inculcating the prejudices of a class.

STRENGTHS AND FAULTS OF PUBLIC SCHOOLS *VIS-À-VIS* INDUSTRY

The public schools would not, of course, have flourished if they had not also served loftier purposes. They had great merits as the nursery of political leaders and administrators for several generations, and their products proved their mettle in the government of the British empire. The standards of behaviour they inculcated were a marked improvement on those of the aristocracy in earlier times. The men they trained helped to bring order and a large measure of fair dealing over much of the globe, and the infrastructure which they built up in the underdeveloped countries was a major legacy of Britain to the successor states of its empire. In a word, the schools helped to form an élite, with the character and self-confidence appropriate to the needs of Britain as an imperial power. The members of this élite were taught to accept a special responsibility for serving the common weal, and this responsibility the best of them bore without arrogance. Perhaps because of their isolation from their fellows in other classes during their formative years, they may have found it all too easy to reconcile their personal ambitions, their desire for power and the maintenance of their privileged status, with their idea of themselves as Platonic Guardians, but they were not alone in confusing personal advantage and the common good. The chief weakness of the schools, when judged from the standpoint of the present inquiry, was their failure to provide leaders equipped to manage Britain's economy in general, and her industry in particular, in an era when her former commercial supremacy

was waning. Their deficiencies in this respect became more evident with
the passing of empire, but they had been perceived long ago by critics
troubled by the early signs of Britain's economic decline. The schools
even instilled a distate of the pursuits which had made the country rich
and powerful. Their most able pupils made their careers in politics, the
civil service and the professions. Too few of them entered business life.

Many of the pioneers in the nineteenth-century steel industry, having
achieved success, fell victim to the social infection which has been the
source of lively contributions to the English comedy of manners, but has
done much to debilitate economic leadership in this country. The
prosperous steel masters, most of whom had themselves been educated
in local schools, followed the now customary practice among the
successful members of the business community and despatched their
sons to the public schools. In many instances their families' social status
was subsequently elevated by the marriage of these sons into the landed
and professional classes whose outlook they acquired. High achievement in industry and commerce thus often came to be regarded as a
route to the satisfaction of social aspirations. Britain, to its loss, was
ceasing to produce, in the older industries at any rate, a class of leader
who found sufficient scope for his ambition and adequate satisfaction
for his pride, in his business accomplishments. The form of snobbery
prevalent among businessmen may have had especially mischievous
effects in steel manufacture because that industry furnished very few
instances of ambitious and capable young men of humble origin whose
path to managerial eminence was smoothed by the traditional and
admirable expedient of marrying the boss's daughter! Of course, there
were many substantial family businesses that maintained their entrepreneurial vigour from generation to generation. Examples can be found
in the glass, confectionery and brewing industries among others, and
these manufactures continued to make progress.

FAILURE OF THE UNIVERSITIES TO SUPPLY INDUSTRIAL LEADERS

The inadequacy of school education in equipping the new generation of
industrial leaders was not remedied by the universities. Despite the
founding of the civic universities at the turn of the century, the higher
education of the upper-middle class was dominated by Oxford and
Cambridge, and has remained so to a diminishing extent until the
present time. The older universities had little interest in, or understanding of, industrial affairs. Indeed, the educational principles, to which in

the half-century before the first world war they were wedded, were not compatible with the type of training devised in other countries for men who were to occupy key positions in industry or commerce. The purpose of a university, it was held, was to make a 'whole man' and not to equip him to follow a specific calling, to prepare pupils for 'everything in general and nothing in particular'. This doctrine, in its more extreme form, declared that the more practically useless a subject, the higher its claims as an instrument for mental discipline. Mr Harold Macmillan, in his charming and moving reminiscences of Oxford in the years before the war, quotes with evident approval the opening words of a lecturer to his class. After referring to the careers they were likely to follow, the Church, the Bar, politics, the civil service and Army, teaching and even industry and commerce, he declared that, except for those who were to teach,

> nothing that you will learn in the course of your studies will be of the slightest use to you in after life, except this . . . that you should be able to detect when a man is talking rot, and that in my view is the aim, if not the sole purpose, of education. (Macmillan, 1975)

It does not seem to have occurred to Macmillan that the history of Britain during the last 60 years shows that this education, in practice, provided a most ineffectual defence against the seductions of humbug and rhetoric, for one of the outstanding defects of Britain's lèaders in that period has been their lack of realism in confronting the problems they faced. He has also not perceived that the definition of education presented to him was idiosyncratic and parochial. Traditionally universities have been the home of *professional* education. In the Middle Ages they prepared men for the ecclesiastical profession and, after the rise of the nation-states, they became the home of Cameralistic studies designed to equip men to serve *religioni et reipublicae*, to quote the motto of one of the Tudor foundations. The anti-vocational bias, the concept of a general mental culture divorced from professional needs as the sole, or the chief. *raison d'être* of a university, gained wide acceptance only after Oxford and Cambridge, about a century ago, acquired a body of resident lay tutors. That this peculiar definition of the purpose of a university survived the introduction of numerous vocational studies, as the training for the professions passed to the universities, can be ascribed mainly to the prestige of Oxford and Cambridge. The proposition that vocational training is not inconsistent with the education of the 'whole man' was considered in those quarters as unworthy of debate. In consequence, until a generation or so ago, few of those recruited into the ranks of industrial managers from the universities had received a training in subjects in any way related to their calling. In the second place, men who had been educated in vocational or professional subjects generally occupied, and still occupy, both in the civil service and in many of the big corporations, subordinate or advisory posts; they were seldom elevated to the ranks of the policy-makers.

THE CULT OF THE AMATEUR

The persistent belief in the merits of leaving high policy to the amateur was associated with the dominance of the classics in the university curriculum. For the majority of civil servants in the administrative class, classics formed the foundation and superstructure of their education. This was true of the governing class in general. The chief criticism that may be directed against the system was not that these men spent an excessive proportion of their university life in studies that were 'useless', for the distinction between 'useful' and 'useless' subjects is difficult to draw. Whether one believes that 'learning Greek teaches Greek and nothing else, certainly not common sense', or that those who have been taught to refer the great questions of civilised society to the oracles of Hellas are rendered immune against the malady of cultural chauvinism and the folly of extremes, the classics must always find an honoured place in western education. The English educational system was not open to criticism because it assigned a high place to the classics but simply because it left little room for anything else. Science and technology, in particular, were grossly neglected, a remarkable state of affairs when one considers the distinction of British scientists from the time of Bacon. This charge applies not only to the universities, but to English education as a whole.

15. The Imperial Bureaucracy*

Anthony Sampson

The characteristic danger of great nations, like the Roman, or the English, which have a long history of continuous creation, is that they may at last fail from not comprehending the great institutions they have created.

Walter Bagehot

My dear young man, there is a good deal of ruin in a country.

The dying Adam Smith to Sir John Sinclair
(who said that Britain would be ruined), 1790

How far have Britain's institutions and rulers stood up to their historic challenge to revive and modernise a nation which carries a heavy weight from the past and faces a highly competitive future? Has Britain survived the classic fate of so many ex-imperial nations, from Egypt to Spain, of becoming trapped in bureaucracies and attitudes which are too inflexible to adjust to new problems? The question becomes more insistent in the face of bleaker winds of world competition, recession and unemployment.

INSTITUTIONS

Twenty years ago Britain was already full of reforming zeal and determined to modernise her institutions—even before Harold Wilson proclaimed his own white-hot revolution to transform whole areas of administration, from schools to scientists to civil servants. How

*Reproduced from A. Sampson, *The Changing Anatomy of Britain*, (London, Coronet Books, 1983), pp. 462–76. Reprinted by permission of Hodder and Stoughton Limited.

seriously the politicians pursued many of those reforms is open to question. Certainly their failures gave much ammunition to true conservatives who insisted that all change was for the worse, and who believed in those pessimistic laws which explain that changes achieve the opposite of what they intend, that more means worse, and that if something can go wrong, it will go wrong.

The move to democratise education succeeded in strengthening the fee-paying schools and abolishing most grammar schools, the traditional poor boy's ladder to the top. The huge spending to apply science to industry succeeded in making scientists still more academic. The attempts to open up Whitehall and the Foreign Office made the mandarins more embattled and relatively more secure. The failed reforms, in contrast to the successful Victorian reforms a century earlier, gave a special poignancy to Bagehot's warning in the mid-nineteenth century; for those 'great institutions', reinforced by their own trade unions and professional pride, had shown how effectively they could close ranks against change. As Sir Monty Finniston found when he tried to reform the engineering profession, Machiavelli's warning was still valid: 'The innovator has for enemies all those who have done well under the old conditions.'

Inside its own castle each profession can present its defences as part of a great tradition of autonomy and freedom, and everyone else's as selfish greed. Lawyers complain about trade union monopolies, while they fortify their own monopoly; dons talk about academic freedom and journalists about the freedom of the press, when they often mean their own freedom from reform. The huge extension of white-collar trade unionism in the 1960s, which was expected to moderate the trade union movement, soon made it more extreme; and the TUC became more helpless as each union refused to see beyond its own claims. Union attitudes were still less attractive when they spread to Whitehall. Many younger public servants would privately criticise their institutions as much as any outsider, but once attacked from outside they would close ranks to defend their overmanned offices or index-linked pensions, in a kind of reversal of Voltaire's principle: 'I agree with everything you say, but I will fight to the end to prevent it happening.'

It is much too early to assess the full consequences of many reforms of the 1960s: long after the Victorians reformed education, the Army or the civil service, conservative critics were mocking their democratic zeal. Any changes which depend on shifting attitudes will have a long time-lag. Twenty years after Macmillan integrated the Ministry of Defence the armed forces are only beginning to adopt a 'tri-service outlook'. The effects of comprehensive schooling—the most fundamental of Labour's changes—will only become clearer after a new generation has grown up in that context. But the faith in 'social engineering' which marked much radical thinking in the 1950s and 1960s, whether in Britain or the United States, is now less evident, as old patterns of behaviour and institutions reassert themselves below the political surface. It is still, as Disraeli said in 1881, 'a very difficult country to move.'

In all their attempted reforms governments and commissions were reluctant to interfere with the traditional autonomy of professions or groups. They liked to assume that civil servants, scientists or teachers would cooperate in reforms from within; they shied away from statutory changes or imposing their own direction, and when they failed they preferred to conceal their frustration. The institutions remained largely immune in their autonomy while they had become increasingly separated from the centre or from each other. The conspiratorial notions of a single 'establishment' holding together over the overlapping circles are all too untrue. The obstacles to Britain's reform have lain in the lack of effective coordination and control, and the circles are always threatening to pull themselves further apart.

The civil service which influences so many other bureaucracies remains basically unreformed. The criticisms of the early 1960s—about its amateurism, unaccountability and lack of experience of industry and technology—remain almost as valid as ever. The scandal of the Crown Agents, the civil servants who in 1974 had squandered £180 million in irresponsible investments, provided a kind of caricature of Whitehall amateurism and separatism which the fiercest critics could not have imagined. The Ministry of Overseas Development, the Treasury and the Bank of England all knew that something was going wrong, but shuffled papers between each other: 'The situation cried out for someone to use some common sense, show some initiative, and grapple with the problem,' as the Report of the Tribunal concluded in 1982. 'But nobody took the lead.' It was a story which illustrated all the worst fears of an overblown bureaucracy.

Of all the legacies of empire the most dangerous is surely an immobile bureaucracy which can perpetuate its own interests and values, like those ancient hierarchies which presided over declining civilisations: the Pharaonic bureaucracy which still casts its spell over the chaos of contemporary Egypt; or the Byzantine bureaucracy which grew up in the Ottoman empire; or the court of Imperial Spain which could not face the new challenges of the sixteenth century:

Heirs to a society which had over-invested in an empire, and surrounded by the increasingly shabby remnants of a dwindling inheritance, they could not bring themselves at a moment of crisis to surrender their memories and alter the antique pattern of their lives.

As the British mandarins reinforce their defences, awarding each other old imperial honours, do they hear any echoes from Castile or Byzantium?

BIGNESS AND CENTRALISATION

In the first post-war decades the decline of British power was mitigated by two special circumstances. The first was the Anglo-American relationship, which could conceal many of the humiliations–at least for those at the top—in the appearance of a common transatlantic identity, so that the British (as Macmillan put it) could be 'Greeks in their Roman Empire'. The second was the long western boom, which allowed the British in spite of their industrial weakness to double their standard of living in a decade, and to expand as they never could during those pre-war decades when half the globe was still coloured red. Britain was never so rich as when she had off-loaded her empire.

In this expansive mood the British embarked on many of their ambitious reforms: building new universities, hospitals or motorways, planning new towns, tower blocks and civic centres. But the pursuit of bigness soon became a cult, encouraged by prosperity and American precedents: skyscrapers and neckties, tower blocks and television sets, hospitals and cars—they all got bigger and supposedly better. British institutions enlarged themselves without much questioning from economists, sociologists or politicians. Governments and civil servants enthusiastically merged ministries, counties or airlines.

Already by the early 1970s the failure of many mergers—whether of companies or Whitehall departments—was becoming clear. After twenty years expansion was succeeded by contraction, optimism by pessimism and mergers by de-mergers. In Whitehall whole armies of civil servants had marched up the hill and down again. The Departments of Trade, Industry, Transport or Energy re-emerged as separate entities from their monster ministries; the Tory Secretary for Social Services tried to remove the extra tier which his Tory predecessor had added; British Airways planned to split up again into Overseas and European airlines. The Treasury survived its rivals, the Department of Economic Affairs and the Civil Service Department, and was once again the sole arbiter of national priorities.

But the age of expansion and bigness in the 1960s had left many relics which could not easily be dismantled, like the tower blocks which remained symbols of the past arrogance of planners. The bigger bureaucracies had added to Britain's inflexibility, when she needed to be more flexible than ever: the town halls and county headquarters, the extensions of Whitehall, the irremovable dons in contracting universities, were all reminders that yesterday's experiments had become today's heavy commitments. While private companies were compelled to lose some of their fat, public institutions were much harder to reduce; and the gap widened between the security inside them and the insecurity in the cold world outside. The great bureaucracies were like pie-crusts which had risen with the rising prosperity, and were now left as high superstructures while the rest of the pie had subsided.

Within government there had been a relentless trend towards the centre, and the spiders' webs of the Treasury and the Cabinet Office were now still more centralised. The countervailing powers of local government had been eaten away, the plans for regional devolution had been shelved and the private sector was far weaker. The Treasury model and the Treasury's control of public spending, with all its vagaries and missing billions, dominated a larger sector of the economy, while the Treasury itself was more tightly held by a group of Conservative ministers.

The combination of bureaucracy and centralisation in the metropolis had marked many declining empires, whose hopes for revival lay in provinces which were less demoralised by extravagance and overmanning. But the flow of power towards Whitehall and the Treasury has increased over recent years as local authorities, lacking their own proper accountability, have lost still more of their autonomy. Each mistake at the centre has been reflected round the periphery. When the Treasury retrenches, every university, school and local council has to retrench: the centre can only keep all these overlapping circles in check by the crudest yardstick of money. Banks, industrial corporations, insurance companies and newspapers have followed the centralising trend, draining more of the decisions from Edinburgh, Manchester or Liverpool; while the London concentration has increased the preoccupation with control rather than opportunities . . .

While many businessman blamed governments for this accretion of centralised power, the private sector had created its own extravagant concentrations. Many of the company directors who pressed through mergers showed little sign of thinking seriously about who should run them, or how; they often expected them to produce their own logic and disciplines. They argued that larger units were essential to the new global scale, which was true for many high-technology and heavy industries, but the mergers which swept up breweries, service industries and entertainment into new conglomerates showed few benefits to the consumers; and the original mergers had more to do with unexploited assets and the stock-market than with serious economies of scale. With relatively easy profits and without effective shareholders' control the companies could build up their armies of executives and workers, and when they merged, ostensibly to produce economies, they often (like British Leyland or British Airways) kept both staffs intact. (It was another echo of Imperial Spain, where aristocratic households grew still larger because of the Castilian custom that when a nobleman bought an estate he kept on all the predeccessor's household, while adding his own. It was the numbers of workers which gave him his status, rather than their effectiveness.)

Politicians on both sides of the House were inclined to prefer giant corporations which seemed to make planning and negotiations easier at the top: Whitehall liked to deal with big companies and big unions while the TUC and the CBI agreed about the advantages of a merger which increased the monopoly power on both sides. The meetings of Neddy at the peak of the triangle began to look like Adam Smith's picture of men of business conspiring against the public. It was the consumer who paid the price for many of the mergers, but he was left out of the picture . . .

THE RULING TRIBES

Behind all convulsions was there any meaning left in the old idea of the establishment, which had cast such a spell over the Macmillan years? Certainly the political leadership now shows little connection with that many-branched family tree of the Devonshires and the Salisburys which spread out to many of the key emplacements of power in the early 1960s. Certainly school and university backgrounds have lost some of their significance in parliament. In the Labour Party Michael Foot and Tony Benn (however disguised) both come from the old Oxford and public school tradition; but as the Party has moved to the Left it has broken most of its links with the patrician or Fabian tradition, and new leaders such as Eric Heffer, Neil Kinnock or Eric Varley have come up from proletarian backgrounds.

The Conservatives have broken with their aristocratic leadership since they chose and rejected the Earl of Home as their leader and Margaret Thatcher sees herself as owing no debts of loyalties to the old guard as she appeals directly to the people. After the 1983 election the Tory Cabinet appeared much more in her own self-made mould, with two of her closest supporters—Cecil Parkinson and Norman Tebbit—both from modest backgrounds. Outside Parliament, too, there is now less aristocratic influence; nearly all chairmen of big corporations, scientists and vice-chancellors come from grammar schools; and none of the leading entrepreneurs has been to university at all.

Yet alongside this new meritocracy the old education élite maintained its continuity and influence through all the political upheavals. Few people in the early Wilson years would have predicted that in July 1983 the Lord Chancellor, the chairman of the BBC, the editor of *The Times*, the Chief of the Defence Staff, the heads of both foreign and civil services and the Governor of the Bank of England would be Old Etonians, while another array including a bevy of judges would come from the rival foundation, Winchester. Perhaps it was never likely that two medieval institutions which had survived King Henry VIII, Cromwell, Victorian reformers and two world wars would lightly surrender their influence to Harold Wilson or Anthony Crosland. But far from retreating, they have advanced into new areas of influence, and their success today is more marked than in Macmillan's time or (as far as I can trace) than in any earlier time. The Victorian professions were full of self-made men who worked their way up to the top, and several schools prepared the way to power. Even Macmillan's Britain included outsiders such as William Haley editing *The Times* or Sir Norman Brook running the civil service. But since then the products of these two ancient schools have reasserted all their old ability to climb the ladders of power, with a continuity which has no parallel in other industrial countries.

The success of Etonians does not represent a straightforward defence of the landed interest, or a reactionary response to social change. Many of the present crop are not rich or aristocratic; and three Old Etonians in Thatcher's first Cabinet—Gilmour, Soames and Thorneycroft—were sacked for being too 'wet'. Etonians nowadays are servants as much as masters, and it was Thatcher who appointed Pym to the Foreign Office, and Armstrong to run the civil service. It is their political skill, their confidence and flexibility, which accounts for their rise much more than their wealth or family connections, and which equips them to serve as the power-brokers who can be so useful to.any government. They have retained all their dedication to the power game, competing with their contemporaries all the way to the top; and it is power which remains their *métier*. The traditional élites have retained their own communication system which still gives them a tribal cohesion in the midst of contemporary Britain. As society becomes more complex and the circles pull apart, so the people who can make connections between them become more useful as the fixers, the lubricants or brokers between one sphere and another. In the world of finance, which depends on quick communications and trust, the old boy network still plays a special part; and the disasters of 1974 only underlined the dangers of newcomers. And in the City the continuity of old tradition seems to merge with deeper tribal patterns of trust . . .

Is there a price to pay for these 'bizarre customs'? In the City, which is surrounded by risks, the rituals of trust have their obvious advantages. But in the wider context of Britain the rule of the Eton and Winchester tribes seems to reflect a degree of regression: a fear of disruptive forces and a preoccupation with controlling and containing new people from the centre. It is not very plausible that such a narrow élite could effectively represent the diversity of people with such different backgrounds from theirs; and their success lies more in restraint than in adventure. These traditional British nurseries of power remain very cut off from the world of technologists and industrial managers who offer the most promising hopes for Britain's future; while the old cross-purposes between engineers and administrators remain as extreme as ever. When the British really need bold industrial leaders who can combine technical mastery with political confidence they often have to look right outside their own class system—to the South African Edwardes in Leyland, the Scots-American MacGregor in British Steel, or the American Giordano in British Oxygen.

Every advanced country, of course, includes very separate élites: New York bankers are cut off from Detroit industrialists. *Inspecteurs des Finances* in Paris from manufacturers in Lille. But the traditional British élite, fortified by their ancient schools and Oxbridge colleges, have maintained their edge over others—at some cost to the country. Their values are less closely related to technology and industry than to pre-industrial activities such as banking and the Army, and their influence reached its apogee in the administration of the empire. Britain achieved the dismantling of the empire with remarkably little political revolt, but found it much harder to change her social structure to ensure her commercial survival.

THE QUIXOTE COMPLEX

It was the public response to the Falkland war—25 years after Suez, 40 years after the second world war—which suggested most clearly that the older British values and attitudes were still lurking close to the surface, as if the war and the empire had happened only yesterday. As the armada set sail for the Falklands so the language of politicians and the press seemed to have reverted back four decades as they exchanged war cries against the new-found enemies, the 'Argies'.

The armada's promptness and efficiency seemed out of character with other British nationalised industries; everyone knew his place in the structured class system of the army and navy. Parliament debated the Falklands with more passion and interest than they ever gave to technology and exports, and for a few weeks the British seemed to discover a national purpose and unity which they never brought to the problems of economic survival. The resounding echoes from the second world war were another reminder that advanced societies can still have a primitive basis. The sense of returning to old values and relationships was heightened when the Pope arrived in the midst of the war, visiting the Queen and the Archbishop of Canterbury as if to complete the medieval backcloth to the pageant.

Was Britain's surge of military pride another sign, as Dean Acheson warned us twenty years ago, that Britain had lost an empire but not yet found a new role? Or was it—as Thatcher suggested—a renewal of the spirit of national confidence and self-respect, infusing all its other activities and relationships? 'We have proved ourselves to ourselves,' she said in July 1983. 'The faltering and self-doubt have given way to achievement and pride.' And the theme was constantly re-stated up to the general election the next summer.

Certainly the British response to the Argentinian invasion involved a genuine element of high principle which would have been humiliating to ignore. But that principle was rapidly overlaid by the war fever and military momentum; and Britain's allies were soon more alarmed by her intransigence than impressed by her honour. It seemed to some of them like a quixotic enterprise, in the literal sense; for Don Quixote—as Cervantes created him in the twilight of the Spanish empire—was fascinated by the romances and past glories of Imperial Spain, embarking on his excursions of honour and principle to rescue damsels or tilt at windmills, with a romanticism which baffled the rest of the world.

16. What is the British Predicament?*

Henry Phelps-Brown

What is the reason for this predicament? One much discussed diagnosis lays its stress on the extent of government expenditure and taxation. Another regards the antagonisms of industrial relations and the class structure of British society as together forming a distinctive handicap of the British economy. Let us examine these diagnoses in turn.

THE PUBLIC SECTOR

The greatly growing expenditure by the public sector, it has been said, has brought high taxation but also a vast borrowing requirement. The burden of taxation has been held to be discouraging to exertion and enterprise at all levels, but especially where marginal rates rise steeply. The borrowing requirement absorbs savings that should be available to industry; or is met by increasing the supply of money; or something of both.

We have to ask not simply whether there is force in these observations but whether they apply to Britain with much more force than to others. So far as they relate to the total amount of taxation, they do not. International comparisons come out somewhat differently on different bases, and those of Table 16.1 exclude capital taxes, and reckon the gross national product (GNP) at factor cost; but on that basis the table shows the total raised by national and local taxation as a percentage of GNP in each of a number of industrial countries. Where the UK stands in the ranking order depends on whether or not social security contributions are included in taxation. Whether they are or not, in 1974 the tax take was a smaller proportion of the GNP in the UK than in

*Reproduced from *Three Banks Review* 116 (1977), pp. 3–29, by permission of The Royal Bank of Scotland plc.

Table 16.1: The tax take compared

Total raised by national and local taxation (excluding capital taxes) in 1974
(USA 1973) as a percentage of the given country's GNP at factor cost in that
year

	Social security contributions	
	included %	excluded %
Using the United Nations' new system of national accounts		
Denmark	53.4	52.4
Norway	52.9	37.7
Netherlands	50.6	30.4
Sweden	49.1	39.4
France	41.1	24.9
Canada	39.7	35.9
UK	38.7	32.0
USA	32.0	24.3
Using the United Nations' old system of national accounts		
Austria	44.9	34.8
West Germany	42.5	29.0
Belgium	41.4	28.5
UK	38.0	31.4
Japan	24.6	20.0

Source: Economic Trends, 277, November 1976, 107–10.

Denmark, Norway, Sweden, Canada and Austria, though a larger
proportion than in the USA and in Japan. When the contributions are
included the UK's proportion was also lower than those of the
Netherlands, France, West Germany and Belgium, but when they are
excluded it was the other way about. The comparative lowness of the
Japanese proportion is outstanding: but if the Japanese economy had a
great advantage relatively to the British in the lightness of its tax
burden, the British should have had an equal advantage relatively to the
Dutch and the Swedish economies.

A given volume of taxation, however, can be raised in many different
ways, and these can have very different impacts on the feelings of the
taxpayer. In particular, indirect taxes are less likely than direct to enter
into workers' judgements about whether extra exertion for extra gain is
worthwhile; once imposed they become fused with prices, and any one

purchase may be optional, whereas direct taxes involve overt and compulsory abstractions of the taxpayer's income. If there are disincentive effects of taxation, then, be they on a rational calculus of marginal cost and benefit, or more simply through a mood of resentment, it is from direct taxation that they are most likely to arise. But during the last ten years the British tax system has moved massively away from indirect towards direct taxation. In 1960 direct taxes together with social security contributions amounted to about 14 per cent of total personal income, against 16 per cent for indirect taxes; by 1974 the corresponding percentages had become 21 and 15. One reason for this was that the 'fiscal drag' of inflation was lowering tax thresholds, so that many income earners were becoming liable to tax at the basic rate for the first time, and those in the middle ranges of income were having to pay tax in the higher rates on a greater part of their income than before without necessarily having had any rise in real income before tax—in the last three years, indeed, their real incomes may have fallen.

There seems, then, to be a case for holding that at least in recent years, whatever may hold of the British tax take as a whole, income tax has borne so hard as to be a disincentive. The case has been supported by reference to the high marginal rate of tax on earned income—83p out of every £1 earned over £20,000 (latterly £21,000) of taxable income. On an international comparison that rate and its threshold certainly stand out, though Sweden is not very different, and the Netherlands is not far away. But a wider basis of comparison is the total levy on the typical salary of a business executive holding a post at a given level in each of a number of countries. Table 16.2 is derived from evidence submitted by the CBI to the Diamond Commission when that Commission was preparing its report on the higher incomes from employment. Some 50 or more firms that operate in a number of countries were asked to give the salaries they were paying in given countries overseas to local nationals holding posts in their branches or subsidiaries there, with responsibilities that would carry a salary of £10,000 or £20,000 in this country. The salaries of the local executives, converted into sterling at the exchange rate of January 1975, were in all cases higher than those of their British counterparts—in 7 of the 11 overseas countries more than 80 per cent higher, and in several more than double. The local tax laws were then applied to these overseas salaries, and Table 16.2 shows what proportions were taken in tax: we see that at each job level the British executive had actually to give up a smaller proportion of his salary in tax than did his counterpart in a number of countries—in 8 of them at the £10,000 level, in 5 at the £20,000 level. This outcome, it will be rightly said, depended not only on the relative tax structures, but on the

Table 16.2: International comparison of tax takes for posts of equivalent responsibilities

Direct taxation as a proportion of the salaries of business executives located in and being nationals of the given countries, and holding posts with responsibilities deemed equivalent to those carrying salaries of £10,000, £15,000 and £20,000 p.a. in the UK, as at 1 January 1975. All are taken to be married, with two children, and to claim only basic deductions.

UK post of £10,000	Tax as % of gross pay	UK post £15,000	Tax as % of gross pay	UK post £20,000	Tax as % of gross pay
Sweden	61.3	Sweden	66.4	Sweden	69.3
Denmark	54.1	Denmark	56.0	Netherlands	58.9
Netherlands	48.4	Netherlands	55.1	Denmark	57.1
Australia	46.1	Australia	51.7	Australia	55.7
Belgium	41.7	USA	46.8	USA	51.8
USA	38.0	Belgium	46.5	UK	51.1
Canada	37.2	UK	44.2	Belgium	50.1
W. Germany	36.7	Canada	43.0	Canada	47.1
UK	34.7	W. Germany	42.5	W. Germany	45.9
France	33.0	France	38.9	France	43.6
Italy	31.0	Italy	36.1	Italy	40.0
Switzerland	30.2	Switzerland	34.8	Switzerland	35.9

Source: Royal Commission on the Distribution of Income and Wealth, *Selected Evidence submitted to the Royal Commission for Report No. 3*: Higher Incomes from Employment (1976). Evidence from the Confederation of British Industry, Annex B (prepared by Employment Conditions Abroad Ltd), Tables 1 and 2, p. 133.

salaries being so much higher overseas. The outcome remains significant, however, if appeal is made to the discouraging impact of the proportionate tax burden. Those who would return the argument from the average or effective rate of tax and base it on the marginal rate alone have to consider Sweden, in which a marginal tax of the same order as the British, and a higher average rate, have proved compatible with the attainment of the highest levels of efficiency . . .

AN EXPLANATION IN OUR SOCIAL STRUCTURE?

Other explanations of our poor performance have rested on factors that are commonly called sociological. They have laid stress on what they

hold to be the distinctive social structure of our society, and its division
by class differences of outlook, manners and speech. The consequences,
it is said, are to be seen not only in our 'adversary system' of industrial
relations and our strike record, but in a general sense of strain and
conflict at the place of work, and the witholding of effort by workers
from managers to whom they are inherently opposed by differences of
class. In these respects, it is said, we differ from our more democratic or
egalitarian neighbours and competitors.

There are two ways in which we can narrow the field of discussion of
this view at the outset, by examining some of the facts it assumes. First,
there is our strike record: Table 16.3 compares it with the records of
some other countries. Such comparisons have to be handled cautiously,
for standards of reporting vary, and differences in the prescribed lower
limit of size that makes a stoppage reportable can make a great deal of
difference to the number reported. Yet with this caution in mind it is
still clear from Table 16.3 that the UK is not marked off sharply from
other western countries: a comparison with the democracies of
Australia, Canada and the USA is particularly instructive. On a
reckoning of rank order, the UK appears as standing third below the
median in both 1965–69 and 1970–74. Thus on a comparative showing its
record is not good but not of the worst: among these 18 countries it falls
in the lower part of the middle group.

The stoppages in the UK, moreover, have been concentrated in a
relatively few plants, while most plants, and many industries, have
remained largely free of stoppages. A study of the Department of
Employment shows that in 1971–73, when the number of days lost from
stoppages was running well above the average, 98 per cent of
manufacturing plants were free of reported stoppages in any one year,
and 95 per cent of them came through all three years without a reported
stoppage. The idea that British workers as a whole are prone to strike,
or that British managers as a whole are incapable of conducting orderly
industrial relations, is not borne out by the facts.

None the less a real problem remains. Our record appears poor in
comparison with that of our European neighbours. The study by the
Department of Employment already cited remarks that 'Great Britain
apparently suffers from a concentration of stoppages in the docks, in
coal mining and in a small proportion (between 2 and 5 per cent) of
plants in manufacturing industry'. Observers from Europe and the
United States, struck by the difference between our social attitudes and
their own, feel sure that our attitudes account for much of the
shortcomings in our industrial relations and economic performance, and
their intuition deserves examination.

Table 16.3: Stoppages internationally compared, 1965–74

Number of days lost annually per 1000 persons employed, through industrial disputes, manufacturing, construction and transport. Countries are arranged in ascending order of the number of days lost on the average of the whole ten years 1965–74.

	Averages for	
	1965–69	1970–74
Switzerland	—	2
Sweden[a]	28	64
West Germany	10	90
Norway	4	116
Netherlands	12	118
Japan	198	288
France	242[b]	300
New Zealand	242	402
Belgium	156	512
Denmark[c]	110	912
UK	300	1186
Finland	206	1414
Australia	482	1344
Ireland	1348	688
India	1010	1292[d]
USA[e]	1230	1380
Canada	1556	1732
Italy	1584	1746

[a]Before 1972 covers all industries.
[b]Excluding 1968.
[c]Manufacturing only.
[d]Not including 1974.
[e]Including electricity, gas and sanitary services.
Source: *Department of Employment Gazette*, December 1975, p. 1276, 'based on information supplied by the ILO'.

We owe the second way in which we can limit the field of discussion to the remarkable study by C.F. Pratten (1975) of productivity in 100 international manufacturing companies making similar products by similar processes in the UK and other countries, for this suggests how much of the difference in performance may be assigned to the employees themselves. When international companies compare the performance of their plants in different countries they are seldom if ever comparing like with exactly like: though management is subject to common standards and surveillance it may still be local in its style, plants are of different ages, and they have different product mixes. None the less the experience of these companies should provide a much clearer view of the contribution of particular factors to differences in productivity than is afforded by statistics of output and employee hours in the aggregate. What this experience brings out is, first, that output per employee hour in the British plants is exceeded by some 56 per cent in North America, by 35 per cent in Germany and 28 per cent in France. The causes of these differences are divided into the economic and the behavioural. It is the economic that contribute most to the differences with North America and with France. They consist mainly of the rate of output and the length of production runs, in which lies by far the most important advantage of North America; the type of plant; the product mix; and the degree of utilisation of capacity. The difference with Germany is reckoned to owe less to the economic than to the behavioural causes, but even so the economic account for nearly half. The behavioural causes are made up of strikes and restrictive practices, manning quotas, and differences in personal efficiency. In these respects the other countries are found to have a substantial advantage over the UK, except that France has none in respect of strikes. But even so, causes associated with the attitudes and performance of employees account for only 12 or 13 percentage points out of the 56 given for the total differential with North America, 19 out of the 35 for Germany, and 10 out of the 28 for France. Evidently these causes are far from being a sufficient explanation in themselves.

None the less they are substantial: they mark a real handicap for the British economy. Here again we must conclude that though the field of discussion is narrowed, the view that attitudes and relations distinctive of British society prevent the British economy from working as cooperatively and vigorously as do some of its neighbours still deserves examination.

ARE OUR CLASS DIFFERENCES DISTINCTIVE?

Some foreign observers have assigned much significance to our traditional class distinctions: they contrast the way of life, the manners and bearing they know in their own country with the segregation by rank, title, speech and mode of address that forms part of their image of the United Kingdom. Certainly the trappings that make up that image appear on the surface of our affairs—indeed, we have thrust them into notice abroad as tourist attractions. There are our great country houses, our hereditary peers and our titles which, be they only conferred for life, still come down from the age of chivalry. Pictures are shown of Eton boys in top hats, of the Royal Enclosure at Ascot, of the Household Cavalry. Novels of the nineteenth century display a society in which human relations were regulated by differences of class both harsh and subtle. The more recent visitor from America has still been aware of differences in speech associated with class, and of a general tendency to sense where a newcomer ranks in the social pecking order and treat him with deference or condescension accordingly, that stands in distasteful contrast with the democratic manners of his own country. Observers from many countries have been struck by the segregation, often from the earliest years of schooling, that has separated children according to the socioeconomic levels of their homes.

There is no question about the trappings, and little question about speech and manners, though this form of differentiation has rapidly decreased in recent years; but on the substantial issue, of how far we are divided into strata, whether these are antipathetic, and how far movement from one stratum to another is difficult, there is no evidence that we are very different from other western countries. So far as comparisons can be made between the distributions of household income before tax, it appears that income is more equally distributed in the UK than in the USA, Japan, France and West Germany, though less so than in Australia. That people tend to associate with those of their own educational level has been found even in Czechoslovakia, where the inequality of incomes has been reduced more than in most Soviet-type economies. Table 16.4 shows that in England and Wales in recent years the men who have been making their way into the top occupational class have come in substantial numbers from homes at all occupational levels, including those of manual workers. In so far as studies in this and other countries of the son's occupation and his father's can be compared with one another, the rates of mobility upward and downward seem for the most part to be much the same; and American sociologists have been surprised to find that by this test at least their country does not stand out from the others as 'the land of opportunity'. Not many of the managers in British industry today have come through the traditional educational channels of the upper class. On the contrary, we shall see grounds to believe that these channels have done the country a disservice by diverting ability away from industry. In industry, as distinct from finance, a great part of management has entered industry with not more than a local secondary education or a technical training, and worked its way up.

In so far as the belief that we are deeply divided by class does not rest on an inherited pageantry, it rests upon a view of our society as it used

Table 16.4: Social origins of men in class I occupations in 1972

Nuffield sample of 1092 men who were in class I occupation in 1972 and who reported their earnings, divided according to the class of the occupation followed by the father when the son was aged 14.

Father's class	% of all men in class I	% of all men in class I earning £6,000 per annum and over
I Higher-grade professional, administrators and managers	25.3	53.2
II Lower-grade professional, administrators and managers; higher grade technicians	13.1	10.4
III Clerical non-manual service workers	10.4	6.5
IV Small proprietors; self-employed	10.1	16.9
V Lower grade technicians and foremen	12.5	2.6
VI Skilled manual	16.4	2.6
VII Semi-skilled and unskilled manual	12.2	7.8
	100.0	100.0

Source: Royal Commission on the Distribution of Incomes and Wealth. Report No. 3, *Higher Incomes from Employment*, Cmnd, 6383, January 1976. HMSO, London. Table 16, p. 237. Preliminary results extracted by Catriona Llewellyn and J.H. Goldthorpe.

to be rather than as it is now. Since the great divide formed by the general election of 1906, that society has been profoundly changed by social democracy, the two world wars, the rise in the standard of living of the last quarter-century, and the redistribution of income by taxation and social benefits. Attitudes and perceptions formed by the old order persist and in some quarters are deliberately fostered, but the order itself is now very different from what some foreign observers take it to be.

THE LIVING PAST OF OUR INDUSTRIAL RELATIONS

But while our society has changed so much, our industrial relations remain the prisoners of their history. The institutions and procedures of today, and still more the assumptions and attitudes that activate them and are in turn fostered by them, cannot be understood save by reference to their past. Institutions like trade unions seem to have a law of their own being: as they begin, so they go on, not only in their structure, but in the perceptions they inculcate of their own function and of the environment in which they have to operate. For British trade unions that propensity has been enhanced by another feature that strikes the foreign observer of our inviolate isles—the extraordinary continuity of their history: they have had no revolution, no defeat in war and no foreign occupation to give them a fresh start. How understandable it is, then, that the structure and outlook of British trade unionism should still bear the marks of the hard world in which it fought its way up. At the end of his outstanding study of industrial relations in electrical engineering firms in England and Japan, Ronald Dore wrote:

> The way a country comes to industrialisation can have a lasting effect on the kind of industrial society it becomes. It will be a long time before Britain loses the marks of the pioneer, the scars and stiffness that come from the searing experience of having made the first, most long-drawn-out industrial revolution. The slowness of the process gave time for the classes gradually to draw apart and over generations to develop their own quite separate cultures before the élite awoke to a realisation of what was happening to the cohesion of their society and began grudgingly to accept a new collectivism. That is a feature underlying many features of Modern Britain, like the antique inflexibility of her trade union institutions' (Dore 1973).

There is one particular feature of our industrial relations today that our history makes more intelligible—the great sensitivity of employees to any loss of jobs and the consequent maintenance of overmanning, which is the correlate of low productivity. What resistance workers will offer to loss of jobs depends on their view of their chances of getting other jobs that are as good or better. In an expanding economy like that of the early USA, with a high ratio of natural resources to population, the risk of not being able 'to find a place' was small, the chance of bettering oneself by moving was real. In this country, on the other hand, the industrial revolution came about at a time when a population explosion was bringing more and ever-more job-seekers into the towns. The value that those who have undergone this experience set upon keeping 'a place' may be contrasted with the more adaptable attitudes engendered when the resources of a continent were open to frontiersmen. The early British experience was different again from that of European countries which industrialised later and were able to expand their industrial equipment more rapidly relative to the growth of their population at that time.

But the tradition of insecurity coming down from the early days of industrialisation in the UK has been reinforced in the present century by the experience of the permanent loss of jobs, the shutting down of mills, mines, yards and stations, in industries that were once among the chief sources of employment in the country. The number employed on the railways is today only three-fifths of what it was before the first world war. Outstanding is the contraction of the number of jobs in coal mining and in textiles. In both these industries the number of jobs decreased by about 30 per cent between the eve of the first world war and the eve of the second; and then from the latter date to the present day it was about halved. These and other contractions occurred while, over the whole span from 1913 to the present, the working population was increasing by nearly a third. What happened in the industries concerned may well have had its effect on the outlook of more than those who lost their jobs, or lost their pride in their vocation, or were unable to follow in their fathers' footsteps. It seems that the concentrations of hardship, the frustrated lives and stricken communities, made a greater impact than the diffusion of new employment that was in fact going on meanwhile: so that a general sense arose of high priority to be given to job security among the aims of the individual worker, and to resistance to labour-saving changes among the functions of the trade union.

But in referring to these contractions we have touched already on the main constraint on our development, for the possible change of our industrial structure during the present century has been bound up with a deep-going change in our trading position in the world.

THE MAIN CONSTRAINT

Our review of factors to which the shortfall of British economic performance has been attributed has found some of them to have been given much more weight than they deserve. A substantial handicap did appear in the resistance to change built into the attitudes of employees at all levels and into the structure of industrial relations. But no doubt other countries that have advanced more rapidly than we have had their various handicaps too. The distinctive and basic constraint on the advance of the British economy remains to be examined. It shows itself in our inability to maintain the balance of our external payments. It was the constant tendency of this balance to run into deficit as domestic activity rose that cut off the rises of the 1950s and 1960s. But more deeply, the imbalance of imports and exports has marked a lack of adaptation of our economy to the manufacturing and trading require-ments of the contemporary western world. It is this slowness of adaptation that has constituted the basic constraint on our development. Here if anywhere we have the core of the British predicament. Unhappily it goes a long way back in our history. The trading relations out of which our external deficit arises had established themselves in their essentials before the end of the last century. They were intensified by the first world war. Since then they have persisted with too little change.

They first made themselves felt through the increasingly effective competition of other countries, especially Germany and the United States, in the sale of manufactures. It was only to be expected that as other countries industrialised our own share of the growing total of world trade would decline; but by 1900 what was happening clearly carried the threat of a setback that would be much more than a matter of arithmetic. For while our production and exports remained concen-trated upon the old staples of textiles, coal and iron and steel, our competitors were developing the technology of electricity, chemicals, oil and internal combustion, with which so much of the future was to lie. This was one reason why our competitors' exports not only rose faster than ours in neutral markets, but invaded our home market. Down to 1914 the effect on our balance of payments was more than offset by an expansion in our exports of the old staples, our receipts of interest on overseas investments, and our rising earnings from shipping, insurance and the finance of trade throughout the world. The first world war cut all these back, but our exports continued very much on the old lines. The staples of coal, iron and steel, cotton and wool, which had made up 52 per cent of our exports in 1900–13, still made up 46 per cent in 1920–38; the newer-style products of chemicals, electrical goods, vehicles and aircraft expanded only from less than 6 per cent of our exports in the earlier period to 8 per cent in the later. That the balance on current account was not upset during the interwar years sufficiently to be a matter of great concern was due—apart from continuing large invisible exports—to our imports of foodstuffs and raw materials being kept down, in quantity by the restrained level of domestic activity, and in price by the world-wide depression. Neither of these factors operated to keep the import bill down after the second world war; but on the side of exports, we emerged from the war with our productive capacity and our marketing still not realigned.

Thus a country that had led the world in the development of an earlier phase of technology, and established thereby what was called at the time its commercial supremacy, moved towards a new phase of technology only slowly and in the wake of other countries, so that it lost sales to them abroad and bought more from them at home . . . Export markets won by by technical pre-eminence came to be lost, in part through political changes and the raising of tariffs, but mostly through the rise of competitors selling new products and using new methods. What was needed in all these countries was an adaptation and realignment amounting to a fresh start. It might seem that none was more likely to achieve it than those who had done so well in the first place. What was there to prevent peoples who had been outstanding for their energies and their capacity for innovation and development in one era, from finding new opportunities in another? The UK was held back in part because it lacked the differential endowment of natural resources for the new processes that had helped to give it is earlier lead in the old, but also because its very success with the old methods made its managers reluctant to learn the new. The minds of practical men became bounded by the processes and products that they had mastered in long apprenticeships. In an age of technology, moreover, the UK was ill-equipped to develop processes that were science-based. The philosophy of liberal education not only denied the manufacturer and manager their due status in society, but put the arts before science, and drew a firm line between 'higher education' and applied or vocational courses. The fresh start was inhibited by cultural values and social attitudes that had come down, little affected meanwhile by the industrial revolution, from a society dominated by the leisured landowner . . .

The remedy for the long term is, in a word, to change our culture. This is not to be done by exhortation. The misfit between our traditional values and attitudes and the way of life by which we can get a living in the world, is a question of fact. Given the facts, people will draw their conclusions. Economic issues can be pursued into deep recesses, but the most important issues are simple. On what conditions the inhabitants of these densely-populated islands can support themselves in the world; what activities and what types of people enable us to do that; how a change in the terms of trade affects the standard of living available to us; where at any time a rise in real pay can.come from—these and other basic issues of our national housekeeping are not so recondite that they cannot be brought home to us. Probably the sharp changes of recent years, with incomes policy and price control, and the broadcast discussion of their implications, have done a good deal to increase general awareness. More firms are making their accounts intelligible to their employees by providing a breakdown of value added. But our political system, that should provide the major source of reporting on the state of the nation and the constraints on our choices, has spoken with an uncertain voice; the game of ins and outs tempts each party to attribute our difficulties to the mistakes of its opponents, and promise better times for all when it is itself in power. When we consider what the effect must be in misleading the public judgement about where change is needed in our economic affairs and how to effect it, this present working of our parliamentary system constitutes a strong argument for proportional representation.

We have touched above on the effect of the tradition of liberal arts, in separating higher education in the UK, and indeed British educational and cultural standards generally, from the needs of the industry by which the cultured were kept alive. Here again the spirit has been troubling the waters. A discussion paper on 'Industry, Education and Management' issued over the signatures of the Secretaries of State for Industry and Education observes that 'attitudes towards industry, and particularly manufacturing industry, are less favourable in Britian than in other major industrial countries and are reflected in our educational system.' 'Britain has a two-culture system based on the distinction between arts and science, whereas continental society distinguishes a third culture in *Technik* (or the art of making things).' The paper is meant to lead to action on both sides that will bring education and industry together, not merely as sectors subordinated to the same public purpose, but as bodies of equal status sharing common values.

A major effect of a clearer view of the facts of our present case should be to make us realise how far our institutions stand in need of change. We have been spared the sweeping away of existing institutions that other countries have suffered by war or revolution, but we have missed their fresh start too. There came a time during our first industrial revolution when contemporaries observed how ill their inherited institutions were assorted to the actualities of their own day, and 1830–60 has been called the Age of Reform. In our own day the currents of activity are breaking through the banks of the traditional channels— in the relations between trade unions, industrialists, parliament and government; in industrial relations; within trade unions; within the firm. The half-century and more in which so much else has changed since the end of the first world war has been remarkable for the lack of change meanwhile in our institutions: by now we stand in need of a new Age of Reform.

17. Banking on Britain*

Harold Lever and George Edwards

Many of Britain's economic ills can be traced in whole or part to the historic distortion in our credit system: the lowest rate of private sector investment in any OECD country, low output and productivity; a workforce with low wages and morale—and aggravated inflation. The average life of all plant and machinery in Britain is 35 years—almost double that of France, Germany and the US. This is not simply an hypothesis about what happens when credit is concentrated in certain ways. It is an observable reality.

It can be seen on the ground in Japan, Germany, France and other countries. If investment credit is provided to industry, with little credit for consumption and government budgets, then economic growth will be high, housing will be of poor quality, the social infrastructure investments (roads, parks, sewage) will be unsatisfactory, and personal savings will be high. That is Japan. If, at the other end of the scale, credit is provided to households and governments, while investment credit for industry is restricted, then there is a high level of public amenity and good housing—with a low-productivity industrial sector. That is Britain.

It does not sound too uncomfortable by comparison with Japan perhaps, but look at Germany, where the mix of investment provides more amenity too—and, on its present course, Britain is guaranteed further decline, retrenchment in public welfare and amenities, with rising unemployment and inflation, while the Japanese and Germans can count on massive improvements in all these benefits. Higher wealth can lead to better welfare; but welfare alone does not result in wealth.

The difference between Britain and these other countries is that they chose during the 1950s and 1960s how savings were to be used for

*Reproduced from *The Sunday Times*, 2 November 1980, pp. 16–18.

180

industrial, personal or government purposes and tailored loans to that end. In Britain, the forces of history, errors of government and the conventions of the financial system made the choice by default, providing consumption credit and inflation and restricting investment credit and economic growth. The tragedy is plain to see in North Sea oil. This bounty is not going to strengthen Britain's economy. Our system makes it result in a high exchange rate and higher consumption (largely of imported goods) and the weakening of our export potential.

Here is the central blindness of British economic discussion and policy. For the monetarists in power today, and their Keynesian critics who were in power yesterday, share a common error with continuously damaging consequences: both are unselective between consumption and investment. Monetarists act as if the central question is the quantity of money, their opponents as if it is the quantity of demand. What this government has produced, expressed through monetary mechanisms, is in reality a classic deflation of demand—a squeeze, which has hammered investment and employment far more than consumption. By limiting bank lending Mrs Thatcher is modestly limiting consumption but producing a devastating blow to the infrastructure of the British economy.

She berates excessive money demands for wages—but at the same time allows the expansion of consumption credits to go ahead largely unchecked. Sir Terence Beckett of the CBI is right. The basis of our future prosperity is being destroyed. The rhetoric of monetarism is that we shall emerge from the squeeze leaner and in better health. The fact is that every such unselective deflation of demand ensures that we emerge debilitated.

There is a similar blindness among the neo-Keynesian critics. In post-war Britain, disciples of Keynes, not so responsive to the modern world as the master would have been, have reflated and deflated with little discrimination. In the depressed 1930s, it did not much matter: the prime urgency was to raise demand any old how to get the wheels turning. But the world has changed.

Our rivals have been selective for decades, channelling saving to investment rather than consumption. We have become less competitive and have gone on making ourselves more so by bouts of consumption-led reflation. Too much saving has gone to consumption, too little to investment, so that in every 'go' period in post-war Britain we have had consumption rising before the productive facilities are there to match it, greater imports as a consequence, inflationary bottlenecks and balance of payments deficits leading to the next 'stop', when, again, productive investment has been the first thing to be hit.

The inflationary effect needs emphasis: consumption credit revolves round the economy very quickly, for the money is spent and redeposited with the banks, who can lend it onwards as consumption credit. By contrast, investment credit can only be spent as rapidly as the investment project absorbs it. It takes time for an industrial plant to be built and for new capital to be put in place. Increases in consumption credit can produce explosive inflation; investment credit increases are more like an expansionary drip-feed to the economy. Every increase in demand caused by increased investment promises a future flow of goods and services and rapidly fulfils that promise. Our lack of selectivity, the failure of our financial system to protect investment, has produced a dynamic which contributes to inflation and relentlessly widens the prosperity gap between Britain and the other industrialised countries.

If we are to create a benevolent instead of a malign dynamic we must by one means or another improve our investment. This is again where observation, not faith, provides the pointer. Observation of the successful post-war economies, Japan and West Germany, produces these conclusions:

1. A much greater proportion of national product is reinvested. Britain's commercial and industrial companies' net investment is about 4 per cent of our gross domestic product in the economic engine of plant and machinery. Japan normally invests 12 per cent net (France and West Germany run at about twice the UK rate). Our private sector net investment needs to be approximately doubled to match our partners in Europe, while for a Japanese rate of economic expansion our private sector investment needs to be more than trebled. Why have we fallen so far behind?
2. British industry has to try to raise most of its investment capital from its own profits. During the six years of 1974 to 1979 something like 70 per cent of the money for expansion came from within industry itself. In Japan, major finance comes from outside the company. The German entrepreneur is able to raise nearly three times as much money from the banks as the British.
3. Britain's banks lend comparatively little to industry, Japan's banks provide five times more money than Britain's for private sector investment. In Japan, bank loans to business amounted to something like 15 per cent of the national product between 1974 and 1978. In West Germany, the comparable figure is 8 per cent. In Britain, it is as low as 3 per cent.
4. Japan's industrialists have really long-term loans of 15 to 20 years. In Germany, the formal term averages 7 years and in Britain the formal

term averages 2½ years (it is more in practice as we shall discuss).
5. The league leaders in the world's productivity growth tables all have
banking systems which make long-term loans to industry. The Stock
Exchange and bond market, though they make a contribution, have
never provided more than a small fraction of the external funds
industry requires.

There is an index to describe and document this hidden dynamic
behind Britain's decline. It is the debt-equity ratio, which displays the
extent to which our industry is forced to rely on raising its own money.
For every 100 pounds a company borrows, the ratio says how much
comes from outside the company (debt), and how much has been put up
by the owners of the company (equity). Japan's debt-equity ratio is 85,
Britain's is 22 . . . .

Clearly the principles governing the system of credit to business and
industry need to be transformed in Britain. Limits have to be put on
consumption credit. That should not only make more saving available to
business but also lower interest rates by reducing competition for funds.
If only a small part of savings is channelled to investment, as it is in
Britain, we are not merely guaranteeing a low rate of investment but
also a high rate of consumption and inflation. Financing investment is
the only sensible anti-inflationary policy—to cure inflation by producing
goods and services. That is where and how the Chancellor should now
reflate. But here we have the great deficiency in our financial
mechanism—which is more fundamental than the current high rate of
interest and will remain a grave handicap when interest rates are cut as
surely they soon must be.

Our banking system has great integrity and the highest reputation but
the principles on which it acts in Britain are not suited to business. The
system works better in practice than the formal system since the average
loan of 2½ years is often allowed to roll over and the banks are usually
prepared to lend more money to repay the original debt. But if the
system works better than it might be thought to do, it works
considerably less well than it needs to do. As long as the possibility
exists of a legal enforcement of short-term debt repayment the
entrepreneur is bound to react differently than if the legal situation
matched reality.

The bank's sense of security is high in our system but it is bought at
the expense of a sense of insecurity in the borrower which discourages
risk-taking and expansion. A manufacturing entrepreneur in Britain
contemplating expansion or innovation knows that when he goes to his
bank he will usually be offered advances of two or three years or less

and that they will not be allowed to exceed the 'gearing ratio' of one-third: he will not be advanced more than one-third of the asset value of his company. At the first tremor of difficulty in the economy he knows that because of the existence of the short-term legal obligation he will be expected to give a good account of himself at his next bank interview. *In theory*, he may expect to be ruined. Of course, the banks do not lightly put people into bankruptcy. What happens *in practice* is that the entrepreneur restricts his credit ambitions and his investment potential. Not surprisingly, many entrepreneurs are reluctant to take loans which may make them hostages to their bankers. The German manager, to take one example, has considerably fewer anxieties. He can borrow much more—up to two-thirds of his assets, effectively double his British rival, and he does—and he can do it over a longer contractual term, and he does.

There is a further difficulty for the British entrepreneur. When his loan application is approved and his assets come to be valued, it will be in part on what they would fetch if he went bust rather than on what they could earn as part of a going concern. Foreign bankers see the value of the company as a productive enterprise; British banks are apt to look at the carcase value. The small number of medium-term or long-term loans our banks advance are often only with property and other collateral, and that is simply not good enough for a venturesome society.

Such prudence can lead to poverty. There is no point in calling Japanese and West German debt ratios 'unsound' when these 'unsoundly' financed companies are out-competing our own industries. The frontiers of risk have to be pushed forward as the Germans and Japanese have done.

If the same rules of ratio-risk, to say nothing of length of term, had been applied by the German banking system the Germans would have had only half the bank lending required to finance their expansion and they would not have got it from anywhere else. If the German rule, in turn, had been applied to the Japanese banking system their expansion would hardly have been greater than the Germans . . . .

The Wilson Committee on the City was told by the CBI that there is never a shortage of investment funds, only a shortage of viable investment projects. But the remark begs the question, for it is the artificial definition of viability which inhibits the flow of investment proposals—projects that in other countries would be generated, considered and approved. A definition which treats a proposals as 'not viable' if it raises the borrowing ratio towards the West German level is clearly one that bears re-examination. The lender's unwillingness to grant enough because of an excessively stringent security ratio and the borrower's unwillingness to accept because of the insecurity of the terms imposed on the loan is bound to produce this result. Investment finance is no different from any other economic factor. If it is long-term and therefore cheap and sure, then using a great deal of it becomes feasible. If it is short-term, dear, unreasonably restricted in amounts, carrying legal risks, and subject to excessive security requirements, then, of course, there will be a shortage of viable investment propositions and less investment than we need.

Banks have been moving to increase the length of their credit, but they have been moving far too slowly. The fact remains that the proportion of our gross national product going to industry remains static at a figure dramatically low by comparison with any of our European rivals or Japan. The figure of total loans by British banks to British industry is about one-half the West German figure and one-fifth of the Japanese figure, taking our different sizes into account—and represents a severe restriction on our businesses. It is one important reason why our private sector investment has declined so gravely. And it is one we could readily remedy.

The greater vitality of an investment credit economy is easily demonstrated. In 1974, the first year of the oil shock, inflation in Japan exceeded 20 per cent and growth was negligible. But inflation has been reduced to single figures and rapid growth is back on trend. Why? The Japanese financial system was a major factor. They ran a money supply similar to our own—14.7 per cent between 1974 and 1977. But theirs did not lead to inflation. While the growth of government and local debt was limited to 3.8 and 0.8 per cent respectively, investment credit grew at 11 per cent. These high levels of investment have transformed the structure of the Japanese economy so that it has moved rapidly away from the dependence on areas like shipbuilding and textiles and into higher value-added areas like electronics.

It is not simply the quantity of investment which is affected by the security of lending. There is a qualitative leap in the kind of investment possible in Japan by comparison with Britain. The financial system has given the Japanese economy not just high growth but flexibility and suppleness—a willingness to go for microchips and not stick simply to shipbuilding, and the like. And all this has been achieved without so much inflation as we have endured because of the transformation of saving into investment credit rather than for consumption . . . .

All this was achieved when the war was beginning to take away manpower and it was achieved with a real increase in the standard of living of 7 per cent. Yet the money supply increased on average by 18.9

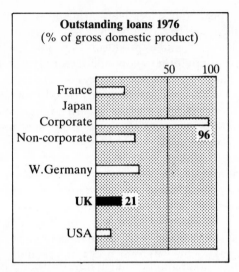

Figure 17.1. How.banks help business

per cent. The vast increase in credit in those years produced more growth than inflation because the boom in the money supply was investment credit. Can we not learn from these observations? Albert Speer, Hitler's Armament's Minister, remarked:

> When the United States entered the war not only Hitler laughed but so did many experts over the reports of production plans that reached us from America. To start from nothing and within five years to produce more than 10,000 heavy bombers seemed to us on the basis of our industrial experience to be Utopia or, as was said then, typical American bragging. But the Americans exceeded their goal.

Britain missed the chance for that kind of advance in the long years of post-war boom when the French, Germans and Japanese advanced and prospered. But we can in future match their advances if we ensure that policy is charged with providing investment credit similar to what the Germans, French and Japanese enjoy. That is the essential base for reversing Britain's stagflation.

Even the most cooperative trade unions, the most brilliant managers, the most inventive technologists, cannot function effectively without it. 'Give us the tools and we will finish the job.'

18. The Effect of Adversarial Politics*

Michael Stewart

What has gone wrong? In 1976, as in other years, there was no shortage of explanations: everyone had at least one pet theory, and some people had several. The examination conducted in this book of the economic policy pursued during the period, and the forces which shaped it, suggests that much of what went wrong can be found in four sets of factors. For convenience they are here called *structural, technical, managemental* and *political*. Although they are all interlinked with each other, they can in broad terms be distinguished, and discussed separately.

STRUCTURAL FACTORS

The structural factors which have played a part in holding back Britain's economy have been not so much physical as psychological. There is, to be sure, the all too visible and tangible legacy of the industrial revolution: industries that are decaying, towns that are rotting, firms that are in the wrong places, factories and mills that are too small and too out-of-date, workers with obsolete skills. But all this would have mattered much less if these structural anachronisms and rigidities had not had their counterpart in the hearts and minds of men. No foreign observer ever fails to note how far British society is still riddled with class distinctions and class antagonisms, and permeated by the suspicious awareness of the difference between us and them. No doubt this explanation of the nation's ills is sometimes overdone: Britain's class divisions have practically become a tourist attraction. It can

*Reproduced from M. Stewart, *The Jekyll and Hyde Years* (London, Macmillan, 1977), pp. 234–45. Copyright © Michael Stewart, 1977.

certainly be argued that class divisions are less marked, and much less destructive, than they were 40 or even 20 years ago.

Nevertheless, there is something in the class explanation of Britain's economic weakness. More than most other comparable countries, Britain is still two nations—not least in the industrial arena. Far too many managers view their workers as the enemy—idle, shiftless, dishonest and irresponsible. Far too many workers see management as the enemy—privileged, inefficient and unaccountable. Managers fail to invest and modernise because 'confidence is lacking' and fail to involve workers in decision-making because decision-making is the prerogative of management, and none of the workers' business. Workers, for their part, refuse to yield an inch to the foe: they resist the introduction of new techniques, stop work for trivial reasons long before grievance procedures are exhausted, insist on manning levels appropriate to a bygone age, and refuse to change jobs in response to changing patterns of demand or technology. This, at any rate, is what it often looks like. The philosophy is the philosophy of the zero-sum game: if one side wins, the other loses, and nobody wants to be the side that loses. In fact, it is a positive-sum game: both sides stand to gain if they cooperate more effectively. Neither side can rise its living standards very far at the expense of the other; this can be done only by joining forces to defeat the recalcitrance of the physical universe and the threatening competition of better-organised foreigners. But, however easy it may be to discern all this from an ivory tower, it is a perspective that folk memories and entrenched attitudes all too often obscure on the shop floor.

But it is not only in the persistence of class antagonisms that the trouble lies. Britain has been slow to adapt its values, its priorities, its policies, its educational institutions to the position in which it found itself after the [second world] war: no longer the centre of a great and economically beneficial empire, but a middle-rank industrial country needing to compete with other highly efficient economies if it was to survive. Even as late in the day as the mid-1970s Britain did not seem to have come fully to terms with its new role. It was not difficult to see it as many foreign observers did—as a lethargic country, clinging to old ways, reluctant to change, unwilling to face up to the implications of the revolutionary shifts taking place around it, and better at debating its problems than at doing anything to solve them.

It may be, of course, that contemporary Britain is not cut out for continual changes and a rapid rate of growth. In a world in which change is often regarded as synonymous with progress, and the new is often confused with the good, such a posture would have something to commend it. But the corollary of such a posture is that average living standards can rise only very slowly and—if intolerable poverty at the bottom of the income distribution is to be relieved—the living standards of the better-off cannot rise at all. Such a corollary has never been accepted. People want to have their cake and eat it too: they want ever-rising living standards, but they also want to stay in the same jobs in the same places and do the same old things in the same old way. Such contradictory demands, and the structural factors which lie behind them, constitute an unpromising background for the conduct of a successful economic policy.

TECHNICAL FACTORS

The technical factors which have had an adverse effect on economic performance are of two main kinds, both arising from lack of knowledge and both, up to a point, unavoidable. Forecasts are rarely highly accurate; and lack of knowledge about how the economy works means that policy measures sometimes have different effects from those intended. Although in practice it may be difficult to tell whether things have gone wrong because the forecast was bad, or because the policies adopted did not work in the way anticipated, in principle the distinction is clear.

On a number of occasions since the early 1960s the forecasts have gone wrong. One case was the failure to foresee the strength of the 1963–64 boom, and the consequent worsening in the balance of payments. Another was the consistent underestimation, over much of the period, of the upward trend of manufactured imports. Another was the failure to anticipate the full effects of the 1973–74 world commodity boom. There were also a number of cases where it was not so much the forecasts of exogenous variables that were at fault, as the inability of the forecasting models employed to relate one variable to another with any great accuracy. One example of this kind of technical failure was the unexpected extent to which the adverse demand-inflation effect of rapidly rising expenditure from 1972 onwards outweighed the favourable cost-inflation effect of rapidly rising output. Another was the way in which big increases in the money supply in 1972 and 1973 led to a rise in the price of existing assets—particularly land and property—rather than to the creation of new assets.

Although none of these errors was unimportant, it is hard to believe that, had they been avoided by a combination of better forecasts and more realistic economic models, policy decisions would have been substantially different. About two other examples, however, it is less easy to be sure. One was the overestimation of the growth of demand at the beginning of 1970. A more accurate forecast here would have led to a more expansionary budget in 1970. This might have resulted in the re-election of a Labour government in June 1970, with effects on subsequent history that can only be speculated about; but even in lieu of that, the recession of 1970–72 would have been less severe, and the measures taken by the Conservatives to get out of it less wildly expansionary. Some of the country's subsequent problems might have been distinctly smaller. The second example is the related phenomenon of the surge in public expenditure from 1972 onwards. Had the extent of this been properly anticipated, steps might have been taken earlier to cut back the growth of public expenditure to something more closely in line with the growth in output.

Nevertheless, it would probably be wrong to ascribe very much of the poor performance of the economy over the past 10 or 15 years to errors in forecasts or economic models. Unless one goes the whole hog with the monetarist or New Cambridge schools and abandons stabilisation policy altogether—and this . . . would probably result in an even more unacceptable outcome—one must accept that there will always be errors in the forecasts, and knowledge of how the economy works will always be less than complete. The more such technical sources of error can be eliminated, the better; but the real trick is to ensure that unavoidable errors of this kind are not compounded by avoidable errors of other kinds.

MANAGEMENTAL FACTORS

A third group of factors which has played a role in Britain's unimpressive economic performance might be described as *managemental*. In this category fall policies and decisions which reflect neither technical judgements on the one hand, nor party political pressures on the other. In practice it is often impossible to say just where technical judgements merge into managemental ones, or managemental judgements into political ones, but in principle the distinction seems useful. . . .

Any list of management misjudgements is bound to be subjective, and is likely to contain examples where technical and political factors were present in some degree. But there are certainly a number of instances since 1964 of bad managemental decisions having an adverse effect on the country's economic performance. One such instance was the failure of the Labour government to devalue in 1964 or, failing that, in 1966. Although there was a political element in this—Harold Wilson's fear that Labour would be damagingly branded as the Party of devaluation—it was essentially a managemental decision based on a misjudgement of the seriousness of the disequilibrium in the balance of payments, and of the role of Britain and sterling in the world economy. It was almost entirely a ministerial decision. While many government economists (particularly the temporary ones brought in by Labour) were in favour of devaluation permanent officials—while in many cases probably against—recognised that it was an issue of such importance and of such possible political ramifications that they bent over backwards to maintain a neutral posture. The failure to devalue at the right time . . . was to have an adverse effect on the economy for many years.

If Labour's greatest managemental mistake lay in not devaluing earlier in a move to get securely-based, export-led growth, the Conservatives' greatest managemental mistake lay in giving far too great a stimulus to private consumption and public expenditure, in a way that practically guaranteed that the economy would be brought to a halt by a balance of payments crisis. Although the Barber boom was triggered off by strong ministerial concern with the implications for the Party's image of high and rising unemployment that the government seemed to be doing nothing about, it seems to have been supported, in general terms, by the civil service and the Treasury economic establishment. They correctly perceived the recession of 1971–72 to be the result of the failure of the government to apply orthodox Keynesian remedies to a situation of sluggish demand. But the hope that a sufficient expansion of domestic demand would soon stimulate productive investment and—helped by a floating exchange rate—lead to an adequate growth of exports proved much too optimistic. A similar managemental miscalculation had been made on a smaller scale in 1963–64, when Maudling tried his dash for growth. There was little excuse for its being made again.

Another adverse managemental factor lay in the failure to realise how rapidly public expenditure was rising, and a failure to bring its growth under more effective control. This miscalculation was first made under the Conservatives, but continued under Labour during 1974 and 1975. To some extent, as was indicated earlier, this was a technical failure, in that the Treasury was slow to grasp the implications of controlling public expenditure at constant prices at a time of rapid inflation. To some extent, too, it resulted from the fact that the scale and nature of public expenditure is one of the main sources of disagreement between the two main political parties. Nevertheless, the fact that between 1972 and 1976 public expenditure rose very much faster than the GNP must be regarded as to a very large extent a failure of economic management which in various ways had damaging consequences for the performance of the economy as a whole.

POLITICAL FACTORS

The final reason for Britain's poor economic performance since 1964 lies in the way the political system has been working. Both Labour and Conservative Parties, while in opposition, have succumbed to the temptation to condemn a large proportion of the government's policies and have promised to reverse many of these policies when they themselves took office. The result has been a fatal lack of continuity. Incoming governments have spent their first year or two abolishing or drastically modifying the measures—often quite sensible—of their predecessors, and pressing ahead with the measures—often unrealistic or irrelevant—which they have formulated in opposition. After a year or two they have come to closer terms with reality, and changed course, but by that time much harm has been done, and the benefits that would have accrued from continuing the policies they inherited have been lost.

    The most important victim of this Jekyll and Hyde syndrome has been incomes policy. This is a crucial new policy instrument. If one rejects the monetarist thesis that a complex modern society, with powerful trade unions capable of crippling the economy almost overnight if their demands are not met, can be satisfactorily run simply be regulating the money supply, then an incomes policy is essential if reasonably full employment is to be combined with a tolerable degree of price stability. But an incomes policy, usually widely welcomed when first introduced because it offers relief from mounting inflation, always becomes unpopular before long, as those affected come to focus more on the restraints it imposes on them than on the benefits they receive from the restraints it imposes on others. Such a policy can only succeed in the long run if it consistently supported by both the main parties, and not regularly repudiated by the one in opposition in the hope of gleaning electoral dividends. Conservative attacks made inevitable Labour's abandonment of its incomes policy in 1969, and led to the 1969–70 wage explosion; and Labour attacks on the belatedly adopted incomes policy of the Heath administration made inevitable the round of 30 per cent wage increases in 1974–75 which gave Britain in inflation rate from which full recovery is proving exceedingly difficult. If the opposition had in each case refrained from making party capital out of the government's incomes policy, the rate of inflation during the 1970s would probably have been considerably lower, and the general performance of the economy considerably better. It was a welcome change that Conservative attacks on Labour's 1975–76 incomes policy were, at any rate at first, muted and oblique—indeed, from the Heath wing of the Party the policy received some support; but as 1976 wore on, opposition speakers increasingly ignored its advantages and emphasised its disadvantages.

Incomes policy, however, is a necessary rather than a sufficient condition of a satisfactory economic performance. What really matters is the efficiency with which resources are utilised, and the extent to which productive potential is increased by investment and the introduction of new technologies. Here Britain's record has been dismal and here too, political factors have been partly to blame. Quite apart from the adverse effects on investment of the 'stop–go' cycle—partly a product of technical and managemental errors, but also the result of the pre-election boom required by party-political considerations—have been the effects of the chopping and changing of governmental attitudes, and assistance, to industry. Labour replaced investment allowances by investment grants; the Conservatives, changed back to investment allowances. Labour introduced SET; the Conservatives abolished it. Labour introduced REP, to make more use of idle resources in the regions; the Conservatives made no attempt to maintain its effective value. Labour set up the IRC; the Conservatives did away with it. This process shows no signs of coming to an end: in 1976 Michael Heseltine, the Conservative opposition's chief spokesman on industrial matters, pledged that the next Tory government would repeal Labour's 1975 Industry Act and abolish the NEB. Nor were the nationalised industries immune: put on a realistic footing by Labour's White Paper, they were subjected in the early Conservative years to haphazard interference with their financial targets, and futile attempts to hive off their profitable activities. Similarly, the Conservatives agreed a long-term policy for the steel industry in the early 1970s; in the mid-1970s Labour drastically amended it. And so on. . . .

At the heart of the Jekyll and Hyde problem lies the role of the opposition. The existence of an opposition free to criticise the government as it chooses is widely regarded as the acid test of a modern democracy. It is clear that the democratic system will be something of a sham if the opposition opposes in only a formal and ritualistic way, in practice rubberstamping whatever the government does. This will deny legitimacy to genuine opposition, compelling it to take extra-parliamentary or illegal forms. The system of parliamentary democracy will be jeopardised: the stage will be set for revolution or totalitarian repression. It is presumably considerations of this kind which underlie the doctrine that 'it is the duty of the opposition to oppose'. First formulated in the eighteenth century by George Tierney, this doctrine became widely accepted in the nineteenth century, and still enjoys wide currency today. It was an article of faith with the late Richard Crossman, and was recently propounded by Reginald Maudling, Shadow Foreign Secretary and former Chancellor of the Exchequer.

In the nineteenth century this doctrine may have been harmless enough: the government's role in the economy was a limited one, and so correspondingly was the impact of abrupt changes in government policy. Nowadays, with extensive government intervention in the economy, things are different. Modern democracy may not work properly if parliamentary opposition is of no more than a token kind; but neither will it work properly if the opposition automatically and vociferously opposes everything that government does. In a world of limited resources and virtually unlimited wants, any government must make many hard and unpopular decisions. If the opposition regularly tries to cash in on this unpopularity for electoral reasons, by condemning such decisions, however justified and necessary, and promising to reverse them, a different kind of threat is posed to the democratic system. The electorate will be encouraged to believe that there is an easy way out, that hard choices can be avoided, and that all their problems stem from the mistakes of a confused and incompetent government. The result will be precisely what has so frequently been witnessed since 1964: the government is deflected from the path of responsible action by the need to protect its flank against opposition attacks in an attempt to ward off electoral disaster; and when the opposition in due course becomes the government, it is committed by its conduct and promises in opposition to reversing many of its predecessor's policies, however sensible, and pushing through new measures of its own, however silly and irrelevant. The resulting poor performance of the economy can itself become a potential threat to a democratic system of government.

This is not at all the same thing as saying that *all* the early policies pursued by incoming governments since 1964 have been misguided, and that it has taken a year or two for common sense to break through. The two main political parties . . . have different values and philosophies, and are largely supported by different groups within the community. It is not only inevitable, but right, that many policies should be changed or modified when one party replaces the other in government, and sometimes the problem is not that the changes are too easily made, but that they meet too much resistance from the civil service and the establishment generally. Active Labour supporters, for example, who work for the return of a Labour government so that it may change society, argue that the first year or two is the time when it fights to put its principles into practice, and the later period is when it surrenders to the forces of reaction, worn down and outmanoeuvred by the civil service. This view is not without some validity, particularly where it is a question of Labour's egalitarian policies for income distribution and the social services. But it is not a compelling case as far as the main consensus objectives of economic policy since 1964 are concerned. Here, the Jekyll and Hyde analogy seems the more accurate one. . . .

Peering into the future one can disern, however dimly, a world in which the problems of resource depletion and the disposal of the by-products of industrial civilisation loom increasingly large; in which the Malthusian nightmare of the planet's population being controlled by famine and plague becomes ever-more real; in which the huge imbalances between the wealth and living standards of the world's have and have-not nations threaten the most explosive possibilities; in which material living standards in countries like Britain must cease to rise and perhaps start to fall. In such a world Britain will no longer be able to afford the luxury of making or breaking economic policies for the sake of party politics or the whims of particular politicians. There will be plenty of things for the parties to disagree about without their disagreements paralysing the operation of the economy. It is high time the parties sorted out the difference between the things which, as a nation, we can afford to disagree about, and the things which we cannot.

19. The Treasury's Contempt for Production*

Sidney Pollard

In our search for a cause of the British failure to invest we have come upon one single overwhelmingly important answer: investment in Britain was low because the whole panoply of government power, as exercised above all by the Treasury, was designed to keep it so. Again and again, in the course of the past 30 years, governments have set out to discourage, cut back and stifle investment, and in the long run they have succeeded. This was done at two levels. There was, on the one hand, a battery of measures to hit investments directly and specifically, but there was also, and perhaps more insidiously, the paralysing effect of the recurring and in the end permanent 'stop' phases on all hopes and plans for the future. It is without doubt a remarkable tribute to the inherent drive of capitalism towards the creation of capital, and to capitalists' urge to invest, that in the fact of all the official discouragement, any investment is still taking place at all in Britain.

However, by pointing to government as the immediate cause of low investment we have merely shifted the problems one step backward. For the obvious question that then demands to be answered is why successive governments should wish to go out of their way to inflict such grievous, ever increasing damage to the British economy. One possible impression left by the kaleidoscope of events over the past three decades may well be that the country merely suffered from a chapter of unconnected accidents. Alternatively, we may come to the despairing conclusion that the Treasury will always choose, from any set of options available, the one which will do the most damage—an assumption that will certainly help as a first approximation for putting the events of the past into some logical order and predicting those of the future. Yet both of these explanations would be wrong: an alternative does exist, and in

*Reproduced from S. Pollard, *The Wasting of the British Economy* (London, Croom Helm, 1981), pp. 71–86, 151 *et seq*.

following it in the search for a unifying principle that will make sense of the many apparently contradictory reactions of British policy-makers, we are beginning to approach the heart of the matter.

Let us be clear what we are looking for. We are looking for a body of ideas and of principles strong and pervasive enough to make governments continue with their policies even though they have led over a period of three decades, as a matter of experience, to the most devastating economic failure recorded in modern history and do not even make sense in their own terms. For as we have seen . . ., the adopted policies were bound to lead, after every 'go', necessarily and inevitably into another crisis; policies supposedly devised to lead to deflation were bound to lead to rises in costs; and policies supposedly devised to cut the PSBR were bound to lead to its increase. Moreover, we are looking for principles held by British governments and policy-makers but not by others—except those, like the United States in recent years, that have shown equally dismal economic results.

There is one and only one principle which will fit the bill: it is the principle of concentrating first and foremost on symbolic figures and quantities, like prices, exchange rates and balances of payment, to the neglect of real quantities, like goods and services produced and traded. In particular, the subordination of one to the other is such that whenever there is a clash of interests, the real must be sacrificed to the symbolic. This scale of values is of course the reverse of that held by ordinary citizens who make up the population of this country, and indeed of every other country in the modern world.

Not that members of British governments have set out to do harm to their economy. On the contrary, they will be found in the past to have supported particular industries, firms or regions, to have supported research and development of new technologies, and in general to have shown all signs of wishing, like the citizens themselves, to ensure the prosperity and full employment of all sections of their country. But these laudable policies have in the majority of post-war years been in direct conflict with the line of high or 'macroeconomic' policy pursued by the Treasury, and it has, as a consequence, been a common feature of the period that different departments have worked simultaneously in opposite directions.

No one who has lived through the period and has read or listened to the media will require proof of the single-minded obsession of the Treasury with such issues as balance of payments or inflation: it is the single most consistent thread running through official propaganda and discussion. It is true that for a time the objective of full employment also played a significant part and that British policy zig-zagged between the

'Pavlovian responses' of Treasury and bank officials dreading a 'run on the reserves' and of politicians dreading an unemployment figure over the critical half-million mark. But the latter barrier has now been broken. Employment itself has more recently, like production and investment, been used as means with which to get the symbolic balance right, rather than the other way round.

There is no question but that the objectives were in themselves worthy and desirable ones. The point is that they were considered more urgent, and more significant, than real productive power and real goods and services available for consumption which were repeatedly sacrificed for the sake of the symbols. In the last resort, therefore, the attitude of the authorities can only be described as one of contempt for production and of the productive sectors of the economy.

The contempt for production thus stood at the centre of British policy in this period. It informs fundamentally all the actions of the Treasury and other central policy-making bodies. At the same time, it is what most clearly distinguishes the British government from all others.

As a policy principle it also proved to be thoroughly destructive. For it preferred the empty symbol to the living reality, and by utterly confusing ends and means, it lost both. Britain, sacrificing her productive power on the altar of monetary symbols, suffered not only in real welfare, but in the end damaged also the symbols for which it had been sacrificed; whereas the countries that got their priorities right and devoted their efforts to improving the productive base found that their symbols, the value of their currencies and the balance of their payments, also turned out successful and positive.

The callousness on the part of the authorities towards the real problems of British productive industry was in sharp contrast to the constant care and concern which they lavished on trade and finance. There was never any question of harming them in the interest of short-term adjustments, still less would it have been conceivable that currency or trade might have been sacrificed in the interests of the productive industry on which the prosperity of Britain ultimately depended.

Nor was this emphasis accidental. The Treasury works in an atmosphere in which the voice of industry is heard but weakly, while the voice of the banks, particularly the Bank of England, and of the overseas trade 'lobby' reverberates daily around its corridors. As all of them clamoured and pushed for their one-sided and finance-orientated priorities, one is left wondering sometimes if there was anyone there who spoke up for Britain.

The contacts with the Bank were naturally the closest of all. Among the Bank's main functions were the management of the foreign exchanges and the marketing of government securities and, like all other institutions, its viewed its own activities as of quite overriding importance in relation to all others; unlike other institutions, however, it was in a position to get its self-centred views largely accepted. The exact relations between the Treasury and the Bank of England were and are complex and shifting, and depend from time to time on personalities, particularly of those of the Chancellor of the Exchequer and the Governor, and since in recent years their objectives have been so similar, Governors do not now, as they did in some post-war years, air their disagreements in public over the heads of their nominal superiors in the government. However, it is clear that the constitutional authority of the government over the Bank, which is there to fulfil certain technical duties on behalf of the Treasury, has never been fully or even approximately implemented.

It is the Bank and the banking community that have been largely responsible for fixing the absolute constraints within which the Treasury has assumed that it has to work. . . .

The bankers were, of course, pushing against open doors: the Treasury's own immediate interest was also with such matters as balancing the budget, maintaining the external value of sterling, and conducting the affairs of the 'sterling area' while monitoring and steering the movements of the so-called sterling balances, the funds held by other countries in London. This constellation of forces, at any rate in such pure form, is almost unique to Britain. Elsewhere, central banks as well as economic policy-makers and planners see themselves as responsible for the welfare of the whole of the national economy; if they have any particular interests, then frequently, as in Germany, Italy and Japan for example, they are likely to lie in home productive industry. The danger of mistaking the foreign balance as an overriding policy goal and the currency as a 'kind of national virility symbol' would therefore hardly arise.

In Britain, the tradition was otherwise. Traditionally United Kingdom banks do not generally acknowledge the need to be more integrated with industry. The City and the merchant banks have placed their main interest in trade and overseas investment. These are important, but it is bound to lead policy-making astray if the special concerns of a narrow section of the economy, refracted by the distorting mirror in which everyone sees his own role in society, are allowed to dictate national priorities. The egocentric views arising therefrom might have appeared amusing in the past. . . . Moreover, there will be little doubt in most people's mind that that one particular official's blinkered attitude, typical for the Treasury at the time, arises essentially because the foreign trade balance happens to be his concern, and industrial production is not. But the tragedy is that there has at no point been a major change of direction in the Treasury obliging it to change its priorities, and the same sentiments, no doubt overlaid by Keynesian theory, still hold sway. Industry has every time to be sacrificed on the altar of the City's and the financial system's primacy:

> How much this has cost Britain in terms of lost economic growth it is impossible to say. But it far outweighs whatever benefit has come from the invisible earnings which the policy has generated.

Again, this is not only a highly dubious scale of priorities; it is also self-defeating. By confusing ends and means, base and superstructure, grievous damage was done to both. The fortunes of British industry have never depended on the soundness of the finance sector; it has always been the other way round. London's original rise as a financial centre was grounded firmly on the strength of the British economy as a whole, and the growing industrial power of, successively, the USA, Germany and Japan, has brought them financial power and helped to undermine London's premier position. In the end Britain's productive weakness contributed to the waning power of the City itself, and to its falling net earnings. . . .

The Treasury is not only a centre of thought about policy, but above all a centre of power. The question is why that power should have been used consistently in the direction of throttling back and damaging the productive part of the economy in order to rectify unbalances on the monetary side. Part of the answer is to be found in [the fact] that the Treasury's macroeconomic power was, for historical reasons, wedded to responsibility for one narrow segment of the economy, namely its foreign exchange and currency balance. In the inevitable strain of loyalties between single-faceted responsibility but multifaceted power, it is not entirely surprising that the Treasury's own tasks took precedence over the long-term interests of the country as a whole, that it refused to engage in medium-term planning, and that 'what has passed for policy has consequently consisted of reaction to short-term crises.'

There was also a second reason. It is to be found in the traditional job of the Treasury, which is to keep down the expenditure of the other government departments. Expenditure is therefore traditionally seen as the enemy, the evil to be kept down; the actual efficiency of the expenditure in terms of the social or economic good it might do, or the comparative efficiency of two competing claims, are completely outside the Treasury's traditional range: 'The time-honoured Treasury attitude to spending is summed up by candle-ends'—the phrase used by Gladstone to describe minute saving of detail; and a former Economic Secretary, Nigel Birch, found that

> [t]he Treasury can argue for months on end with all the subtlety of Duns Scotus about what a day's subsistence allowance ought to be for Bogotá, but when really large sums are at stake there tends to be a certain withdrawal of interest.

'Instead of worrying about candle-ends,' said one Treasury minister, 'they should have asked themselves the question "in what sense should Britain still be a great power?"'

This blindness to economic reality, as distinct from departmental accounting, was particularly disastrous in the failure to see the difference between current expenditure and productive investment. In times of stress they were treated as equally worthy of cuts—indeed, capital expenditure was generally treated as more easily dispensable, since it offered fewer toes to be trodden on: 'Few civil service jobs are at stake and there are no awkward negotiations with unions or large redundancies.' Similarly, when actual cuts had to be imposed, the tendency was for the burden to be shared out equally between the departments: the exercise was therefore a political rather than an economic one, which would have been to minimise the economic or social damage of the cuts. One could go further and say that the Treasury function as the nation's watchdog over public expenditure was altogether seen as a political task, geared mainly to the power a minister could pull in the Cabinet, or to the influence of a particular permanent secretary as against another. It was as far as it possibly could be from the economic logic of looking at the government's activities as a whole, which might well at times require an increase of expenditure in certain directions, even in tight times, and a more than proportionate cut elsewhere. It was this kind of approach, and only this kind of approach, which made it conceiveable for the Treasury to react to all crises with the standard formula: 'produce less and eat up your seedcorn' . . .

The Treasury's power no doubt derives in part from the native talent of Treasury men; but very largely it rests on the solid fact that it holds the purse-strings and acts as the personnel department for the whole civil service. What we have therefore is a department standing on three legs. By the fateful constellation of historical development and of its own inherent talents, its most important leg, overall economic policy, is poisoned by its second leg, the direct responsibility for currency and exchange matters, but is made dominant by the third leg, the control over the civil service.

Planning in the real sense, the direction of private citizens, the apparatus of *étatisme* were more foreign to the British Treasury and civil service than to the traditions of the continentals and even of the Japanese. Not that the range of functions of the modern British state was any less—according to some critics, it was even greater—but in the absence of a tradition and of a willingness to recognise the modern reality, it was *ad hoc*, less coordinated, it made less sense and it was less effective. It was generally left to the politicians in charge, less well versed in financial matters, but more aware of the general social implications, to force the permanent Treasury officials to think in sensible economic cause and effect, rather than departmental accountancy and internal politics terms: the famous incident of Winston Churchill's misgivings over the return to gold in 1925 has been repeated many times since.

Beyond the Treasury itself, the character of the whole top layer in the civil service also played a part in permitting the unchallenged pursuit of disastrous policies without change over 30 years. It is difficult to believe that a group like the French civil service élite, with their mathematical/ technical training and their relative independence from the politicians, or the American top appointees who come in with each new administration and are therefore less tied to previous policies, or indeed any group less sure of itself would not have acted differently in the same external circumstances. . . .

Essentially what counts is the administrative class. Within it are to be found all the officials who coordinate the actions of different ministries with or without the consent of the politicians nominally at their head, who provide and select the advice submitted to ministers, and who can exert direct personal influence on the ministers themselves. The administrative class of the British civil service is without doubt an intellectual élite, devoting itself to its tasks with honesty and dedication; but, it is also a social and power élite. It is part of the British 'establishment' and the selection process with all its variants and variations since the war has zig-zagged between the twin poles of a bias towards intellectual ability and bias towards the 'right' background of class and upbringing. It had produced a group overwhelmingly from the professional and managerial middle classes, from the public schools and the ancient universities, with a training overwhelmingly in the humanities. In all these respects, the bias of the direct entrants has been even greater than that of the entrants by internal promotion.

By initial training, therefore, most of them are unprepared for the task of administering a complex economy, and while the numbers trained in economics, statistics or accountancy are growing, they are still pitifully small within the overall totals. Add to this the tradition of a different posting every two or three years, and the taunt of amateurism will not appear misplaced: in particular, even top administrators often lack a mathematical sense and a feel for quantitative relationships, preferring to trust their own alleged sense of values. Sometimes, as revealed for example in the bank rate leak investigation of 1957, this kind of decision-making is little removed from frivolity. 'Our whole national life is permeated with easy-going self-satisfaction, and the toleration of incompetence.'

The further training within the departments which is part of the working life of the young top civil servant essentially teaches him two things. One is the manner of proceeding. Here he quickly finds that what is rewarded is the ability to write good papers, the ability to compromise and the skill to avoid treading on too many toes; major innovative thoughts are not encouraged, particularly in junior administrators, and habits acquired then tend to stick. As far as the subject-matter itself is concerned, he learns by the time-honoured method of 'sitting next to Nellie', or learning by doing what the others have done before him. It would be difficult to think of a system more designed to perpetuate the basic policies carried on to date and to inhibit their questioning. The occasional secondments to formal training periods, though valuable in themselves, cannot be a substitute for the grasp of overall principles which alone provides the power and self-assurance to question transmitted assumptions.

This is not to impugn the ability of the top echelons: on the contrary, it may well be argued that the power and prestige attached to higher civil service jobs has drained too much of the nation's intellectual élite into the administrative class. What is at stake is the misapplication of so much brain power. It is precisely because of their innate ability, fostered by the peculiar skills developed in the service, that leading officials have been able for so long to defend the indefensible; one can only wish that an equal effort had gone into devising policies that would not need to be defended because they were successful. It is not even clear that the British civil service, with all its weaknesses, is in any sense inferior to that of the more successful countries. It may just be that it is placed in a setting in which both its virtues and its failings work in the wrong direction. . . .

The British civil service has many virtues and was in many ways an ideal instrument for the later Victorian and Edwardian era; this is particularly true of the Treasury. Even today it can be relied on to complete a set task with admirable dedication and reliability. But the very virtues become faults in the light of the present need to look with fresh eyes at the role of Britain in the world, and the need to realign fundamentally the course and premisses of economic policy. The peculiar strengths and weaknesses of the civil service, and of the Treasury in particular, form a powerful contributory cause of our decline.

20. The Impact of Foreign Economic Policy*

Stephen Blank

There were two sets of contraints on Britain's economic performance after 1945, one internal and the other external. The internal constraints included inefficiently organised industries, dated capital structures in many industries, low levels of replacement of capital goods, widespread restrictive practices, an outmoded system of industrial relations, and trade union and management practices that inhibited industrial modernisation and economic expansion. The external constraints related primarily to Britain's extraordinarily vulnerable international financial position (a function of limited reserves), consistently unfavourable balance of payments, and extensive international financial and economic commitments.

The history of the British economy in the 30 years after 1945 is, for the most part, the story of Britain's inability to overcome the internal constraints on its economic development. This failure has thus increased Britain's vulnerability to the external constraints. Most analyses of the British economic situation focus on the failures of the domestic economy. Included here would be the failure to increase production, to maintain stable prices, to invest more, to get more satisfactory returns in productivity from investment, to export more, and so on. But economic issues *per se* are not always seen to be the primary reasons for these failures. Increasingly, observers of Britain have come to believe that the fundamental reasons for the problems of the British economy are more political than economic. It is argued that the structure of British society and, more particularly, the way in which the political system operates have made it possible for groups representing limited interests to warp

*Reprinted from S. Blank, 'Britain: the politics of foreign economic policy, the domestic economy, and the problem of pluralistic stagnation', *International Organisation*, 31(4), Autumn 1977, pp. 674–90, 715–21, by permission of the MIT Press, Cambridge, Massachusetts.

or undermine government policy. These groups are even seen to assume the powers of government and thus to inhibit or prevent governments from carrying out policies which are in the interests of the entire nation. Organised groups—workers or businessmen—ruthlessly exploit their power within the British political system to enhance their welfare at everyone else's cost. Political parties have made this situation still worse by promising far more than governments can deliver and, thus, by creating expectations doomed to be frustrated.

This essay argues that a major source of the constraints on British economic performance since 1945 has indeed been political. It disagrees, however, with those who say that the differences lie primarily in the abilities of groups in British society, particularly industrial or labour organisations, to thwart or undermine government policies. It suggests that frustrated expectations and the actions to which they give rise are the result more than the cause of Britain's economic and political difficulties. The argument of this essay is that Britain's economic problems in the post-war years have been caused in large measure by the policies of successive governments, especially those policies which dealt with Britain's role in the world.

It is not meant to suggest by this that organised industrial and labour groups in Britain have had no influence on government policies or that they have never undermined economically and socially-productive policy objectives. In particular cases, under particular circumstances (not necessarily unique or even infrequent), trade unions and industrial associations have been able to influence policy outcomes substantially. When issues are finely focused rather than broad, administrative rather than political, when the expert knowledge of the group can be brought to bear, or when government's own policy is uncertain or the members of the government divided, there is considerable scope for influence. Regardless of policy outcomes, groups can also influence policy as it is implemented.

But these groups had little influence on the determination of domestic or international economic objectives or on the formulation of the broad outlines of national economic policy. In Britain, the permeability of the economic policy-making process has been considerably less of a problem than the insulation of the policy-making process from the impact of criticism and new ideas. What one finds in post-war Britain is not so much weak government, unable to resist the demands made by powerful interest groups, as government which made many wrong policy choices and persisted in following these policies with remarkable stubbornness. In the field of economic policy, British government has been neither weak nor vacillating. It rigidly adhered to the policies which it determined, even when the adverse impacts of those policies had become all too clear.

The external constraints on British economic performance differed from the internal constraints in that, to a large extent, they were the result of a series of political choices made by post-war governments to restore and preserve Britain's role as a world power. For much of the post-war period, domestic and international economic policy was dominated by and subordinated to the goals of foreign policy; goals which Britain was incapable of realising. Yet, the attempt to achieve these goals led successive governments to sacrifice the domestic economy again and again. By the end of the 1950s, a vicious cycle had evolved in which efforts to maintain its international position became themselves the very causes of Britain's continuing international financial vulnerability. Efforts to create new policies and institutions whose purpose was to confront the problems of the domestic economy and to improve domestic economic performance foundered on the willingness of political leaders to abandon the most cherished symbol of Britain's international position by devaluing the pound.

Eventually, although not until the second half of the 1960s, British political leaders came to see that the international role Britain had sought to play since 1945 was beyond its capacity. By then, however, enormous damage had been inflicted on the domestic economy. Moreover, largely because of the retardation of economic growth that had been the result of these earlier policies, Britain was in a poor position to cope effectively with the new challenges of the 1970s; domestic and international.

This essay looks much more at the impact of élite attitudes, particularly those dealing with Britain's international role, on domestic economic policy than at the major structural determinants of foreign economic policy. The essay seeks to examine the interrelationships of international and domestic economic and political objectives and policies. It looks, in particular, at the impact of foreign policy goals upon international and domestic economic policies. It contends that economic policies in Britain after the second world war, both domestic and international, were dominated by foreign policy goals and that this domination provides the primary explanation for Britain's poor economic performance during the post-war years.

Without the constraints which were the result of British foreign policy goals, Britain's economic performance would surely have been more satisfactory. But it still would have been limited by internal economic factors, not least of which are attitudes and values concerning the role of the state in the economy and the relationship of public and private

208 The View from the Centre

power. Equally important are the rights and responsibilities of such bodies as the trade unions and the appropriate limitations, if any, on collective bargaining and price-setting throughout the economy. To alter these attitudes as well as the practices and institutions in which they are embodied is perhaps the most vital task of national economic policy. The heightened level of social conflict in British society, the failure of governments to give adequate consideration to the needs of institutional development, and the politicisation of economic policies and the instruments of economic management have made this task far more difficult at the present time than it might have been earlier.

In the end, in large part as a result of the continued failure of the economy to perform more successfully, Britain may be approaching a point at which its governments are exhausted, the legitimacy of its political leadership undermined, and its political parties deeply divided. Britain may thus be reaching a point at which there are no longer effective political barriers to protect society from groups which seek to defend themselves at all costs from a continuously declining economic situation. At such a point, the basic structure of Britain's economy and democracy will be undermined.

There is an extensive and well-known literature which deals with Britain's long-term descent as a leading economic power. Much of this rests on the notion of Britain's precipitous industrial decline, relative to the expanding industrial economies of such nations as the United States and Germany, sometime during the last decades of the nineteenth century—the British 'Climacteric' . . . (Supple, 1963) . . . The analysis of Britain's 'climacteric' of the late nineteenth century, because it is so well documented and compelling, has had the unfortunate effect of encouraging scholars and, even more, a large number of non-scholars to see Britain's present economic situation solely in terms of this long drawn out economic collapse.

The major problem with the analysis of long-term collapse, aside from a frequent vulgar economic determinism, is that it simply misses the subtle parts. The real story is better and, perhaps, sadder. Many indications exist to suggest that Britain's economy has not been in a state of continuous decline since the end of the nineteenth century. Rather, they suggest that it was substantially revitalised in the period which began in the late 1930s and continued through the second world war into the late 1940s. . . .

Despite the enormous economic losses of the war, Britain's post-war economic recovery was remarkable by any standards. Indeed, one can, with some justice, speak of Britain's recovery in the first post-war years as Europe's first 'economic miracle'. The economic instability which had characterised Britain after 1918 was avoided, and impressive gains were made in total production, in productivity, and in exports. Between 1945 and 1950, industrial production increased by between 30 and 40 per cent. (Indeed, between 1948 and 1960, the rate of real growth in total industrial output was 3.7 per cent, compared to 3.1 per cent between 1920 and 1936 and 1.6 per cent between 1877 and 1913). The rate of increase in industrial productivity was almost 3 per cent between 1949 and 1960. Between 1924 and 1935 it had been 2.2 per cent and was 1.6 per cent between 1907 and 1924.

Perhaps most significantly (and frequently overlooked), Britain's international trade performance improved dramatically. Visible exports increased by 75 per cent over pre-war levels in the first post-war years, with no increase in imports. Although British exports declined after the late 1940s as a percentage of all world exports, they continued to increase absolutely and imports into Britain rose no more rapidly than in other developed nations. Britain's net trade gap had run around 30 per cent in 1900–10 (that is, there were 30 per cent fewer visible exports than imports), 20–30 per cent in 1920–30, and 40–45 per cent n 1930–39. Since 1945, it has run consistently below 10 per cent, and often lower than 5 per cent. The remaining deficit has been more than made up each year by an invisible surplus. As a result, Britain consistently ran a *surplus* balance on the *private* account after the war (at least through the late 1960s) as favourable as that of France or Germany.

All of this was acomplished against the background of the creation of the welfare state, a fairly large redistribution of personal income in favour of wage earners, and the maintenance of full employment. Although some observers of the British economy saw the economic crises of 1947 and 1949 as stages in a longer-term process of decline, others believed these problems to be more temporary and caused by the inevitable difficulties of adjustment after the war. The going was tough enough in Britain after the war, particularly in the winter of 1947. But the achievements of these years were clear too, and there was a widespread sense of national purpose in the country. Besides, compared to the political and economic situation in Europe, Britain's difficulties hardly seemed insurmountable. . . .

British economic policies after the second world war were dominated and shaped by two overriding policy objectives. British governments were committed to consolidate and maintain the welfare state, the system of economic and social security which ensured that the human suffering and deprivation of the interwar years would not be repeated. Its most vital element was the policy of full employment. The domestic roots of these commitments are obvious, but they have significant international foundations as well. By the end of the war, the British were convinced that the fundamental causes of the war were the economic and social conditions of the interwar years. British economic commitments and policies in the postwar years were greatly influenced by the belief that it was necessary to avoid the recurrence of such conditions at almost any cost. Thus, the consolidation of the welfare state and the guarantee of full employment at home went hand in hand with Britain's efforts to recreate a stable and liberal international commercial and financial order.

British governments after the war were committed, in the second place, to restore and protect Britain's international position. This was necessary not only in diplomatic and military terms (where it soon became clear that Britain would have to play second fiddle to the Americans) but in commerce and finance as well. Britain would maintain the 'special relationship' with the US and would continue to play, alongside the United States but also independently, a major world political and economic role. The Commonwealth provided a power-base which was independent of the US and Europe and, in particular, enabled Britain to maintain its position as the world's foremost commercial and financial centre. Within this arena, the sterling system served as the prime mechanism which linked the Commonwealth into a coherent economic entity. Thus, the sterling system, resting on fixed exchange rates and London's role as banker, was seen as the key support for Britain's position as a world power. The stability of the international financial and commercial system that was created under Anglo-American supervision at the end of the war was felt to be essential for the operation of the sterling system and, thus, for the maintenance of Britain's international role. This was so despite the fact that Keynes and others had been aware of the system's defects in so far as British interests were concerned. The continued successful operation of the international financial system both ensured a better world and guaranteed that Britain would be one of its leaders. These had been the two linked aims of British international economic policy since the early nineteenth century.

All of this—the consolidation of the welfare state at home, the recreation of a liberal world economic system with sterling at its centre, and the restoration of Britain as a major world power—presented enormous commitments whose economic cost seems never to have been calculated. The 1950 budget, for example, which committed the nation to massive rearmament, led to the resignation of three members of the Cabinet. But the resignations focused on much more minor (although symbolically important) domestic issues, and the debate over these new defence and military commitments was minimal. Similarly, William Wallace observes that Eden's pledge in 1954 that Britain would maintain a sizeable defence force on the Continent for an unlimited period was given 'almost without reference to the future cost to the balance of payments'. The same was true, he states, in the negotations which led to Germany's admission to NATO as well as to Britain's military commitments in the Far East. Conservative governments in the 1950s continued to press for the restoration of full convertibility, but it does not seem that the burdens this would create for the domestic economy were carefully evaluated . . .

The weight of tradition was extremely powerful. Britain had been a dominant international and imperial power since the early nineteenth century. Although its own resources were clearly insufficient to support this role after 1945, its position at the centre of the 'three circles' provided Britain with the unique access to resources and a basis for international power and influence. The 'three circles' were, of course, Churchill's description of the strategic base of Britain's power in the post-war world, those overlapping circles of Britain's relations with the United States, with Western Europe, and with the Commonwealth.

It was by no means obvious during the first post-war years that Britain's international position had been fundamentally altered. Various factors served to disguise the situation. These included the image of British political and economic superiority over Japan and the nations of Western Europe, and the belief that the Commonwealth would provide Britain with a major source of strength. Finally,

> The British political system militated against a public admission that Britain's status had been reduced, either by the government of the day or by the Opposition, although some of their members may have held and privately expressed much more skeptical views than those in public announcements.

No government would, or could, announce that it was presiding over the decline of Britain from a first- to a second-class power.

There were few differences, in any case, among party leaders, officials or leaders of the major producer groups with regard to Britain's post-war international commitments. Frankel notes that:

> Both parties agreed that it was Britain's role to maintain peace, law and stability in the world . . . Not only did the leaderships and majorities of the two main parties appraise Britain's major national interests in fundamentally similar terms, they also held similar views on maintaining her world role. Whichever party had been in power, the general trends of her post-war policy would probably not have been appreciably different. (Frankel, 1975, pp. 33–4)

Although some officials in the Foreign Office and Treasury were deeply concerned at the end of the war about Britain's capacity to resume a leading world role, their voices remained in a minority. There was little debate about Britain's international role and the commitments this involved, either within government or Parliament or outside of Westminster and Whitehall.

There is another dimension to these perceptions of Britain's role as a world power. The British tended, in the early post-war years in particular, to envisage their international role very much in terms of a range of responsibilities, the responsibilities of a world power. They were determined not to duck these responsibilities. This was especially true in so vital an area both to the future of world peace and to British interests as the re-establishment of a liberal world trading and financial system. Younger observes that, while Britain's power to discharge its responsibilities might have been limited, 'She none the less rightly felt herself to be still the same sort of power that she had been before, handicapped indeed by lack of resources but still cast for a world part, which no one else, for the time being, could play in her stead'. (Younger, 1964, p. 3) . . .

A broad consensus on the structure of the post-war economic system, the objectives of economic policy, and the instruments of economic control had developed among leaders in the public and private sectors during the last years of the war. The policies of the 1945 Labour government scarcely constituted a revolution and were easily assimilated into this broad consensus. Debates over nationalistion, for example, were largely symbolic. It was widely recognised that the means of production would remain almost entirely in private hands but that government would assume responsibility for a broad spectrum of economic and social goals, including social security, full employment, and rising standards of living. It would exercise this responsibility by 'managing' the economy, but it would do this 'indirectly,' mainly by regulating the overall level of demand in the economy. Governments would not intervene directly in the affairs of individual firms or in collective bargaining.

The consensus predicated a very delicate balance between public and private power in the British economy. The Labour government's social reforms did not essentially alter this balance and, as the wartime economy was dismantled, the clear demarcation between the public and private sectors was reestablished. From 1947 until the very end of the 1950s, government policy-makers as well as business and labour leaders sought to restore the traditional distance between government and the economy. They also tried to minimise government's role in the entire range of decisions affecting investment, the determination of wages and the conditions of work, and industrial relations. They attempted to limit the government's economic policy instruments to global mechanisms which would minimise administrative discretion. Government's economic policies, it was widely believed, should function globally, as simply and as automatically as possible. It was this dramatic reassertion of the liberal state after the second world war that prompted Andrew Shonfield to remark in 1965 that 'The striking thing about the British case is the extraordinary tenacity of older attitudes towards the role of the state' (Schonfield, 1965, p. 88).

These liberal views were emphasised much more by the Conservatives, who would recall how they returned to power in 1951 under the banner of free enterprise, but they were widely shared among British leaders. Attlee's government never seriously attempted to institute a more interventionist style of economic management. The British labour movement had not developed an economic strategy which focused on planning or on more selective forms of state intervention. The Left opposition within the Labour Party continued to call for further nationalisation and the imposition of physical controls rather than economic planning. The trade unions sought, above all, to preserve maximum autonomy in the determination of wages and in all aspects of industrial relations.

The movement away from sectoral wartime economic regulation was well underway by the time the Conservatives returned to power in 1951. It had been Harold Wilson who, as President of the Board of Trade, had lit the 'bonfire of controls' in November 1948. The Conservatives, after 1951, tried to rely almost exclusively on global forms of economic regulation and emphasised, in particular, monetary policy as the master control of the level of economic activity. They were uninterested in developing sectoral policies in areas such as industrial structure and organisation, investment, or industrial relations. Increasingly, they sought to make domestic economic management automatic as well, by utilising the external strength of the pound as the principal regulator of the level of activity in the domestic economy.

The consensus in Britain in the late 1940s and 1950s on the objectives and mechanisms of international economic policy was perhaps even more broadly based than that on domestic economic policy. The function of international economic policy was to restore and enhance Britain's role as a world power and, in particular, to contribute to the maintenance of the Commonwealth and sterling system (as well as the 'special relationship' with the United States), upon which Britain's international power rested so heavily. To be sure, there were differences in emphasis between the international economic policies of the first post-war Labour governments and the Conservative governments of the 1950s. In the years just after the war, the outstanding problems were still reconversion and shortages and the government was prepared to rely on physical controls to guide the economy. The emphasis at that time had been on the Commonwealth and overseas sterling area as a 'defensive currency area', where, in particular, scarce dollars would be pooled and conserved. After 1951, the emphasis shifted to the achievement of convertibility and multilateral trade, to 'the re-establishment of sterling as a general international currency and of London as an open financial market-place' (Strange, 1971, p. 64).

But while emphases differed and evolved through time and changing conditions, basic commitments did not. What these came to involve was the creation of an interlocking network of policies which related to the preservation of Britain's role as a world power. Included were the restoration of sterling's international transaction and reserve functions, fixed exchange rates, overseas investment directed particularly toward the sterling area, government spending and lending in the Commonwealth and sterling area, and the maintenance of a British military and defence presence in these areas.

There was little debate, and little discussion, in Britain about these international economic policies. International (and domestic) economic policies emerged in large measure as a response to perceptions about Britain's position, interests, and responsibilities as a great power in the international arena. But post-war economic policies were also shaped by the nature of the policy-making process, by commitments to particular techniques of economic management and by the nature, as well as the objectives, of national economic policy.

There are few case studies of policy-making within the British government, and little material is available to illuminate the decision-making process. At best, a few general notions can be provided. Within the British government, the Treasury has had primary responsibility for the implementation of both domestic and international economic policy. The Foreign Office has not had the economic expertise, even if it had the will (which is doubtful), to contest this role. The Board of Trade played a far less central role in international economic policy, limited largely to the area of overseas commercial and trade policy. Twice in the post-war years, efforts were made to create a rival centre within the government which would have primary responsibility for domestic economic, as opposed to financial, policy. The first was the formation of the Ministry of Economic Affairs under Cripps in 1947; the second, the Department of Economic Affairs, with George Brown as minister, in

1964. In both cases, the Treasury soon reasserted its traditional control over the entire scope of domestic economic and financial policy. In neither case, however, was the Treasury's preponderant responsibility for international economic policy and, in particular, for the defence of sterling questioned.

The Treasury has had primary responsibility for the implementation of economic policy rather than for the determination of policy objectives. The very efficiency of the government machinery in Britain, and especially of the Treasury, frequently leads observers to misunderstand the role of the civil service in policy making in Britain. The Treasury, in particular, is superbly efficient at carrying out policy. Indeed, sometimes it is so efficient at running the machine and implementing policy that insufficient attention is paid to the basic policy decisions themselves. Hugh Heclo and Aaron Wildavsky have recently observed that the great weakness of the American political system lies in implementation, in executing policy which is so laboriously pieced together. The danger in the British system, they note, is just the opposite:

> The government may agree all too quickly, before the major implications of the policy are understood or the affected interests realise what is about to happen to them, leaving all concerned agape and aghast as the machine implements the policy with its usual splendid impartiality, that is, with equal harm all round. (Heclo and Wildavsky, 1974, p. 12)

Perhaps this takes the point a little too far. Obviously, in a government in which the number of political leaders and senior officials is so small, there is no absolutely clear distinction between the policy makers and the policy implementors. Yet, despite the small number of people involved at the peak of the policy process and the absence of absolute clarity between functions, the different roles are deeply internalised. Civil servants carry out policies made by their masters, although, like a fine horse or automobile, the master who is not strong or able enough will soon find that the machinery has run away with him.

There are, of course, important feedback links. Officials in government, especially in the Treasury, have been less concerned with ultimate objectives than with means and instrumentalities. But this very concern for means or instruments of implementation can influence the shape of policy objectives. Indeed, given a lack of strong policy guidance from the political leadership, it can determine policy objectives by default. Certainly, the strong commitments of Treasury officials with regard to the means and techniques for the management of the economy influenced the shape of Britain's domestic and international economic policies after the second world war. There are a number of reasons why this was undoubtedly so. 'High foreign policy' was relatively insulated from international economic policy and political leaders (particularly Prime Ministers) lacked interest in international economic issues. There was also very little discussion and argument in the government about the whole structure of British economic policies and about the implications of political decisions (especially foreign policy) on economic policy.

For the Treasury, domestic and international economic priorities and policies are closely linked, and its highest priorities were clearly focused on protecting sterling's international position. Britain's international role and its international commitments and responsibilities were all symbolised in the pound sterling and the sterling system. The domestic economy was viewed largely in response to international developments, particularly international confidence in the pound. What this seems to indicate is an extraordinary primacy of political over economic considerations within the Treasury itself. Treasury thought was dominated by a variety of 'political myths' about Britain's role in the world, sterling, and so on, which, in fact, operated against Britain's economic interests. The Treasury approach, far from being ruled by narrow economic considerations, too often evaded such economic realities as Britain's capacity to pay the costs of its international role.

The Treasury had readily assimilated a Keynesian approach to economic management during the war. Keynesian techniques, *as interpreted by officials*, provided government with the capacity to overcome the economic problems of the 1930s—unemployment, overproduction, the downside of the economic cycle—and yet to preserve the basic structure of the liberal economy. By regulating a single macroeconomic lever, the overall level of demand in the economy, these problems could be remedied without seriously disrupting the balance between public and private power in the economy. As late as 1959, Sir Robert Hall (who served as the government's economic adviser from 1947 to 1961) observed that in the British government 'there is still a tendency to speak in magical rather than scientific terms of the use of interest rates and monetary controls generally' (Maddison, 1964, p. 124).

The overriding goal of the Treasury after the war was to re-establish an international economic order. This system was to rest on fixed exchange rates and the free movement of currencies. Sterling, supported by its privileged position in the Commonwealth and overseas sterling area, would serve as the primary international reserve and transaction currency. A further goal of many officials lay in linking Britain's domestic economic management to the international economy.

The level of domestic economic activity would be regulated as automatically as possible by the international economy. When the pound was strong in the world economy, domestic economic activity would be stimulated; when the pound weakened, the level of domestic activity would be cut back. A system quite this automatic was never established, although it was seriously discussed in the early 1950s. This discussion was characterised by Angus Maddison as 'another case of wishful hankering after the will-of-the-wisp of automatic devices, which springs from a desire to abandon the heavy responsibility of formulating policy.' Britain's domestic economic policy options were severely limited by several internationally-oriented commitments. The first of these was the basic policy commitment to maintain the external strength of sterling as an essential support for Britain's international position. The second was the determination to support sterling internationally by deflating the domestic economy when the pound came under external pressure. Finally, there was the Treasury's deep commitment to more global and automatic techniques of economic management. . . .

CONCLUSION

The objective of this essay has been to discuss the political and economic impacts of certain policy choices made by British governments after the second world war, particularly policy choices which involved efforts to restore Britain's role as a major world power. The essay is meant to be a response to those who claim that the fundamental causes of Britain's unsatisfactory economic performance in the post-war period are to be found primarily in the attitudes of British workers and managers, in its labour and industrial organisations, and in the failure or inability of British government to exert its will more forcefully over the economic decision-making process.

The attempt has been made in particular to assess the responsibility of interest groups for the problems of the British economy since 1945. The conclusion reached here is that the responsibility of organised industrial and labour groups, while not negligible, is far from substantial. The responsibility for Britain's economic difficulties, in so far as these were within Britain's capacity to control, lies mainly with successive British governments and with the polices they adopted. Britain's economic problems have risen less from the subversion of government policy by powerful agencies or groups, either in the bureaucracy or in the private sector, than from the impact of the attitudes, commitments, and politics of Britain's top political leaders. . . .

It is not the intention of this essay to suggest that all of the economic problems that Britain faces today grow out of a set of foreign policy choices and decisions made in the years which followed 1945. A wide range of serious defects of industrial structure, labour organisation, and work and management practices would have to have been confronted and solved if Britain's economic situation were to have been improved. But the pattern of policy which characterised the post-war era severely limited the options of policy makers in dealing with these issues. The result of the government's commitment to maintain Britain's international position was continuing domestic economic stagnation and a failure to develop new techniques and instituions to cope with the structural problems of the economy. This, as has been seen, made it much more difficult for the British to deal with new challenges when they arose at the end of the 1960s.

The argument of Britain's long-term economic decline does not take into sufficient account the impressive gains Britain enjoyed in technological and managerial development from the end of the 1930s through the war years, nor the remarkable recovery of the British economy after the war. It must also be remembered that the 'margins of failure' of the British economy, at least through the 1960s, were narrow indeed. The balance of payments crises of 1955, 1957, 1961, and even 1964 represented quite small adverse movements against the pound when compared, for example, with the yearly or even quarterly totals of British trade. The impact of government's response to these crises was far more damaging to the British economy than were the problems represented by the balance of payments difficulties. There were several points at which the direction of Britain's economic development might have been altered during this period. This is where the failures of perception and policy are most vivid.

Perhaps the greatest failure was the lack of attention given to the problems of the domestic economy in the first post-war years. Yet it is easy to see how Britain's very success blinded its leaders to this need for a full-scale attack on the structural inadequacies of the economy. Britain's military, political and economic achievements during the war and in the first post-war years were remarkable. Defeat forced the French to confront head-on the underlying defects of their economy; the achievements of the British economy were so substantial that it was all too easy to overlook its fundamental problems. The war divided the French and held up their weakness for everyone to see; the war united the British and disguised their weaknesses. The failure of the war economy forced the French to re-examine their national economic and industrial policies; the British successes encouraged them to believe that existing policies and techniques were sufficient for peacetime purposes. . . .

The most tragic failure to change the direction of British economic policy was Harold Wilson's. It is not so much a question of devaluation, which was a necessary but by no means sufficient step to revive the domestic economy. The real failure was Wilson's inability—unwillingness—to utilise the resources which were available to him to reverse the course of British economic development. From the late 1950s, a new consensus had begun to emerge within British leadership. This consensus focused on the need to energise Britain's economy, to modernise its industry, and to overcome the deeply-ingrained inhibitions in British society which limited economic growth. Among leading industrialists, in particular, who were deeply disturbed about the damage that 'stop–go' policies were doing to business expectations, the nucleus of a group similar to that which surrounded Jean Monnet had begun to form. They were excited by Wilson's promises of radical (which is to be distinguished from, although not necessarily opposed to, socialist) leadership and were prepared, I believe, to take on significant new responsibilities, in his administration. The government's failure to exploit this resource and, indeed, its alarming capacity for making the most conservative choices at critical moments destroyed this movement and undermined what remained of business confidence. Increasing fatalism and aggressiveness characterised business response to government after 1966.

PART IV:
Marxist Views of Industrial Decline

Marxist explanations of contemporary economic difficulties add a number of themes to our story. Overridingly, of course, they add the theme of capitalism itself—the argument that industrial production here, as elsewhere in the OECD, is organised within social relationships (of capital and wage labour) which are inherently and necessarily prone to instability, change and crisis. The recent problems of the British economy have then to be understood as in part common to all capitalist economies' experiencing as they are the particular form of contemporary capitalist crisis (stagflation) common everywhere since 1973. Marxist explanation also add the recognition that, as a world system, capitalism necessarily develops in a combined but uneven way, and is subject to processes of capital accumulation (and geographical relocation) which move resources away from some economies and towards others; such that industrial production is something which has to be captured and retained, and can be so only by the provision of suitable kinds of social, economic and political environments. The Marxist explanation of why Britain's manufacturing base is in decline is, in essence, one which emphasises the growing absence of those environmental prerequisites in a world in which the competition to retain industrial plant and equipment is everywhere growing more intense.

When Marxists ask why those environmental preconditions are absent now, in an economy which was once the heartland of industrial capitalism itself, they invariably trace the story back to that early stage of world monopoly and to its social and political consequences. They draw attention in particular to the resulting interplay of a capitalist class divided into financial and industrial sectors, a labour movement entrenched in a defensive posture by the relatively easy competitive conditions of the monopoly phase, and a state (with a power bloc of classes around it) insufficiently locked into local accumulation and more

223

concerned with capital export and imperial glory. That is, they trace the origins of the cumulative decline of British industrial capital back to the 1880s, and to the emerging challenge to British industrial dominance occasioned by the rise of German and American political power. This is how the extracts from *Ron Smith* handle the origins of economic decline, and how the problem is approached by *David Coates* in the final extract in this part. Both rely heavily on some version of the *Hobsbawm* thesis, namely that the arrival of foreign competition did not bring industrial restructuring on any significant scale. Instead, the earnings on foreign investments cushioned the impact of foreign manufactures on the British balance of payments for at least a generation, and imperial markets were exploited to absorb British surpluses no longer competitive on the world stage.

No agencies or social forces arose to stop that retreat into empire. The labour movement did not; nor did the state. As *Tom Nairn* argues, the British state was and remains hopelessly anachronistic, quite unprepared to initiate a process of industrial modernisation if that required, as it must, breaking Treasury domination, compelling the City to fund industry, reforming Oxbridge and leaving the alliance with the United States. The fusion of internal state conservatism and external imperialism occurred, in Nairn's view, through the victory of southern financial and commercial interests over northern industrial ones after 1880. The subordination of industrial capital to City interests, the persistence of a mercantile capitalist ideology, and the traditionalism associated with pre-capitalist elements within the British ruling class, all combine, in Nairn's view, to block any state initiative to regenerate local industry.

That blockage was consolidated too by the fracturing of financial and industrial interests within the twentieth-century ruling class (as argued in the short extract by *Andrew Glyn* and *Bob Sutcliffe*) and by heavy recent expenditure on armaments (as argued by *Nigel Harris*). What is more contentious is whether working-class strength has been, and remains, also a blockage on industrial development under capitalist control. *Andrew Kilpatrick* and *Tony Lawson* put the case that workplace conflicts over the organisation of production have affected adversely rates of labour productivity, and have done so for a long time. *Laurence Harris* puts the counter-case—that industrial capital in Britain has not been forced into modernisation by a sufficiently militant trade union movement. Certainly that impulse to modernisation still will not come from the state; and *Bob Rowthorn* demonstrates quite clearly the class reasons why this is so.

David Coates' survey chapter then offers one orthodox Marxist specification of the character and origin of Britain's economic decline. He too goes back to the character of early industrialisation to trace the emergence of divisions within the capitalist class between finance and industry, to document the low rate of manufacturing investment and the political weakness of industrial capital, and to show how this was compounded by trade union defensive strength and the particular international ambitions of the British political élite. His argument makes two periods of recent British history critical. With Hobsbawn, he attaches importance to the late nineteenth-century retreat into empire; and with Pollard and Blank, he recognises the missed opportunity of the 1950s. On his argument, it is the cumulative impact of those two periods, and of the class forces which created them, which makes the situation of industrial capital in Britain so dire.

21. Economic Trends and Crisis in the UK Economy*

David Currie and Ron Smith

In examining this process of relative decline, we would emphasise the role that the early industrialisation and subsequent internationalisation of British capital under the umbrella of imperial power had in making it more profitable to expand abroad than to innovate and accumulate in Britain. This created a ruling class and a policy regime dedicated to the international interests of British capital rather than the development of the domestic economy. The policies adopted, which remain the focus of conflict—free trade, high exchange rate, high military expenditure and a monetary policy and system geared to the City of London's role as world banker—were and are a major brake on domestic accumulation. Low domestic accumulation and the international orientation of the most dynamic element of capital also reduced the ability of the British economic and social system to adjust to domestic needs. The pattern of class relations and financial institutions which developed was well adapted for a role of servicing the internationalisation of capital, but was a major obstacle to rapid industrial transformation. And once established, this pattern of characteristics perpetuated itself in a cumulative process. Thus low accumulation resulted in slow growth in output and real wages. The low wage growth and ossified social relations produced by domestic stagnation and international orientation increased class conflict and worsened industrial relations. The defensive strength and strategy of the British labour movement can then be seen as a result, rather than as a cause, of this failure of development. But this strength and the conflict over wages and control of the work process did then become an important material force in the subsequent cumulative process. But to attribute the origins of this process to working-class strength itself seems misleading. While early instances of

*Reproduced from D. Currie and R. Smith (eds.), *Socialist Economic Review* (London, Merlin, 1981), pp. 10–13.

may be cited for the UK, as for other countries, the relative failure of UK economic performance pre-dated the main growth in the strength and scale of working-class organisation.

However, the development of defensive attitudes was not confined to working-class organisations alone, but was shared more widely by domestic capital and British society in general. Slow growth in output led all the major domestic social groups and institutions to become primarily concerned with defending what they had, producing the social rigidity and arthritic inability to respond that characterises British social relations. This rigidity and inability then of course became an obstacle itself to growth and transformation.

In the same way, the sluggish pace of innovation so characteristic of Britain from late Victorian times to today . . . is better regarded as a symptom than a cause of the decline. Although it is often argued that there is some specific national malaise that afflicts British management manifesting itself as entrepreneurial failure, this seems inadequate as an explanation. British capitalists showed no lack of entrepreneurial drive in their overseas expansion and in many cases failure to innovate or invest in the UK can be shown to be the most profitable behaviour given the environment capital faced. Various elements made innovation unprofitable. The large existing capital stock embodying a traditional technology together with low expected growth made scrapping all the old plant and equipment and starting afresh more costly than merely making marginal additions which reinforced the existing structure and ossified the system further. The international links created both the opportunities to expand more profitably abroad, and a financial system geared to servicing international rather than domestic accumulation. Government policy which puts international expansion and interests before domestic development reduces the profitability of accumulation and innovation in the UK and reinforces the prospects of continued low growth. High military expenditure, needed to support imperial aspirations, constituted a drain on the surplus available for accumulation and diverted scarce scientific and technical skills away from industrial R & D. Although government policy played an important role in subordinating domestic development to international expansion the mechanism is quite different from that suggested by the argument that the expansion of state expenditure depressed growth through crowding out private accumulation and distorting incentives through high taxation. . . . There is little evidence that the post-war pattern in Britain differed from the average for the advanced industrial countries, except in the higher share of military expenditure. In addition the problems of the British economy pre-date the expansion of public expenditure.

Thus by the beginning of this century a stable pattern of interconnected characteristics which are still maintained was established—
international orientation; domestic social rigidity; the low profitability
of domestic accumulation and innovation; and class stalemate. These
characteristics are still typical of British capitalism. The process of
relative decline they engendered, perpetuated itself in a sequence of
cumulative causation—low accumulation leading to low profits, increasing class conflict and further obstacles to accumulation—which reinforced the pattern. Although the process is highly stable it is not
inexorable: there have been periods when major crises have forced
substantial restructuring of British capital. During the 1930s, despite the
massive unemployment, the economy continued to grow and a whole
range of new industries developed, though protection through high
tariffs was essential to this process. In the late 1940s there was rapid
growth in industrial production, with protection and state intervention.
But the possibility of the creation of sustained rapid accumulation was
not realised because again governments subordinated domestic development to imperial aspirations. The Korean war rearmament with its
destructive effects on investment and exports; the return to free trade,
the rebuilding of the City with convertibility and increased foreign
investment, all worked to re-establish the traditional pattern. . . .

The roots of the British crisis lie in:

1. The ossification of the relations of production and the associated
   widespread class conflict, and failure of innovation and accumulation.
2. The damaging effects of the very high degree of international
   orientation of British capital and the general internationalisation of
   capital.
3. The effects of the first two factors in producing low growth of output,
   employment and real wages, creating a vicious circle of cumulative
   decline.

In summary [As Ron Smith has put it elsewhere (R. Smith 'The
historical decline of the UK', in S. Aaronovitch and R. Smith, The
Political Economy of British Capitalism (McGraw Hill, 1981), p. 72] our
argument is that Britain's early industrialisation led to the development
of a mature working class with a strong political and economic
organisation before its competitors, while the early international
expansion led British capital to focus on investment and operation
abroad. The British ruling class thus became dominated by international
and financial capital. The structure of production and social organisation that arose in the course of this early start were initially very

effective, but with the growth of competition from other industrial countries and the transformation of the technology of production they became increasingly inappropriate.

By the end of the nineteenth century these structures had become a major barrier to the expansion of domestic production and there developed a contradiction between the international orientation and interests of British capital and the growth of the British economy. To transform these structures required extensive state intervention in the organisation of production and control of international trade and capital movements. Both of these were opposed by important sections of capital: the former because during the twentieth century the potential strength of working-class organisation meant that there was always a danger that state intervention might be used in a manner hostile to capital; the latter because control of trade and capital movements would endanger the freedom to pursue profitability on a world scale and endanger existing overseas investment. The control and intervention adopted were thus severely limited and as a result domestic production stagnated. This stagnation meant that Britain fell behind relative to her competitors and this deterioration generated recurrent crises.

22. The Beginnings of Decline*

Eric Hobsbawn

The relative decline of Britain is, broadly speaking, due to its early and long-sustained start as an industrial power. Nevertheless, this factor must not be analysed in isolation. What is at least equally important is the peculiar, indeed the unique, position of this country in the world economy, which was partly the cause of our early success and which was reinforced by it. We were, or we increasingly became, the agency of economic interchange between the advanced and the backward, the industrial and the primary producing, the metroplitan and the colonial or quasi-colonial regions of the world. Perhaps because it was so largely built round Britain, the world economy of nineteenth-century capitalism developed as a single system of free flows, in which the international transfers to capital and commodities passed largely through British hands and institutions, in British ships between the continents, and were calaculated in terms of the pound sterling. And because Britain began with the immense advantages of being indispensable to underdeveloped regions (either because they needed us or because they were not allowed to do without us), and indispensable also to the systems of trade and payments of the developed world, Britain always had a line of retreat open when the challenge of other economies became too pressing. We could retreat further into both Empire and Free Trade—into our monopoly of as yet undeveloped regions, which in itself helped to keep them unindustrialised, and into our functions as the hub of the world's trading, shipping and financial transactions. We did not have to compete but could evade. And our ability to evade helped to perpetuate the archaic and increasingly obsolete industrial and social structure of the pioneer age. . . .

However strongly the winds of change blew elsewhere, as soon as

*Reproduced from E. Hobsbawm, *Industry and Empire* (London, Weidenfeld & Nicolson 1969) pp. 2, 149–62.

they crossed the Channel to Britain they grew sluggish. In every key aspect of the economy . . . Britain fell behind its rivals; and this was all the more striking, not to say painful, when these occupied fields which Britain had itself been the first to plough before abandoning them. This sudden transformation of the leading and most dynamic industrial economy into the most sluggish and conservative, in the short space of 30 or 40 years (1860–90/1900) is the crucial question of British economic history. After the 1890s we may ask why so little was done to restore the dynamism of the economy, and we may blame the generations after 1890 for not doing more, for doing the wrong things, or even for making the situation worse. But essentially these are discussions about bringing the horse back into the stable after it has gone. It went between the middle of the century and the 1890s. . . .

Why . . . this was so has been much debated. Clearly, the British did not adapt to new circumstances. They could have done so. There is no reason why British technical and scientific education should have remained negligible, in a period when a wealth of rich amateur scientists and privately endowed research laboratories or of practical experience in production clearly no longer compensated for the virtual absence of university education and the feebleness of formal technological training. There was no compelling reason why Britain in 1913 had only 9000 university students compared to almost 60,000 in Germany, or only 5 day-students per 10,000 (in 1900) compared to almost 13 in the USA; why Germany produced 3000 graduate engineers per year while in England and Wales only 350 graduated in *all* branches of science, technology and mathematics with first- and second-class honours, and few of these were qualified for research. There were plenty of people throughout the nineteenth century to warn the country of the dangers of its educational backwardness; there was no shortage of funds, and certainly no lack of suitable candidates for technical and higher training.

It was no doubt inevitable that British pioneer industries should lose ground relatively as the rest of the world industrialised, and that their rate of expansion should decline; but this purely statistical phenomenon need not have been accompanied by a genuine loss of impetus and efficiency. Still less was it predetermined that Britain should fail in industries in which she started with the arguable disadvantages neither of the older pioneer, nor of the latecomer, but substantially at the same time and point as the rest. There are economies whose lag can be explained by purely material weakness: they are too small, their resources too scarce, their supply of skills too meagre. Britain clearly was not one of them, except in the vague sense that any country of its size and population had, in the long run, more limited possibilities of economic development than much vaster and richer countries like the USA or the USSR; but certainly not significantly more limited possibilities than the Germany of 1870.

Britain then failed to adapt to new conditions, not because it could not, but because it did not wish to. The question is, why not? An increasingly popular explanation is the sociological one, which puts it down to lack (or decline) of enterprise among businessmen, to the conservatism of British society, or to both. This has the advantage for the economists of throwing the burden of explanation on the historians and sociologists, who are even less capable of bearing it but just as willing to try. There are various versions of such theories, all quite unconvincing, but the most familiar runs something like this: the British capitalist aimed at eventual absorption into the socially more respected and higher stratum of the 'gentlemen' or even the aristocrats, and when he achieved it—and the British hierarchy was only too willing to accept him as soon as he had made his pile, which in the outlying counties might be quite a modest one—he ceased to strive. As an entrepreneur he lacked that built-in urge to maintain a constant rate of technical progress almost for its own sake, which is believed to be characteristic of American industrialists. The small family firm, which was the characteristic type of enterprise, was fairly effectively insulated against excessive growth, which risked the loss of family control. Consequently each generation became less enterprising, and, sheltered behind the vast ramparts of pioneer profits, had less need to be.

There is some truth in such explanations. The aristocratic scale of values, which included amateur status and not apparently trying too hard among the criteria of the 'gentleman', and inculcated them in the 'public schools' which indoctrinated the sons of the risen middle class, was indeed dominant. Being 'in trade' was indeed an awful social stigma; though 'trade' in this sense meant small-scale shopkeeping much more than any activity in which really big money—and therefore social acceptance—could be gained. The wealthy capitalist could certainly, upon shedding his more provincial crudities—and from Edwardian times even without shedding so much as his accent—win his knighthood or peerage; and his children slid into the leisure class without any difficulty whatever. The small family firm certainly predominated. The ramparts of profit were indeed high. A man might have to work hard to raise himself into the middle class, but once in a moderately flourishing line of business, he could take things very easily indeed, unless he made some appalling miscalculation, or hit an abnormally bad patch in the course of an unusually bad slump. Bankruptcy was, according to economic theory, the penalty of the inefficient businessman, and its spectre haunts the novels of Victorian England. But in fact the risks of incurring it were extremely modest, except for the very tiny and marginal man in such occupations as small shopkeeping, the fringes of the building trade, and the underside of a few still dynamic industries such as metals. In Edwardian England, including two years of crisis, the average bankruptcy was for liabilities of no more than £1350. Indeed, the risk of loss through bankruptcies became steadily less during the last 30 years before the first world war. In important industries it was negligible. Thus in 1905–9 (which includes a depression) out of the 2500 or so firms in cotton manufacture, an annual average of only eleven went bankrupt (i.e. something less than ½ per cent).

Freed from the spectre of sudden impoverishment and social ostracism—the very horror of bankruptcy is itself a symptom of its comparative rarity—the British businessman did not need to work much. Frederick Engels may not perhaps be a typical specimen; but there is no sign that until his retirement at the age of 49 with a comfortable life income for himself and the Marx family, he failed to pull his weight in the flourishing firm of Ermen and Engels, cotton merchants of Manchester, though the world knows that he spent as little time as he could on their business.

It is equally true that British business lacked certain non-economic spurs to enterprise; a nation which is already at the top politically and economically, and tends to look down on the rest of the world with self-satisfaction and a little contempt, inevitably does. Americans and Germans might dream of making their destiny manifest; the British knew that it has manifested itself already. There is no doubt, for instance, that a nationalist desire to catch up with the British was largely responsible for the systematic German reinforcement of industry by scientific research: the Germans said so. Nor can one reasonably deny that the typically American desire to have the latest and most up-to-date piece of mechanical equipment, while providing a constant impetus to technical progress, is also often—perhaps mostly—quite economically irrational in origin. The average firm which instals elaborate computer equipment today gets less benefit from it even than the average man who exchanges the simple, small, adaptable, cheap and superior razor blade for the electric razor. An economy which makes capital as well as consumer goods into social status symbols—perhaps because it has no others—has an undoubted advantage in the matter of technical progress over one which has not.

Nevertheless, the value of these observations is limited, if only because very many British businessmen did not conform to them. Before the twentieth century the average British businessman was not a 'gentleman' and never became either a knight, a peer, or even the owner of a country house. It was Lloyd George who made provincial towns into 'cities of dreadful knights'. The absorption of the sons of grocers and cotton spinners into the aristocracy was a *consequence* of the loss of impetus in British business, not its cause; and even today, the acutal management of medium-sized firms (the sort of people who would in 1860–90 certainly have been owner-managers) contains not more than one in five who have been to a university, not much more than one in four who have been to a public school, including not more than one in twenty who have been to one of the top twenty or so public schools.

Sociologically, the incentive to make money fast was by no means weak in Victorian Britain, the attraction of the gentry and aristocracy by no means overwhelming, especially not to the cohorts of middle-class conscious and often nonconformist (i.e. deliberately anti-aristocratic) Northerners and Midlanders, their heads filled with mottoes like 'where there's muck there's brass', and solid pride in their productive achievements. They were proud of the soot and smoke in which they drenched the cities in which they made their money.

Moreover, earlier in the nineteenth century, Britain had certainly not lacked that acute, even irrational, joy in technical progress as such, which we think of as characteristically American. One can hardly imagine the railways being developed, let alone built, in a country or by a business community, which was not *excited* by their sheer technical novelty; for . . . their actual business prospects were known to be relatively modest. It is true that the large literature, of popular science and technology petered out after the 1850s, and that perhaps it had always aimed at a public of 'artisans' rather than at the middle class: at those who wanted to, or ought to, rise rather than at those who had already risen. And yet these were precisely the recruits to the bourgeois army most likely to finger the field marshal's baton in their knapsack. And even in the second half of the century there were enough of them to make the fortune of Samuel Smiles, the bard of the engineers. His *Self Help* came out in 1859. Within four years it has sold 55,000 copies. The romance of technology remained strong enough to make engineering the choice of 75 per cent of boys in at least one large public school of the 1880s.

What is more, there were plainly sectors of the British economy to which few of the complaints of torpor and conservtism applied. There were the West Midlands, whose capital was Birmingham: a jungle of small firms producing essentially consumer goods—often durable metal goods—for the home market. The Midlands did transform themselves after 1860, having previously been very incompletely captured by the industrial revolution. Old and declining industries were replaced, and sometimes actually transformed themselves, as in Coventry, where textiles went down after 1860, but the local watchmakers became the nucleus of the bicycle industry, and through it later of the motor industry. If Lancashire in 1914 was recognisably what it had been in 1840, Warwickshire certainly was not. There were industries, such as parts of the increasingly important engineering and metals manufacture, which had all the bubbling instability of the dynamic private enterprise of the theorists; where men rose and fell, and were on the move. While an average of only eleven firms in the cotton industry went bankrupt every year in 1905–9, an annual average of 390 were bankrupted in the metal industries in the same period, mainly small men attempting independent production with inadequate resources. And there were parts of the economy like the distributive trades, where no one could conceivably speak of stagnation. These also were based on the home market and not on exports.

Simple sociological explanations therefore will not do. In any case, economic explanations of economic phenomena are to be preferred if they are available. There are indeed several, all resting tacitly or openly on the assumption that in a capitalist economy (at all events in its nineteenth-century versions) businessmen will be dynamic only in so far as this is rational by the criterion of the individual firm, which is to maximise its gains, minimise its losses, or possibly merely to maintain what it regards as a satisfactory long-term rate of profit. But since the rationality of the individual firm is inadequate, this may not work out to the best advantage of the economy as a whole, or even of the individual firm. This is partly because the interest of the firm and the economy may diverge in the short run or the long, because the individual firm is to some extent powerless to achieve the objects it would wish to, because it is impossible for the accountancy of the individual firm to determine its best interests, or for other analogous reasons. All these are merely different ways of expressing the proposition that a capitalist economy is not planned, but emerges from a multitude of individual decisions taken in the pursuit of self-interest.

The commonest, and probably best, economic explanation of the loss of dynamism in British industry is that it was the result ultimately of the early and long-sustained start as an industrial power. It illustrates the deficiencies of the private enterprise mechanism in a number of ways. Pioneer industrialisation naturally took place in special conditions which could not be maintained, with methods and techniques which, however advanced and efficient at the time, could not remain the most advanced and efficient, and it created a pattern of both production and markets which would not necessarily remain the one best fitted to sustain economic growth and technical change. Yet to change from an old and obsolescent pattern to a new one was both expensive and difficult. It was expensive because it involved both the scrapping of old investments still capable of yielding good profits, and new investments of even greater initial cost; for as a general rule newer technology is more expensive technology. It was difficult because it would almost certainly require agreement to rationalise between a large number of individual firms or industries, none of which could be certain precisely where the benefit of rationalisation would go, or even whether in undertaking it they were not giving away their money to outsiders or competitors. So long as satisfactory profits were to be made in the old way, and so long as the decision to modernise had to emerge from the sum total of decisions by individual firms, the incentive to do so would be weak. What is more, the general interest of the economy would very likely be lost sight of. . . .

The traditional methods of making profits had as yet not been exhausted, and provided a cheaper and more convenient alternative for modernisation—for a while. To retreat into her satellite world of formal or informal colonies, to rely on its growing power as the hub of international lending, trade and settlements, seemed all the more obvious a solution because, as it were, it presented itself. The clouds of the 1880s and the early 1890s lifted, and what lay before the eye were the shining pastures of cotton exports to Asia, steam-coal exports to the world's ships, Johannesburg gold mines, Argentine tramways and the profits of City merchant banks. In essence, what happened, therefore, was that Britain exported its immense accumulated historic advantages in the underdeveloped world, as the greatest commercial power, and as the greatest source of international loan capital; and had in reserve, the exploitation of the 'natural protection' of the home market and if need be the 'artificial protection' of political control over a large empire. When faced with a challenge, it was easier and cheaper to retreat into an as yet unexploited part of one of these favoured zones rather than to meet competition face to face. Thus the cotton industry merely continued its traditional policy when in trouble, of escaping from Europe and North America into Asia and Africa; leaving its former markets to the exporters of British textile machinery, which made up a quarter of all the country's rapidly increasing machinery exports. In so far as they exported, British coal flowed rapidly in the wake of the British steamship and the vast merchant fleet. Iron and steel relied on the empire and the underdeveloped world, like cotton: by 1913

Argentina and India alone bought more British iron and steel exports than the whole of Europe, Australia alone more than twice as much as the USA. In addition, the steel industry tended—like coal—to rely increasingly on the protection of the home market.

The British economy as a whole tended to retreat from industry into trade and finance, where our services reinforced our actual and future competitors, but made very satisfactory profits. Britain's annual investments abroad began actually to *exceed* her net capital formation at home around 1870. What is more, increasingly the two became alternatives, until in the Edwardian era we see domestic investment falling almost without interruption as foreign investment rises. In the great boom (1911–13) which preceded the first world war, twice as much, or even more, was invested abroad than at home; and it has been argued—and is indeed not unlikely—that the amount of domestic capital formation in the 23 years before 1914, so far from being adequate for the modernisation of the British productive apparatus, was not even quite sufficient to prevent it from slightly running down.

Britain, we may say, was becoming a parasitic rather than a competitive economy, living off the remains of the world monopoly, the underdeveloped world, its past accumulation of wealth and the advance of its rivals.

23. The Nature of the British State*

Tom Nairn

It would be more accurate to say that the nature of the state is the proximate cause of the British crisis. It is our constitution, our political and administrative system, and an associated penumbra of civil hegemony, powerful yet hard to define, which maintain society on its hopeless course.

What is this nature? The subject is so well known that I need spend little time on it here. The unwritten constitution reposing sovereignty upon the Crown in Parliament rather than the people; a two-party political order placing stability before democracy; an élite-controlled bureaucracy no one has ever been able to reconstruct; and a civil structure exhibiting low individual mobility, high group deference, and prominent forms of idological control like the monarchy and the famous British media. The term 'system' has had a bad press recently, because of the ultra-left usage denoting a baleful and omnipotent monster who has thought of everything. However, although far from omnipotent, there is a 'system' here in the sense that these elements do support one another unusually strongly, and have been remarkably slow to disintegrate.

The resultant overall mixture is one of anachronism and strength . . . the two things are inseparable. The ever-recurrent economic crisis is, by near universal consent, caused by failure to 'modernise' the industrial sector. This conventional view identifies weakness with backwardness. It deplores (in the language of the Hudson Institute) such culpable failure to re-orient British Society to fit it for the high industrialism of the twentieth century'. But actually this blatant social archaism has its own strength, too. Furthermore, radical modernisation would probably destroy that strength. It would dramatically augment mobility, under-

*Reproduced from T. Nairn, The future of Britain's crisis', *New Left Review* 13–14, January/April 1979, pp. 49–56.

mine traditional class-consciousness, make the old hierarchies unworkable, menace the comfortable sloth of everyday existence, alter the political party system, upset the City and the Treasury dreadfully . . . and so on.

Of course,such conservative strength actually conserves. The great majority of actors in UK politics depend upon this fact. They *all* want Great Britain to catch up and (in the words of Sir Alan Cottrell, Master of Jesus College, Cambridge, a former chief scientific adviser to the government) 'have a second go at what it has failed so dismally to achieve during the past century: true regeneration of British industry, based on commercial policies, investment, technology, understanding leadership.' Well naturally, who has ever been able to carp at this objective. But wait a minute: not *at any cost*—not, for example, if it means letting a lot of French-type technocrats run the economy, instead of the Treasury, nor if it means compelling the City to direct investment into domestic industries, comprehensivising the public schools, turning Oxbridge into a polytechnic, sacking most of Whitehall, thoroughly annoying the United States and ceasing to be the 'good boy' of the western alliance. The trouble is that any actual programme of crash 'modernisation' is bound to mean things like this. It implies giving up a lot of the good, comfortable habits everyone depends on, as well as the notorious bad habits holding us back. These comfortable habits include the way we are ruled. In short, 'modernisation' is not, and perhaps never has been, a merely economic strategy under UK conditions. It could only be enacted, as distinct from endlessly prospected, through what would really be a revolution. That is, a relatively radical upheaval in the state and the governing ethos. In the past it was only under the special and transient circumstances of war-time that anything like this was ever seriously attempted, particularly between 1940 and 1945.

A revolution, *or* a counter-revolution; a movement of the Left, *or* of the Right. One need not prejudge this issue, when predicting that at some point a political break must occur, and a new regime must actually try to realise the content of all those modernisation programmes. By 'break' I mean that the change of route must be forced, by some novel combination of circumstances. It is inconceivable that it will be chosen through any agency of the existing system. . . . In the long descent to the real crisis, I believe that the conditions of such a break are now relatively imaginable. And I *will* prejudge the issue by suggesting that it is most likely to be of the Right, rather than the Left. Also, I believe . . . that its form is more foreseeable than is usually thought . . .

However, some further development of our predictive model is needed first . . . we are discussing a society where, contrary to many

received opinions, the political culture is all-important and economics—
at least in the sense of industry—is secondary. The true purpose of that
culture, manifested in what its leaders do as distinct from what they
write down in their diaries, is self-preservation. Behind all the new
resolutions is a kind of Venetian consensus, built around a number of
familiar taboos and constraints. And this consensus has been erected
against 'modernsiation' in precisely that sense trumpeted by a century of
economic pundits and other apparent scourges of the *status quo*. But—it
is bound to be objected—this awards a somewhat mysterious character
to the state. Marxists, especially, would be prompt to see the hand of
Idealism at work. How can a system of hegemony be said to enjoy this
degree of autonomy, if not outright independence, *against* the body of
economic and social relations it stands on?

In approaching this problem, let me draw attention to one outstanding recent analysis of the economic crisis. Stephen Blank has argued
that, in any overview of these persistent failures and false starts, one
remarkable fact stands out plainly: the domestic economy was consistently sacrificed to a variety of *external* factors. The repeated body-
blows of 'stop–go' deflation were administered to UK industry in order
to maintain 'Britain's position' *vis-à-vis* the outside world. What was
that position? 'The function of international economic policy was to
restore and enhance Britain's role as a world power and, in particular,
to contribute to the maintenance of the Commonwealth and sterling
systems (as well as the "special relationship" with the USA)', comments
Blank (1977, pp. 686–7) and the core of that role was 'the re-
establishment of sterling as a general international currency and of
London as an open financial marketplace (ibid.). This aim was the
consistent obsession of the state. It was upheld by the Treasury, with
approval from the City, and with scarcely any critical opposition. This
was the general strategy worked out by Keynes towards the end of the
war, and implemented at Bretton Woods. Afterwards, finance capital
did not have to fight to impose its view upon the state; its assumptions
and world-view were, by and large, taken for granted inside the general
tableau of the British great-power mentality. Britain had to stay great;
this meant putting sterling first; that in turn implied balance of payment
constraints and manhandling the industrial sector to fit.

The tale has been told so often, and to the accompaniment of so much
gnashing of teeth and futile rage, that one hesitates even to mention it
again. 'Every single measure taken by British governments in the
post-war period, whether Labour or Conservative, to spur exports . . .
led to a curtailment of exports,' writes one typical commentator.

Every single one penalised the efficient and technologically advanced industries on which growth and exports depend. Sometimes these measures hurt the domestic economy more than they did at other times. But none of them produced permanent improvement in British international accounts even though this was the sole aim of the policy (Peter Drucker, 1969).

Still, we can see now what the goal of the vicious circle has been: preserving the UK's place in the capitalist world, both politically and economically. This dominant aim bears an ancient and unfashionable title: imperialism. The 'external' strategy meant putting the empire first, and it clearly made almost no difference to this attitude that there was less and less empire to defend. What was left, at any given stage, was somehow always more important than the long-suffering industrial sector. Efforts to redress the balance, like Sir Stafford Cripps' Economic Ministry after 1947, or George Brown's Department of Economic Affairs after 1964, were weak and short-lived. After only a year or so, Treasury mandarins could be heard scrunching their bones with discreet relish.

Imperialism, therefore, in the sense of maintaining this special, outward-leaning equilibrium of the UK economy, has been the counterpart of internal, conservative cohesion. . . . Not only do the various elements of our state support each other in that comfortable stagnation the critics have so deplored; they are all in their turn supported by this particular inclination of the economy. This is the material reality. It is for this reason that I believe a generally Marxist model of Britain's condition is sufficient. But it has to be a historical and specific model, one which takes in the *longue durée* of British capitalist development—this means the longest in existence—and, above all, locates that development in wider context. One may then perceive that it is no Hegelian *Geist* which maintains the remarkable, entrenched authority of the British state. It is a set of equally remarkable entrenched interests which, because they have been in the saddle for generations, have assembled around themselves an unusually extensive and varied battery of political and civil hegemony.

Some other recent work helps us gain insight into how this was achieved. In a brilliant article titled 'Wealth, Élites and the Class Structure of Modern Britain', Rubenstein argues that it is a fundamental mistake to overlook the internal contradictions of the capitalist class in modern UK development. One can get nowhere with a one-dimensional model of capitalism, above all in this case. 'It is a logical fallacy,' he points out

to infer from the central importance of industrial capitalism in the dialectical

process the central importance of industrial capitalism for the bourgeoisie.
The notion of the preeminent importance of industrialism and the industrial
revolution has, moreover, affected our view of 19th century British history
totally, and in so insidious a way as to be accepted virtually without thought.
(W.D. Rubenstein, 1977, p. 126)

In reality, one may more accurately read the history of later
nineteenth-century Britain as first the containment, then the defeat, of
industrialism by an older, more powerful and more political
bourgeoisie. This was, of course, the southern, London-based élite, first
mercantile and then financial in its interests, which during this epoch
built up about itself what Rubinstein calls 'its London-based associates
of great influence in 20th century society, like the civil service and the
professions—the familiar "Establishment" of fact and fiction.' This
strong hegemonic bloc then colonised and took over the growing state
power of the Edwardian decade and afterwards.

Consequently, the sinister mystery of 'deindustrialization' has fairly
ancient but quite understandable roots. It lay in the ever-more
dominant interests of what became the most successful and politically
crucial sector of British capitalism: the City of London. By 1914 the
northern-based industrialists had been reduced to a subordinate role. It
is in this quite secondary position that one may trace the origins of the
extraordinarily feeble struggle they have put up against the policies
imposed upon them. The imperial interest made industrialism its
tributary. In this manner the only social class likely to fight effectively
for 'modernization' has been neutered, over most of the period of
Britain's modern 'crisis' mythology. At approximately the same
time—say between 1900 and 1918—both wings of the bourgeoisie
enjoyed combined victory over the emerging political forces of the
working class. This wider class struggle was institutionalised in the form
of the new Labour Party. Through an able strategy of 'social
imperialism' its leaders were persuaded of the soundness of constitution
and parliament, from their point of view; once inside the state, and
exposed to its proditious range of ideological influences, they found it
impossible to get out.

But there is no space here and now to expand too much on this theme.
Suffice it to say there is a quite non-mystical explantion of the
'anti-Ogburn cycle', Great Britain's peculiar resistance to change, or
what Peter Jay used to call 'Englanditis'. I doubt—for example—if
British intellectuals are more irrecuperably Tory in instinct than those of
any other society. A vociferous minority among them has always been
outraged by the system; and in any case anti-technological humanism
and pre-capitalist fantasy appear to be endemic in all capitalist states.

However, it is certainly true that in Britain objective conditions have favoured a rather insouciant, romantic traditionalism on their part. . . . The same conditions have awarded real weight to such attitudes by locking them into a larger, more pervasive ideology which binds together the educational system, politics and the state. It is in this way that the distinctive 'climate' of modern British society was formed. While this can be called a 'capitalist ideology' in an almost uselessly vague way, it is much more important to recognise its specific nature: it is a mercantile, old-bourgois *weltanschauung* and not a neo-capitalist one. Many of its impulses are frankly hostile to 'capitalist' ideas in this narrower, more modern sense; and, of course, this is one important reason why the working class, which has its own motives for hatred of such factory-capitalist virtues, finds traditionalism palatable.

I have no time either to say much about the history of British archaism. In a longer perspective it can be traced to the characteristics of the post-revolution mercantile state. In the more limited context of interest to us here, its founding moment was undoubtedly the containment and curbing of the industrial revolution: at that point, the state chose a strategy of predominantly external development—the kind of imperialist consolidation most congenial to its inherited (and already quite ancient) structure. Set in comparative context, one may say it elected *not* to separate itself more authoritatively from civil society, and become the 'interventionist' guiding structure which the great majority of radical critics from Matthew Arnold onwards have pleaded for in vain. The cost of this strategy was a peculiarly decentred development, and hence a peculiar dependence upon the wider framework of the capitalist world. Priority was given to overseas investment, and to the great complex of banking and other capital institutions which so effectively serviced world capitalism for so long. These had little concern for the lagging industrial economy, but an overwhelming interest in the state of world-wide trade and investment. So, therefore, did the British state. Since the second world war especially, all its governments have subscribed to a uniform foreign policy consensus which (as Blank says) effectivly determined all the internal economic vicissitudes there was so much fuss about. There were periods of dispute between the parties over Europe, true; but they were fairly easily resolved, and nobody challenged the primary policy of adhesion to America's definition of the new Free Trade world.

Depictions of the coming Great Crisis have normally contained an image of the hard, cut-throat world of advanced industrialism—those conditions to which the British had either to adapt by modernisation, or suffer some even worse fate like revolution. As a matter of fact, the UK *ancien régime* did not find world conditions all that distressing, until very recently. Notoriously, it benefited from victory in 1945, then from the post-war boom of the 1950s—when most of the competitors were in no state to cut anyone's throat—and afterwards established a tolerable place within the sustained growth of the 1960s. This was an ever-more dependent place, certainly. Yet as long as a general expansion was proceeding, 'dependency' was classified as sin only by the modernising, industrial-minded pundits. They could complain that the British overseas-oriented economy was being confirmed in its parasitism by these conditions, and sinking back into the ruts of anachronism. But the spokesmen of the establishment could reply, also quite correctly, that the really successful sector of British capitalism was flourishing anew and keeping the entire system afloat.

These were, surely, the general conditions referred to initially, the crisis which has been ever with us yet never truly critical. The industrial base fell farther and farther behind, its periodic troubles provoking ever wilder schemes for Great Leaps forward, and ever-increasing cynicism when, inexorably, these faltered into a few nervous sideways steps. But it was kept in forward motion none the less, by the massive advance of the whole world economy. And as long as this was the case, the booming City sector could afford to ignore the problem. Once the spectre of white-hot technological revolution had been exorcised, the state too evolved normally. Social imperialism was pursued into the last age of a shrunken empire, as state expenditure and employment continued to mount. Right-wing critics found this growing top-heaviness of the state insupportable, and identified it as the newest cause of 'Britain's economic problem' . . . . so far as the external force-field is concerned, things have begun to change since 1973. The global economy has sunk into stagnation. With its peculiar degree of dependence, Britain has begun to suffer much more severely than at any time since the 1930s. From Bretton Woods up to the IMF rescue operation of 1976–77, we enjoyed a relatively complaisant international framework. But if the recession continues for years—the most widely held view at present—then this will disappear. The circumstances of her negotiated decay are on the way out.

24. The Rivalry of Financial and Industrial Capital*

Andrew Glyn and Bob Sutcliffe

One cause of competitive weakness [has been] the relatively low level of investment in industrial capacity, especially since 1900. This led to a slower growth of productivity than in rival countries. One of the major reasons for this low investment was low profitability. Profitability was not always higher in other industrial countries, but German and American industry has never relied as much as British on the supply of finance from its own resources often instead borrowing from banks and outside investors. This exposes another of the recurrent themes: the comparative separation of industrial from financial capital.

There have been many examples of the rivalry of finance and industry at work. At times finance has preferred free trade (because it coexisted with free movement of capital) when protection would have been beneficial for industry. This was certainly true in the years between 1880 and 1913 and again after the first world war. Finance favoured a high exchange rate when industry needed devaluation, and this was true not only in the years after 1920 when the rate was forced up to an absurd level and held there until 1931, but again from the late 1950s, until 1967 at least. Finance has pressed for high interest rates to attract foreign funds and maintain the reserves while industry has wanted low interest rates to cheapen the finance of investment: again, the 1920s were such a time, and so were the 'stop' phases of the cycles of the 1950s and 1960s. Finally, finance has opposed increases in government spending to avoid shaking international confidence in the currency at times when industry undoubtedly needed a higher level of demand: 1931 provides the most obvious example of this, though fewer industrialists realised it at the time when it happened again in 1966. Of course, this conflict is not

*Reprinted from A. Glyn and B. Sutcliffe, *British Capitalism, Workers and the Profits Squeeze* (Harmondsworth, Penguin, 1972), pp. 41–3, by permission of Penguin Books Ltd. Copyright © Andrew Glyn and Bob Sutcliffe, 1972.

absolute: now and again the interests of the banks and of large sections of industry, especially the large exporters, have coincided.

However, over the years the divergence has grown bigger. It first became substantial in the years of imperialism before the first world war. It grew again over the period from 1930 to 1950, during which time industry was restructured to rely much less on foreign and more on the home market than in the nineteenth century. For a time after the second world war their interests seemed to merge over the sterling area, which formed a protected market for exports of goods and capital and for financial services. But as trade liberalisation was extended and the competitive position deteriorated, the Sterling Area was of less and less benefit to industry. The financiers nevertheless believed in the importance of sterling's world currency role in maintaining London's position as a financial centre; and they resolutely opposed all talk of devaluation, which, it was correctly thought, would end the reserve role of sterling by confirming the worst fears of those whose confidence in it was waning.

This important contradiction in the structure of capitalism in Britain seems itself to be the result of two things. One of these is the even pace of development of industrial capitalism in different countries during the nineteenth century; the other is the basic contradiction between capital and labour. The appearance of the division between industry and finance coincided with the accentuation of foreign competition for British industry. To face this competition vast new investments in modern industrial plant had to be financed; that would have required in Britain the same integration of industry and finance as existed in Germany, France and America. This did not happen and the alternative structural change in capitalism which did take place was that financial capital decided to look outwards and invest abroad. By this route capitalism in Britain became imperialism.

The banks and the City did not want to involve themselves directly in domestic industry because they evidently expected larger—or at least more secure—profits outside England. And it is very likely that one of the underlying reasons for this was the realisation that the growing strength of the working class would make the profitability of industrial investment at home increasingly precarious. And on the whole, although the advantage in the class struggle has shifted back and forth, they have proved to be right.

25. The Role of Defence Expenditure in Industrial Decline*

Nigel Harris

What are the reasons for the industrial decline? Since at least the mid-1950s, British capitalism has apparently had a consistent tendency for profit rates in domestic industry to be low relative to its nearest rivals. Immediately after the second world war, only British and US industry remained intact, and profit rates were high in supplying the devastated rivals in Europe and, for the US, Japan. The return to British capitalism were not used to renovate the old depreciated stock, or at least not on the scale adequate to compete with the leading overseas rivals. Some went abroad, some into services, and an important chunk into the very substantial military spending programme. Defence spending was—when added to the much larger US programme—vital for the stabilisation of world capitalism, and served the external purposes of British imperialism, but its effect on British manufacturing was disastrous.

The cumulative effect of a sustained failure to invest is at the heart of the growing crisis of British capitalism. By now, the British workforce is, relative to the workforce in other advanced capitalist countries, required to work increasingly hard, for longer hours for lower pay, and, because of the relatively low capital per worker, at disastrously low levels of productivity: at some 40 per cent below the levels of Germany and France in manufacturing in the mid-1970s.

Low profit rates induce poor investment performances. Since the early 1950s, both British and US capitalism have had the lowest rates of investment of the advanced capitalist countries. The US level hovered aroung 17 to 18 per cent (investment as a proportion of gross domestic production) in the 1960s, declining to 15 per cent in 1975. Britain's 15

*This is an extract from an article which first appeared in *International Socialism*, quarterly journal of the Socialist Workers Party, available from IS Journal, PO Box 82, London EC.

per cent rate in the 1960s rose very slightly to 18 per cent in 1975. Most recently, Italy's former rates of around 22 per cent have declined to 18 per cent. Compare these proportions to West Germany's 25 to 27 per cent (although by the mid-1970s, the German rate had declined to 23 per cent) or the spectacular performance of Japan, rising from 24 per cent in 1960 to 37 per cent (1973), and still hovering around 32 per cent.

British employers have annually created the lowest level of gross fixed capital per head of the population (but Britain has been overtaken over the past decade by Italy). Gross fixed capital formation per worker in manufacturing has run at about a quarter of the US figures and a third of its other nearest rivals.

All elements of the central strategy of British capitalism have become subordinated to this question, which in its turn flows from the past structure of British imperialism. Thus, the programme of scientific and technology research has been wilfully twisted to defence questions, producing far fewer innovations for civil industry to develop. Government finance, the major part of R&D spending, has been directed to improve aircraft, particular military prototypes, to aerospace and military electronics; that is, the British ruling class has endeavoured to compete with the leading rivals in the system, the US and the Soviet Union, but with nothing like the industrial base to support such activities. By contrast, the much lower levels of R&D spending in West Germany have been devoted heavily to civil industry; as a result, the value per ton weight of German machinery exports is about double that of Britain. Expenditure on training workers has followed the same direction, so that now Britain has one of the lowest rates of participation in full time education in the 16–18-year-old group. The numbers completing engineering apprenticeships fell by one-third in the 1970s.

But the most dramatic and recurring demonstrtion of the incapacity of British industrial capitalism to compete with its rivals is the external balance of trade. When British capitalism expands, imports rise much more sharply than exports—that is, British industrial capacity cannot meet home demand, nor can it export enough to cover the cost of imports. This produced throughout the 1950s and 1960s the familiar lurching of 'stop–go', a mild expansion, followed by a payment crisis and the braking of expansion. The payments problem is just as severe now in trade terms but masked by the arrival of oil exports.

Take four key sectors of manufacturing, at the heart of the engineering industry. By 1976, imports took—of the domestic market— 53 per cent in instrument engineering, 32 per cent of electrical engineering, 42 per cent of shipbuilding and marine engineering, and 31 per cent of vehicle production. In the case of vehicles, the downward trend has been very long in the making and very rapid in its final results. 4.5 per cent of the domestic market was taken by imports in 1963, 11.5 per cent in 1970, and now—nearly 60 per cent. In fact, exports now are limited in the main to a narrow range of luxury cars and the internal transactions of multinationals (General Motors, Ford, Chrysler-Citroën). Only a couple of years ago, car component manufacturers consoled themselves that, for every £1 of assembled car imports, there were £2 of car component exports. In the first half of 1979, however, for the first time, the exports of cars and components failed to cover the deficit on the import of vehicles (£210 million).

The high value of sterling acted as the final straw. In textiles, the trade deficit has nearly doubled in the past year. Chemicals, which recorded massive export surpluses in the 1960s, is now threatened with massive imports. Finally, services themselves have begun to show signs of weakness as well.

The balance between imports and exports is not the most accurate index of the performance of British capitalism. The structure of informal state controls, domestic monopolies, public subsidies (whether direct or through tax concessions, credit terms, etc.) changes any simple reading of the meaning of the trade balance. to a greater or lesser extent, all advanced capitalist countries cheat the spirit of the formal rules of international trade to push up exports, robbing the domestic population to subsidise foreign buyers. so that as imports have 'invaded' Britain so British manufacturing sold abroad has risen from 15 per cent in 1966 to 19 per cent in 1971 and 22 per cent in 1974. In the case of the four engineering sectors mentioned earlier, they are also the sectors with the highest share of output going to exports—55 per cent for instrument engineering, 37 per cent for electrical engineering, 34 per cent for shipbuilding and marine engineering, and 44 per cent for vehicle production. In addition, 45 per cent of mechanical engineering output is exported. But the total value of exports does not rise as rapidly as the value of imports nonetheless.

26. The Strength of the Working Class*

Andrew Kilpatrick and Tony Lawson

I

In the past few years a considerably body of literature has focused on the relatively poor competitive performance of the UK economy since the second world war . . . and in particular has highlighted its relatively low productivity growth. . . . These studies however have tended to ignore workplace conflict over the organisation of production, although the resolution of this conflict significantly influences overall factor productivity.

The labour process has also been largely neglected in those studies which have recognised that the relative industrial decline of the UK economy has been underway for over a century. The supply side of the economy has of course by no means been completely ignored: many studies have detailed how since at least 1870 Britain has been systematically slow at widely adopting new products and processes even when these were invented (and sometimes even manufactured) in Britain, while others have drawn attention to relatively high manning levels in the UK. Even so, the focus of attention has usually been on 'entrepreneurial failure' or on so-called 'institutional' factors such as Britain's failure to develop a comprehensive technical education system in the nineteenth century. While the importance of factors such as the educational infrastructure is not disputed we shall argue that Britain's industrial performance cannot be understood without some analysis of the labour process.

The role of collective bargaining and the strength of job-based worker organisation are factors which must be carefully considered. In the UK, collective bargaining over all aspects of work takes place at local as well

*Reproduced with permission from *Cambridge Journal of Economics*, vol. 4, 1980, pp. 85–102. Copyright 1980 by Academic Press Inc. (London) Limited.

as at national level. However, the ability of workers to bargain with management at the plant level is essentially a defensive strength: workers attempt to maintain working conditions and living standards. Through the bargaining process workers can only check management's intentions to reorganise production. Even so the highly decentralised structure of bargaining which exists in the UK is not without significance. It tends to inhibit long-term planning and coordinated decision-making . . . and works against quick responses to changes in the organisation of work, and generally restrains productivity growth. Bargaining over conditions in the workplace can delay the adoption and diffusion of new techniques and/or lead to manning levels above what they would otherwise have been. Disagreement in negotiations often leads to disruptions which give rise to unmet delivery dates and generally affect availability, while the resulting slow productivity growth usually means low quality or poor reliability.

Section II of this paper looks at the relatively early acceptance of mass trade unionism and the evolutionary nature of industrial relations in the UK and draws some comparisons with the experiences of other industrial countries. The main intention of this section is not to explain the development of the highly decentralised structure of bargaining in the UK, but to indicate its present-day economic significance. The nature of collective bargaining cannot be regarded as unchanging, of course, but neither should the influence of job-based worker organisation on economic development be seen as a temporary 'aberration' which can be easily undermined by government strategies designed to restore competitiveness.

II. THE LABOUR PROCESS

Early 'acceptance' of trade unionism in the UK
The end of suppression of organised collective resistance by the military and the courts occurred in Britain in the nineteenth century. Between 1867 and 1875, a series of Acts were passed which made it easier for workers to strike without being imprisoned (Master and Servant act 1867; Employers and Workman Act 1875); which helped secure the legal status of trade unions (Trade Unions Act 1871); and which legalised peaceful picketing (Conspiracy and Protection of Property Act 1871).

Partly as a result, there was a rapid growth in the number of trade unions, with membership of those affiliated to the newly-formed Trades Union Congress (TUC) more than doubling from 250,000 in 1869 to

510,000 in 1873. At first, these were organisations of skilled workers only, defending acquired customs and their privileged status as craftsmen. However, by the 1880s unskilled workers were also able to form stable organisations. These 'new' unions of unskilled workers started out critical of the older craft unions for their inward-looking nature and élitism, and tended to concentrate their energies on national issues. But, by the turn of the century, they too had adopted craft union practices and were possessive of past gains and acquired customs.

This establishment of customs or standards has been an important element in the development of the labour process. As soon as any situation has been regarded as the norm—whether it refers to levels of pay or conditions of work—then efforts by management to reduce the standard, to erode past gains, have, where possible, been resisted. This last qualification is important: if the interests of similar groups are the same everywhere, then differences in ability to further or to defend those interests partly explain systematic divergences in paths of development. It is therefore significant that, unlike in other countries, trade unions in the UK were legalised and experienced a sharp increase in membership well before the turn of the twentieth century. Thus, growth of real power by workers to resist changes and to defend standards coincided with customs and norms that existed before the introduction of mass production techniques. It appeared when the forms of organisation and bargaining took place on a craft-type basis. the system of industrial relations which evolved was thus highly decentralised, uncoordinated and relatively unsuited to the later needs of mass production.

Of course changes in the organisation of production were continually enforced by management, although worker resistance reduced the speed of change. Where management had accommodated itself to workers' organisations, through the establishment of procedures and the recognition of norms and customs, these procedures and standards were not easy to overcome. Confrontations did occur and workers' organisations were not always able to maintain even the pretence of 'skill' status. As Penn (1978) illustrates, in a comparison of the development of cotton and engineering workers' organisations, the ability to maintain craft status was largely 'a direct function of the relative strength of labour prior to the development of mechanised factory production' (Penn, 1978, p. 27). However, while the strength of resistance within Britain was unevenly distributed, it remains the case that the relative strength of labour prior to these developments tended generally to be greater everywhere in Britain than in other countries, so that craft union practices were better able to survive.

Britain's evolutionary system of industrial relations

Some international comparisons. While early development is an important factor in explaining the unique degree to which trade unionism has penetrated the workplace in the UK, the latter phenomenon is also due to the fact that 'Britain has had the most evolutionary system of industrial relations in the twentieth century' (Thompson and Hunter, 1978, p. 85). Indeed, Britain's experience contrasts sharply with events that occurred in other countries which also industrialised in the nineteenth century. Not only did these countries undergo upheavals due to more rapid industrial transformation, but they also experienced political traumas, sometimes associated with (defeats in) war and with strong state or legal influence over development.

In Germany, for example, the labour movement was suppressed by the Nazis, with unions being abolished in 1933 and unable to re-form until 1945. By this time organisational impediments to industrial unionism had disappeared. Moreover, the western forces supervising the German reconstruction favoured total centralisation. This latter objective was only dropped following strong opposition from the British TUC. German trade unionists aimed to create a unified structure to avoid the ideological, religious and craft divisions of the Weimar period, with the result that the present day structure is highly centralised.

The suppression of the 1871 Paris commune effectively broke up the French unions. . . . Although legal recognition was granted in 1884, it implied only the right of association; there was no obligation on the part of employers to negotiate. Unlike in Britain, no system of collective bargaining arose to give legitimacy to existing customs or procedures. 'The very notion of the obligation to bargain has always met with strong opposition from the courts, and it was only in 1971 that a law was enacted providing for penalties against the party that would not answer a demand for bargaining' (Dunlop and Galenson, 1978, p. 220).

In Italy, Mussolini replaced the Confederation of Labour by government-controlled syndicates, which persisted until the overthrow of Fascism in 1945. Moreover, the state-controlled unions which he set up were never properly dismantled in the post-war period, so that the centralised nature of organisation has continued. Indeed, for most of the post-war period there has been no direct union presence in factories in Italy or in France. Only since 1970 in Italy and since 1968 in France has this begun to change.

The growth of collective bargaining was also a slow process in the USA. The major development came in the 1930s with the passing of the National Labour Relations (Wagner) Act, and the subsequent expansion into union organisation. Even so, federal government employees are denied the right to strike and, in practice, the right to bargain is limited. A number of union practices have been banned since 1947, when employers successfully challenged the Wagner Act on the basis that it conceded too much to unions (Labour/Management Relations Act [Taft-Hartley]). The legal framework of collective bargaining has remained essentially unchanged since 1947.

The conciliatory approach to industrial relations in the UK. The development of industrial relations in the UK stands in sharp contrast to some of the experiences of other old industrial economies. As British management in the late nineteenth century came to accept the reality of workers' power in many industries, it took a more conciliatory approach to workers' organisation than its overseas counterparts and attempted early on to institutionalise current practices, customs and the resolutions of disputes into workplace or firm 'procedures'. In this way management sought to minimise the number of disruptions, not through challenging the basis of worker resistance, but rather by attempting to limit its effect. Friedman (1977), in discussing the use of procedure and 'other forms of conciliation' from 1870 onwards, suggests that 'the most crucial development of the capitalist mode of production in Britain during the 1870s to 1914 was the acceptance by many employers of organised worker resistance as a permanent reality in their day-to-day dealings with workers (American acceptance came somewhat later)' (p. 97). Unions were an active party to forming agreements with employers for they saw in them a means of defence against further losses of control over the organisation of work. Moreover, there were sectional gains to groups of workers, as procedures were established which related to promotion and discharge. In this way, although many of the workers were relatively unskilled, they gained some protection from the competitive forces of the 'external' labour market. Thus the structure of decentralised decision-making and internal 'collective' bargaining was further reinforced.

The conciliatory approach to industrial relations adopted by management must also be set alongside the existence of formal and informal imperial markets, which reduced the necessity for prolonged confrontation with workers over the restructuring of work. Thus, at the turn of the twentieth century, British firms sought to make profits through foreign investment in, and exports to, semi-protected regions, rather than to embark on a path of continuous confrontation with British workers over large-scale modernisation and integration of British industry.

Contracting. The maintenance of a decentralised structure of bargaining seems also to have been partly due to the existence of systems of internal labour contract that were widespread in the nineteenth and early twentieth centuries. Many of the early British trade unions were primarily associations of subcontractors and it seems likely that the internal contract acted as a means of job control, and structural support of craft-type organisations. . . . In so far as the subcontractor controlled hiring and firing, this power could be utilised to maintain exclusiveness and control of access to jobs. This structure of control may have been preserved because the elimination of contracting was brought about by unskilled workers rather than by employers. In the steel industry, for example, the end of subcontracting was brought about by underhands in separate unions opposed to contracting, but who

> retained much of the contractors' control over the pace of work. Scientific management made little or no impact and employers were unable to easily adjust manning levels and were obliged to take disputes through the disputes procedure where unions were as successful in establishing precedence over manning and work rules as they were over wage rates. (Elbaum and Wilkinson, 1979, p. 300.)

The experience of war. The experience of two world wars is yet a further consideration. Unlike the continental industrial countries Britain was neither occupied nor defeated, and it seems that the experience in the second world war reinforced resistance to centralisation, and actually strengthened job-based worker organisation in the UK. For example, the 'spirit of cooperation' which the 'war effort' demanded led to the establishment of Joint Production Committees, particularly in the engineering industries. These committees were factory-based, with the union members (often shop stewards) elected by ballot, and were concerned with all aspects of wartime production within the factory. These committees spread in factories throughout Britain, including in those with no previous tradition of shop stewards. . . . Thus, while temporarily performing a major role in 'national interest corporatism', these committees formalised and reinforced the institution of shop-floor trade unionism. Moreover they gave workplace-based organisation an even greater independence from trade union officials than had previously been the case and eventualy came to be regarded by workers as the custom or norm.

The labour process and industrial decline
Factors such as those outlined above all played a role in the maintenance of a highly decentralised structure of bargaining in the UK.

That the Donovan Report (HMSO, 1968) found 'that the craft system is deeply rooted in much of British industry' is testomony to the early strength of British unions and to the active role workers' organisations have played in shaping the technical and social conditions of production. And although amalgamations have greatly reduced the total number of unions in the twentieth century—from 1269 in 1913 to 488 in 1975—it remains the case that they have done very little to simplify the overall pattern, or to centralise control. . . . Decentralised bargaining has constrained productivity growth in the UK, compared with elsewhere. In particular, it has tended to lead to higher manning levels and slower rates of adoption and diffusion than would otherwise be the case.

The reorganisation of production continually took place, of course, but where resistance—or the threat of resistance—was strong, concessions were obtained, concerning either pay or the conditions of work in general. Frequently these concessions provided the basis for further resistance so that one way or another industrial change proceeded more slowly than it would have done in the absence of resistance; and proceeded much more slowly than in other countries.

We have concentrated at length on the active role of workers' resistance in shaping the labour process because this is an important element in understanding the uneven development of the structure of production across countries. The role of management has not been, and cannot be, ignored—although management designs are not the only important factor, as some American radicals are apt to imply. By the same token it is not obvious that the relatively weak competitive position of the British economy can be seen to be the result of 'entrepreneurial failue'. For example, if British management, when faced with increased competition in certain export markets, chooses to exploit protected markets rather than to modernise the methods of production, then the role played by its awareness of workers' ability to resist cannot be ignored. Rather, the outcome must be seen as the resolution of conflicting interests at all levels of society; certainly conflict over the reorganisation of production cannot be neglected. . . .

The labour process cannot be omitted from the deindustrialisation debate. While we can still agree with Landes (Gomulka, quoted in Beckerman, 1979, p. 18) that: 'All evidence agrees on the technological backwardness of much of British manufacturing industry—on leads lost, opportunities missed, [and] markets relinquished', it is clear that this outcome cannot be interpreted as a series of 'mistakes', but as the logical result of the opportunity for change being constrained by organised resistance and obviated by the existence of relatively protected markets, among other factors.

However, this history has given rise to attitudes, structures of organisations and procedures for decision-making, which work to inhibit rapid adjustment to changing trends. The social and institutional factors which make for a relatively slow rate of growth of productivity are now deeply rooted in the social structure of British society. . . .

This discussion should not, of course, be seen as implying criticism of worker organisation. Rather, it is a comment on the nature of the competitive system and its uneven development. Worker resistance can usually only check management intentions; it cannot control developments. Nor are unions opposed to new technology *per se*. It is clear from the TUC's position on technological developments, as set out in 'a programme for action' that it accepts the need for, and indeed wishes to encourage, the adoption of new technology. Understandably, the programme is also concerned to avoid redundancies and to improve conditions of work. The important point is that it takes for granted the right of workers to bargain and negotiate over all aspects of investment. . . . Indeed, it argues that 'full agreement of negotiating issues should be a precondition of technological change' (TUC, 1979).

The ability to achieve collective bargaining is essentially a defensive strength. Workers bargain to maintain living standards and working conditions, or at least to be partly compensated for detrimental changes to work conditions, skill status, and so on. However, negotiations can take time, and the likely opposition of workers may even deter management from taking up the potential for change. Of course, the defence of standards or 'norms' is carried out by all members of all societies. The important factor in the sphere of international competition is the relative ability to achieve these aims. If UK workers achieve the ability to bargain over the conditions of introduction of a new process, where in another country it is brought in without negotiation, the latter country will tend to experience faster productivity growth. Of course, contrasts are never so sharp, but on the other hand nor are conditions everywhere equal. Development across countries has been uneven. . . .

Britain is an old industrial country with a highly decentralised system of collective bargaining. The job-based strength of worker organisation is such that management has often only embarked on confrontations over restructuring production when alternative strategies have appeared more costly than the ensuing disruptions (usually in terms of lost sales). In fact, in the face of international competition, a typical management strategy has been to use this situation to threaten a plant's closure unless such a restructuring is accepted. With a domestic market partly sheltered from such competition this argument loses force; and, indeed, the management incentive to restructure production is reduced, as the result of import controls plus fiscal reflation, with the consequence that productivity growth will tend to be lower than it would otherwise have been. This latter tendency will be partly or wholly offset in the short run, if there is spare capacity in the economy which can be utilised to raise the level of productivity. However, in the longer run, given the nature of worker resistance and the relatively monopolistic position in which firms operating in the domestic market would find themselves, the temptation to increase profits through raising prices, rather than through introducing new technology and restructuring work, would be large. Moreover, these factors would also provide the temptation for exporters to switch from producing for the competitive export market to producing for the protected domestic market—a move which again would reduce the incentive for producers to adopt the latest techniques and raise productivity growth. Indeed, the situation would be not unlike that facing Britain in the late nineteenth century, when competition was increasing in domestic and export markets after 1880, while protection was afforded by the markets of the empire. In this situation, UK exporters found it to their advantage to avoid conflict with workers over an accelerated remoulding of the structure of production, and instead redirected sales to the new or protected markets often with the aid of capital exports.

27. Working-Class Strength: A Counter-view*

Laurence Harris

The view that labour's strength and commitment to class struggle has been the cause of low profitability and industrial decline has had an international dimension which argues that profitability is not only low in absolute terms but low relative to other countries and this has resulted from a uniquely militant strain in British labour. The figures do show that profitability was low relatively to other countries. In the UK, the net rate of return on capital in manufacturing industry was lower than that in West Germany, the USA and Canada throughout the period 1955 to 1978. The year 1970 gives a striking illustration: in that year the (gross) rate of return in UK manufacturing industry was 10 per cent as compared with 40 per cent in Japan, 19 per cent in West Germany and 17 per cent in the USA. The comparative weakness of UK profits tempts many to accept that it has been caused by the strength of British trade unions compared to other countries, but has it? The short answer is no; but a longer answer is warranted to establish the point.

Trade union strength could affect profits in two ways: first, by forcing wages up at the expense of profits and, second, by effectively fighting for control of the methods and pace of work thereby limiting productivity (in the extreme, by blocking new technology and working practices). Wage earnings did rise relatively fast and productivity did rise relatively slowly in the UK during the 1970s. The net effect of changes in wage costs (per hour of labour) and changes in productivity (as output per hour of labour) is a change in the wage cost of each unit of output. In the UK wage costs per unit of output went up 15.5 per cent per year between 1970 and 1980, while in West Germany they rose at a rate of only 5.5 per cent, in the USA at 6.2 per cent, and in Japan at 6.6

*Reproduced from L. Harris, 'British capital: manufacturing, finance and multinational corporations', in D. Coates, G. Johnston and R. Bush (eds.), *A Socialist Anatomy of Britain*, (London, Polity, 1985), pp. 14–17.

per cent. Figures like these are used to lend support to the idea that Britain's trade unions have caused low profits, but a closer look at the evidence does not support the argument.

First, the data for the previous decade, 1960 to 1970 show that wages increased relatively slowly and productivity relatively fast so that UK wage costs per unit of output went up no faster than other major countries, yet, as we have seen, UK profit rates were declining throughout the 1960s and they remained low compared to other countries. In the UK wage costs per unit rose at 2.8 per cent per annum in that decade, which was the same rate as Japan and West Germany experienced (2.7 per cent). If labour militancy was the problem, its effect on Britain's comparative performance was not strongly evident in the 1960s even though those were the years when developments such as the powerful shop stewards' movement in the car industry were at their height.

Second, there is no reliable evidence identifying trade union militancy as a cause of either high rates of wage increase or low productivity growth. Given the certainty with which employers, governments and Fleet Street claim that trade unions are at the root of Britain's problems, it is important to be clear on what the evidence does show.

The most entrenched idea which gives credence to the employers' claim is that Britain is very strike-prone, and much more so than countries with more successful industries. In fact, in a comparison of working days lost through strikes in 16 major countries, the UK was almost half way up the league. It ranked seventh in working days lost (averge number per thousand employees per year) between 1967 and 1976, while Canada, Italy, the USA, Australia, Finland and Ireland lost a greater number of days in strikes. Throughout the period 1964 to 1976 the United States lost many more days in strikes each year than the UK, but wage costs per unit of output rose less than in the UK (reflecting lower wage increases or higher productivity growth, or both). The figures for annual average days lost per 1000 employees in 1964–66 were 870 in the USA and 190 in the UK; between 1967–76 they were 1349 and 788 respectively. Yet in the USA unit wage costs rose only 1.5 per cent per annum from 1960 to 1970 and 6.2 per cent per annum from 1970 to 1980 while in the UK they rose at an annual rate of 2.8 per cent and 15.5 per cent in those periods. Thus, not only has the strike record in the UK not been particularly high, but also a comparison of the UK and USA suggests that there is no direct, simple link between days lost in strikes and industrial performance.

International comparisons of the UK strike record are one way to assess their importance; another is to judge how widespread strikes have been. Strikes in British manufacturing industries have been highly concentrated in a few large firms so that their direct impact on wages and productivity, if any, was not widespread. Thus, for the period 1971 to 1975 (when union membership and strike activity was rising) the Department of Employment found that 98 per cent of manufacturing establishments employing about 80 per cent of that sector's workforce experienced no official strikes in an average year.

But the strike record is not the only way to judge whether trade unions have led to excessive wage increases or low productivity growth: trade union strength could be high even if the number of days lost in strikes is not. Economists have attempted to measure trade union strength in a variety of more or less arbitrary ways and then calculate statistically whether it has been related to either wage increases or productivity growth. These studies have not produced reliable evidence that wage increases have accelerated as a result of trade union strength or that productivity has been held back by it. Certainly casual impressions held by people who have lived through the changing struggles of the 1970s and 1980s can lead to a feeling that trade union strength has been a major fctor in industry. After all, the high wage increases in the early 1970s coincided with a considerable expansion in trade union membership, and the declining union membership in industry in the early 1980s has coincided with low nominal wage increases. But several statistical studies have now established that changing union membership is the effect of such economic conditions in contrast to their cause.

Industrial capital, and especially manufacturing industry, is relatively weak in the UK and has been in decline. Its condition does depend ultimately on the relation between capital and workers, but this does not imply that the cause of its weakness lies in its workers' strength; industrial relations should not be seen as a zero-sum game. There is no hard evidence showing that trade union strength has been the cause of industrial capital's problems. But there are several reasons for thinking that if trade unions had been *more* militant industrial capital would have been forced to be more competitive. Workers in British industry have not won high real wages. They are among the worst paid of the advanced capitalist countries. This is a sign of trade union docility and it has enabled British industrial capital to persist with old, inefficient plant. Cheap labour has meant that such old equipment could continue to generate profits while industrial capital in other countries modernised and eventually came to undercut the British, but a militant trade union movement struggling effectively for high wages would have made labour costly and forced capital to modernise. That type of trade union strength would have involved a struggle for the planned, agreed and controlled implementation of modern technologies.

Thus, a focus on British workers' unique militancy does not help us understand the character and weakness of the industrial fraction of British capital; the weakness of the forms of struggle British workers have adopted is more significant. This, however, is an unusual view. The stylised facts that have dominated public images of the unions, together with some more rigorous research, support the opposite view. The image of workers in the car industry, for example, engaged in demarcation disputes between themselves and in shop steward-led struggles to wrest control of production from management leads automatically to a view that union strength hindered productivity; why else would aggressive managers like Sir Michael Edwardes have had to try to smash that union power in the late 1970s? Similarly, the research which suggests that the increased output achieved on average from investment in new plant is lower in Britain than elsewhere, is taken to imply that it is not lack of new machinery but workers' resistance against operating it intensively that is the root of the problems.

But such conclusions are not warranted. The fight to defend demarcation lines and the shop stewards' movement were a mark of the fragmentation and weakness of British unions. Those sectional and local strengths were a symptom of the weakness unions suffered from in confronting capital at the level of the industry, or the firm, or within tripartite corporatist bodies such as NEDC. Unable to enforce demands at those levels for a high-wage economy with rational coordinated investment (on French or, in part, Japanese lines) union members were only left with the possibility of defending their position at sectional and local levels. This was encouraged by the fact that British management in its turn has been fragmented, plant-based and with short-term orientation rather than a force for coordinated, rational accumulation of industrial capital. The Edwardes' strategy was not a sign of union strength; instead, his easy victory in labour relations was a sign that what had been presented as workers' strength for decades was in fact very precarious and was lost as soon as the management structure and style that had facilitated it was rationalised.

The relatively low productivity achieved with new plant in British industry is also explained by the general conditions under which capital is accumulated and particularly the absence of a long-term rational plan for Britain's industrial development. It is not legitimate to attribute it to a single cause such as workers' militancy; indeed, the inability of unions to impose a strategy of high wages and rational accumulation on capital is a major part of the explanation.

The failure of industrial capital to adopt such a strategy was not only connected with the character of the labour movement. The form and nature of the British state have also been crucial factors in preventing it from adopting the strategic role played by the French or Japanese states. And the impact upon industry by a separate fraction of British capital, financial capital (or the lack of such an impact in the case of Germany and Japan) has been a major problem in its own right.

28. The Passivity of the State*

Bob Rowthorn

It is a commonplace to point out that Britain's present crisis is the culmination of more than 100 years of economic decline, during which its position as the world's leading industrial power has been destroyed, and that its economy is now one of the weakest in Western Europe. The prospect of such a decline, and its consequences for the British people, were already clear to such writers as J.A. Hobson at the end of the last century, and have been a familiar theme of commentators ever since. Despite such warnings, however, governments have been unwilling to confront the problem of decline or to act decisively so as to halt it.

The British state has displayed an extraordinary passivity and incapacity in the face of growing economic difficulties, and has never seriously pursued a concerted modernising strategy of the kind implemented, on occasion, in countries such as France or Japan. This is true even in the post-war period when, apart from a brief flirtation with the idea of planning, governments have not even tried to develop a coherent and positive programme for the regeneration of British industry, nor to create the kind of civil service and state apparatus required to implement such a programme.

The hesitant and ineffectual character of government policy since the war is the outcome of a particular balance of class forces in Britain during this period. Capital has in general been opposed to a policy of vigorous planning and detailed state intervention in industry, whilst the working class has lacked the consciousness or unity of purpose to impose such a policy. The reasons for capitalist 'opposition' are both economic and political. On a political level, most capitalists are frightened of any really determined and coherent policy to modernise

*Reproduced from B. Rowthorn, 'The past strikes back', in S. Hall and M. Jacques (eds.), *The Politics of Thatcherism* (London, Lawrence & Wishart 1983), pp. 63–68.

industry and plan its development. They believe that such a policy is the thin end of the wedge and, if successful, would legitimise socialist ideas in popular consciousness, and give rise to pressure for more radical forms of state intervention, or even for outright expropriation. Such a belief is well founded and reflects a sound appreciation of the way in which capital maintains its hegemony in British society. Britain is a highly proletarianised country. It has a small petty bourgeoisie, the peasantry disappeared long ago, and the bulk of the population consists of wage and salary earners and their dependants. There is a strong trade union movement and, until recently, a substantial proportion of the working class supported the Labour Party. Ever since 1918 this Party has been formally committed to the establishment of a socialist society, based on the 'common ownership of the means of production, distribution and exchange', and there has always been a significant element in the trade unions and Labour Party who take this commitment seriously. Given the numerical importance of the working class, the very existence of such a strong and potentially radical labour movement has posed a permanent threat to the continued survival of capitalism in Britain.

One of the main political objectives of the capitalist class has always been to contain this movement and to isolate its more radical elements. To achieve this objective, capital has been forced to forgo the economic advantages of certain kinds of state intervention because their success would legitimise socialist ideas and strengthen the Left within the labour movement and society at large. Planning and nationalisation, for example, are widely associated with socialism in the public mind, and they have either been opposed outright by capital—or else, where such measures have been unavoidable, efforts have been made to give them a form which minimises the political dangers involved. In conformity with capitalist opinion, planning agencies such as the National Economic Development Council and the ill-fated Department of Economic Affairs were denied the powers they required to function effectively; there has been a persistent emphasis on the voluntary character of relations between capital and the state; and the National Enterprise Board, the Industrial Reorganisation Corporation, and many other government agencies, have been set up as semi-autonomous bodies—which are explicitly not part of a coherent central planning framework. Capital has also sought to prevent detailed intervention into the day-to-day workings of industry by forcing the government to deal with trade associations and similar bodies, rather than with individual companies. In these and in many other ways, capital has kept the state at arm's length and prevented the establishment of a strong and integrated planning system, whose very existence might have been politically dangerous.

Quite apart from any political motives, capital has also had strong economic reasons for opposing the establishment of an effective central planning system in Britain. Much of this capital has extensive international connections and is worried that detailed state intervention in its affairs will inhibit its global freedom of manoeuvre. This is most obvious in the case of the City of London whose role as a world banking and commercial centre requires great flexibility and involves the perpetual transfer of funds across national boundaries. It is less obvious in the case of industrial firms, but over the past 30 years they too have become increasingly international in character. British industry is now dominated by great multinational companies, which own productive facilities in many different countries and organise a complex international division of labour within their own enterprise. Most of these firms are British, some are American and some are continental; but no matter what their legal nationality, all of them think in international terms and wish to minimise detailed state intervention in their operations. Thus, although there have certainly been conflicts between industry and the City during the post-war period, they have shared a common interest in opposing state policies which might disrupt their international operations. This is even true as far back as the 1950s when, although still mainly national in operation, big British industrial firms were already thinking in international terms and beginning to invest heavily overseas. Given the excellent long-term prospects for such investment, these firms were quite unwilling to sacrifice their freedom of action in the interests of national economic growth. Even when British firms later became worried about economic decline and began to support planning in the early 1960s, the kind of planning they had in mind was so weak as to be almost useless.

So, there are both economic and political reasons to explain why, throughout the post-war period, capital has opposed the kind of planning and state intervention required to halt Britain's economic decline. By legitimising socialist ideas such measures could have been politically dangerous and undermined the hegemony of capital; and by controlling the international operations of industry and the City these measures could have jeopardised the profits they derived or hoped to derive from such operations. This opposition from capital has been remarkably successful both in preventing the emergence of an effective planning system and in discrediting the whole idea of systematic planning in popular consciousness. It is, perhaps, the main reason why government attempts to halt Britain's economic decline have been so ineffectual.

29. The Character and Origin of Britain's Economic Decline*

David Coates

The question we must answer here is why British capitalism has proved so vulnerable to the world recession and why, as a result, employment levels, output figures, trade balances and standards of living have all been so adversely affected since 1973. There is, of course, no shortage of answers already available to that question. The excessive power of trade unions, on wages, working practices and levels of manning (and the associated propensity of British workers for idleness and restrictive practices), is a favourite of many commentators on the Right and Centre of British politics. So too is the thesis of excessive government activity. Modern monetarist doctrine often points to the way in which politicians overspend in the pursuit of votes, fuelling inflation as they do so, and helping to consolidate outmoded working practices by their 'artificial' maintenance of over-full employment and their 'cosseting' of workers through excessive welfare provision. Monetarists too tend to blame governments for protecting and subsidising firms, and for making credit too easily available, all of which only lessens, in their view, the impact of those important market pressures which alone can spur essential innovation and rationalisation in methods of industrial production, in product design and in marketing. There is also the argument, often seized upon by those with right-wing political leanings, that it is the excessive expansion of state employment that holds the key to Britain's relative economic decline (the Bacon–Eltis thesis). This often joins other monetarist arguments as a justification for reductions in both the scale and range of government activity as a way of re-establishing the economy's competitive edge, no matter what the short-term costs may be (and they are invariably high ones) in public sector unemployment and the diminished provision of hitherto essential social services.

*Reproduced from D. Coates and G. Johnston (eds.) *Socialist Strategies* (London, Martin Robinson, 1983), pp. 35–62.

Explanations from the centre of British politics tend to be gentler, emphasising a whole range of relatively disparate factors as causes of economic decline: the low level of demand in the home market, poor quality management, inadequate provision of industrial retraining, deficiencies in our education system, the damanging impact of perpetually changing government policies, inadequacies in the machinery and personnel of governments, the excessive centralisation of decision-making, or even the decay of those social values of thrift, discipline and a respect for authority that are widely thought to be crucial to the industrial renaissance of others. The parliamentary Left, for its part, tends to emphasise low levels of industrial investment, the absence of economic planning and the persistence of social inequalities as causes of industrial decay. The Labour Left criticise the Thatcher government for failing to reflate the economy, arguing that a lower level of demand is itself a cause of stagnation and inefficiency. They are also highly critical of the financial institutions of the City, especially the banks, the insurance companies and the pension funds, because of their encourgement of capital exports and their preoccupation with high exchange and interest rates. Parliamentary socialists tend to draw attention to the excessive concentration of ownership in manufacturing industry, and to its increasingly multinational character, and point to the problems of controlling and harnessing industrial activity behind nationally-specified goals without an extension of public ownership, the tight supervision of private industry and some form of import controls. And left-wingers too tend to stress the low quality and restricted social background of many leading figures in British industrial life, 'dead-wood in the boardrooms' that in their view is maintained there by an archaic class structure and the absence of industrial democracy.

Sections of the extreme Left often bring the argument full circle, going beyond the theses of the parliamentary Left to recognise the way in which the strength of the British labour movement has provided a barrier to the effective restructuring of British capitalism. Much recent Marxist scholarship has concluded that since the war industrial capital here has been too weak to enforce significant industrial change on a strongly defensive working class, whilst that class has been too conservative politically to force through a socialist alternative to capitalist decay. From these arguments, as from all the others, very clear political programmes directly emerge, with the solution to the economy's ills necessarily dependent on the mobilisation of forces strong enough to sweep away the impediments singled out for attention. For that reason, if for no other, it will be necessary in the argument that follows to consider the strengths and weaknesses of each of these theses too; to build, that is, not simply an explanation of our current malaise but also a critique of the commentaries upon it. . . .

II

It is, presumably, generally recognised that British industry has been undercapitalised for a very long time, and that it has never been able to restructure itself to the degree necessary to re-establish the kind of industrial dominance that it enjoyed before 1900. Instead, the competitiveness of its products has eroded in a cumulative fashion down the years, with existing inadequacies in investment levels, productivity and profitability then discouraging still further the investment and changes in working practices vital to break the circle. I shall discuss this process of cumulative decline later. What has first to be established is when it began and why, and here it is clear that developments in the last quarter of the nineteenth century, when industrial capital first began to experience serious international competition, are of crucial importance.

It was in that period of industrial challenge, and in the years of world monopoly for British-based industrial capital that preceded it, that the balance and character of class forces in Britain settled into a particular form. It was in that period that there emerged a labour movement of a certain kind, which we shall need to examine in detail in a moment. It was from that period too that the organisation of industrial production in Britain emerged as too small in scale, too defensive in orientation and too anchored in old industries, methods of production and markets, to be able to withstand easily the growing scale, intensity and quality of foreign competition. But it was also in that period that we can locate the foundation of a particular relationship within the British ruling class between financial and industrial interests—a relationship which even today continues to play an important part in the continuing political weakness and economic vulnerbility of British-based manufacturing industry. In any proper explanation of that vulnerability, it is with the power of the City that we need to begin.

Initially, British industrialists did not need bank capital to anything like the degree that characterised the fledgling industries of Germany and Japan. Britain's world monopoly position gave its industrial capitalists surpluses on which internally-financed, long-term investment could proceed apace. It also gave sterling a particular role in the nineteenth-century world economy (broadly similar to that of the dollar between 1944 and 1971), and attracted to London foreign borrowers keen to draw on those surpluses for their own industrial take-off. From the 1870s the English banking system found it more profitable to finance foreign trade and to handle portfolio investment abroad than to seek out domestic industrial demand for long-term finance. This established both a distance between industrial and financial interests and an international focus for British banking practices that had no close parallel elsewhere. When challenged by the rise of German and US competition in the last quarter of the nineteenth century, this first capitalist class did not respond by a rapid and far-reaching restructuring of its domestic manufacturing base. Instead its industrailists turned increasingly to the security of protection within the markets of the empire, and its bankers found even greater reasons for concentrating on the expansion of the overseas interests and role of British-owned capital. Between 1880 and 1914 those financial interests established a position of dominance for themselves in the councils of the state, so that by 1914 at the latest, because of the way in which

> early industrialization and subsequent internationalization of British capital under the umbrella of imperial power had [made] . . . it more profitable to expand abroad than to innovate and accumulate in Britain [nationally-based industrial interests found themselves facing] a ruling class and a policy regime dedicated to the international interests of British capital rather than the development of the domestic economy. (Currie and Smith, 1981, p. 10)

Initially, this fracturing of interests between nationally-based industrial and internationally-oriented financial capital was mutually beneficial;

> So long as Britain was the principal 'work-shop of the world' for both capital and consumer goods, this specialization did not constitute a serious obstacle to industrial acccumulation in Britain but actually stimulated it through the creation of overseas demand' (Jessop, 1977, p. 30)

But once British domination of world trade and industrial production had gone, the interests of the two sections of British capital proved increasingly incompatible, and nationally-based industrialists found themselves locked into increasingly outmoded industries and production methods, whilst at the same time being both disadvantaged in their access to long-term credit relative to their competitors, and subject to a political class in which financial interests had a disproportionately strong voice. Unlike their counterparts in Japan and Germany, British industrialists found their bankers geared to the export of capital, and preoccupied with maintaining the 'conditions in which exported capital was safe, sterling defended and international commercial and financial operations could freely function' (Aaronovich and Smith, 1981, p. 61). They found it difficult to persuade bankers to make long-term loans to industry on any scale, or to put up risk capital in sufficient quantities, and hence were driven back into a disproportionate heavy reliance on their own by now inadequate sources of internal funds to fuel the investment process.

Financiers for their part, because of their world-wide interests, lacked any great concern with the successful expansion of the domestic productive base, and instead used their considerable political leverage (which accrued to them through the City's centrality whilst sterling remained a reserve currency, and via the Bank of England's connections to the Treasury and, lately, the IMF) to hold successive British governments to policies that were vital to London's role as an international money market but detrimental to any restructuring of British manufacturing industry. The defence of free trade before 1914, of a return to the Gold Standard in 1925, of a high exchange rate in the 1950s and 1960s and of the high interests rates and deflationary policies with which the defence of sterling was associated, are all examples of the way in which financial interests had the political leverage to establish a popular connection between their needs and 'the interests of the nation as a whole' that actually eroded the capacity of the industrial sector to maintain economic growth, market share, profits and jobs. Then the resulting underperformance of that industrial sector became a force shaping investment patterns in its own right, reinforcing the banking network's antipathy to the risks involved in supporting industry, and encouraging them to continue to concentrate a high proportion of their considerable resources on government debt, property speculation, capital export and short-term, small-scale industrial loans. In this way, it is now quite legitimate both for critics of the banking system to call for greater bank involvement in industrial investment, and for others to retort that more money is available within the City for industrial use than is currently being taken up by industrialists. The arm's length relationship of financial and industrial interests that has persisted for so long, and the *political* dominance at critical moments of financial interests over industrial ones, have by now helped to establish a situation in which the simple logic of market forces and relative competitive performance keeps the banks and the factories apart.

III

One consequence of this is that British industry has for over 60 years been 'characterized by low investment, technical backwardness and an outmoded industrial structure' (Cambridge PEG, 1974, P.7). This weakness of industrial capital is thus an important contributory factor to the economy's present competitive difficulties, but it too needs careful delineation and explanation, not least because of the considerable disagreement in the relevant literature on both the problems of industrial capital and their origins.

Left-wing critics have often pointed to the low levels of investment in manufacturing plant and equipment as the crucial factor in Britain's economic decline—a pattern of underinvestment by international standards that stretches back at least to 1900, and means that now 'the average life of all plant and machinery in Britain is 35 years, almost double that of France, Germany and the US' (Lever and Edwards, 1980). But other commentators, equally left-wing in their sympathies, have doubted the adequacy of this as an explanation and hence, by implication, as a solution as well. For there is no simple and direct correlation between rates of economic growth and shares of gross domestic product going into manufacturing investment; and even where that correlation holds, it is by no means certain whether it is investment or growth that comes first. In any case, the undoubted gap between the British investment ratio and that elsewhere in the OECD countries has diminished lately without any concomitant equilisation of growth rates. On the contrary, in the years immediately before 1973

> the proportion of GDP which the UK mobilised for investment rose fairly steadily . . . and the gap between the investment countries *narrowed* to a difference of 2 or 3 percentage points . . . at precisely the same time as the UK was falling further behind them in the rates of growth of per capita income and real wages. (Purdy, 1980, p. 73)

What has persisted is a lower rate of *productivity* of investment in the UK relative to its foreign competitiors, and it is the technical reasons for that, and the social conditions which produce them, which we particularly need to explore.

The weakness of British industrial capital here is now fully documented: 'that differences between the growth rate of the UK and eleven other advanced economies from 1955 to 1962 [were] much more associated with differences in the productivity of capital than with differences in investment ratios' (Stafford, 1981, p. 40). The growth of output per unit of investment between 1961 and 1972 in Britain 'was only half that of Britain's major competitors such as France, West Germany and the USA and two-thirds that of Japan, whereas Britain's investment ratio was only marginally lower' (Purdy, 1976, p 313). This deficiency in capital's productivity has many causes. One is undoubtedly the defensive strength of the labour movement, to which we shall come.

Another, and much more important cause, to which we have alluded already, and to which we shall return, can be found in the persistent deflation of levels of demand in the post-war economy made necessary by the prior commitment of government to the protection of sterling and the international role of the City. These causes worked in conjunction too with a whole cluster of other factors which varied in importance in different industrial sectors: factors such as inadequate levels of capital and its outmoded distribution between industries, technologies and products; the inability of particular industries and firms to exploit economies of scale because of limited production runs, too small a capital base, or too restricted a home demand; and the weakness of innovation and generally unadventurous style of management that is common across large sections of British industry.

This last feature seems vital, but is difficult to isolate or to quantify—a particular lack of intensity and innovative ruthlessness in large sections of British industrial management which has resulted in 'technological backwardness . . . leads lost, opportunities missed, markets relinquished that need not have been' (Beckerman, 1979, p. 189). Some parts of that managerial weakness may well be explicable in terms of long-established deficiencies in technical and managerial training (themselves, of course, in need of explanation); or by the way in which low rates of economic growth and capital accumulation even during the long post-war boom failed to create the market conditions and profit rates favourable to major technological and industrial change. Some part of the explanation for the quality and style of British management may lie with working-class industrial strength or with the particularly easy competitive conditions experienced by British industry in the first ten years after the war, niether of which predisposed managements to rapid technological change or major shifts in the character and location of investment, and both of which helped to consolidate a complacency in managerial circles that was to be rudely shattered by the recession of the 1970s. But it is also clear that British management teams abroad have been quite capable of confronting labour movements and quickening the rate of exploitation of labour; and that suggests that the underlying reason for the poor performance of domestic management lies much further back in the history of British industrial capitalism as a whole.

The fact that Britain industrialised first meant 'that British capital was locked into areas and techniques of production that became obsolescent as more advanced products and technologies were discovered' (Jessop, 1977, p. 34). The long period of nineteenth-century world monopoly consolidated industrial capital in Britain into small production units that were slow to cartelise in the face of competition from far larger overseas units of capital, and which accordingly lacked any strong central coordinating structure which could bring effective pressure to bear in their defence on the banking network and the state. More impressionistically, because they industrialised first, and did so in a political alliance dominated by the personnel and attitudes of a non-militarised aristocracy and an internationally-oriented financial establishment, British industrialists lacked that 'growth culture' and aggressive nationalism vital to the class of industrial owners in second-wave capitalist countries (like Japan and Germany) who were bent on catching up already existing capitalist competitors by 'showing a high degree of openness to foreign expertise' and to promoting 'values and attitudes which helped to stimulate the process of pursuit of the world's technological leaders' (Beckerman, 1979. p. 192). It was for this reason that British education and government policies were never systematically geared to the adoption and dissemination of foreign innovations in technology (as happened particularly in Japan). Instead, British capital reacted to the rise of foreign competition in a defensive way, seeking protection in the markets of an expanding empire and remaining for too long tied to outmoded methods of production and declining industrial sectors.

The weakness of this impulse to innovate and restructure both reflected and then reinforced the political weakness of industrial interests within the British ruling class to which I have already referred. The initial coalition between industrial and financial interests that was consolidated after 1870 shared a common commitment to free trade, imperial expansion and a non-interventionist state; and this increasingly unsuitable political programme was shed only slowly and with difficulty in the twentieth century because it continued to suit the needs of the City and because industrial interests were often hesitant to adopt a close relationship with the state that was common among their major European competitors but which was canvassed in Britain most strongly by the rising political voice of organised labour.

In any case, the industrial lobby's strength politically always reflected to some degree the market power of the industries on which it was based; and yet another consequence of Britain's early start was that, in the crucial years between the wars, the ability of industrial interests to offset the political pressure of the City was undermined by the fact that those industrial interests—based as they were in coal, cotton, railways and heavy engineering—were themselves in secular economic decline. Even the industrial interests that were to replace them in leadership by the 1960s—in the second-wave growth industries of cars, chemicals and light engineering—lacked the political weight of the financial sector, because from the beginning they were industries of the second league, dwarfed by their US equivalents on whom they drew for technology and capital and, as such, lacking the world-wide resources that the City remained able to mobilise. Only the oil companies (and the occasional giant firm such as Unilever) stand as long-established exceptions to this; and neither they, nor the multinational monopoly concerns that emerged in British industry after 1960, altered significantly the balance of pressures operating on the state from capital. On the contrary, the interests of the new multinationals were as global as those of the City, and their arrival largely left nationally-based industrial capital in the political position it has occupied all century, namely that of junior partner to financial interests that were not directly geared to national economic reconstruction. Indeed,the continuous political weakness of this locally-based industrial capital can be judged quite simply by the amazingly late date (1965) and the initiating force (of all things, a Labour government) that at long last created for industrial capital a single all-embracing spokesman organisation, the CBI.

I shall argue . . . that this historical weakness—both political and managerial—of industrial capital played a crucial role in the 1950s, in 'missing the opportunity' to exploit the temporary dislocation of other capitalist economies in ways that could have locked British capitalism on to a new growth path. Once missed, that opportunity did not return. By the late 1960s, the competitive weakness of British industrial capital was evident for all to see, most visible in the general fall of profits across the sector as a whole. That did at least prompt a new centralisation and concentration of capital, a merger movement of an unprecedented scale that has left British industry as monopolised as ever (the top 100 companies are now responsible for nearly two-thirds of all industrial production). But that merger movement was itself defensive, a reaction to market weakness and to the rise of foreign competitors, and did not provide the institutional base for any dramatic increase in industrial investment or rates of capital or labour productivity. For the cartelisation of British industry coincided with the end of the long boom and in the new competitive conditions of the 1970s, when markets had not so much to be created as captured, even the new giants of British industry found themselves too limited in size relative to their competitors, too undercapitalised, too short of internally-generated funds, and too deficient in organisational coherence, managerial skills and labour discipline, to compete effectively.

The new industrial structures still reflected in their internal organisation, existing technologies, scales of operation, main markets, labour practices and rates of return, the way in which the opportunity of the

1950s had been lost. Take British Leyland as one example. Formed in 1968 in a merger to give a home-based car company the size to compete with the US giants (Fords, Chrysler and General Motors), British Leyland lacked the internal reserves to sustain even a modest investment programme. Moreover, it faced competitors whose existing strength enabled them to raise vastly greater sums for their new models than BL could ever hope to do, and it found itself saddled with a product range and widely scattered number of production units that were already outmoded and uncompetitive when compared to the rising power of the Japanese. When the recession after 1973 left the world car industry at least 25 per cent over capacity, British Leyland was bound to be in crisis, the weakest of the giants in an industry in recession, put there by the cumulative failure of an entire national industry over 30 years to restructure its industrial location, capital base and labour practices in line with the dictates of a by now fiercely competitive world market system.

What the creation of vast monopolies across the whole of British manufacturing industry after 1960 did was not to facilitate the reindustrialisation of the home economy. Rather, it acted to permit the more profitable sections of industrial capital to move abroad, and to reduce their own dependence on (and therefore interest in) the viability of production within Britain itself. In this way, City interests found new and powerful allies within the industrial sector, and the CBI found itself wracked by internal tension between large companies and small. In fact, big or small, industrial capital in Britain is now in serious difficulty. On the world scale, the multinational companies that dominate its growth sectors are themselves caught in a serious crisis of profits that is encouraging them to redistribute their investment away from high-tax, strong labour movement economies to more compliant political regimes. Small and medium-sized businesses increasingly lack the capacity to compete with foreign penetration of the home market that has been precipitated by the same crisis of profits on a world scale; and neither national nor multinational industrial capital possesses ̃ the political leverage to pull the Conservative Party under Margaret Thatcher away from monetarist policies of high exchange and interest rates, and restricted levels of home demand. As the recession deepens and factories close at an unprecedented rate, the historic weakness of British industrial capital is rapidly turning into a rout.

IV

This long-established and ever-increasing competitive weakness of industrial capital in Britain has been compounded by two other social forces of importance: the general character of the political class to whose leadership it has been subject; and, since the war at least, the defensive strength of the labour movement that it faced. There is no denying 'the fact that the British working class is [now] integral to the fundamental problem of the British economy, the slow rate of growth of productivity'; (Elson, 1981, pp. 66–7) but nor can it be denied that this problem of worker resistance to capitalist restructuring is a secondary and derivative one, of relatively recent centrality. It is important to get the timing and position right, and to see that 'while early instances of class conflict may be cited for the UK, as for other countries, the relative failure of UK economic performance *pre-dated the main* growth in the strength and scale of working class organisation' (Currie and Smith, 1981, p. 11).

The roots of that defensive strength do, however, lie far back, 'in the nature and timing of Britain's industrialisation and its nineteenth century dominance in the international system' (Jessop, 1977, p. 33). Trade unionism was established early among skilled workers, and Britain's initial industrial monopoly and subsequent period of imperial expansion enabled at least those unions to establish a degree of job control (and traditions of militancy in its defence) that were only slowly challenged by an employing class predisposed to avoid class confrontation by a retreat into the protected markets of an empire. There were challenges. The 1890s saw one and the first world war another; and craft control was under threat from the Great Depression onwards; but there is plenty of evidence too of 'entrepreneurial failure' brought about by the 'constraints which the sharing of control over work with strong unions placed on the possibilities for redivision of labour and the introduction of new technology' (Kilpatrick and Lawson, 1980, p. 91). It was this combination of strong craft unionism and imperial expansion that 'postponed the necessity to improve productivity in many of Britain's main industries, including cotton textiles, and railways' as UK exporters found it to their advantge to avoid conflict with workers over an accelerated remoulding of the structure of production, and instead redirected sales to the new or protected markets often with the aid of capital exports' (Kilpatrick and Lawson, 1980, p. 98)

This industrial power was restricted to certain craft unions until 1945, and was even there eroded by the general defeat of working-class militancy in 1926 and the prolonged unemployment of the interwar years. It was only after 1945 that the balance of class forces generally changed, and unions (and work groups within unions) among even semi-skilled and unskilled workers in the new industries of engineering, vehicle construction and chemicals, established a significant degree of control over many key aspects of the work process. These included, in well-organised factories, demarcation, apprenticeships, manning levels, work rates, and overtime and the ability to maintain effective resistance to managerial attempts to reorganise the work process. The strength of such work groups and their stewards was a direct consequence of three major processes at work in late capitalism. It was a feature of industries with the high capital/labour ratios that were characteristic of many of the growth sectors of the post-war boom, where capital could easily be immobilised by the strategic withdrawal of relatively few units of labour. It was a consequence of the lack of fierce competition in the product markets of those industries in the immediate post-war years, and indeed has been a casualty of precisely the intensification of that competition brought on by the world recession. It was predicated on government maintenance of full employment for a whole generation, and on the only restricted availability in Britain of the reserve armies of unskilled labour (of peasants, women and immigrants) available to the West German and Japanese industrial bourgeoisies. Skilled workers in particular were in short supply, and enjoyed industrial power accordingly.

The maintenance of full employment, and the financing of welfare services by the taxation of profits that shifted GNP away from capital and towards labour, were the political consequences of the enhanced power of the British labour movement after 1940. It was as a consequence of working-class political strength that up to the crisis of 1973–74 adherence to a full employment regime [was] . . . a major parameter of ruling-class policy', reducing that 'class's ability to make use of unemployment and recession as a disciplinary instrument against the working class (and, incidentally, as a renewal mechanism for weeding out backward and inefficient firms)' (Purdy, 1976, p. 274). As a result, shop floor bargaining on wages kept hourly earnings in manufacturing rising ahead of output per man hour well into the 1960s, and meant that 'Britain became the only imperialist power which proved unable to increase the rate of exploitation of its working class significantly during or after the Second World war' (Mandel, 1975, p. 179) The contrast here with the experience of Japan and West Germany is striking. The weakness of plant bargaining in those countries during the long boom left their capitalists stronger, and the fact that their labour movements were less extensive in their recruitment, divided internally on religious, political or skill lines as the British TUC was not, and seriously weakened or destroyed by pre-war Fascisim and post-war employer and state offensives (as again the British labour movement was not), all affected the relative strength of class forces in the various national capitalisms and helped to erode British industrial capital's competitive position. For

> it was the lesser ability and willingness of the average capitalist enterprise in Britain to subordinate the working class to the requirements of rapid growth, whether in introducing technical innovation or in raising and maintaining the intensity of labour with given technical conditions . . . which differentiated British capitalism from its rivals in the post-war period. (Purdy, 1976, p. 311)

and whose origins lie in the degree of defensive industrial power achieved by a well-organised and class-conscious labour movement in a context of full employment.

The result, of course, in capitalist terms was 'an erosion of the rate of profit and a much slower rate of economic growth and accumulation' (Mandel, 1975, p. 179) in Britain than in other OECD countries. Even successive British governments found that they too lacked the resources to tackle this defensive power directly: both because they lacked any legal means to alter class practices at factory level, and because they found a labour movement that was willing in the 1970s to strike against the introduction of such legal changes, and that was unwilling to tolerate prolonged bouts of incomes policy and productivity bargaining that attempted the same erosion of working-class power and living standards by a more conciliatory route. Indeed state employees—both manual workers and the increasingly unionised white-collar strata—proved particularly intransigent in the face of policies of income restraint that discriminated against them, as governments tried to set a good example to private employers by taking a tough line themselves. They, and a miners' union strengthened in its bargaining by the rising price of oil, effectively destroyed two Labour and one Conservative governments in the decade after 1969, in a process of defensive labour militancy which (1968 apart) had no parallel elsewhere in the advanced capitalist world.

Industrial regeneration in Britain in the 1970s, by either capitalist or socialist routes, was blocked by this balance of class forces in industry, in which

> workers [could] stop management taking certain positive action but [could] not stop them exporting capital; and management [could] stop workers realising money wage increases by passing these on in higher prices, but [could] not get them to increase output from the same machinery and plant. (Coates, 1979, p. 51)

The significance of the Thatcher government's monetarism lies precisely here, as a dramatic attempt to break that stalemate in favour of certain sections of capital by creating mass unemployment, falling living standards and tougher labour laws.

V

Finally, this process of industrial competitive decline was compounded by the particular character of the political leadership offered by successive British governments over a long period. The whole policy thrust of the entire political class (and that, to their shame, has included every Labour government to date) has been to maintain the world role of British imperialism—either as an autonomous power, as with Conservative governments up to 1965, or in a junior relationship with the USA or latterly with Europe (a project so dear to the hearts of the social democratic wing of labourism). Governments of either party have, as a result, been reluctant to shed a level of military spending and a scale of military operations reflective of an earlier period of industrial monopoly and world empire, and have proved disproportionately sympathetic to the political programme of the City because of the symbolism afforded to this world role by the possession of a strong currency.

The cost of the defence of sterling in the post-war years has been a heavy one. It has necessitated high interest rates, to hold speculative capital in London and to reassure a nervous financial community, at the cost of discouraging private manufacturing investment. It has cheapened imports in ways that have eased the foreign penetration of the domestic market. It has gone along with a proclivity for free trade in capital and goods, and only limited state intervention in industrial restructuring, that has corresponded less and less well to the actual needs of a weakening industrial base. It has left the economy vulnerable to periodic flights from sterling by nervous foreign holders of a patently overvalued currency—sterling crises often precipitated by balance of payments difficulties that have then necessitated cutbacks in state spending and the deflation of the entire economy, to the detriment of industrial sectors that rely on buoyant home markets and on extensive state orders and financial assistance.

The maintenance of a military budget no longer in keeping with the competitive strength of the civilian economy that has to sustain it has been equally burdensome. Defence spending in Britain in the post-war years, though moving from its peak of 11 per cent of GDP at the time of the Korean war to only 5 per cent in the 1970s, still exceeded that of any OECD country other than the USA. The cost of that defence spending to the civilian economy was at times quite direct, taking investment funds (particularly at the critical time of the Korean war) that might otherwise have assisted in the restructuring of the civilian engineering industry. At other times, the effect of high defence spending has been less direct but equally serious, slowing the general rate of accumulation by its unproductive absorption of surplus, and trapping as many as 40 per cent of all research scientists and engineers in R&D programmes geared to military ends. It is noticeable that those industrial bourgeoisies denied the right to sustain a large national army (the Japanese and the West German after 1945) proved to be the most technologically efficient and competitive thereafter, as their engineering sectors were forced to operate entirely in the open markets of civilian production, as their research scientists were obliged to concentrate on civilian projects, and as their salesmen were denied the 'feather-bedding' afforded to military producers by the 'cost-plus' basis of so much armament procurement by the state.

This pattern of political leadership and stalemated class forces in industry was particularly important in the 1950s, for it was then that West German and Japanese industrial capital established the basis for its subsequent strength and British capital did not. In retrospect, it is relatively easy to see why. 'The necessity for a favourable balance of class forces and for an entreprenurial class able to take advantage of production and trading opportunities,' (Aaronovitch and Smith, 1981, p. 164) played into the hands of the German and Japanese ruling groups just as it did not into the British. As militarily defeated and economically-weakened classes, under direct US political control until the late 1940s, the West German and Japanese industrial bourgeoisies had fewer established patterns of production, trade and finance on which to fall back. Their political élites had no world role to play that might divert resources from industrial reconstruction into wasteful military expenditure. They each had to reconstitute their war-damaged economies through a rapid expansion of their manufacturing sectors, with its attendant favourable consequences for general labour produc-tivity. They each had large reserves of cheap and non-unionised labour on which to draw (in their urban unemployed, in the Japanese countryside, in Eastern Europe and in the poor economies of the Mediterranean). Their labour movements had been destroyed in the 1930s, and the accumulated profits of the resulting period of intensified labour exploitation remained to be harnessed for manufacturing reconstruction. When those labour movements were reconstituted, their moderation was guaranteed, initially by deliberate employer offensives against militants (in Japan) and communists (in West Germany), and then consolidated by particular institutional arrangments (the famous company unions and cradle to grave employment practices of the Japanese *ziabatsu*, and the industrial democracy schemes of the US-designed and highly-centralised West German trade union movement). Since both countries came to possess a crucial strategic importance to the USA in the emerging battle lines of the Cold War, so the industrial bourgeoisie in each had no difficulty in attracting large amounts of US military spending, foreign aid and private corporate capital. As Ron Smith had described the situation:

> These factors, together with the 'catching up' process as war torn economies started to restore output levels, led to generally rapid growth in manufacturing industry. The dynamic benefits from this . . . meant sharp gains in productivity. Real wages could also rise quickly, although the existence of labour reserves meant that this increase generally was not large enough to threaten the high profitability on which it was based. Rapid growth in demand was ensured by the heavy demand for capital goods, the rapid expansion to consumer expenditure consequent upon large real wage increases, and the general expansion of world trade as tariff barriers and other obstacles to trade started to fall in the fifties. Those countries that were initially able to expand rapidly found that the correspondingly higher growth in productivity acted to sustain this, avoiding too rapid a depletion of labour reserves and helping to maintain their competitive position internationally (a factor that assumed particular importance in the sixties, when international competition intensified). By contrast, initially slow growing economies found themselves caught in a vicious circle of slow growth, low investment and low productivity gains. (Aaronovitch and Smith, 1981, p. 165)

Britain was one of those slowly-growing economies because there the situation in the early 1950s was so different. British manufacturers enjoyed a temporary easing of competitive pressures because of the war-time destruction of many of their competitors and because of the heavy demands for manufactured goods created by the programmes of post-war reconstruction. The underinvestment that had characterised British industry between the wars had been compounded by the exigencies of war-time production, and yet the market conditions of the early 1950s made production viable on even the oldest and most exhausted of machinery. Not until the balance of payments crisis of 1961 did it really become generally obvious that the easy market conditions of the immediate post-war years had gone, and could no longer be maintained even by favourable terms of trade with the Third World or the semi-protection afforded by the existence of the sterling area.

Then too there was the labour movement, undefeated in Britain since

1926, with its own political party in or on the edge of power, standing as a barrier to any substantial shift in social or public resources away from consumption to investment, or to any major reorganization of methods of production. Only relatively limited supplies of ready available labour stood easily to hand (West Indian and Pakistani immigrants in particular, and women in general); and the legacies of empire, not least in the Nationality Act 1948, prevented the use of immigrant labour as guestworkers of the West German kind. The English peasantry had long vanished as a source of cheap labour to fuel an 'economic miracle' that could parallel the Italian and the Japanese ones; and imperial connections still froze British trade into markets that were to grow more slowly than the emerging European community from which the British political élite chose to exclude itself. As we have seen, that political class was still in the 1950s preoccupied with the maintenance of a world role for themselves that their economic base could no longer sustain and, as a result, military adventures (at Suez and in the colonies) continued to drain resources and manpower; and the exchange rate of sterling (fixed and protected at $2.80) came to diverge more and more from a level appropriate to the actual international position of the economy that it was taken to symbolise. With little market pressure, a profoundly conservative and imperialist political and financial ruling class, and a strongly defensive labour movement, it is hardly surprising that industrial capital in Britain was slow to see the threat posed to it by the rise of West German and Japanese economic power, and that instead 'at least up to the late 1950s, habituation to the protection of Empire and the expectation that this could be perpetuated removed any strong incentive from the average enterprise to overhaul its means and relations of production' (Purdy, 1976, p. 318).

VI

The missed opportunity of the 1950s was difficult to recapture. A domestic economy weak in investment, low in managerial and innovative skills, and with a strong labour movement, quickly found itself locked into a series of self-sustaining disabilities, a syndrome of economic decline, where low investment bred low profits that in turn attracted even lower investment. The very absence of rapid economic growth in the 1950s removed the possibility of rapid gains in labour productivity, and so left the economy disproportionately vulnerable to inflation, to international competition as that intensified, and to the persistence of low rates of economic growth. That same low rate of growth 'hardened worker resistance. The sluggishness of markets meant that new labour saving techniques generally brought redundancies in their wake' (Glyn and Harrison, 1980, p. 521) and so encouraged worker opposition to technical change vital to strengthened competitiveness. The absence of that competitiveness precipitated balance of payments deficits that required internal deflation, and increased still further the inability of British industry to offset its weakening position by a sustained growth in demand and the associated exploitation of economies of scale. Instead low investment, low rates of return on capital, and a low productivity of labour produced a manufacturing sector less and less capable of sustaining high levels of government spending and employment without creating inflation; and the inflationary pressures (stronger here than elsewhere because of the strength of political support for high welfare spending, and the low productivity of the manufacturing sector that had to sustain it) eroded international competitiveness still more, and intensified class conflict as governments were forced by their own need for economic growth to make a late but quite sustained attack on working-class living standards and control over the labour process.

But by then it was too late. The mistake was to have fallen behind. The British economy had already become locked in a 'low growth spiral' by which 'from being a high wage economy at the end of the Second World War [it] progressively became a low wage [but high cost] economy with consequent exacerbation of class stalemate' (Aaronovitch and Smith, 1981, p. 26). Once weak in international competitive terms, that weakness became and remained cumulative, with each deflation making for further decline and each relative expansion in the economy's overseas competitors putting them further ahead. The Marxist law of unequal development was never more obvious than in this. So that when, after 1973, the whole of the capitalist world was in recession and beset by inflation, the degree of restructuring that was then necessary for Britain industrial capital to survive in the intensified competition which the recession called forward was quite literally beyond the grasp of governments seeking to persuade a labour movement to cooperate in the dismantling of its members' hard-won industrial gains. The 'corporatist' road to industrial regeneration beloved of Labour governments since 1964 just could not stand the strains of the restructuring it required; and when that is recognised, the rise of Thatcherite monetarism can then be seen for what it is—the application of the ruling class's other and latest strategy for the restoration of capitalist profits: a forced increase in the rate of labour exploitation through the escalation of unemployment, state repression and tightened industrial discipline. It is the social costs of that particular strategy, and its bankruptcy even as a mechanism of saving national industrial capital at the workers' expense, that makes the forging of a socialist alternative all the more pressing.

It should now be clear why the explanations mentioned earlier need to be revised if an appropriate socialist strategy is to be forged in Britain in the 1980s. The defensive power of the unions has not created, but has only compounded, a competitive weakness whose roots lie elsewhere, and much nearer to the class forces with which monetarists identify. The social costs of their solutions are, in any case, appallingly high, and disastrous even for the industrial interests they claim to represent. State spending is no artifact of electoral politics alone, but has been a crucial strand in the consolidation of 25 years of economic growth by private industry. If inflation and stagnation are now its legacy, these arise from contradictions in the class structures and monopoly institutions of late capitalism, and cannot be resolved by a return to a free market economy that had lost its economic rationale for British industrial capital as long ago as 1914. The inadequacy of management and education, the amateurishness of a civil service without direct industrial experience, and the twists and turns of government policy, are not accidental or easily removable phenomena either. They reflect the particular history of the first industrial capitalism, and the character of the political and social élites that have dominated it. That is why the Left is on stronger grounds when calling for the expropriation of that class, the subordination of finance capital to public ownership, and the redistribution of power within industry. but that solution will necessarily meet heavy resistance, and unless it can generate new structures of decision-making to harness the untapped productive potential of a classless society, will degenerate quickly into a 'statism', a bureaucratised state capitalism, in which problems of labour alienation, low productivity and dwindling international competitiveness will continue behind a hollow rhetoric of socialist advance.

PART V:
Over-views of Decline

This collection ends with a series of survey articles, each written from different political and intellectual vantage points.

We begin with *Sam Brittan*'s examination of some of the explanations canvassed earlier in the volume: 'stop–go', low investment, import penetration, excessive government spending and high average tax rates. Brittan rejects all of these on the basis of international comparisons. He stresses instead, as a set of immediate causes, high marginal tax rates, monetary over-expansion, and the combination of state intervention and egalitarian social policy resulting from excessively democratic political institutions. In looking for longer-term causes, Brittan is prepared to give some weight to peculiarities in the British class structure, but mainly emphasises the monopoly power enjoyed by producer and special interest groups, not least the trade unions. 'The disease,' as he puts it, 'is that of collective action by special interest groups preventing a reasonably full use being made of our economic resources.'

The argument by *M.J. Weiner* is quite different. It is included here, rather than in Part III, because of its sense of the limits of what he calls 'economic explanations', particularly those of the Hobsbawm variety. Weiner argues for a sensitivity to local variations and to cultural processes, insisting that for a long time the English have not been happy with notions of progress, and have been in fact deeply suspicious of material and technological development. He observes the paradox of what he terms 'the inner tension in modern British culture . . . hostility to industrial society' persisting 'in the world's first industrial society'. Weiner finds the roots of that inner tension in the nineteenth-century social structure, in the absence of total bourgeois domination and the maintenance of cultural hegemony by a *rentier* aristocracy. The 'humanising' of the industrial process which resulted led to the

289

'containment of capitalism within a patrician hegemony which never either then or since actually favoured the aggressive development of industrialism or the general conversion of society to the latter's values and interests.' Weiner cites the Marxists Anderson and Nairn in developing his case, and one suspects he actually could have cited Hobsbawm too.

Geoff Hodgson also sees the source of Britain's industrial decline in the relationship between classes. But unlike Weiner he lays the emphasis not on relationships within the ruling class so much as on the social relationships immediately surrounding the production process— the relationships of capital to labour. Like Brittan, Hodgson arrives at his conclusion after a survey of some of the alternative explanations which we have already encountered in this volume: in this instance policy mistakes, excessive taxation and government spending, pillage by multinational corporations, profits crises, low investment and trade union defensive strength. He rejects some as empirically unfounded, and others as consequences rather than causes—parts indeed of the problem to be explained, and explained in terms of the class contradictions of capitalism.

Bernard Stafford is also sympathetic to that conclusion, or at least to a particular version of it. In a major article, he examines both Keynesian and Marxist explanations of Britain's economic decline, and finds both wanting. Keynesian explanations can show the mechanisms by which decline becomes cumulative, but not why it begins. Marxist explanations of the Hobsbawm variety lack empirical support for their view of the impact of capital export and differential banking practices. For Stafford, the stronger Marxist arguments are those, such as Kilpatrick and Lawson's, which attribute centrality to the defensive power of trade unionism. It is this conclusion which *Sam Aaronovitch* challenges so succinctly in the discussion note which follows.

Finally, *John Hillard* brings the collection to a close by considering the contribution to Britain's economic decline made by the policies of the Conservative government led by Margaret Thatcher.

30. The Role and Limits of Government*

Sam Brittan

Why has British performance fallen so far behind other countries? . . .
Both the inequities of British society and excessive egalitarian zeal have
been blamed; so too have inadequate competition and insufficient
government intervention. Some people cite the enormous institutional
obstacles to change and others the excessive ease with which policies are
reversed under a two-party, winner-takes-all system; and one could go
on indefinitely.

Some of the suggested explanations of British economic performance
may shed light on recent years, but cannot conceivably explain the
long-term lag in growth rates. Some dwell on transitory phenomena
already disappearing or unlikely to last. Some are factually dubious on
any basis whatever.

For instance, a once-popular diagnosis was that British growth was
held back by cyclical fluctuations in output, caused by 'stop–go'
financial policies. Numerous studies have, however, shown that
deviations in UK output, measured in relation to trend, were less than
in most other countries. (NEDO, 1976).

A related explanation was low investment, especially in manufacturing, since the second world war. Close examination reveals, however,
that gross investment in manufacturing, as a percentage of value added,
was no higher in Germany than in the United Kingdom. Where the UK
did come clearly at the bottom of the league was in the effectiveness of
investment in terms of output generally. It is therefore not surprising
that profitability and the return on investment were low by international
standards. (The ordering in the second column of Table 30.1 is still
roughly appropriate.)

A contemporary vogue diagnosis is 'deindustrialisation', which has

*Reproduced from S. Brittan, *The Role and Limits of Government* (London,
Temple Smith, 1983) pp. 219–39

Table 30.1. *Investment in manufacturing 1958–1972[a]*

	Investment ratio[b] %	Increase in net output[c] per unit of investment Index no. UK = 100
UK	13.0	100
USA	12.2	145
Germany	13.0	190
Sweden	14.4	145
France	16.3	163
Japan	24.6	157

Notes: [a]Or nearest comparable period to eliminate cyclical distortions.
[b]Manufacturing gross investment as % of value added.
[c]Incremental output to capital ratio.
Source: Confederation of British Industry, *Britain Means Business 1977*, 38 (1977).

Table 30.2. *Changes in employment in the UK ('000s of employees)*

	1959	1959–71	1971–76	1976–81
Private industrial sector	9137	−296	−755	−1251
Other private sector	6912	+175	+396	+533
Public sector (non-manufacturing)	5108	+721	+817	−79
Total employees	21 417	+705	+421	−834
Unemployment	512	+184	+569	+1130

Source: Central Statistical Office.

been used to describe a pathological fall in the ratio of industrial to total employment. But comparative international figures make it clear that if this is a disease at all, it is a very new one. The United States, Sweden, the Netherlands and Belgium all had falls in the ratio of industrial to total employment in 1965–75 of comparable size to Britain's. Germany and France just about maintained the same manufacturing ratio, while Japan and Italy were exceptional in increasing theirs. (Brown and Sheriff, 1979).

One aspect of a relatively slow growth rate has been the fall in the British share of world trade or world exports of manufactures. Repeated investigations have shown that this decline cannot be explained by any special features either of the commodity composition of British exports or of the market outlets for them. It is simply that if the UK has a lower growth rate than competitor countries, one would expect, other things being equal, a declining share of world exports relative to those countries' share. It is thus a consequence rather than a cause.

There is a more specific doctrine relating Britain's slow growth to trading performance. This is that the country has a special difficulty in earning enough overseas to support a full-employment level of activity. The doctrine is the theme song of the annual reviews of the Cambridge Economic Policy Group. The essential argument is that even if exchange rates move so as to keep British money costs competitive with those of other countries, imports will be too high and exports too low to maintain full employment. This would imply that British products are not merely inferior in design, performance or delivery, but are continually deteriorating in these respects. The Cambridge Group's case rests on the very strong assumption that the annual fall in terms of trade required to stay in equilibrium would be so steep and meet such strong union resistance that it could not be brought about without an inflationary explosion.

The whole diagnosis of output being limited by a demand or balance of payments constraint is open to serious question. The rise in import penetration took place in a series of jumps during periods of boom or supply bottlenecks or during periods of sterling overvaluation. The increase in British exports, relative to any given increase in world real incomes, has been substantially less than that of exports of other countries; but it is disputable whether such ratios are a true measure of the income elasticity of demand for British exports. Failures on the supply side—even when the unemployment statistics have been high—have limited the response of British industry to increases in overseas demand.

SPENDING AND TAXES

The level of government spending is also often blamed for recent poor performance. We should, however, be very careful in citing figures of the ratio of public spending to the national product, as different definitions produce widely different figures. The UK is in the middle rather than at the top of the international league, despite an exceptional bulge in the early 1970s.

Was there a dangerous switch of workers from private manufacturing to public services? Up to 1971 the shifts closely paralleled trends in other countries. The shift into public service employment after 1971 up to 1975 seemed more worrying, but we should, however, note that of the 850,000 workers who entered public service employment between 1971 and 1975, nearly 650,000 were females, over half part-time. It is stretching credulity to suppose that these women and girls would otherwise have been employed in factories at a conventionally acceptable wage. The rise in public employment has in any case been subsequently reversed.

Let me not be misunderstood. Large parts of public expenditure are not devoted to genuinely public goods and do little to transfer resources to the poor. These expenditures take place only because of the imperfections of the political market. But there is no need to claim that public spending is (a) out of control, (b) higher than in other countries, or (c) in itself a likely cause of economic breakdown or political collapse.

Not surprisingly, international tax comparisons lead to a similar picture. On comparable definitions, the UK has a tax burden of about 42 per cent of GNP, half-way down the list just below France and Germany, higher than that of the United States, but a good deal less than the Scandinavian countries. In these comparisons, social security levies are included with taxation, where they properly belong.

We come nearer to the source of complaint if we notice that the UK raises a relatively high proportion of revenue from taxes on households; and the *personal* tax burden did rise sharply in the mid–1970s. Most of the increase in the personal tax *burden* was due not to any increase in tax *rates*, but to the failure to index the tax starting-points and higher rate brackets against inflation until the very late 1970s.

For most of the post-war period the real trouble was, however, not the average tax rates, but the very high marginal rates, both at the top and at the bottom of the income scale. The top marginal rates were not only higher until 1979 than in other industrial countries, but were reached at a much lower level of income. They were entirely political taxes. The revenue collected at the top was trivial in statistical terms; and the real effect was likely to lower revenue, thus reducing what was available for redistribution. As important, from the point of view of the British growth rate, was the diversion of scarce energy and talent into trying to convert income into capital or into benefits in kind not taxable at these rates.

What proportion of the lag in Britain's growth rate do these tax rates explain? We can only guess, but two facts are worth pondering. One is that the confiscatory marginal tax rates of the mid–1970s cannot explain any of the lag before the second world war.

Secondly, the western country which most nearly approached the UK in the severity of its tax progression, Sweden, has been much higher in the growth league for most of the post-war period. Despite a recent setback, Sweden has a level of GNP per head which is comparable to that of the United States.

STATE INTERVENTION

Nor can we really ascribe the UK growth lag to any generalised fault known as state intervention. For the greater part of the post-war period, there is no evidence that there was more state intervention in the market-place in the UK than in other western countries. During the 1950s and most of the 1960s—even during the Labour governments of 1964–70—most industrial decisions were made in the market-place. Moreover, among industrial economies there is little connection between growth rates and the degree of state involvement in the economy. Germany has prospered under free-market doctrines, while Japan and France have often prospered under a sort of right-wing *dirigisme*—a common front between government and industrial organisations designed to bypass the market wherever possible. At the level of specific industries, agriculture has been subject to more government intervention than almost any other industry in most western countries. Yet it has been characterised by a high rate of productivity growth.

A generalisation worth venturing is that a country can get away either with a great deal of state intervention or with a great deal of egalitarian social policy, but not with the two together. Sweden, for instance, had a high level of social services and fiscal redistribution but, until well into the 1970s, was a model market economy. Industrial policy was geared to encouraging workers to shift as quickly as possible to the most profitable industries, and investment was guided by world markets rather than by government planning. In France and Japan, on the other hand, 'planning' was combined with a highly unequal distribution of income and the bulk of taxation tended to come from sales and turnover levies.

One further tentative generalisation may be suggested. The more democratic a country's institutions, the more likely is government economic intervention to hold back rather than encourage growth. Growth depends on change; and change can be disturbing. The general citizen has a dispersed stake in change and efficiency spread over thousands of different decisions. Particular industries and interest groups have a much more concentrated interest in stopping change or in securing inefficient decisions for their own narrow benefit. In a highly democratic society, geographically or professionally concentrated groups have much more influence than do general citizen interests. A

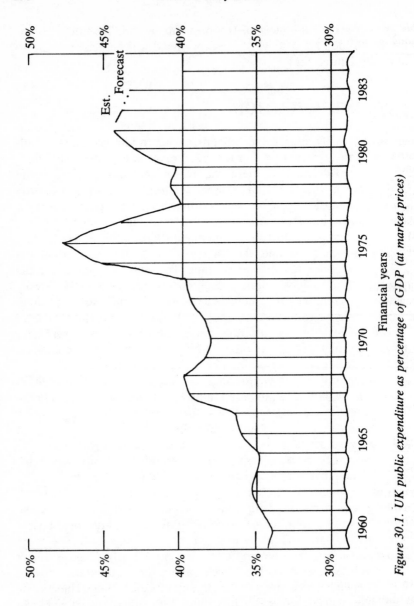

Figure 30.1. UK public expenditure as percentage of GDP (at market prices)

concrete example of what I have in mind was the decision of Conservative Prime Minister, Harold Macmillan, in a conflict over the location of a steel mill between Scotland and Wales at the beginning of the 1960s. The resolution was to have two smaller, sub-optimal mills, one in each area.

Table 30.3. Taxes and social security contributions as a percentage of gross national product at factor cost

| | 1970 | | 1975 | | 1980 | |
	%	Rank	%	Rank	%	Rank
Norway	48	1	54	1	59	1
Sweden	46	2	49	2	55	2
Netherlands	42	5	49	3	52	3
Austria	43	4	46	4	49	4
France	41	6	42	6	48	5
Belgium	39	8	45	5	48	6
West Germany	39	7	42	7	44	7
United Kingdom	43	3	41	8	42	8
Finland	36	10	40	9	39	9
Italy	30	12	31	13	38	10
Canada	37	9	37	10	36	11
Australia	28	13	33	11	35	12
United States	33	11	32	12	33	13
Switzerland	25	14	30	14	31	14
Japan	21	15	24	15	28	15

Source: Economic Trends, (London, HMSO, December 1982).

Table 30.4. Impact of UK personal tax

Year	Effective rate of income tax plus national insurance contributions (married man with two children on average earnings) (%)
1964–65	9.7
1970–71	21.3
1973–74	21.6
1976–77	26.3
1977–78	24.1
1982–83	30.2*

Source: Hansard.

In its time the steel-mill decision was untypical. Most such decisions would then have been taken in the market-place. After 1972 there was a notable increase in the quantity of government intervention in the UK and a deterioration in quality. We have had a multiplication of discretionary subsidies to individual concerns with no realistic prospects of paying their own way and with no genuine spillover benefits to justify subsidy. The standard of living of UK consumers was reduced and the development of poorer countries impeded by putting barriers on low-cost imports. In these respects the Thatcher government made much less difference than commonly supposed. It was, if anything, even firmer than its predecessors on Japanese and Third World imports. It did however start reversing the union legislation of the mid–1970s, which seemed almost deliberately designed to make worse the pricing out of work of the less skilled, the less able, the victims of prejudice, the young, the old, women and coloured imigrants—all in the name of high-sounding principles such as 'the rate for the job'.

INCOMES POLICY AND INFLATION

Perverse regulation, especially in the labour market, has increased in most European countries. If it has at times been worse in the UK, it has been from a desire to keep the unions sweet for pay controls. Indeed many of the occasional perversities of British economic policy have stemmed from the belief that inflation must be fought by regulation of specific pay settlements. To create a climate in which the unions will tolerate such intervention has been the object of much government activity, when an incomes policy has been in operation, which it was during most of the 1960s and 1970s. The UK seemed to be experiencing a respite from attempted pay controls in the 1980s, although it would be unwise to make firm predictions about its duration. To obtain support for pay restraint in 'incomes policy' phases, governments have introduced (often against their better judgement) price control and high marginal tax rates, and have expressed a special sensitivity to union leaders' views on many aspects of policy. The 1972–79 period of especially perverse intervention began, not with a change of government, but with a conversion of the Heath Conservative government to pay and price controls.

   This conversion, and the emphasis of subsequent governments on pay restraint, can itself be explained by the fact that the United Kingdom had a much larger jump in inflation rates than most other countries in the great inflation which hit the western world in the 1970s. Sudden and severe inflation nearly always increases the pressure for direct pay or price controls, however questionable their economic logic.

   The exceptionally severe and explosive British inflation was, however, both a superficial and an ephemeral aspect of the British disease. It lasted, as already mentioned, for only a decade, and its passing may lessen the temptation to some policy perversities. The main enduring temptation to misguided intervention which arrived with the 1970s arose of course from an understandable preoccupation with soaring unemployment. Severe recession or stagnation, whether or not combined with inflation, increases pressure for make-work policies. The vogue of ideas such as the National Enterprise Board and 'Planning Agreements', or the ability of politicians to dress up make-work policies as industrial regeneration, together with the recurrent bouts of pessimism about the future of capitalism, are all characteristic of severe inflation or slump, and still more of the combination of both.

Unemployment has much intensified since the 1960s, but inflation in Britain fell back to the OECD average or less in the late 1970s and remained there apart from a temporary resurgence in 1979–80. Some of the improvement was due to the effect of the North Sea oil on sterling, but much the greater part reflects the monetary and fiscal guidelines eventually adopted by the British governments—both Labour and Conservative.

More important is the fact that the lesson has been learned from the inflationary period. By this I do not mean that inflation has been conquered or that some ideal monetary rule will be followed, but simply that the British authorities have now had irrefutable evidence that beyond a very limited point creating money to finance budgetary deficits leads to an inflationary crisis rather than the much-desired real growth.

The great temptation to monetary overexpansion comes from the temporarily benign effect of such expansion on output and employment, and the delayed effect on prices. Even this temporary gain to output is very much smaller than it used to be in the UK, if indeed it exists at all. This is partly because the foreign exchange and other financial markets are now fully alert to monetary indicators. An expansion of the money stock, or mere *fear* of a future budget deficit likely to be financed in this way, has a much more immediate effect than it used to have on the exchange rate and on inflationary expectations, and little if any of the stimulus affects output. A temporary trade-off between inflation and employment is nowadays more likely to exist in a continental economy with little experience of rapid inflation than in an open economy with such experience.

THE ARGUMENT SO FAR

Let me summarise so far. The lag in the British growth rate goes back at least a century, although it took on a new dimension in about 1960 when the level as well as the growth rate of British real income began to fall behind similarly placed European states. In addition the UK has shared in the poor output and employment performance of the post–1973 economic cycles. But I have suggested that British inflationary excesses were ephemeral and therefore not fundamental aspects of the British disease. Many other much-criticised British policies are also followed to a comparable degree by other governments, working under similar political pressures. Moreover, these errors are too recent or temporary to explain the longer-term weaknesses. The tax rates of the 1970s hardly shed light on weaknesses of British management which worried Lord Haldane before the first world war.

Can anything be said, then, of the deep-seated lag in British growth rates? And does British experience thrown any light on the stagflation problem, which still remains serious, even if it is likely henceforth to show itself in Britain more in stagnant output and employment than in runaway inflation?

These broader questions bring us to two subjects which are always raised in any discussion of long-run British economic performance. These are the class system and the trade unions.

THE CLASS SYSTEM

Contrary to travellers' tales, the UK is *not* more stratified than other societies in any obvious statistical sense. Income disparities, even before tax, are less in the UK than in the USA, Japan, France or West Germany. Rates of occupational mobility between father's and son's occupation are substantial—over 60 per cent of men in the top occupational classes have parents two or more classes below them. Indeed 40 per cent are the sons of manual workers or lower-grade technicians. There is at least as much upward mobility in the UK as in the USA; and a greater proportion of British university students have working-class backgrounds than is the case on the Continent of Europe. Nor are these overnight developments. Economic divisions in the society have been lessening since the turn of the century if not earlier (Phelps Brown, 1977).

Yet, there is a sense in which Britain is more class-ridden than other capitalist or mixed economies. It is to be found in the features of British society furthest removed from pecuniary matters. It lies in such things as emphasis on the social pecking-order, concern with subtle differences of speech and manner, and the educational segregation from an early age of a so-called élite in fee-paying and often unpleasant residential institutions, strangely known as public schools. These features have given us the British novel; and they are a boon to the travel industry. If anyone doubts that they add to the bitterness as well as the gaiety of British life, he should take the first opportunity to see—or at least read—John Osborne's play of the 1950s, *Look Back in Anger*. One important feature of this type of class division is that it cuts right across the higher echelons of society. Most British managers have not had the traditional upper-class education; and a captain of industry can feel socially inferior over a glass of sherry with a country parson or a retired army major. The old school conservative and the socialist reformer come together in a common dislike of merely commercial values. In all societies people care about their status in the eyes of their fellowmen. In Britain, however, social status has less to do with merely making money than in almost any other western society.

UNION POWER

The other old-established British institution, which needs to be mentioned, is the trade union movement. But here again we must be careful of misdiagnosis. The number of days lost in British industry through strikes, even in the troublesome period of the early 1970s, was less than in the United States or Canada (although more than in Germany or France). The quantities involved are insignificant—just over 1 day per man-year on average. Strikes are overwhelmingly in large concerns. Well over 90 per cent of workers in establishments employing less than 500 do not have any experience of strikes from one year to the next (Phelps, Brown, 1977).

Monopolistic union practices are a different matter. Their effect on productivity is difficult to quantify, although the international productivity comparisons cited earlier may give a clue. A good analysis of the logic of unionism was provided in the 1940s by the American economist, Henry Simons. He shows that unions derive their influence over wages from the power to exclude and the main losers are other workers. He cites severe restrictions on entry such as:

high initiation fees, excessive periods of apprenticeship and restrictions upon numbers of apprentices, barriers to movements between related trades, and, of course, make-work restrictions, cost-increasing working rules, and prohibition of cost-reducing innovations, not to mention racial and sex discrimination . . .

There is every prospect that opportunities for collective, collusive, monopolistic action in particular labour markets will increase indefinitely wherever organisation is possible. This prospect alone suffices to explain the ominous decline of private investment and the virtual disappearance of venturesome new enterprise.

Investors now face nearly all the disagreeable uncertainties of investors in a free-market world plus the prospect that labour organisations will appropriate most or all of the earnings which would otherwise accrue if favorable contingencies materialised (Simons, 1948).

Even this is not the worst of it. Partial unionism is 'a device by which the strong may raise themselves higher by pressing down the weak'. It makes 'high wages higher and low wages lower'. This works when 'everybody does not try it or when few have effective power. Attempts to apply it universally are incompatible with order.' Simons goes on:

In an economy of intricate division of labour, every large organized group is in a position at any time to disrupt or to stop the whole flow of social income; and the system must soon break down if groups persists in exercising that power or if they must continuously be bribed to forgo its disastrous exercise . . . The dilemma here is not peculiar to our present economic order, it must appear in any kind of system. This minority-monopoly problem would be quite as serious for a democratic socialism as it is for the mixed individualist-collectivist system of the present. It is the rock on which our present system is most likely to crack up; and it is the rock on which democratic socialism would be destroyed if it could ever come into being at all.

He did not pretend to have a remedy but spoke about the possibility of 'an awful dilemma: democracy cannot live with tight occupational monopolies; and it cannot destroy them, once they attain great power, without destroying itself in the process.' His remarks can be regarded as an elaboration of Dicey's contrast at the beginning of the twentieth century between the effects of the individual pursuit of self-interest and its collective pursuit (Dicey, 1963). This is the distinction glossed over by British trade union leaders when they say with monotonous regularity: 'If there is to be a free-for-all, we are part of this all.'

DEMOCRACY AND INTEREST GROUPS

Simons' forebodings were followed in the USA by over three decades of unparalleled prosperity in which the membership and influence of US trade unions declined. Unfortunately, a premature prediction is not necessarily a wrong one. We still do not know whether the gloomy forebodings of Dicey and Simons were averted or merely postponed.

The underlying question concerns the impact, not merely of unions, but of all producer and special-interest groups on the functioning of the economic system . . . The problem is not one of inflation, as so often wrongly supposed, but in part of unemployment. If the total effect of the monopolistic activities of producer groups is to price so many people out of work that the resulting unemployment rate is higher than the electorate will tolerate, then our system of political economy is doomed (Jay, 1976). If the government in such a situation tries to spend its way into full employment, the result will be not just inflation, but accelerating inflation. Despite the apparent calm of Britain in the prolonged afterglow of the Falklands campaign, we do not know if the sustainable unemployment rate is too high for democratic stability or, if it is, what the role of union-type monopoloy is in making it so. The fact that we cannot rule out the pessimistic hypothesis is itself important.

The Simons quotation also raises the question of the effects of uncertain property rights on investment. Investment can take place under state ownership, under workers' cooperatives, or under untrammelled private ownership. The private enterprise system can probably adapt to the capture by unions of a large proportion of the return on new investment—provided that proportion is predictable and stable. The main eventual effect might then be higher profit margins and higher gross returns. But a system of confused and unpredictable property rights under a nominally private enterprise system is highly discouraging to investment—and thereby also depressing to employment in the longer run.

It is difficult to pronounce on the breakdown hypothesis in general terms. A great deal depends on things such as the proportion of the population unionised—which is much greater in the UK than in the USA—as well as on the degree of toleration of undercutting of union suppliers by others. Much also hangs on the electorate's toleration of higher unemployment in today's circumstances, on which premature judgements could easily turn out to be wrong.

Moreover, we should not conceive the producer-group threat too narrowly. Collective action to secure real wages incompatible with full employment may come not just through the strike threat alone, but also through political action—import-price ceilings, minimum wage laws and farm support are only some of the more obvious areas. The uncertainty and insecurity of property rights which Simons feared can be the result of regulatory agencies or of legislative hyperactivity as well as of unions. The real danger is that the end result of action taken by people through collective activity will be unacceptable to the same people in their capacity of consumers and voters—a perverse 'invisible hand'. The fact that Simons was premature in his forebodings in the case of the USA does not mean that they can be dismissed.

Why have restrictive policies, not only by unions, but by all producer groups, had more impact in the UK than in many other countries?

Professor Mancur Olson has an interesting hypothesis derived from his theory of comparative growth rates . . . The central conclusion that Olson draws is that

the longer the period in which a country has had a modern industrial pattern of common interest and at the same time democratic freedom of economic organisation without upheaval and disorganization, the greater the extent to which its growth rate will be retarded by organised interests.

Thus it is not surprising that the British disease should have come first to the country which pioneered the industrial revolution and had the longest record of civic freedom and settled institutions.

But there is no need to end this paper on a fatalistic note. As the output gap widens between a slowly-growing country held back by restrictive interest groups and other countries employing best-practice techniques, the incentive to catch up also becomes larger. The more atrophied become a country's techniques and habits, the greater becomes the return to innovation. The gains can become so great that it may be possible to make agreements to share them with the restrictive interest groups. Moreover, restrictive practices are never of the same severity across the economy; and if innovation is blocked in traditional or well-organised sectors, talent and capital will drift to newer areas, where group loyalties have not yet 'solved' the freerider problem. In the last resort, too, the returns to political entrepreneurship from trying to change the institutional or political rules in favour of better economic performance may become so great that the changes are made.

The conclusion to which I am leading is not that the UK is about to have an economic miracle, but that its problems are from now on likely to become typical of mixed advanced democratic economies in general. The British disease pertains not to a particular country but to a stage in political and economic development. The disease is that of collective action by special interest groups preventing a reasonably full use being made of our economic resources. There is some hope that the disease, like many others, may eventually produce its own cure.

31. The Decline of the Industrial Spirit: An Overview and Assessment*

M. J. Weiner

The leading problem of modern British history is the explanation of economic decline. It has not always been thus. Until the later 1960s the generally accepted frame for the history of Britain over the previous century was that of a series of success stories: the bloodless establishment of democracy, the evolution of the welfare state, triumph in two world wars, and the enlightened relinquishment of empire. Such a happy frame, however, became increasingly hard to maintain as, having steered clear of the rocks of political turmoil or military defeat, the British found themselves becalmed in an economic Sargasso Sea. As successive governments, Labour and Tory, saw their varying panaceas for lifting the economy to the level of growth of Britain's neighbours and competitors yield only frustrating failure (despite even the unforeseen windfalls of North Sea gas and oil), the realisation began to sink in that the problem had a long history. 'The English disease,' Correlli Barnett argued in 1975, 'is not the novelty of the past 10 or even 20 years . . . but a phenomenon dating back more than a century' (Barnett, 1975). The intractability of the problem made it ever clearer that it was rooted deep in the nation's social structure and mental climate. The more closely Britain's twentieth-century economic decline is examined, the more social and psychological elements are to be found intertwined with economic factors. The German Director of the London School of Economics. Ralf Dahrendorf, concluded after studying Britain for some years that 'economic performance and cultural values are linked', and that 'an effective economic strategy for Britain will probably have to begin in the cultural sphere' (Dahrendorf, 1976).

All manner of historical explanations for British economic decline have been put forward, ranging from the exclusively economic to those

*Reproduced from M. Weiner, *English Culture and the Decline of the Industrial Spirit 1850–1980* (London, Cambridge University Press, 1981) pp. 3–10, 157–66.

involving political, social and psychological components, and spanning the ideological spectrum from Marxist to Keynesian to free-market standpoints. It is without doubt a complex problem, and lacks any simple or generally accepted solution. Although it is true that, as E. J. Hobsbawm has sternly enjoined, 'economic explanations of economic phenomena are to be preferred if they are available', such explanations as have been put forward, by their inadequacies, have only made clearer the problem's character. Strictly economic explanations either have been based on questionable assumptions or have left large space for 'residual' factors, which would appear to be social and psychological.

In a world perspective, it seems difficult—and unhelpful—to separate sharply culture and economics. Development economists have repeatedly come up against the limitations of purely economic analysis. Most leading development theorists have agreed that economic motivations alone—however necessary—are not sufficient to redirect a society's path (see Lewis, 1955; Rostow, 1960). Culture, society and ideology have been portrayed as central to the development process. This awareness has spawned a large body of literature, emanating particularly from social psychologists and development specialists, that elaborates models of social–psychological change undergone by members of modernising societies. These studies all brought out the importance of such factors, difficult to quantify, as character, world outlook, values and attitudes in the economic transformation of societies (see e.g. McClelland, 1961). This approach has not been limited either to social psychologists or to American scholars. The Swedish Nobel Laureate Gunnar Myrdal, in his massive *Asian Drama* (1968), showed in detail the social and cultural upheaval involved in—and apparently necessary to—development. The example of India virtually overwhelms anyone following a narrow approach to economic development. India's experience since independence has been frustrating for economic planners at home and advisers from the West. Repeatedly, schemes of fiscal and financial policy, foreign aid and programmes of industrial and agricultural investment foundered on the intangible resistances built into perhaps the world's most conservative culture.

Another Asian society, Japan, by its contrasting success, has also underlined the fact that economic behaviour does not take place in a cultural vacuum. We have come to see that Japan's startlingly rapid development owes at least as much to peculiar characteristics of Japanese society and culture—the 'tribal' character of work relationships and the inner discipline that makes possible remarkable adaptability, for example—as to the country's specifically economic techniques. No one can fully understand the Japanese economic miracle without grasping the working principles of Japanese culture.

How did specifically English cultural elements influence economic life? Despite all the publicity given trade union 'obstructionism', this question is in the final analysis primarily about 'bourgeois,' or élite, rather than popular English culture (although there exists no precise line of division between them). Élites have disproportionate influence upon both the effective climate of opinion and the conduct of affairs. The values of the directing strata, particularly in a stable, cohesive society like modern Britain, tend to permeate society as a whole and to take on the colour of national values, and of a general *mentalité*. In economic matters, as has been observed, bosses tend to get the workers they deserve; the attitudes and behaviour of workers are deeply influenced, even if only in reaction, by the attitudes and behaviour of employers. How, then, has English middle- and upper-class culture affected the nation's economic development?

PROGRESS AND ITS DISCONTENTS

For a long time, the English have not felt comfortable with 'progress'. As one social analyst has perceived, 'progress' is a word that in England has come to possess a curiously ambiguous emotive power. 'It connotes tendencies that we accept, even formally approve, yet of which we are privately suspicious' (Allison, 1978). It is an historic irony that the nation that gave birth to the industrial revolution, and exported it throughout the world, should have become embarrassed at the measure of its success. The English nation even became ill-at-ease enough with its prodigal progeny to deny its legitimacy by adopting a conception of Englishness that virtually excluded industrialism.

This suspicion of material and technological development and this symbolic exclusion of industrialism were intimately related in Britain. They appeared in the course of the industrial revolution but, instead of fading away as the new society established itself, they persisted and indeed were extended and strengthened. In the later years of Victoria's reign they came to form a complex, entrenched cultural syndrome, pervading 'educated opinion'. The idealisation of material growth and technical innovation that had been emerging received a check, and was more and more pushed back by the contrary ideals of stability, tranquility, closeness to the past and 'non-materialism'. An 'English way of life' was defined and widely accepted; it stressed non-industrial non-innovative and non-material qualities, best encapsulated in rustic imagery—'England is the country' in Stanley Baldwin's phrase (by his time already a cliché). This countryside of the mind was everything industrial society was not—ancient, slow-moving, stable, cozy and 'spiritual'. The English genius, it declared, was (despite appearances) not economic or technical, but social and spiritual; it did not lie in inventing, producing or selling, but in preserving, harmonising and moralising. The English character was not naturally progressive, but conservative; its greatest task—and achievement—lay in taming and 'civilising' the dangerous engines of progress it had unwittingly unleashed.

Over the years, this outlook contended with an industrial reality that sometimes was proclaimed as a source of pride. The resulting conflicts of social values—progress versus nostalgia, material growth versus moral stability—were expressed in the two widespread and contrasting cultural symbols of workshop and garden (or shire). Was England to be the Workshop of the World or a Green and Pleasant Land? This question, with its presumed incompatibility of industrial and rural values, lay at the back of a great many English minds.

Rural myths did not have to be opposed to industrialism. In late nineteenth-and early twentieth-century America, nostalgia abounded for what was often seen as a simpler and happier time; rural life was often idealised and much was made of its moral importance to the nation. These sentiments, however, rarely came together into a critique of progress itself or of economic development, as in England, except in the hands of a few intellectuals, whose distinctive strain of almost anarchic individualism reflected their awareness of being outside the cultural mainstream. Even rural panegyrists, and those nostalgic for an earlier America, rarely disdained manufacturing or commerce. The ideal of the American yeoman-farmer was of an agrarian technologist and capitalist, a businessman producing for a market, ever ready to invent or adopt technical or commercial improvements. Men like Jefferson welcomed the development of commerce and manufactures as an essential part of civilisation, while idealising the 'rural republic'. Industry would and should come, planted in the rural landscape, the one as American as the other. Even nostalgia had a modernising character in America, as made clear by Henry Ford and his historical reconstruction of Greenfield Village in the 1920s. This project was a sentimental evocation of the simpler America of Ford's early years, and at the same time a celebration of technological progress. Americans may have idealised their 'garden', but it was, in contrast to the English vision we shall explore, an economically dynamic, technically progressive garden.

In England, the symbols of machine and garden, workshop and shire, were in more direct opposition. These symbols embodied a tension that had become implanted deep within middle- and upper-class culture over at least the previous century. Much of the peculiar character of English domestic history over this period was the result of a nation, or at least an élite, at war with itself.

This inner tension in modern English culture is something of a puzzle. Why did hostility to industrial advance persist and even strengthen in the world's first industrial society? Why did such hostility so often take the form of rural myth-making? Some answers lie in the peculiar pattern of nineteenth-century British social history.

THE REVOLUTION THAT NEVER WAS

Nineteenth-century Britain was a pioneer of modernisation. Yet, the path it took to modernity was one all its own. Britain's transition was marked by admirably peaceful gradualism, but also, thereby, by a certain incompleteness. From this incompleteness stemmed long-lasting cultural consequences.

Modernisation has never been a simple and easy process. Wherever and whenever it has occurred, severe psychological and ideological strains and stresses have resulted, though they have not always taken the dramatic form they found in Germany, or received so much attention. In Britain these tensions have been particularly easy to overlook, as the transition to modernity was relatively smooth and involved no political upheaval. However, that very mildness, I shall suggest, fostered a self-limiting element in Britain's development. The industrial revolution in other countries came at least partly from without and thus challenged and disrupted traditional social patterns. In Britain, on the other hand, industrialisation was indigenous, and thus more easily accommodated to existing social structures, which did not need to change radically.

The often-hailed Victorian achievement, seen in this light, was Janus-faced. If society was transformed, with a minimum of violence, the extent of the transformation was more limited than it first appeared to be. New economic forces did not tear the social fabric. Old values and patterns of behaviour lived on within the new, whose character was thus profoundly modified. The end result of the nineteenth-century trans-formation of Britain was indeed a peaceful accommodation, but one that entrenched pre-modern elements within the new society, and gave legitimacy to anti-modern sentiments. The cultural and practical consequences would become clear only in the twentieth century.

The ambiguity of the Victorian achievement has been perceived by some observers, both on the Right and on the Left. Conservative politician, Sir Keith Joseph, has located the source of Britain's contemporary economic problems in the fact that it 'never had a capitalist ruling class or a stable *haute bourgeoisie*'. As a result, he has argued, 'capitalist or bourgeois values have never shaped thought and institutions as they have in some countries' (Joseph, 1975). This interpretation has expressed an important truth, but in a partial and misleading form. It blurs capitalism and bourgeoisie. The key to the peculiar pattern of modern British history is that the two have been distinct. The nation had the world's first (except perhaps for Holland) essentially capitalist ruling class: the eighteenth-century landed aristocracy and gentry. What Britain never had was a straightforwardly bourgeois or industrial élite. This crucial distinction has been usefully elaborated by two Marxist historians, Perry Anderson and Tom Nairn. Anderson and Nairn emphasised the importance of the fact that the industrial revolution began in Britain while the ruling landed aristocracy was becoming still richer, more self-confident and an even more tightly-knit oligarchy. This aristocracy, however, was no longer feudal but was essentially capitalist.' There was thus, 'Anderson argued,' from the start no fundamental antagonistic contradiction between the old aristocracy and the new bourgeoisie' (Anderson, 1964). Consequently, no bourgeois revolution ensued; in its place was accommodation. Yet these two classes, if both capitalist, were not capitalist in the same way. The capitalism of the aristocracy, although varying in individual cases, was basically *rentier*, not entrepreneurial or productive. Thus the accommodation between aristocracy and bourgeoisie meant an adaptation by the new middle classes to a comparatively aloof and passive economic role. The rentier aristocracy succeeded to a large extent in maintaining a cultural hegemony, and consequently (as we shall see) in reshaping the industrial bourgeoisie in its own image. The Victorian retreat of the aristocracy was more political than psychological. The landed élite gave way only slowly to the industrialists, so that, as Peregrine Worsthorne put it not long ago, 'the transference of power, protracted over a century, resembled a merger rather than a conquest; a marriage (in many cases literally) rather than a rape.' The result was, in Worsthorne's phrase, the 'civilizing [of] the bourgeoisie' (Worsthorne, 1977).

Aristocratic hegemony persisted also—indeed, more obviously—in Britain's emerging rival, Germany. Because the political histories of the two nations contrasted so dramatically, for a long time Britain was wrongly seen as taking a path of development opposite to that of

Germany—a path of complete bourgeois triumph as against Germany's holding onto 'feudalism'. Britain was supposed to be the archetypal 'nation of shopkeepers'—a Napoleonic gibe that was false when first uttered, and still false, if less obviously so, when repeated by German writers before and during the first world war. In truth, Britain and Germany both underwent powerful industrial revolutions in the midst of strong and resilient aristocratic societies.

That this encounter of industry and aristocracy led to different economic (not to mention political) outcomes in the two countries can be explained by many factors, chief among them the chronology of economic change, the degree of aristocratic openness and, perhaps most crucial, the character of each aristocracy. Because the industrial revolution in Germany took place later and more suddenly than it did in Britain, the German industrial bourgeoisie had less time to become accepted by and absorbed into the older élite. Second, the Prussian aristocracy in particular was less ready than the English aristocracy to accept wealthy businessmen into its ranks, regardless of how much they hastened to remake themselves on the *Junker* model. for both these reasons, the new industrialists and entrepreneurs of Imperial Germany were more likely than their longer-established English counterparts to retain their preoccupation with production.

Beyond this, however, the two aristocracies were different enough to influence their respective middle classes in quite distinct ways. The Prussian aristocracy was still an aggressive, authoritarian military caste; English lords and gentry had, with prosperity, long since shed that character. Moreover, the *Junkers*, for all their caste pride, were not wealthy on the English scale, and had to continue to struggle ruthlessly to protect and develop their economic and political position. In spite of their romantic pretensions, the *Junkers*, became, as Fritz Stern (1977) observed, ever more 'agrarian industrialists'. It was perhaps this combination of militarism and economic pressure that made Bismarck's government appreciate the geopolitical value of economic development, and that underlay the historic arrangement of 1878–79, in which industry traded political support for the economic support of tariff protection (and, ultimately, *Wetpolitik*). Particularly after 1879, the industrial bourgeoisie in Germany was moving toward an aristocratic model less hospitable than the English to 'free enterprise' or political liberalism, but more suitable to maintaining a fierce drive toward economic growth (closely associated with national power). In Germany, thus, capitalism and liberalism were devalued far more than industrialism, whereas in England it was industrialism and not capitalism or liberalism whose development was inhibited. In this way the conjunction of modernisation with an entrenched aristocracy led in Germany to obstructed political development, and in Britain to inhibited economic development.

The British form of accommodation yielded both gain and cost. The gain was political and social stability, and a 'humanization' of the rawness of early industrialism. The cost was, as Nairn put it, 'the containment of capitalism within a patrician hegemony which never, either then or since, actively favoured the aggressive development of industrialism or the general conversion of society to the latter's values and interests' (Nairn, 1977). Lasting social and psychological limits were thus placed on the industrial revolution in Britain. As Correlli Barnett (1963) concluded in his history of modern British military leadership, 'the social and intellectual values of industrial society never ousted those of the aristocracy'. Out of this successful aristocratic–gentry holding action a distinctly English 'culture of containment' developed. The social conflict was never clearly resolved, but internalised within the compromise that emerged: a new dominant-bourgeois culture bearing the imprint of the old aristocracy. The tensions within this compromise culture were reflected in anxieties and discontents surrounding the idea of material progress, and in the emotions laden onto the cultural symbol of England as a garden. Beyond this, these tensions shaped not only bourgeois culture, but also, through culture, behaviour. A variety of modern British practices that has served to humanise urban industrial society—new towns and green belts, the love of gardening, even a weariness of most modern architecture—owes a debt to this social compromise. Less attractive patterns of behaviour also show their mark—chief among these is persistent economic retardation.

The consolidation of a 'gentrified' bourgeois culture, particularly the rooting of pseudo-aristocratic attitudes and values in upper-middle-class educated opinion, shaped an unfavourable context for economic endeavour. Economic historians, economists, civil servants, and even political leaders held sentiments and ideals that served to restrain rather than stimulate economic growth. Often even those seeking growth showed at the same time the influence of their cultural environment, which worked to 'muffle' or 'domesticate' such growth. Industrialists themselves were crucially affected in developing their view of the world and their role in it. They too gravitated toward what they saw as aristocratic values and styles of life, to the detriment, more often than not, of their economic effectiveness. The outcome was the spectacle (not necessarily all for the bad) of an industrial society diffidently led by men with 'mind-forg'd manacles' restraining their concepts and their actions. How this came about is our story . . .

THE CULTURAL DOMESTICATION OF THE INDUSTRIAL REVOLUTION

At the time of the Great Exhibition of 1851, Britain was the home of the industrial revolution, a symbol of material progress to the world. it was also the home of an apparently triumphant bourgeoisie. Observers like Carlyle and Marx agreed in pointing to the industrialist as the new aristocrat, a figure that was ushering in a radically new order and a new culture. Yet they were misled. From the time of their assertions, social and psychological currents in Britain began to flow in a different direction.

By the 1970s, falling levels of capital investment raised the specter of outright 'deindustrialisation'—a decline in industrial production outpacing any corresponding growth in the 'production' of services. Whether or not such a spectre had substance, it is true that this period of recognised economic crisis in Britain was preceded by a century of psychological and intellectual deindustrialisation. The emerging culture of industrialism, which in the mid-Victorian years had appeared, for good or ill, to be the wave of the future, irresistibly washing over and sweeping away the features of an older Britain, with itself transformed. The thrust of new values borne along by the revolution in industry was contained in the later nineteenth century; the social and intellectual revolution implicit in industrialism was muted, perhaps even aborted. Instead, a compromise was effected, accommodating new groups, new interests and new needs within a social and cultural matrix that preserved the forms and even many of the values of tradition. Potentially disruptive forces of change were harnessed and channelled into supporting a new social order, a synthesis of old and new. This containment of the cultural revolution of industrialism lies at the heart of both the achievements and the failures of modern British history.

The new society created by the later Victorians rested on a domestication of the wilder traits of earlier British behaviour; the rioutous populace, the aggressive and acquisitive capitalists, and the hedonistic aristocrats of the Georgian world became endangered, if not extinct, species of Englishmen. Their descendants were more restrained, more civilised and also more conservative, in that they now had an established and secure place in the social order, or, in the case of the aristocracy, had come to terms with social change and recemented their place in the *status quo*. By Victoria's death, British society had weathered the storms of change, but at the cost of surrendering a capacity for innovation and assertion that was perhaps the other face of the unruliness and harshness of that earlier Britain.

In particular, the later nineteenth century saw the consolidation of a national élite that, by virtue of its power and prestige, played a central role both in Britain's modern achievements and its failures. It administered the most extensive empire in human history with reasonable effectiveness and humanity, and it maintained a remarkable degree of political and social stability at home while presiding over a redistribution of power and an expansion of equality and security. It also presided over the steady and continued erosion of the nation's economic position in the world. The standards of value of this new élite of civil servants, professionals, financiers and landed proprietors, inculcated by a common education in public schools and ancient universities and reflected in the literary culture it patronised, permeated by their prestige much of British society beyond the élite itself. These standards did little to support, and much to discourage, economic dynamism. They threw earlier enthusiasms for technology into disrepute, emphasised the social evils brought by the industrial revolution, directed attention to issues of the 'quality of life' in preference to the quantitative concerns of production and expansion, and disparaged the restlessness and acquisitiveness of industrial capitalism. Hand in hand with this disparagement went the growth of an alternative set of social values, embodied in a new vision of the nation.

The dominant collective self-image in English culture became less and less that of the world's workshop. Instead, this image was challenged by the counter-image of an ancient, little-disturbed 'green and pleasant land'. 'Our England is a garden,' averred the greatest poet of imperialism; another imperialist, a poet laureate, celebrated England at the height of imperial fervour for its 'haunts of ancient peace'; and an anti-imperialist socialist has inspired his readers with the aim of making England once again, as it had been before the industrial revolution, the 'fair green garden of Northern Europe'. The past, and the countryside—seen as inseparable—were invested with an almost irresistible aura. These standards and images supported a very attractive way of life, geared to maintenance of a *status quo* rather than innovation, comfort rather than attainment, the civilised enjoyment, rather than the creation, of wealth.

British political opinion bore the imprint of the aristocracy long after the demise of the aristocracy's power. The politicians, civil servants, churchmen, professional men and publicists who did so much to shape modern British political opinion and policy moved in a climate of opinion uncongenial to the world of industry. Most of them showed a striking fondness for gentry tastes and standards, making such tastes an essential part of the modern British style of government. Political calls for economic growth went against the grain of the values and style of life actually believed in by most politicians and civil servants, as well as by the rest of the élite.

Industrialists themselves were far from immune to this anti-industrial culture; like others, they breathed it in ever more deeply the higher they rose in social position. The new British élite was open to industrialists, if they adapted to its standards. With few exceptions, they were ready to do so, although such adaptation required a degree of disavowal of their own former selves and their very function in society. By modelling themselves—in varying proportions—upon civil servants, professional men, and men of landed leisure, industrialists found acceptance at the upper reaches of British society. Thus, the famed "Establishment" and its consensus was created. Social integration and stability were ensured, but at a price—the waning of the industrial spirit . . .

APPENDIX: BRITISH RETARDATION—THE LIMITS OF ECONOMIC EXPLANATION

Economic explanations of British retardation begin with the classical factors of supply—capital, labour and natural resources. yet these by themselves explain little. Late Victorian and Edwardian Britain boasted capital resources unprecedented in world history, resources clearly adequate to support continued rapid growth. Charles Kindleberger (1964) concluded after a careful study of the period from 1851 to 1950 that 'by any reasonable test the supply of British capital was sufficient'. To explain why domestic investment was not greater, he felt it necessary to discover why it was not more attractive. The size and competency of Britain's labour force posed no obvious obstacle to growth. There was neither a shortage of labour nor such a surplus as to discourage industrial investment. Supplies of the chief industrial resources—coal, iron and other minerals—were more than adequate to maintain vigorous expansion. It was, as Kindleberger concluded, the *use* made of resources, of labour and of capital that was crucial.

The other side of the classical economic equation—demand—offers equally insufficient illumination. Overseas demand was not slackening. Quite the contrary. The economic development of the world, broken only by the Great Depression of the 1930s, was providing ever-growing opportunities to British industry, which were on the whole not taken. The loss of the empire has been popularly seen as a fundamental cause of economic difficulties. In this view, Britain's Victorian economic pre-eminence had been supported by its worldwide possessions and power. 'Trade follows the flag', as the nineteenth-century slogan went. Yet students of the question over the past several decades have agreed that the empire was not, on balance, a crucial economic asset.

If material conditions were not wanting, was there then a social or psychological obstacle to continued economic leadership? Was at least one important part of the emerging problem a *human* one? Two otherwise quite different schools of thought have converged in denying this.

The first of these have been Marxists. E. J. Hobsbawm, the most distinguished of British Marxist historians, insisted in 1968 that, understood rightly, British economic retardation involved no 'irrationalities'. The 'fault' lay not with the temperament, attitudes or abilities of businessmen or workers, but with the self-defeating nature of the capitalist *system*. How, specifically, was this system self-defeating? It depended for its dynamism on one unreliable motor—private profit:

> In a capitalist economy (at all events in its nineteenth-century versions) businessmen will be dynamic only in so far as this is rational by the criterion of the individual firm, which is to maximise its gains, minimise its losses, or possibly merely to maintain what it regards as a satisfactory long-term rate of profit. But since the rationality of the individual firm is inadequate, this may not work to the best advantage of the economy of the whole, or even of the individual firm.

Given this mechanism of change, as Hobsbawm saw it, Britain's early start as an industrial power ultimately proved its undoing. Pioneer industrialisation naturally created a particular pattern of both production and markets that would not remain the one best fitted to sustain economic growth. Yet to change to a new pattern involved both the scrapping of old investments still capable of yielding goods profits, and the venturing of new investments of even greater initial cost. 'So long as satisfactory profits were to be made in the old way, and so long as the decision to modernize had to emerge from the sum-total of decisions by individual firms, the incentive to do so would be weak' (Hobsbawm, 1968). Britain thus—almost inevitably (to Hobsbawm), given its capitalism—stuck with the *status quo* while the rest of the advanced world developed.

Much of this line of reasoning is plausible, and indeed does not preclude the importance of social and psychological factors. Yet Hobsbawm's insistence on the inherent weakness of capitalist economic organisation bordered on dogma. To base an explanation of British economic performance upon the general nature of capitalism makes it very difficult to account for the very real differences in national experiences. If British retardation stemmed from the universal inherent flaws of capitalism, they are strange universals that are so easy to locate in Britain and so hard to find elsewhere. It seems much more likely that we are dealing with a phenomenon at least in part shaped by factors peculiar to late nineteenth- and early twentieth-century British society.

Ironically, an even stronger tendency to dogmatism and universalising abstractions is evident in the work of a new school of non-Marxist and indeed often anti-Marxist economic historians who also deny the need for non-economic explanations. Addressing the problem of British performance up to 1900, a group of econometricians have concluded that there really *was* no problem (McCloskey, 1971). Business and industry did about as well as they possibly could have. 'There is, indeed, little left,' Donald N. McCloskey summed up, 'of the dismal picture of British failure painted by historians.' In its place McCloskey unveiled a portrait of an economy 'not stagnating but growing as rapidly as permitted by the growth of its resources and the effective exploitation of the available technology' (McCloskey, 1970). Applying the new model-building techniques of econometric analysis, McCloskey and his colleagues discovered eminently rational behaviour everywhere they looked. Like Hosbawm, McCloskey (from a very different ideological standpoint) saw businessmen, investors, workers and consumers as tightly fixed within an economic system that operated according to immutable laws. If the pace of economic development in Britain slowed, or if Britain's relative position fell sharply, this was explained by the prevailing market situation. Nobody was to 'blame'; profit was being maximised. In the analyses of these 'Cliometricians' (after Clio, the Muse of History), social institutions, values and sentiments played no role. Whereas Marxists often failed to appreciate the power of social and cultural context, Cliometricians were virtually indifferent to— almost contemptuous of—any evidence merely 'qualitative'.

Does the method of the Cliometricians fit this subject? Many economic historians doubt it. Sidney Pollard observed that *Essays on a Mature Economy*, the product of a conference of 'new economic historians' devoted to this issue, tended to prove 'that the econometric method works well and beyond cavil only where it is used to answer an econometric question'—which the general performance of a national economy is not. Two drawbacks in the use of econometric methods here stand out. First, in such an enterprise, Pollard warned, 'It is the definitions that will determine the conclusions.' It is perilously easy to assume, for instance,

> that competition will force entrepreneurs to take the optimal decisions open

to them, and then to arrive, after lengthy argument and calculation, at the conclusion that [one has] (on these premises) proved that entrepreneurs did take the optimal decisions.

Second, it is all too easy to rely on inappropriate data, or data so weak that they could not carry the conclusions built upon them. Pollard found McCloskey's particular contribution to this controversy, a 'proof' that British productivity in steel and coal before the first world war was ('given the differences in factor endowment and prices') as great as, indeed greater than in the United States, to be riddled with this type of error. Other historians, as versed in econometric techniques as McCloskey and his colleagues, have begun to question their findings as highly 'sensitive to debatable assumptions and tentative estimates.'

The determination to explain all economic phenomena with a self-contained model of purely economic factors pushes much of social life to a dimly-lit periphery. It excludes much of what is most interesting to a general historian. Behaviour not conforming to the assumption of 'rational', profit and wage-maximising action is attributed to a catch-all category such as 'imperfections in the market. When this obscure category is opened to the light, it turns out to be a pathway back to the social world enveloping economics. 'Market imperfections' often resolve into social and political structures or patterns of behaviour that, although not 'rational' in the strict economic sense, are none the less real. Efficient allocations of resources, for example, may be impeded by a variety of such imperfections (as one British sociologist has pointed out):

> Skilled labour is unwilling to migrate, governments legislate against unfamiliar activities, communities demand protection against threatening disruptions of their environment, management cannot assimilate new forms of organization, businessmen foresee only the kinds of demand and technical developments already allowed for in their experience (Marris, 1974).

The question of the causes of British economic decline remain beyond the sole grasp of the economists. 'The problems [involved]' Peter Mathias has concluded, 'cannot be explained just in simple terms of economic hypotheses such as wage rates, shifting terms of trade or deteriorating natural resources' (Mathias, 1969). Similarly, as an economist, Michael Fores, reminded an audience of businessmen and civil servants, 'The variables acting on growth are many, and not concerned only with quantities of economic resources and with industrial techniques' (Fores, 1971). But the need for extra-economic explanation should not be taken as an admission of ignorance. John

Saville (1970), a social and economic historian, has reminded business historians that

Historial analysis involves different levels of precision and imprecision, and once we become more aware than is common at present of the considerable margins of error in many of our statistical series—which are often so effortlessly moulded into unnatural shapes without any indication being given of what the dimensions of error are likely to be—we shall perhaps be less worried about the admittedly more difficult problems of evaluating cultural, social or ideological factors.

32. The Underlying Economic Crisis*

Geoff Hodgson

It is possible to draw up a representative list of explanations that have appeal, at first sight, as explanations of the underlying crisis. All of them claim to pay some regard to peculiarly British conditions. These theories idenitfy the following causes of the British crisis:

1. policy mistakes of government and civil servants;
2. excessive taxation;
3. excessive government spending;
4. high degree of penetration by multinational firms;
5. a decline in corporate profits;
6. insufficient investment;
7. the strength and resistance of the trade unions.

The list as a whole is not exhaustive, neither of course are the items on the list mutually exclusive. A number of the explanations have a wide adherence from both Left and Right of the political spectrum: in particular (1), (5) and (7). In addition, the Right has tended to emphasise (2) and (3), while the Left has emphasised (4) and (6).

The point of making a critical excursion through these theories is to try to reach a more adequate, historical and non-monocausal explanation of the underlying economic crisis in Britain.

1. THE CRISIS AS A RESULT OF MISTAKES IN POLICY?

In an extensive and imaginative study, Posner (1978) provides insights into the comparison of the different effects of various approaches to

*Reproduced from G. Hodgson, *Labour at the Crossroads* (London, Martin Robertson, 1981), pp. 142–66.

economic policy. The striking conclusion is that variations in policy make a difference, but not big enough to account for Britain's historic decline. This answer runs against the entire orthodox tradition in economics, which assumes that the basic economic structure is sound and that minor adjustments are required to put the economy on an optimum path. Posner's study indicates that solutions to the British crisis cannot be found in terms of mere adjustments to, for example, the money supply, or the level of public expenditure, or the value of the pound, or the level of imports.

In Posner's study, four groups of researchers were asked to review two historical periods: 1964 to 1969, and 1970 to 1975. Their task was to determine, with hindsight, if the governments of the day could have arrived at better settings for tuning the economy, and with the help of econometric models of their choice to determine the benefits of an improved set of macroeconomic policies. Four contemporary schools of thought were represented. The monetarist approach was developed by Laidler. A Keynesian approach was taken by Surrey and Omerod from the National Institute of Economic and Social Research. Cripps, Fetherston and Godley represented the Cambridge Economic Policy Group. Finally, Ball and Burns worked with the models and ideas developed at the London Business School. Each of the four groups was allowed to adjust the standard variables of macroeconomic policy, such as the supply of money, the level of corporate and personal taxation, the level of public expenditure and the exchange rate of sterling. If desired they were allowed to experiment with incomes policies or restrictions on imports. Neither the external environment nor the structure of industry could be changed.

The four groups came to some general agreement on certain mistakes of policy: it was held that sterling should have been devalued earlier than 1967; the 1970–74 Heath government was criticised for setting sterling too high a value in 1971, and for the threshold agreements in its 1973–74 incomes policy. However, there vas less agreement on the gravity of these mistakes and the optimal policy alternative. Moving from the 'obvious' mistakes to the less obvious, there was even less agreement. Wide divergences existed between the optimal settings for policy instruments that were suggested by each group. Similar divergences existed on the expected benefits from each 'optimal' policy. The lack of a consensus on such crucial issues of economic management makes it difficult to suggest that Britain's crisis clearly or wholly results from mistakes in policy.

Even more significantly, none of the four teams was able to come up with a 'golden route' to economic success by mere adjustment of the instruments of economic policy. In each case, each team came up with relatively small adjustments towards the perceived optimum; but this 'optimum' was still a Britain with the symptoms of crisis and ongoing decline. . . .

2. BRITAIN TOTTERING UNDER AN EXCESSIVE TAX BURDEN?

Although the British economic predicament is frequently explained in the media as resulting from excessive tax burden, there is little empirical evidence to support this proposition. Several writers have pointed this out and there is no need for anything more than a short statement of the most important facts here.

First let us compare total taxes in Britain with other major OECD countries. Table 32.1 gives a summary of relevant data for the 1969–75 period, when tax levels in Britain were higher than at any time in its preceding history. It can be seen that several major and more prosperous countries have overall tax levels higher than Britain. In fact, in 1975 Britain came at about the middle of the range.

A longer historical view gives even stronger results. As Phelps Brown has pointed out, for the fifteen years immediately before the first world war the highest rate of income tax was under 7 per cent, and from 1909 most taxable earned income paid less than 4 per cent. Yet this was not a time of vigorous economic growth; it was a period of stagnation with little advance in productivity. And it is clear in retrospect that the current decline of the British economy has roots that can be traced back to that period, and earlier.

More detailed analysis of the British tax structure (Kay and King, 1978) reveals many defects of the present system, but does not give clear support to the notion that the 'excessive burden' of taxes exists or is responsible for the British malaise. For example, it has been suggested that the taxation system in Britain has had little perceived effect on work effort or overtime working by employees (Brown and Levin, 1974). Similarly, evidence indicates that top managers have not changed their hours of work, their work effort, their propensity to move to other jobs or their attitude to moving overseas as a result of perceived and actual increases in the taxation of those on high incomes (Kay and King, 1978).

Turning to the corporation, again there is little evidence that taxation has been excessive or responsible for lack of investment. In a classic article, King (1975) showed that corporation taxes have fallen con-

Table 32.1: International tax levels

Country	1969	1975
Norway	45.9	54.9
Netherlands	43.1	53.2
Sweden	44.5	52.2
Denmark	42.0	50.4
Austria	42.1	46.1
Belgium	38.0	44.7
West Germany	40.0	42.9
France	40.7[a]	41.2
United Kingdom	42.7	40.8
Finland	36.1	40.5
Canada	36.7	37.8
Australia	29.4	34.2
Italy	28.4[a]	34.0
United States	31.1	32.5
Switzerland	25.0	30.1
Greece	28.8	27.2
Japan	20.8	27.4

Source: *Economic Trends*, December 1977, London, HMSO
Note: Taxes including social security contributions as a percentage of GNP at factor cost on common OECD system of national accounts. Countries ranked in terms of 1975 percentages.
[a]1970 figures

tinuously since the 1950s, reaching an effective average rate of only 12 per cent in the early 1970s. Corporate taxes in Britain amount to 1.7 per cent of GDP, compared with figures as high as 3.5 per cent in Japan, 3.0 per cent in the United States, 2.3 per cent in France and 2.2 per cent in Italy. The figures for West Germany and Sweden are 1.7 and 1.8 per cent, respectively. There is little substantial evidence to support the repeated diagnosis, of the CBI and others, that taxation has removed much of the incentive from work and investment in the British economy.

3. BRITAIN SUFFERING FROM SPENDTHRIFT GOVERNMENTS?

Perhaps the most sophisticated argument that has connected Britain's economic problems with high levels of public expenditure is that of Bacon and Eltis (1977). As is well known, they argue that a growing shift of resources from the production of marketed goods and services to unmarketed public services reduced the rate of growth of the British economy, weakened the balance of payments, reduced investment and fuelled inflation. In recent years, however, their thesis has come under increasing criticism. One frequent criticism of their underlying theory is that, even if the share of non-marketed output has increased, it is not in itself evidence that the marketed sector has sufferd as a result of being 'crowded out'. It would be necessary to show that the non-marketed public sector had made a claim on resources that otherwise the marketed sector would have used. This has not been done. In fact, more than three-quarters of the workers who entered the expanding public sector in the early 1970s were women, so high government demands on labour resources have been largely offset by an increasing female participation rate; at the same time, male unemployment rates have increased considerably. Crowding-out, it seems, has not occurred on the labour market. . . .

Other crowding-out theories have placed more emphasis on shortages of finance. It is impossible to do justice to this argument, and the fierce controversy surrounding it, here. On balance, however, the theoretical and empirical evidence do not seem to back up the thesis that public spending has constrained finance for the private sector. . . .

But, of course, there are other well-tried ways of blaming public spending for the crisis. Perhaps the most popular of all is the suggestion that excessive public spending has increased the public sector borrowing requirement which, in turn, has led to an increase in the money supply which, according to monetarist arguments, leads to inflation. Naturally, this issue is far too complex to be discussed fully here. However, it will be sufficient to point out some serious flaws in the argument. First, the PSBR was never a serious problem until about 1973, when, for the first time ever, it exceeded 6 per cent of GDP. By 1975 it had reached a peak of more than 11 per cent of GDP. Before 1973, with the single exception of 1967, the PSBR had never exceeded 4 per cent of GDP, and it had actually been zero or negative in 1969 and 1970. Second, the link between the PSBR and the money supply is often tacitly assumed, but it is highly questionable. In reviewing evidence for the connection, Blackaby concluded: 'the association of changes in the money supply and the public sector borrowing requirement has ceased to hold' (Blackaby, 1979). Kaldor reached an even more forceful conclusion when he showed that changes in the PSBR could explain no more than 5 per cent of the variation on money supply for 1966–79 (Kaldor, 1980). Even with an alleged connection between the rate of inflation and the money supply (which is increasingly being subjected to doubt), the connection between public spending and inflation is not proven. Although the control of public spending (and its allocation) may be a real problem, public spending cannot be blamed for a crisis that had begun to mature well before the rise of the PSBR to over £4 billion and to the tabloid headlines. . . .

4. PILLAGE BY THE MULTINATIONALS?

The idea that modern multinational firms are largely responsible for the decline of the British economy is popular in the labour movement. But, in addition, it has been argued at length by economists, particularly Holland (1975). There is clear evidence that multinational firms have been growing at an alarming rate, moving towards a situation where the entire world capitalist economy is dominated by just a few hundred large firms. . . . However, a concentration of economic power is not necessarily deleterious, *in terms of the standard indices of economic performance*. And there is a danger of confusing a genuine political concern about an enormous concentration of unaccountable and undemocratically controlled economic power with the actual effects of multinational penetration upon the performance of the British economy and with the economic causes of unsatisfactory performance by the multinationals located in Britain.

Holland has suggested that multinational firms have exported capital abroad and taken up foreign markets by producing overseas rather than in Britain. . . . Let us accept that there has been a serious export of capital (as Hobsbawm and others have suggested) from Britain. Let us accept that multinationals have facilitated this transfer. The question still remains as to why the transfer has taken place. *The inescapable conclusion is that the capital has been transfered because of unfavourable conditions for production and profit within the British economy.* If this were the case it would apply to *any* firm operating in the same circumstances, multinational or otherwise. The implication, quite clearly, is that it is primarily the unfavourable environment for capitalist production in Britain that has caused the export of capital, not the existence of *multinational* firms themselves.

In any case, from an historical perspective, the multinational penetration thesis is also found wanting. On all accounts the rapid growth of the multinational firm in Britain has been a post-second world war phenomenon. Yet, compared with Britain's past, this has been a period of relatively high economic growth for Britain. And if the decline of the British economy dates from at least as far back as the end of the

nineteenth century, which I believe it does, then multinationals cannot
be indicted as the main cause of the decline. In the interwar period,
Britain experienced an early and exceptionally severe depression, yet
there were very few multinationals in existence and their operations
were not nearly as significant as they are today. Thus they cannot be
regarded as *the fundamental cause* of the crisis. To find the latter our
attention must shift to the structure and development of the British
economy itself.

5. A PROFITS SQUEEZE?

In the meantime, there are other inadequate explantions to be
discussed, although it must be noted that the seven explanations have
been ranked in increasing order of plausibility, each in turn containing a
larger germ of truth. At this point we turn to the persuasive argument of
Glyn and Sutcliffe (1972) which was very influential in the mid-1970s.
These authors showed, in their now famous book, that the level of
profits in Britain, as a share of national income, had declined from the
early 1960s. It was argued that British capital had been ground down by
the twin millstones of strong international economic competition and a
defensive and well-organised national trade union movement. As a
consequence, the working class was able to claim an increasing share of
the cake by bargaining for higher wages relative to the total value of
output. This meant, of course, a squeeze on profits, a consequent failure
of investment and a self-perpetuating decline. . . .

Since the publication of their book, a great deal of discussion has been
generated around the empirical aspects of their argument. Yaffe (1973)
pointed out that if after-tax wage incomes are considered, their share of
national income has remained at about 50 per cent for the entire period
under consideration. However, this could simply displace the cause of
the squeeze from disposable wages to increasing taxes on incomes. It
does not show that a profits squeeze had not taken place. More poignant
is the criticism of King (1975), who has shown that the decline in the
share of profits in Britain is exaggerated if it is taken into account that
taxes on profits have fallen dramatically since the 1950s. However, as
would be expected, there was a decline in profits in the late 1970s
leading up to the 1980 recession. It seems that profits have been affected
by events in Britain in the 1960s and 1970s.

A more substantial critique of the Glyn–Sutcliffe thesis would be
along theoretical and methodological lines. Whilst in many ways the
thesis is attractive and innovative, it is found wanting on a number of

counts. Accepting that workers have pushed up real wages, a direct effect on profits would occur only if productivity did not increase. The account given by Glyn and Sutcliffe seems to suggest that there has been a struggle between capital and labour over a *given quantity* of output. Against this, it can be established quite easily that vastly different levels of productivity exist int he advanced capitalist countries, that Britain is at the bottom of the league, and that possible increases in output should not have been ruled out. . . . There is no escaping from the fact that output per worker in British manufacturing industry is about one-third of what it is in the United States and significantly less than in most of the large competing capitalist countries. With productivity differentials such as these it is difficult to support the notion that constraints in the productivity of output have been less important than the wage-induced profits squeeze. After all, an increase in productivity of 20 per cent, with up to half going to increased wages, could totally alleviate a reduction of gross profit shares from say 20 to 10 per cent. . . . This and other evidence indicate that it is not primarily a profits squeeze that has been the problem, but a failure of capitalist firms to *respond* to pressure for higher wages by increasing productivity. . . .

Figures for the growth in overall national productivity . . . give a slightly different picture. They show that annual growth in productivity was lower in the UK than in any other major competing countries, with the single exception of the United States, for the 1963–73 period. It was in this period, according to Glyn and Sutcliffe, that severe squeezes on profits took place. Since 1973, productivity in Britain has fallen dramatically, but other countries, such as Italy, have experienced the same phenomenon.

Does this persistently low and flagging productivity in the UK indicate that there is no way of reversing a deep-rooted trend, that growth rates in output should be regarded as constrained, and that the profits squeeze hypothesis should be regarded as valid after all? One single event suggests that this is not the case. In 1974 the Heath government restricted work in manufacturing industry to a three-day week for six weeks. Although labour power and capital equipment were utilised for no more than 60 per cent of the time, output was about 90 per cent of its normal level, indicating an immediate jump of labour productivity per hour of around 50 per cent.

I have been at greater pains to stress the issue of low productivity Britain because, as well as the Glyn–Sutcliffe thesis, it is crucial to my further argument below, when I shall address the question of the causes of low and flagging productivity. . . .

6. LOW INVESTMENT AS THE CAUSE OF THE CRISIS?

There is little doubt that the level of investment is much lower in the UK than in other advanced capitalist countries. Although it has risen in recent years, from around 13 per cent of GDP in 1967–68 to more than 16 per cent in 1974–77, it is still comparatively low, and Table 31.2 shows. As a result of this consistently poor investment performance, the amount of capital assets per employee in manufacturing industry in Britain is much lower than elsewhere. It has been estimated that a worker in the manufacturing sector in West Germany and the United States is backed up by about three times more assets than his or her colleague in Britain, and in Japan the value of assets per employee is four times greater.

Table 32.2. Gross investment per employee in manufacturing; 1960–75

	1960	1965	1970	1975
United Kingdom	334	460	604	1006
United States	—	1675	2145	2947
West Germany	—	—	—	1707[a]
France	—	905	1439	2682
Japan	492	460	1317	1768
Italy	332	367	751	1469[a]

Note: All figures in US dollars at current prices and exchange rates.
Source: F. Blackaby (ed.), *Deindustrialisation* (London, Heinemann Educational Books, 1978,) p. 297.
[a]1979 figures.

However, whilst these differences must be important, and offer a partial explanation of the British malaise, they prove, on close inspection, to be inadequate as a complete explanation. I consider differences in investment first, and differences in amount of plant and machinery per employee second.

As Brown and Sheriff (1979) and Purdy (1976) have pointed out, it would be wrong to place sole stress on the *quantity* of investment as an explanation of poor economic performance. Qualitative considerations should be involved as well. Purdy and others have shown that the increase in output per unit of investment is much lower in Britain than in several other advanced countries. This is shown in Table 31.3. Despite differences in the two sets of figures, the comparatively low level of investment productivity in Britain is plain to see. Amongst the countries listed, only Japan has a similarly poor performance, and this is overcome by much larger levels of investment overall. It is clear that *even if* investment had been higher in the UK, increases in output would not have been as dramatic as in the USA, West Germany, France and Italy.

Table 32.3. Comparative investment productivity

	Increase in GDP per unit of investment in plant and machinery 1968–72	Increase in per capita GDP per unit of gross fixed capital formation, 1970–77
United Kingdom	0.23	0.52
United States	0.49	0.89
West Germany	0.43	0.80
France	0.49	1.06
Japan	0.32	0.52
Italy	0.51	1.03

Source: D. Purdy 'British capitalism since the war', *Marxism Today*, September/October 1976, p. 313; M.E. Blume, in R.E. Caves and L.B. Krause (ed.) *Britain's Economic Performance* (Washington, The Brookings Institution, 1980), p. 266.

For comparison of the effects of absolute differences in plant and machinery, the study by Pratten (1975) is invaluable. He examined 100 multinational companies located in Britain, the USA, West Germany and France, and found that when comparing productivity differences between the UK and the other three countries differences in plant and machinery were a fairly minor causal factor. In the comparison between West Germany and the UK, differences in plant and machinery appeared to be responsible for only about one-fifth of the average difference of productivity of 35 per cent. There were other factors, such as the length of the production run, the efficiency of capital utilisation and the final product mix, that together were much more important than differences in the stock of capital.

The conclusion must be that whilst low investment is a problem, and also very much a symptom of the British crisis, it is not the principal cause of low productivity and relative economic decline.

7. TRADE UNION POWER AS THE ORIGIN OF THE CRISIS?

Since Glyn and Sutcliffe's pioneering work in the early 1970s, a number of writers, including some of socialist persuasion, have followed their lead in suggesting that the strength and nature of the trade union movement has something to do with the economic crisis in Britain. Perhaps the most persuasive contributions of this type are those of Purdy (1976) and Kilpatrick and Lawson (1980). All these writers emphasise the long-term nature of the British economic decline. They note that the British trade union movement was one of the earliest to be established, it has a continuity of organisation unfractured by invasion or internal reaction, it is densely organised at the point of production, and it has recruited a large fraction of the workforce. Kilpatrick and Lawson also emphasise the decentralised system of collective bargaining in Britain, and its role in constraining productivity growth. The importance of these studies, as I shall endorse below, lies in their emphasis on the labour process and the need to include an analysis of the sphere of production in determining the causes of economic development or decline. . . .

However, whilst the trade union movement may have resisted technological change in Britain, it cannot be singled out as the only cause of decline. If trade union organisation at the point of production is the only cause, how is the extremely *slow* growth of productivity to be explained in the United States, where the trade union movement encompasses little more than 20 per cent of the workforce? And how is the relatively *high* growth rate of productivity (exceeding that of Britain, West Germany, France and the United States in the 1963–73 period) in Italy to be explained, where the trade union movement is about 57 per cent of the workforce? And what about the Swedish economic 'miracle', in a country where trade union density formally exceeds that in Britain? Reference to the qualifying factors of strength and structure of organisation, mentioned by Purdy, does not seem to account for all these differences.

Another indication of the complexity of the problem is found in comparative strike statistics. Although industrial stoppages do not directly reflect bargaining strength at the point of production, many commentators have seen strikes as a major symptom of the British disease. However, the figures show a high strike rate in Italy and the United States, with Britain significantly behind. . . . The exaggerated picture painted by the national media of a strike-prone Britain is a gross distortion. Even through the 'strike-ridden' 1970s, on the average each

British employee was on strike for less than 1 day in 100. Whilst the existence of a strong trade union movement can act as a *threat*, and force the employer to concede demands *before* a strike is called, the picture of the British economy being dragged to a halt by the activities of militants bears no resemblance to reality.

Whilst the Kilpatrick and Lawson argument is on a sophisticated level, is there not an object lesson in these statistics of strike concentration? Whilst their data are extremely important, and have a sound basis in economic history, the examples given are from studies of relatively few industries and plants. From these would it not be possible to exaggerate the effects of trade union organisation on the shop floor?

In referring to Britain's unique labour history, a danger exists that the role of management in Britain's economic development will be ignored. There is plenty of evidence to indicate that *both* managerial *and* trade union factors are important in understanding Britain's economic decline (Payne, 1978). As a result of the early industrial revolution in Britain, management practices and attitudes were crystallised long before those of their American, West German, French, Italian or Japanese colleagues. Industrial relations and methods were based on the needs of the early and more basic industries: cotton, coal, iron and steel, and heavy engineering. The more precise and sophisticated managerial practices required for modern industry were slow to develop. It was in the United States, not Britain, that the modern techniques of 'scientific management' (the ideas of F. W. Taylor) were first to emerge. Management backwardness in Britain was coupled with a failure to set up new industries and methods of production. It was in Germany, not Britain, that the chemical industry was first to develop on a mass scale. It was in the United States, not Britain, that the mass production of consumer durables was established for the first time with products as the Ford Model T. Backwardness was further perpetuated by low investment in new plant and machinery; managers were not encouraged to learn new ways by the arrival of new equipmnent and new techniques. Minds and social relations became bounded by processes, products and practices that had been mastered in the apprenticeship of the various phases of the industrial revolution. . . .

There is further evidence that Britain's industrial decline cannot be blamed entirely on the trade union movement and that backward managerial practices should also be considered. In a very important comparative study of a large number of British and United States industries, Caves (1980) shows that both managerial and trade union factors can be used to explain relatively low productivity levels in the United Kingdom. Confirming previous studies, Caves showed with regression analysis that amounts of capital equipment did not explain differences in productivity. His most interesting results were obtained with independent variables relating to trade union strength, regional location and need for skilled managers.

The three sets of data for the crucial independent variables were on (1) the proportion of manual employees covered by collective bargaining agreements, (2) the percentage of industry employment in 'older' regions (i.e. Scotland, Wales, North, North West, Yorkshire and Humberside, West Midlands), and (3) the percentage of managerial and kindred employees in the workforce of the US counterpart industry. The first of these sets of data relates, of course, to trade union strength. the second indicates those industries that tend to be located in those regions most affected by older work and management practices. The third starts from the premise that industries differ in the amount and quality of managerial skills they require. The idea was to test the idea that the UK experiences larger shortfalls in productivity in those industries requiring more numerous managers, assuming that the US provided an indication of relative requirements.

Caves experimented with a number of independent variables. When used as an independent variable, he found that (1) was *not significant* as an explanation of differences in productivity, and coefficients of different sign were obtained, depending on the other independent variables chosen. However, (1) became significant *in combination with* (2), which indicates that trade union strength is important in reducing productivity in those industries that are more concentrated in older industrial regions. In other words, trade union strength has an inhibiting effect on productivity when it is located in industries more likely to be dominated by less advanced management practices and forms of organisation. But, to repeat, Caves found that trade union strength was not significant on its own.

By far the most significant independent variable was (3). This implied that British industry's relative productivity falls as the need for managerial sophistication rises. However, the coefficient on this variable is not nearly as large as on the variable formed from the product of the elements of (1) and (2). Caves draws the following conclusion: 'I found strong statistical evidence to support the negative influence on industrial productivity of both poor labour–management relations and deficiencies in British management.'

It appears, therefore, that Kilpatrick and Lawson can be criticised for considering trade union power in isolation from managerial practice and structure. Britain's economic problem does not stem from the single factor of *either* strong trade unions *or* poor management. It stems from backward managerial–worker *relations* and work practices most concentrated in the older industrial regions. More exactly it is the historically-determined *social relations within the sphere of production* that have to be considered. The relatively backward nature of these relations in Britain, resulting from the fact that Britain is the oldest industrial nation, is the most important element in explaining the relatively poor industrial and economic performance since the end of the nineteenth century.

33. Theories of Decline*

Bernard Stafford

The modern Keynesian analysis of the post-war decline of the UK economy is less rudimentary than some commentators on the Left suppose, but also less complete than its advocates often acknowledge. For the London CSE Group (1980, pp. 37–8) and in Blake and Ormerod (1980, pp. 3–34) the message of Keynesianism is that the level of output and employment depends upon the extent to which existing productive capacity is taken up by effective demand in domestic markets. This is of course a central claim of the *General Theory* but the post-Keynesian analysis of the decline of the UK economy, as developed by Cripps and Godley (1978), Eatwell (1982), Kaldor (1975, 1979), Singh (1977) and Thirwall (1980, ch. 2) departs from it in two respects. First, the principle of effective demand is shown to operate in international markets through the mechanism of the foreign trade multiplier and is thus not confined to the operation of the domestic market. And second, changes in demand are shown to generate changes in productive capacity and are thus not confined in their effects to the utilisation of existing capacity. In this way the familiar short-run analysis of employment and output in one economy is converted into a long-run analysis of international growth. The analysis also incorporates the claim that the manufacturing sector is the engine of growth, but in contrast to the claims of the role of effective demand, there is nothing distinctively Keynesian about this argument which is consistent with and accepted within most other explanations of the decline of the UK economy.

The multiplier analysis asserts that the international market mechanism is not self-correcting at full employment levels of activity and shows how trade imbalances between economies will result in changes in

*Reproduced from B. Stafford, 'The class struggle, the multiplier and the alternative economic strategy', in M. Sawyer and K. Schott (eds.), *Socialist Economic Review 1983*, (London, Merlin 1983)

output and employment with relative prices unaffected. Several factors contribute to this result. The oligopolistic manufacturing corporations which dominate trade between capitalist economies operate with planned reserves of capacity and typically respond to demand changes by changing output and employment rather than prices. Domestic labour markets are also non-competitive. Trade unions in an economy suffering from a fall in demand for its products in world markets and a growing trade deficit will struggle to protect real wages from the increase in the price of imports induced by a falling exchange rate. Success in this will result in generalised inflation in the prices of domestic and foreign goods rather than a corrective increase in the relative price of foreign goods. A government may of course finance a growing trade deficit from foreign currency reserves or by borrowing from abroad and run a budget deficit designed to offset the depressive effect of the trade deficit on domestic activity. But this strategy can offer only a temporary respite. The reserves will eventually run out, and the terms on which loans can be raised will become increasingly restrictive. Sooner or later the government will be forced to withdraw the fiscal offset to the fall in net exports and allow a fall in income and employment sufficient to generate a matching fall in imports. The message of the analysis is that the level of output and employment in a trading economy with a given propensity to import depends upon the demand for its exports. This claim is easily converted into a dynamic form which asserts that the growth of output and employment depends on the growth in demand for exports for any given income elasticity of demand for imports.

The link between the expansion of demand and economic growth is established by the claim that changes in demand and output are a principal determinant of both investment and productivity growth. The output–productivity relationship is that described by the well-known 'Verdoorn Law'. The output–investment relationship is the element of the post-Keynesian analysis which most clearly distinguishes it from most other explanations of the decline of the UK economy. The shortest and most general expression of the relationship is that, as capitalist production is the production of commodities by commodities, the growth of output and capital accumulation are merely different aspects of the same process. Capital accumulation is thus the sign that growth is taking place and not the originating cause of it. A fuller expression can be provided by an amalgamation of the post-Keynesian distribution theory and the familiar accelerator theory of investments, the former describing how, within wide limits, capitalists are free to accumulate as they please for profits and savings will depend on the rate of investment;

and the latter showing how investment depends on the prospective changes in demand and the expected level of output. This view of the relationship between demand, investment and profits is the theoretical basis of Kaldor's claim that

> savings and capital accumulation in a capitalist economy do not represent an independent variable—a faster rate of growth induces a higher rate of investment—it also brings about a higher share of savings to finance that investment through its effect on the share of profits.

(Kaldor, 1968, p. 390) and also explains why the post-Keynesian analysis of growth focuses on the demand effects of imbalances between planned exports and imports rather than looking to mismatches between planned savings and investment. The profits-accelerator and Verdoorn mechanisms convert the foreign trade multiplier into a variant of the Hicksian super-multiplier whereby, for a given income elasticity of demand for imports, the growth of output and capacity in a trading economy will be governed by the growth of demand for its exports.

In the world as a whole the growth of exports is endogenous and thus in the multiplier system the growth of world output is indeterminate. But it requires only one economy, or one bloc of economies, to be suffering from falling net exports for all others to be necessarily enjoying rising net exports. In this case the elements of the super-trade multiplier will interact to propel the unconstrained and constrained economies along divergent growth paths. In the former the growth in productivity and investment induced by buoyant export demand will improve competitiveness and attract additional demand in both home and foreign markets, and so on. The reverse process will operate in the bloc of constrained economies—slackening demand will depress investment and retard the growth of productivity, which will undermine competitiveness, which will further reduce demand, and so on. This is the principle of circular and cumulative causation from which the post-Keynesian analysis derives its explanation of persistent international differences in economic growth. The elements of the post-Keynesian account of the relative decline of the UK economy are all now to hand. The originating cause has been a demand constraint imposed by a chronic deterioration in the competitiveness of UK manufacturers in world markets. This contraction in demand has depressed investment and retarded technical progress. These effects in turn have made UK manufacturers still less attractive in world markets and thus set in train a sequence of induced contractions in net exports, output and employment. And all the time these forces have been working in the opposite direction in other more successful economies.

This is a persuasive account of the process of relative economic decline, but does it offer a reasonably complete explanation of the post-war decline of the UK economy? The issue here is adequacy rather than correctness. The question is not whether the specific claims of the analysis are correct or not but whether the system they comprise is reasonably complete as an account of the causes and mechanisms that could have produced the observed outcome. To put the point another way, if each claim of the analysis were valid would we then have a genuine understanding of the causes of the decline of the UK economy. The analysis offers an account of the process of economic growth which explains how differences in economic growth will become self-perpetuating. But the issue at stake is not how differences in growth persist and widen, nor, even, how any trading economy may suffer a progressive decline. What we want to know is why the UK economy suffered such a decline. If the post-Keynesian analysis is to explain why what was possible anywhere actually occurred in the UK it must also say something about the original cause of the failure of the UK to hold world markets. The analysis can tell us that this failure is attributable to a process of cumulative decline, but this does not advance the argument. It can also say that the cause is a low world income elasticity of demand for UK exports or a chronic deterioration in non-price competitiveness—but this is merely to express the unexplained factor in a different form of words. The source of the problem here is of course the structure of the theory of circular and cumulative causation which is that A causes B, which causes C, which causes . . . N, which causes A. As any outcome is explained only in terms of its consequences nothing can be said about what initiates the process of cumulative decline (or expansion). Any analysis which relies on the theory can thus offer no explanation of why the UK has experienced slow growth rather than fast growth.

This difficulty is plainly evident in the response of Keynesian writers to the question 'What was the origin of the cumulative decline of the UK economy?' In answer to the question 'Why, if Britain was the most successful economy in the early nineteenth century, did she not remain a world leader?' (Eatwell, 1982, p. 61), Eatwell replies 'in part this was due simply to the inevitable effect of other countries industrialising—a catching-up process'—(ibid., p. 62), and

the challenge of early British success had forced other countries to adopt new strategies to ensure a high rate of growth of demand for their domestic industry . . . So in France, Germany, Russia, Japan and the United States . . . an active role was played by the state in promoting industrialisation . . .

In France, Germany and the United States banks were organised for the express purpose of promoting industrialisation. (ibid., pp. 65–6).

This seems a plausible and useful extension of the post-Keynesian analysis until it is recalled that the central message of the analysis is that 'in a market economy the princple of cumulative causation ensures that success breeds success and that failure breeds failure' (ibid., p. 60). Eatwell's analysis of the origins of the economic decline of the UK thus seems to require the rider 'except in the case of success of the UK and the failure of Germany, France, Russia and the United States'.

Ward's response is that 'an understanding of how the process (of declining competitiveness and slow growth) came about may not be all that relevant to the question of how it can be reversed and, in any event, certainly ought not to be a precondition for designing policies to protect the British economy from the effects of the historical process' (Ward, 1981, p. 97). The claim that a strategy for economic reconstruction can be formulated without knowledge of the causes of the decline which it seeks to reverse is not a serious argument. It may however be possible to moderate the process of decline by a strategy derived from an analysis which says little or nothing about underlying causes. But this view implies and contains a major redefinition of the purpose and scope of the AES. The strategy to be derived from the post-Keynesian analysis is at best a programme for rescue and protection which cannot offer the prospect of reconstruction and regeneration. The arguments here lead directly to the conclusion that the post-Keynesian analysis offers neither an explanation of the post-war decline of the UK economy nor the basis of a strategy for sustained economic recovery.

Marxist analyses are not vulnerable to the charge of inadequacy of scope. None of them may be accurate but each represents an attempt to uncover the underlying political and economic forces which have governed the progress of the UK economy over the post-war period. The most fully developed Marxist explanations rely on a general theory of self-generated decline and crisis which is first applied to the world capitalist economy to account for the rise and fall of the long boom (for example, Glyn and Harrison, 1980, ch. 1; Pillay, 1981, Glyn and Sutcliffe, 1972, ch. 4; Aaronovitch et al., 1981, ch. 13) and then extended to incorporate the distinctive features of the UK economy which explain the relative weakness of the long boom and the extra severity of the post-1973 slump (Glyn and Harrison, 1980, ch. 2; Aaronovitch et al, 1981, ch. 6). Although all Marxist writers attribute the differential performance of the UK economy to differences in the structure of class relationships, there are substantial disagreements about which class relationships have been crucial and about the mechanisms by which class conflict has been transmitted into the observable outcome of slow growth. The major division is between those who put the conflict between capital and labour at the centre of the analysis and those for whom the primary factor is the orientation of powerful sections of the capitalist class and the conflict which this has generated within the capitalist class as a whole.

The argument that the decline of the UK economy is attributable to the orientation of powerful sections of the capitalist class draws much of its inspiration from Hobsbawm's analysis of the decline in the international position of the UK economy after 1860:

> what lay before the eye were the shining pastures of cotton exports to Asia, steam coal exports to the world's ships, Johannesburg gold mines, Argentine tramways and the profits of the City merchant banks . . . what happened therefore, was that Britain exported her immense accumulated historical advantages in the underdeveloped world . . . and had in reserve the exploitation of the 'natural protection' of the home market and if need be 'artificial protection' of political control over a large empire. When faced with a challenge it was easier and cheaper to retreat into an as yet unexploited part of one of these favoured zones rather than to meet competition face to face . . . The British economy as a whole tended to retreat from industry into trade and finance . . . Britain's annual investments abroad began actually to exceed her net capital formation at home around 1870. What is more, increasingly the two became alternatives . . . The amount of domestic capital formation before 1914, so far from being adequate for the modernization of the British productive apparatus, was not even sufficient to prevent it from running down. Britain we may say, was becoming a parasitic rather than a competitive economy. (Hobsbawm, 1968, p. 161)

Aaronovitch (1981a, 1981b, ch. 2) has applied a much-developed form of this thesis to the post-war UK economy. Detailed comparative material is presented for the UK, West Germany, Italy, France and Japan to demonstrate the cosmopolitan orientation of UK capital which is manifest in three characteristics of the organisation of UK capital: the extent of the overseas operations of UK multinational companies and the City; the historic dislocation between industrial and financial capital in the UK which is institutionalised in the separation of banking and industrial enterprises; and the historic alliance between UK financial capital and the state designed to safeguard the international position of sterling and the City, Aaronovitch acknowledges the relative strength of the UK trade union movement over the post-war period, but judges it to have been of secondary importance—'this largely defensive posture has certainly interacted with other conditions which have contributed to the relatively low growth rate of the UK but this has been, in our judgment, a secondary father than a primary factor' (Aaronovitch, 1981a, p. 69). Two mechanisms are identified by which the specified class characteristics have been transmitted into slow growth. The first involves an investment–growth relationship. The claim here is that domestic accumulation and thus growth has been retarded by (a) a shortage of finance arising from the export of capital and the dislocation between industrial and financial capital, and (b) the deflationary and other policies adopted in defence of the overseas interests of UK capital. The second link involves the political and organisational cohesion which capital requires in order to restructure itself and grow. The claim here is that the coordination of UK capital has been seriously weakened by the dislocation between its financial and industrial sections.

Several writers have analysed the post-war decline of the UK economy within the broad framework adopted by Aaronovitch. Jessop (1980) and Longstreth (1979) emphasise the importance of the brake on domestic accumulation which has resulted from the enforcement of policies designed to sustain the political and economic hegemony of UK financial capital. Jessop also points to the importance of the relative strength of the UK labour movement in retarding industrial reconstruction and in generating the damaging 'stop–go' cycle by its interaction at the political level with the power of financial capital. The London CSE Group (1980) endorses the argument on the structural damage inflicted by the overseas orientation of the City, and also shares Aaronovitch's view on the relative unimportance of the strength of the UK labour movement. Whereas Currie and Smith (1981) see the relative strength of the UK labour movement not as a cause (primary or secondary) but as a result of the decline generated by the promotion of the overseas interests of UK capital—'the defensive strength and strategy of the British labour movement can then be seen as a result, rather than a cause of this failure of development' (Currie and Smith, 1981, p. 10).

An even more radical interpretation of the significance of the UK labour movement is Rowthorn's claim that the neglect fostered by a strategy of overseas expansion was tolerated by a quiescent labour movement and that a more militant movement could have forced the state to give priority to the restructuring of the domestic economy: 'We reach the paradoxical conclusion . . . that British capitalism declined not because workers were too militant . . . but because they were not militant enough and were willing to foot the bill for a suicidal strategy which put overseas expansion before domestic development' (Rowthorn, 1980, p. 144). Coates (1983) also insists on the importance of the historic relegation of the interests of domestic industrial capital but rejects both the claim that domestic investment has been retarded by capital exports and a shortage of finance and that there exists a systematic causal relationship between the quantum of investment and economic growth. The argument relies instead on a less direct transmission mechanism by which innovation and the productivity of investment has been retarded by the political and managerial weakness of UK industrial capital. Coates also acknowledges the relative strength of the UK labour movement but insists that the 'problem of worker resistance to capitalist restructuring is a secondary and derivative one' (Coates, 1983, section 6). In one way or another each writer in this group traces the post-war decline of the UK economy to the motives, orientation and responses of the dominant section of the capitalist class. Their explanations can thus be seen as expressions of the Hobsbawm thesis.

The fullest statement on the importance of the capital–labour struggle in the post-war decline of the UK economy is that of Kilpatrick and Lawson (1980). Other writers adopting a broadly similar position include Purdy (1976), Glyn and Harrison (1980, ch. 2) and Hodgson (1981, ch. 8). The basic argument starts from the claim that the process of industrialisation in the UK economy relied on pre-industrial craft labour to a much greater extent than elsewhere. The emerging labour movement in the nineteenth century thus became organised on the basis or skill differences rather than industrial categories, and as a result, and in contrast to developments in France, West Germany, Italy and Scandinavia the growth of centralised collective bargaining was inhibited whereas a strong union organisation at plant and company level was encouraged. The strength of European labour movements at the point of production has also been weakened by political and religious divisions in France and Italy, and by state suppression and control in Germany, Italy and France during the war and interwar periods of the twentieth century.

The final claim is that the balance of power in favour of labour in the UK retarded economic growth through its effect on the level and growth rate of industrial productivity—

the UK working class's strong organisation at factory level thwarted many of capital's attempts to increase productivity. New techniques, involving a sharp increase in the technical composition of capital were often effectively vetoed by unions which did not want to lose jobs. Where new technology was installed, its effect on productivity was often reduced because unions insisted on maintaining existing operating levels or line speeds. (Glyn and Harrison, 1980, p. 50)

The advocates of this view see the retreat into protected overseas markets as a result of the economic decline of the UK and not a cause of it. The general claim, which appears in one form or another in each of the cited works, is that 'if British capital did turn overseas, this was largely because it was difficult to produce competitively for export from the UK' (ibid., p. 42). The structure of the arguments of these writers suggests that they would not disagree with Kilpatrick and Lawson's specific claim about the relevence to the post-war UK economy of the situation after 1880 in which 'UK exporters found it to their advantage to avoid conflict with workers over an accelerated remoulding of the structure of production, and instead redirected sales to new or protected markets, often with the aid of capital exports' (Kilpatrick and Lawson, 1980, p. 96). This assessment of the relative significance of the strength of the UK labour movement and the overseas orientation of UK capital should be compared to that contained in the arguments of Aaronovitch, Coates, Currie and Smith, the London CSE Group and Rowthorn. The reversal is more or less complete. The factor which is secondary or consequential in these expressions of the Hobsbawm thesis is central to the Kilpatrick–Lawson thesis, and vice versa.

It is not difficult to arrange the various claims reviewed in this section into two competitive explanations of the post-war decline of the UK economy. The post-Keynesian and Kilpatrick–Lawson theses are clearly complementary and the latter can easily absorb the former. There is no inconsistency in the view that the uniquely strong position occupied by the UK labour movement in its struggle with capital has retarded economic growth by setting in train a cumulative process of decline involving slow innovation and productivity growth, a slackening demand for UK products in world markets and a slow rate of accumulation in the domestic manufacturing sector. This formulation does not explain the origins of the post-war decline of the UK economy in terms of the responses of other economies to the relative success of the UK in earlier periods, and thus avoids the inconsistency in Eatwell's argument.

The comparison presented above makes it quite clear that this composite thesis is competitive with almost all expressions of the Hobsbawm thesis. It is possible to hold that the decline of the UK economy, the overseas orientation of UK capital and the neglect of the domestic manufacturing sector have been joint products of the relative strength of the UK labour movement, or that capital exports and the overseas orientation of capital have been of fundamental importance with the struggle between capital and labour occupying a secondary or even consequential position. But it is not possible to hold both views at once. In particular it is not possible to subscribe to the view that in a capitalist economy such as the UK, investment is in the long run self-financing and accumulation is the evidence of growth, and also to hold that UK growth has been retarded by low investment induced by the export of capital and a shortage of investment finance. Both claims may be incorrect but if one is correct the other must be false. What all of this means is that if there is convincing evidence for the post-Keynesian view of the investment-growth relationship and for the Kilpatrick–Lawson argument on the importance of the strength of the UK labour movement then there must be serious doubt about the validity of most formulations of the Hobsbawm thesis.

THEORIES AND EVIDENCE

There is no comprehensive and conclusive evidence of a negative relationship between the strength of the UK labour movement and the post-war growth of the UK economy. There is however an ill-assorted collection of items, many of which relate only to earlier periods or are restricted to a single dimension of the problem. None is very impressive by itself but when taken together they offer some support to the Kilpatrick–Lawson thesis. Kilpatrick and Lawson rely on case studies of innovation from the 1880s onwards in the textile, steel and other manufacturing sectors of the UK and US economies which suggest that productivity and the pace of innovation in the UK have been retarded by the greater degree of job control exercised by the UK labour movement. Pratten and Atkinson (1976) survey a major study of differences in labour productivity within international companies operating in the UK, Germany, France, the USA and Canada in 1972 (Pratten, 1975), and a large number of studies of differences in labour productivity in UK and US industries in the early post-war period. All studies rely on a questionnaire method. The qualitative conclusion that emerges from most of them is that union work rules and practices resulting in overmanning (more workers per machine) and underproduction (less output per machine) have been one cause of lower UK productivity, but that other factors including capital equipment and the scale of production have been equally important.

Pratten's estimate of the proportion of productivity differences between the UK and other countries attributable to labour relations is about 50 per cent of the shortfall relative to Germany, 30 per cent of that relative to France and 25 per cent of that relative to the US and Canada. The lack of statistical evidence on the Kilpatrick–Lawson thesis

arises from the well-recognised difficulty of devising a quantitative index
of trade union strength and militancy. Notwithstanding this problem
Caves (1980) presents a statistical analysis of 71 industries for the period
1963 to 1972 in which the ratio of UK to US labour productivity is
expressed as a function of a number of variables including (1) the ratio
of UK to US gross investment per worker, (2) the proportion of working
days lost by strikes in the UK, (3) the number of strikes in the UK, (4)
the proportion of UK manual workers covered by collective agreements, (5) the proportion of UK employment in the old industrial
regions (the West Midlands, Yorkshire and Humberside, the North
West, the North and Wales and Scotland), and (6) the proportion of
managerial employees in the US counterpart industry. (2), (3) and (4)
are designed to capture the effects of trade union strength, whereas (6)
is entered on the argument that the UK shortfall in productivity is
greatest in those industries requiring more managerial effort. The
implicit assumption here is that US practice provides a true indication of
managerial requirements. Caves' results are that (1) has no explanatory
power, (2) and (3) are significant factors, whereas (4) is significant only
in combination with (5). (6) is also significant.

The overall conclusion is that there is 'strong evidence to support the
negative influence on industrial productivity of poor labour-
management relations and deficiencies in British management' (Caves,
1980, p. 173). It is important to recognise that Caves' and Pratten's
conclusions refer to international differences in the level of labour
productivity, whereas the Kilpatrick–Lawson thesis is concerned with
the importance of trade union strength in the relatively slow growth of
the UK economy, and thus with its impact on the relative growth of UK
productivity. However, there are reasons to expect international
differences in levels of productivity to be associated with international
differences in productivity growth, and this is indeed what Caves finds in
respect of the UK and the US (ibid., pp. 176, 177).

This evidence makes it very difficult to argue that the strength of the
UK labour movement has been irrelevant to the post-war decline of the
UK economy. Whether trade union strength has been secondary to the
factor associated with the overseas orrientation of UK capital depends
on the strength of the evidence for the relationships which the advocates
of the Hobsbawm thesis see as crucial.

Over the post-war period overseas investment rather than exports has
become the characteristic means by which the UK has served foreign
markets, whereas the reverse has been the case in faster growing
economies such as Germany, Japan and Italy. Thus between 1957 and
1965 a 32 per cent increase in UK overseas sales was achieved by a 12

per cent increase in exports and a 20 per cent increase in overseas production. This compares with figures of 24 per cent (exports) and 5 per cent (overseas production) for Italy, 17 per cent and 2 per cent for Japan, and 14 per cent and 2 per cent for Germany (Rowthorn, 1980, p. 55). However, there are several grounds for questioning the general view that more overseas investment has meant less domestic investment. To the extent that UK foreign investment has been concentrated in the production of raw materials exported to the UK, foreign and domestic operations and investment will tend to be complementary rather than competitive. Krainer's (1967) study of post-war UK and US foreign investment offers some support for this view by showing that, in contrast to the US position, UK foreign investment has been concentrated in raw material production and positively related to domestic capacity utilisation.

Complementary relationships may also exist in the production of high technology goods. Overseas investment may be used for the assembly of high technology components or for the production of simple versions of sophisticated products to serve as a base for a full export operation. There is a substantial body of evidence which throws doubt on the more specific claim that UK industrial investment has been retarded by a shortage of funds arising from capital exports and the dislocation between financial and industrial capital. Evidence from several sources suggests that UK industrial investment has not been retarded by a shortage of finance, but governed by changes in capacity utilisation and exported output acting through an accelerator mechanism. That finance is not an independent constraint is what UK businessmen invariably say when asked. The overwhelming view expressed in evidence to the Wilson Committee (Cmnd. 7937, 1980) is that the availability of external finance has not been a significant constraint on industrial investment in the UK. It is not surprising that this should be the case in an economy such as the UK in which the amount of credit money in the system can be expanded without limit by bank lending. The greater importance of the accelerator mechanism is suggested by several formal studies of the determinants of UK investment expenditure.

Changes in capacity utilisation and output have been found to be highly significant determinants of industrial investment in the UK by Nobay (1970), Junankar (1970), Smyth and Briscoe (1969) and Panić and Vernon (1975). In contrast the effect of financial factors measured by interest rates, the user cost of capital and profits appears to be erratic and never more than weak. Feldstein and Fleming (1971) and Nobay (1970) show a composite user cost of capital variable to be statistically significant but relatively unimportant in explaining variations in investment. Nobay finds that profits have had a relatively small but significant effect on manufacturing investment excluding chemicals and steel but no significant effect on total manufacturing investment. Panić and Vernon also find no significant relationship between profits entered as a proxy for internal sources of finance and total manufacturing investment. The results of research in the Bank of England on the relationship between investment and the ratio of the cost of capital to the rate of return of capital 'have not been particularly encouraging, though in some cases (the ratio) has proved to be just as successful as conventional accelerator models in explaining the behaviour of investment' (Bank of England, 1977, p. 157). The overall conclusion that emerges from formal studies is that changes in financial conditions not associated with changes in output have had relatively little effect on UK industrial investment.

To be set against this conclusion is the substantial body of comparative evidence presented, for example, by Aaronovitch (1981a) and the Labour Party (1976) that a feature of economies which have grown faster than the UK is a much closer integration of banking, financial and industrial institutions. But even if the causal relationship between finance and investment is much stronger than formal studies suggest it is difficult in both theoretical and empirical terms to demonstrate a causal relationship between the level of investment and the rate of economic growth. A once-and-for-all increase in the ratio of investment to national income can be expected to increase the level of output but to increase the growth rate of output only over a transitional period. It is well known that over the post-war period the gap between the UK ratio of investment to output and that of other advanced capitalist economies has been much less than the gap in growth rates, and also that the investment gap narrowed over the 1970s as the growth gap increased (see Blume, 1980). This picture has been confirmed by formal studies of the investment-growth relationship. An OECD study (1970, Appendix VI) of 20 advanced economies over the period 1955 to 1967 shows that the ratio of investment to output is very weakly correlated with growth rates. This evidence is consistent with the conclusion of Beckerman's ealier analysis (Beckerman, 1965, chap. 1) that differences between the growth rate of the UK and 11 other advanced economies from 1955 to 1962 are much more associated with differences in the productivity of capital than with differences in investment ratios.

A variant of the investment argument is the claim that productivity growth in the UK and thus growth overall has been retarded by a low level of investment per worker. The level of investment per worker in

UK manufacturing has been significantly lower than in other advanced economies (see Brown and Sheriff, 1979, Table 10.9). But it is very difficult to judge the extent to which this represents underinvestment rather than overmanning. Also several studies including that of Caves referred to above have failed to show that international differences in productivity have been associated with differences in investment per worker.

The clear implication of these results for the Hobsbawm thesis is that the overseas orientation of UK capital and the associated dislocation between financial and industrial capital can have had an impact on UK growth only through a mechanism other than that involving finance and investment. The Aaronovitch formulation of the thesis presents two such mechanisms: those involving state policies and the related but more general factor of the political and organisational cohesion of UK capital. Perhaps the most well-defined argument here is that which attributes slow UK growth to the damaging effects on investment and innovation of the 'stop–go' cycle of the 1950s and 1960s which resulted from an attempt by the state to reconcile a commitment to a fixed exchange rate and the international status of UK capital with the maintenance of full employment which was a condition of the post-war settlement between capital and labour. A major difficulty with this argument arises from its logical implication that an acceptable alternative strategy was available to successive UK governments which would have been significantly more successful. It is probably that no such alternative actually existed.

The issue has been examined in great detail in a study edited by Posner (1978), in which four groups encompassing a wide range of Keynesian and monetarist positions present a set of simulations of the path of the UK economy from 1964 to 1977 under regimes of macroeconomic policy different from each other and from that which actually obtained. There is general agreement on certain policy mistakes (such as the failure to devalue before 1967 and the timing and substance of the policy on Competition and Credit Control introduced in 1971), but no group was able to identify an alternative policy regime which defined a path of sustained and substantial economic recovery. The interpretation of the results of simulations of the economy over long periods is notoriously difficult and this particular finding is not conclusive evidence that a superior alternative strategy did not in fact exist. But in any case an objection to the 'stop–go' argument can be made without reference to hypothetical states of the world for the unimportance of any instability caused by the macroeconomic policies of UK governments is also suggested by the international record.

Whiting's (1976) evidence on seven major OECD economies is that over the period 1955 to 1973 the UK has, in terms of net manufacturing output, experienced the smallest percentage deviation from trend growth and the lowest rate of trend growth, whereas the two fastest growing economies (Italy and Japan) showed the greatest levels of instability. These results are consistent with Wilson's (1969) earlier finding that over the period 1950 to 1965 stability and growth in 13 advanced economies were not positively correlated.

The position now reached can be summarised as follows. Modern formulations of the Hobsbawm thesis gain some general support from the qualitative evidence provided by comparative and historical studies. But formal quantitative studies offer no support for the thesis that the post-war decline of the UK economy is attributable to the adverse effects on domestic accumulation of the devotion of UK capital to its overseas interests. Advocates of this view have specified several mechanisms through which the factors involved have taken their effect but such studies provide no evidence that any of them has actually operated in the post-war UK economy. Thus although the available evidence is contradictory the balance of it seems to lie against the thesis. In contrast there is no inconsistency in the evidence on the claim that the position of strength occupied by the UK labour movement has been integral to the decline of the UK economy and that this factor has been transmitted into the outcome of slow growth by a self-reinforcing process of slow innovation, low investment and a falling demand for UK manufactures in world markets. The evidence is certainly not abundant but the quantitative and qualitative items which are available are consistent in their support of the thesis.

34. Discussion*

Sam Aaronovitch

I shall want a lot more time to think about Bernard Stafford's powerful and impressive paper. At this point I propose only to set out a possible agenda for a reply. I am glad he finds the Marxist approach appealing—one, that is, which looks at the structure of class characteristics as a major source of explanation.

A brief comment first on method. I appreciate his criticism of *cumulative causation* as tending to description rather than analysis and fudging the issue of causality. But I want to defend my own approach. Scientific analysis must try to specify the crucial forces and relationships in any system it examines but if, for instance, we are comparing different countries Marxists should not deduce all that happens in them from the existence of common crucial features e.g. the capital–labour relationship which defines them all as capitalist societies.

No one, for instance, can deduce the way in which Germany was unified from the capital–labour relationship in Germany alone. We require specific and concrete historical analysis; this may well show not only that systems change in significant ways for a variety of reasons but that the way in which capitalist states affected each other depended on the different elements in their social and class structures, the particular alliances arising from their own unique histories.

I entirely agree that the capital–labour relationship is the central distinguishing feature of capitalist societies as such; that class conflict has become a powerful force in such societies; and also that the capital–labour conflict as expressed in the struggle for control over the labour process is a much neglected field. In the picture set out in the *Political Economy of British Capitalism* (*PEBC*), the centrality of the capital–labour relationship is stressed and a large section of the book

*Reproduced from M. Sawyer and K. Schott (ed.), *Socialist Economic Review 1983* (London, Merlin, 1983), pp. 23–5)

devoted to it and to the labour process. It does not follow however that the class struggle in each country must therefore be the major determinant of the way in which a particular capitalist society develops. I find it implausible that the course of British capitalism since the 1850s (and why not from the beginnings of the industrial revolution?) was shaped mainly by the degree of working-class organisation. In any case such an approach ignores the way in which the working class, its composition and organisation is itself shaped by the changes in the system of which it is a part. This is an important element in Marxist method which should not be confused with 'cumulative causation'.

I should explain that my interest in the Hobsbawm thesis arose in the 1940s when I attempted to follow up a phrase of Lenin's that Britain had certain characteristics of an imperialist state before the epoch of imperialism. The ways in which this affected the structure of the capitalist class, its ideology and organisation as compared for instance with Germany and Japan are set out in the *PEBC*. These characteristics in turn help to explain the courses chosen, even though these were undoubtedly influenced by working-class practices and struggles. I think Bernard Stafford claims more for the evidence provided in Lawson–Kilpatrick than they do themselves.

I find it surprising that Bernard Stafford discounts so easily the evidence for what he terms the Hobsbawm–Aaronovitch thesis. I believe that the way in which the financial system has grown up and is even now structured in the UK, its relationship with industrial capital, the manner in which the bulk of savings are now channelled and invested, are important factors in Britain's relative decline and I cannot see how they are countered by repeating the Wilson's Committee's view that there is no shortage of money—only of profitable investment projects.

There is also evidence to support the view that the attempt to maintain the world role of sterling including its overvaluation for long periods, has been (and is now) very damaging and cannot be refuted by evidence drawn simply from 'stop–go' analyses. And I interpret the relatively high level of arms expenditure, the effects of the 1950 rearmament programme all as evidence of the particular direction and ideology developed by the dominant groups of British capital and which weakened the relative position of the UK domestic economy.

One point that needs more discussion is Bernard Stafford's claim that there is little evidence of the relationship between investment, growth and productivity. I did argue in PEBC that the relationships were not invariant and for that very reason it was important to examine other more underlying factors, but Bernard's interpretation strikes me as extreme. There is systematic weakness of the UK in levels and productivity of investment, share in GDP etc and these weakenesses have greatly intensified in the period when the working class has been much weakened by the economic crisis, itself aggravated by deliberate government policy.

Bernard Stafford is wrong to suggest that the Hobsbawm–Aaronovitch thesis implies the 'irrelevance' of class conflict to UK economic problems. I argued that it was a contributory but not the *primary* factor in determining the ways in which British capitalism sought to play a world role beyond its capacity to sustain and which weakened relatively its domestic industrial base.

35. Thatcherism and Decline*

John Hillard

> Where disorder develops
> Words are the first steps.
> > Confucius

> Confusion in her eyes
> Says it all –
> She's lost Control.
> > *Joy Division*
> > © 1979 Factory Records Limited

> We made a promise
> We swore we'd always remember
> No Retreat
> Baby
> No Surrender.
> > *Bruce Springsteen*
> > © 1984 CBS Records Inc.

INTRODUCTION

In the build-up to the 1979 General Election, Mrs Thatcher evoked the vision of a spring-time for Greater Britain by promising a radical break from the politics of persuasion, compromise and appeasement which, in her view, had contributed directly towards the perceived problem of accelerated economic decline. She castigated the voluntaristic corporatism of the Labour government's Social Contract as merely managing the crisis of welfare capitalism rather than resolving it. In advocating the

*Accepting the usual disclaimers, I wish to thank Teresa Brier, David Coates, Rodney Crossley, Bill Gerrard, Stuart Ogden, Hugo Radice, Michael Surrey and Ken Woolmer for constructive criticism and helpful comments. Thanks also to Sue Logan for typing the manuscript.

politics of radical reaction, she claimed that the bipartisan one-nation approach found itself helplessly caught between a nostalgic longing for the October sunshine of the post-war boom and the economic actuality of a winter ingress of hyper-stagflation. In contrast to the muddling-through politics of Butskellite pragmatism, Thatcher expressed the resolute conviction that, by challenging the *status quo*, Britain's slide into economic oblivion could be reversed. In essence, her programme envisaged a progressive reconstruction of the British economy through the removal of one-nation impediments standing in the way of individual free enterprise. In the event, given the exhaustion of middle-of-the road Labourism, and with a little help from the marketing men, Thatcher unbolted Britain's political gate on 4 May 1979.

What, then, of Thatcherism in practice? Mid-way through Thatcher's second term in office an assessment of her impact and continued potential is well justified. But first it is necessary to define the term Thatcherism. It would be tempting to concentrate, as many commentators have, upon Thatcher the individual, the woman. Certainly, Thatcher herself, as leader of the Conservative Party and the first woman Prime Minister of Britain, is a fascinating topic, and much of the political success of Thatcherism can be explained in terms of the symbolic projection of her individual image. In what follows, however, the main emphasis focuses on the notion of Thatcherism as a *political formation* occupying a space on the spectrum to the right of what has been commonly regarded as the conventional pale of the British state. Secondly, Thatcherism can be defined as an *operational strategy* designed to achieve what Sir Keith Joseph envisages as a 'law-abiding free enterprise' (Chapter 9, p. 104 above) reconstruction of Britain's social relations of production. In consequence, an understanding of Thatcherism cannot be based upon conventional methods of assessment which remain fixed upon pre-1979 conceptions of the relationship between capital, labour and the British state. Stripped to its essentials, Thatcherism is best viewed as a coherent and long-term project motivated by the will to convert what Joseph describes as 'romantic and outmoded' socialist aspirations into the acceptance of the 'new common ground of reality'.

For reasons of space, as well as a desire to emphasise those aspects most directly relevant to the debate on decline, the economic dimension of Thatcherism will constitute the major theme of the analysis below. A comprehensive account of the Thatcherite phenomenon would involve a thorough exploration of the political, social and ideological, as well as the economic elements, which constitute the form of the contemporary British state. Naturally, the extreme Right perception of what constitutes the freedom of the individual British subject touches on all quarters. But in the present discussion, the aim is much less ambitious and the main concern revolves around the Thatcher government's Financial Strategy, which comprises the central plank of its platform for the capitalist reconstruction of the British state.

THE FINANCIAL STRATEGY

Unveiled in 1980, the Medium Term Financial Strategy formulated the code of Thatcherite economic practice.

The main statement of the MTFS was set out in the Financial Statement and Budget Report in 1980, as follows:

> The Government's objectives for the medium term are to bring down the rate of inflation and to create conditions for a sustainable growth of output and employment.

The MTFS eschewed the consensual all-party agreement that the government should aim to promote and maintain 'a high and stable level of employment'. Instead, the MTFS substituted a simple monetary rule to dictate the conduct of government intervention. The stated function of the MTFS was the achievement of a significant and lasting reduction in the rate of monetary growth. According to the logic of monetarism, money-supply growth is generated as a consequence of the monetarisation of government debt and the means to controlling the rate of monetary growth lies in controlling the borrowing (in effect, the spending) of central government. The Chancellor's policy stance, therefore, was guided by the prime imperative of attaining a diminishing target range of money-supply growth, and reducing the Public Sector Borrowing Requirement provided the proximate means of achieving that end. The ultimate justification for monetary discipline lay in its function of squeezing inflation out of the system, which constituted 'the necessary condition for growth and stability' (Joseph, p. 98 above).

As a strategic conception, the aim of government economic policy in the monetary sphere, combined with direct tax reductions, was

> to revitalise the entrepreneurial spirit and to achieve an expanding economy. A restoration of high employment would follow through these means, but there was no direct commitment to achieve, or maintain, full employment. (Pliatsky, 1982)

The Treasury jettisoned demand management, and, in 1984, the

Chancellor argued in his Mais Lecture 'that it is the conquest of inflation, not the pursuit of growth and employment, which is or should be the objective of macro-economic policy'.

For all this, it is somewhat of a misnomer to categorise Thatcherite practice as plainly monetarist. Indeed, there are strong grounds for asserting that Thatcherite policy has shattered, the monetarist formula for all time. When the numbers of the inflation game did not add up to the sum of monetarist logic, the government employed the canons of Friedmanite positivism to divert attention away from the intellectual void upon which monetarism is based. Concentration was directed away from the validity of its propositions (a direct, if lagged, relationship between the rate of change in money supply and the level of inflation) and was focused instead on, the outcome (lower inflation). In fact, throughout the first phase of the MTFS (1980–83), the annual rate of growth of M3 was considerably more than double the inflation rate in 1983/84. In all, the 1984/85 M3 target range did not represent a contraction in money supply growth compared with 1978/79. To place Thatcher's 'monetarist' achievement in its proper perspective, the 1983/84 rate of inflationary growth was still around double the annual average recorded between 1951 and 1964, the hey-day of the Keynesian welfare state. Secondly, Britain has not been alone in experiencing a falling rate of inflation, and Thatcher succeeded only in reducing Britain's inflation from 0.6 per cent above the OECD average in May 1979 to 0.3 per cent below the average in May 1984. The final irony lies in comparing the MTFS with the bastard monetarism of the previous socialist Chancellor who succeeded in hitting a narrow target for monetary growth with the aid of an incomes policy between 1976 and 1978.

A more plausible explanation for the decline of the annual inflation rate to just half the level inherited in 1979 derives from the severe deflation imposed on the British economy in the *name* of sound money. Leaving aside for the moment the reasons for the lack of congruence between government rhetoric and action, it is fair to contend that Thatcherism from the outset represented something more than an attempt to transform Britain into a monetarist laboratory. In retrospect, the Government's initial flirtation with monetary mechanics was designed to present a semblance of credibility to the application of age-old deflationary policies. Also, the imperative of reducing the Public Sector Borrowing Requirement engendered a hidden *fiscal* squeeze in the midst of international depression. Although Chancellor Lawson continued to pay lip-service to the MTFS through his pledge to create the sound financial base of zero inflation, the word monetarism has all but disappeared from the government's economic vocabulary. The emphasis has now shifted away from a sole reliance upon monetarist voodoo to the alleged existence of supply side inflexibilities at the micro-economic level. In terms of *total* strategy, the stated objective of Thatcherism is to

> make markets work better . . . by removing the impediments which prevent people and firms responding quickly to changing conditions and market demands. With a more flexible economy we can ultimately have more jobs and growth without inflation. (Treasury, 1984, p. 1)

Central to Thatcherite strategy, therefore, is the creation of a 'free' market for labour and capital. Critical here is the superstructural process which determines the social reproduction of labour power. From the vantage point of capital, the superstructural framework of the One Nation State eroded individual economic freedom by partially removing the responsibility for the social reproduction of labour power from the arena of private property. The semi-capitalist character of social democracy erected a political canopy which partially shielded labour from the full force of capitalist reality. Whereas the concessional approach of the post-war settlement initially paid a high dividend for capital—rising real wages, for instance, created a stimulus from the demand side to sustain high production and profitability—the existence of inbuilt political stabilisers now constitutes a formidable barrier to the reconstruction of capital in the context of over-accumulation. The necessary condition, therefore, for the creation of a stable platform upon which to rebuild the capitalist framework is the removal of non-market 'poisons' from the national economy.[1] In effect, the social reproduction of labour power is to be governed solely by the requirements of capital. The upshot would be a free market of privatised individuals imbued with rational expectations about their position and role within a capitalist economy.

How does this rather abstract schema relate to the Thatcherite policy configuration? For many people, even after six years of office Thatcherism still appears like a journey without a destination, in that the ultimate goal is rarely articulated. None the less, it is possible to construct a Thatcherite scenario which extends beyond a discussion of day-to-day tactics to a specification of the overall strategy and where it will all end. Interestingly, the total strategy was formulated quite clearly in the Ridley proposals which were leaked to *The Economist* in 1978, and to a lesser extent in *The Right Approach to the Economy*. Sir John Hoskyns' recent contribution to the debate on decline merely reiterates the underlying philosophy of these documents. Hoskyns defines the problem as an interdependent totality comprising a checklist of objectives with the imperative of cutting direct taxation at the top of the chart. The main presupposition of the radical Right strategy is the belief that capital accumulation proceeds faster under a low-tax regime. Correspondingly, welfare spending constitutes a direct burden upon capital. In consequence,

> We will not *cut taxation* unless we can *cut spending*. We will not cut the spending unless we can completely *reshape the welfare state*. We will not be able to reshape the welfare state unless we can complete *a reform of the trade union movement*. (Hoskyns, BBC1, 1985; emphasis added)

Here, in a nutshell, is a near complete statement of the Thatcherite strategy for turning back the tide of socialism.

On the above grounds, the acid-test for the Thatcher experiment after five years is the extent to which a real enterprise ethic has permeated British capital. Has the tide of public expenditure been turned? Have changes in the tax system introduced the motivation and incentive required for the resurgence of free enterprise? Are workers driven by a new realism of effort and responsibility towards the achievement of the national good? The simple answer is no. On the surface, and within her own frame of reference, Thatcher has struggled in vain to hold the line of socialist advance. The 1984/85 levels of taxation and public expenditure are both around as high in proportion to gross national product as during the so-called fiscal crisis of 1975/76. *And* the Conservative government inherited the windfall of North Sea oil taxation, which now accounts for eight per cent of total government revenue. Overall, the economic policy pursued since 1979 has reduced national production to its 1967 level and has created record unemployment, but the benefits to the British populace as a whole are still as intangible as the glow worm at the end of the tunnel spotted by a CBI spokesman as long ago as 1982.

ASSESSMENT

What factors, then, militated against the smooth implementation of the Thatcherite strategy? First and foremost, a government obsession with the canons of born-again liberalism created a false optimism about the prospect for market-directed structural change. Although private enterprise still commanded the heights of welfare capitalism, the social democratic parliamentary process occasioned a superstructural metamorphosis of the British national economy. The holotype Keynesian-

faire economy not only protected labour from market pressures by the creation of a social welfare safety net, but many fractions of capital themselves also became what can only be described as wards of the state. In 1978/79, the state provision for capital in the form of grants, subsidies and tax reliefs amounted to a minimum of £7.3 billion. The erection of political supports to underwrite British capital's competitive position in the international economy constituted a significant contribution to the overall outlay on public expenditure. In this way, the stabilising function of demand management simultaneously succoured and eroded the carapace of capital. For the purposes of rolling back the frontiers of the state, it has become practically impossible to delineate between private and public spheres of economic activity. On the other hand, the mutual interdependence of capital and the state proved expeditious only so long as the social and political outlays were exceeded by the economic benefits to capital. In 1957, the Treasury looked on helpless as the link between expenditure and taxation snapped. Thenceforward, British capital accumulation was squeezed by the ratchet expansion of expenditure, borrowing and taxation, and not until the panic reaction of 1976 produced the reinstitution of prior approval cash limits was public spending under anything but informal control. Even then, the high plateau of expenditure remained intact. Yet Thatcher's embarkation upon the 'rolling back the frontiers' mission turned a squinted eye towards the expeditious role of the state as a critical prop supporting British capital's crumbling economic edifice. Not surprisingly, the government quickly discovered that the road to the free-enterprise economy was considerably rougher than that envisaged in the clinical parlours of the Centre for Policy Studies and the Institute of Economic Affairs.

The conflict between abstract theory and actual practice was immediately brought home to the guru himself, Sir Keith Joseph, in his first ministerial post as Secretary of State for Industry. In opposition, the Radical Right had castigated the corporatist-inspired National Enterprise Board as an inefficient and wasteful mechanism for attempting to achieve industrial reconstruction. The prime case for enterprise treatment within the NEB was British Leyland. Unable to operate profitably as a privately-owned corporation, BL had been taken into public ownership by the previous Labour administration. Under the auspices of the NEB, a process of rationalisation was initiated but, as was to be expected, political and social considerations figured alongisde the ultimate imperative of a return to capitalist viability. Naturally, Joseph sought to promote the latter, and he envisaged a rapid phasing-out of public funding to allow free-market forces to dictate the future shape of the British-owned car industry. In the event, he proved unequal to the task. Faced with the unpalatable prospect of an additional million unemployed, as well as the imminent collapse of Britain's industrial heartland, Joseph was forced to swallow his pride. He accepted the continuation of a state-funded, planned reconstruction of BL. When it came to the crunch, therefore, the *political* reality of decline overrode the dictates of economic rationality. Then again, Joseph was persuaded by non-economic arguments to subsidise the Harland and Woolf shipyard in Belfast to the tune of £6000 per employee in 1980/81. Such U-turns as BL and Harland and Woolf (as well as Nexos and others) emphasised graphically the extent to which the familiar spirit of pragmatism remains impervious even to the most resolute of radicals.

Secondly, the deliberate abandonment of demand management policy in favour of a simple monetary rule with the market set free induced 'unforeseen' effects on the real economy. The concept of the self-regulating natural economy was sorely tested in the early 1980s. Despite the prediction that the transition to a privatised economy would be smooth and determinate, the costs of adjustment have turned out to be neither temporary nor small. Moreover, the brunt of disinflation was borne by export-oriented capital. Government endeavours to target money-supply growth brought in their train a sharp increase in interest rates.[2] Not only was capital's debt burden heightened but, as a result of high interest rates, sterling moved strongly against other currencies, particularly the dollar. The over-valuation of sterling, when combined with the effect of the bursting of the wages dam instigated by the return to free collective bargaining and the inflationary boost of Howe's victory Budget of 15 June 1979, led to a 40 per cent deterioration in the price competitiveness of British products between 1979 and 1981. It was not surprising, therefore, that total output fell by 5 or 6 per cent in 1980. Manufacturing industry was hardest hit. Between the fourth quarter of 1979 and a year later, manufacturing production plummeted by 16 per cent, as export demand dried up and import penetration was given a boost by the over-valuation of the pound. In this light, the government's claim that the severity of Britain's recession was simply a function of the chickens of post-war socialism coming home to roost needs to be set against the government's own contribution through its dogmatic belief in market flexibility.

The sole beneficiary of such an outcome appeared to be footloose supra-national capital, which was conveniently provided with the economic justification for rationalising, or even liquidating, British operations. The expected flight of capital following in the wake of the

abolition of exchange controls and dividend restraints in 1979 did not
turn out to be a once-for-all adjustment, and the net outflow of capital
remained consistently high throughout the first six years of the Thatcher
government. While pension and unit-trust managers built up their North
American and Japanese portfolios, capital departed to surplus labour
havens and took advantage of the sterling permium to break into the
United States' investment market. Direct overseas investment virtually
doubled between 1979 and 1981 to £5.1 billion, while portfolio
investment rose from £1 billion in 1978/79 to £4.2 billion in 1981, and to
£6.2 billion in 1982. As a study by Labour Research on the relationship
between overseas investment and exports for the 50 largest manufacturing companies concluded, 'it seems clear that UK companies are
choosing to meet overseas demand for their goods from foreign-based
rather than UK subsidiaries. They have become better at exporting jobs
than goods' (Labour Research, 1980). Nor has freedom of international
capital movements led to a compensatory increase in investment in
Britain by foreign corporations. By 1982 British companies were
investing overseas 'at three times the rate at which foreign companies
were investing in Britain' (Gaffikin and Nickson, 1984, pp. 61–2) and, in
all, Britain's net private assets overseas rose from £15 billion in 1978
through nearly £55 billion at the end of 1982 to £70 billion by end–1984.
The latter figure represents 22 per cent of gross domestic product.
Whereas the trend towards overseas investment was reinforced rather
than created by the abolition of exchange controls, the stampede of
capital from Britain since 1979 poses serious questions both about the
motivation of Thatcherite policy and its long-term impact on the already
chronic problem of under-investment in domestic manufacturing industry. At the very least, the flight of capital represents an unease about the
Thatcher government's ability to achieve its goal of the enterprise
economy. More to the point, in the critical area of manufacturing,
Thatcherism has reinforced the cumulative impact of under-investment
in the national economy and thereby exacerbated the innate contempt
for production which lies at the heart of Britain's poor post-war
productivity performance.

It is against this background that the so-called recovery since the
trough of 1981 has to be assessed. It represents no more than a move
towards the trend-line of economic growth last attained in the halcyon
days of stop–go. In effect, the upturn during the early 1980s was no
more than a pallid replica of a traditional credit-induced, consumption-
led 'recovery'. The latter word has achieved the status of a weasel word,
especially when applied to the £3 billion balance of trade deficit in
manufactures in 1984. In other words, the net result of Thatcherism was

not only reflected in record levels of unemployment and bankruptcies but also in the revelation that in 1983/4, for the first time in 150 years, Britain imported more manufactures than it exported. Britain's economic 'recovery' can be measured by the difference between a £0.5 billion non-oil trade surplus in 1979 and a non-oil deficit of £11.5 billion in 1984. In summary, a combination of the incentive of domestic deflation, price falls in the international economy brought about by prolonged depression, and the effects of an artificially high exchange rate, were largely responsible for the government's medium-term success in bringing down the rate of inflation. The price paid by the national economy was in the form of worsened stagnation and a freeze on productive investment comparable to the effects of returning to the Gold Standard at the pre-war parity in 1925. In the key trading sector of manufacturing, investment has fallen since 1979 by a third. Over the same period, excluding oil, national output has fallen by 3 per cent, which compares unfavourably with the OECD average, and indicates a further deterioration in Britain's relative economic performance.

The major contradiction between the theory and practice of Thatcherism arose in the equation of private taxation and public expenditure. First, measures undertaken to achieve financial stabilisation *themselves* induced, directly and indirectly, increases in demand-determined public spending outlays. Most obvious is the direct cost to the Exchequer of the government's toleration of a high and stable level of unemployment. The annual cost of unemployment is conservatively estimated at £6 billion or around 5 per cent of total public expenditure. Between 1979/80 and 1984/85 the cost of social security rose by 28 per cent in real terms, largely as a direct consequence of the growing number of jobless. But also the expenditure incurred in controlling and policing the process of adjusting Britain's social relations of production to the needs of capital has contributed directly to Thatcherism's strategic failure to reduce overall public expenditure. In practice, the Thatcher government proved less than consistent in applying the profitability test to the various spending departments. The dedicated followers of supply-side fashion would be hard put to provide an *economic* rationale for a 33 per cent real increase in Home Office spending or a rise in defence spending by 29 per cent in real terms over the period of Thatcher's first term of office. Indirectly, the pursuit of free-market policies and the generation of unparalleled austerity has cost the Exchequer dear in the form of lost revenue. In 1984/5, annual receipts are a minimum of £15 billion *lower* than would otherwise have been the case if the government had not pursued a policy of centralised deflation.

Secondly, the government gradually became 'convinced' that a mere holding-operation on the total amount of public spending was the best outcome that could be realistically expected, even in the medium term. As the Treasury reflected on the Chancellor's 1984 Autumn statement: '[he] emphasised the government's continuing commitment to cutting taxation, and *to that end keeping a firm grip on government spending*' (Treasury, 1984, p. 7; emphasis added). The apparent victory of the 'consolidaters' over the 'radicals' amounted to the concession that the Thatcher government had thrown in the towel as far as rolling back the frontiers of the state was concerned.

In any case, the public borrowing targets set by the Thatcher government were achieved not through significant cuts in the flow of public expenditure but by the cosmetic ploy of one-off sales of public assets, like British Telecom. And, for all the government's stated determination, public expenditure as a proportion of GDP has risen under Thatcher by an average of 1½ per cent every year. On the other hand, with expenditure on housing down by more than a third, and spending on industry reduced by 29 per cent in real terms since 1979, the pattern of expenditure has been transformed as well as its overall scope being now considerably higher. The impact of Thatcherism has not been to change the extent of public expenditure but merely to change its composition.

On the other side of the equation, the government's lack of achievement in the spending area has foreclosed the prospect for anything more than marginal reductions in direct taxation. In the Thatcherite vision of an enterprise economy, the incentive effect of direct tax cuts constituted an integral part of the overall package. To be sure, in the post-election Budget of June 1979, the highest rate of income tax was cut from 83 to 60 per cent, but the incentive effect of this measure, and such concessions as the abolition of the investment income surcharge in 1983, have been confined to families living on a yearly income of £18,000 or more. For lower income groups, the main thrust of tax changes has concentrated on increasing the incentive to work by abolishing the earnings-related supplement and by taxing unemployment benefit. Without entering into the dubious argument about the relationship between direct taxation and incentives, such minimal changes that have been introduced in the taxation area since 1979 appear more designed to redistribute the fruits of the existing structure than radically to reward the development of individual initiative and responsibility. Then again, the 1979 cuts in direct taxation at the top end of the scale were accompanied by a doubling of VAT which, by its regressive nature, tends to benefit the better-off at the expense of the low-paid and unemployed. Also, there has been a developing tendency under the Thatcher government to introduce forms of revenue-generation which amount to taxation without parliamentary authority. For example, the imposition of external financing limits for the nationalised industries brought about enforced price increases, which are payroll taxes in all but name, for the provision of basic utilities.

THE PROSPECT

Thus far, the Thatcher government has failed strategically to bring about a significant reduction in public spending through its inability or unwillingness to transform radically the role of the state within the mixed economy. Footloose transnational capital takes heed of the *overall* outlay on public expenditure as a proxy for the social and political constraints upon market imperatives. International capital's confidence in the Thatcher government thus revolves around its ability to transform rhetoric into action; and if the administration's past record means anything, then the omens for the medium term are not propitious. It takes a great stretch of the imagination to share the Chancellor's faith in his stated aim to hold the level of public spending steady in real terms until 1987/88. In the first place, the Chancellor's projections are based on the planned 1984/85 total rather than the actual out-turn, which, with the contingency reserve already exhausted, is likely to overshoot by a minimum of £1.7 billion. Additionally, the real cost to the Exchequer of the 1984/85 miners' dispute is yet to be included. Set against this uncertain background, the Chancellor's spending plans resemble science fiction rather than probable fact. Indeed, there are even elements of fantasy in his presumption that public sector pay will rise by only 3 per cent every year until 1987/88, and that the level of unemployment will stabilise at 3 million. The latter prediction is crucially relevant when it is counterposed against the proposed 60 per cent reduction in spending on industry, energy and trade over the next three years (1985/87), as well as a further 25 per cent reduction in housing. This is not the place to dissect the intricacies of Treasury planning methods and procedures, but even a cursory glance at the official forecasts reveals a sharp disjuncture between the abstract economy perceived by the Chancellor and the reality of intensified crisis. For, even in the most improbable event of the Chancellor achieving his goal of steady-state expenditure until 1987/88, this outcome would merely represent a reduction in public expenditure as a proportion of GDP to the level which the Thatcher government inherited in 1979. Despite the prognostications of Thatcherite ministers, the public expenditure ratchet has not 'gone the other way', but instead looks geared to break the 50 per cent barrier by the end of the decade.

Despite the great emphasis placed upon the 'poisons' of excessive public expenditure and high direct taxation by the Radical Right, the Thatcherite record in these areas, judged by its own standards, must be viewed as a lost opportunity. Indeed, the failure to tackle effectively the fiscal problem in the medium term has itself precluded radical action because of a growing crisis of confidence in the government's will to achieve its stated objectives. In this respect, the Thatcher government has turned out to be no more successful than its predecessors in resolving the contradiction of the mixed economy, but has merely raised the stakes in the struggle and precluded the feasibility of a centrist compromise to overcome the stalemate. Furthermore, the loss of strategic direction extends across the whole range of Thatcherite policy. Nowhere is this more apparent than in its endeavour to shift the balance of power between capital and labour both at the point of production and at the national level.

A recurring feature of the debate surveyed in the earlier sections of this book concerns the extent to which the activities of organised labour constitute either a primary cause or symptomatic expression of Britain's relative economic decline. The Thatcherite position on this matter is unequivocal in that the existence of a politicised trade union movement is regarded as yet another 'poison' responsible for Britain's ills. Trade unions are perceived as a distorting influence upon the workings of the free economy by their ability to prevent the 'normal' adjustments of levels of unemployment and real wages to fluctuations in the business-cycle. Accordingly, the Thatcher government's approach to the labour market has taken the from of a moral and political crusade against what is viewed, *in extremis*, as an 'enemy within' blocking the road to economic renewal. What seems from a rational perspective to be a bizarre and almost farcical attitude of mind, represents, in actuality, a sharp indicator of the inner logic of Thatcherism—one which is rarely manifest but which none the less constitutes the driving force towards the ultimate aim of creating the new 'common ground'. For instance, the Chancellor of the Exchequer described the government's resolution to stand firm indefinitely against the National Union of Mineworkers as an 'investment' in Britain's future. Similarly, Leon Brittan, the Home Secretary, clarified the hard core of Thatcherism in a speech delivered to the Bow Group in December 1984 when he hammered home the conviction that

Britain is only slowly recovering from the effects of years of egalitarianism, . . . the obsessive and unconditional pursuit of equality [which] lies behind most of our country's decline.

Such pronouncements denote an ultimate vision of a trickle-down economy where development precedes distribution and individual freedom waives the rules of egalitarianism.

In this light, the government's obsession with 'poisons' helps to explain the unyielding approach adopted towards the issues raised by the miners' dispute. Having failed to hold the line on public spending or direct taxation, the prospect of humiliation at the hand of the NUM would render Thatcherism as hollow as its detractors have always upheld. Whatever the outcome of the miners' struggle, the price for the government's strategy is measurable in terms of delay. As the *Financial Times* reflected on 1 February 1985:

> The Thatcher experiment is taking much longer to implement than any of its advocates foresaw. It may not have been radical enough, fast enough. It is possible that time is running out.

In the meantime, of course, as was emphasised in the earlier survey of the Financial Strategy, the economic miracle promised by the free marketeers remains a figment of faith rather than a realisable goal; but, given the continued political supremacy of Thatcherism, it is improbable that a change in economic direction will be contemplated. The unkindest epithet to Thatcherism would be 'This Lady's not for turning . . . she never even set out.' In a real sense, however, the government's insistence that there is no viable, coherent alternative to Thatcherism is correct. From the perspective of capital, the crisis of over-accumulation, as it is expressed within the British state, can be resolved only through the implementation of a Thatcher-type strategy: and the patent failure to confront 'the country's central dilemma – our unsustainable post-war political economy' (Hoskyns, p. 124 above) – represents the penalty for Thatcherite 'underkill'. Not surprisingly, therefore, and notwithstanding the Prime Minister's enduring resolve, international capitalist confidence in the UK domestic economy wavered towards the pessimistic in early 1985.

For all this, one of the primary factors which has contributed towards the rigid inertia of Thatcherite resolution derives from its evangelical belief that organised labour is the main barrier preventing productive transformation. Apart from acting as a most convenient black propaganda tool to divert attention away from the government's indolent attitude towards economic stabilisation, trade unions simply underline and reinforce the anti-productive bias of the dominant elements within the British state. The gradualist incorporation of the institutions of organised labour into the ancient structural formation of the British state was well advanced before the bogus compromise of welfare capitalism and 'beer and sandwiches' paternalism. When it came to the crunch, through two world wars and an intervening slump right up to the second Battle of Britain in 1974-75, the official trade unions have proudly and obediently served the Crown-in-Parliament. Even as late as the June 1983 General Election, only 40 per cent of voting trade unionists nailed their flag to the 'socialist' mast.

From these indications, Thatcherite ministers engage in the art of remarkable overstatement when trade unionists are depicted as subversive, militant and bulging with industrial muscle. The reality of British trade unionism throughout the twentieth century has been epitomised by loyal moderation and mindless conservatism. Amongst the mass of British workers, the transition from imperial power to imperial parasite was greeted with passive indifference. Nor has organised labour ever played any significant part in the determination of national strategy which, to all intents and purposes, remains the jealously guarded province of the military/financial fraction of British capital. It cannot be denied that trade unions have acted negatively and defensively in response to the cumulative disintegration of the British economy, but in no respect can such a reflex be described as a fundamental cause of absolute and relative decline. Hoskyns himself admits this:

> the role of trade unions since the war may itself be a reflection of the individual's frustration in a low-growth, high-tax, low opportunity inflation-prone economy. (Hoskyns, p. 133 above)

The Thatcherite approach to organised labour, however, implies that British workers must shoulder the burden of adjusting the productive base in line with international standards of economic performance. Under present conditions, a full-blown privatisation and denationalisation programme to achieve capitalist stability would, in all probability, double the present level of unemployment. Even now, with a third of public spending devoted to welfare, there are 7 million people in Britain existing below the official poverty line, those 'unfed and unfree' to whom Thatcher referred in her address to the joint meeting of the US Congress on 20 February 1985. Also, real wages for the majority in work have continued to exceed increases in the overall price-level even though 7 million British workers live below the European Council's decency threshold.

Whereas the new realism heralded by Thatcherite ministers in 1983 as an indication of the success of government labour market policies now looks like the familiar discontent writ large, the response by the labour movement, particularly in the miners' struggle, has been motivated more by hardy instinct than socialist consciousness. All the same, the Two Nations approach, with its ultra-elitist connotations, implies that any organised attempt to oppose Thatcherism comprises a subversive threat to the security of the British state. In this context, Thatcherism represents a pujadist and populist endeavour to save the bourgeois cause in the United Kingdom. However, the anti-enterprise culture identified by the Radical Right as yet another 'poison' extends far beyond the confines of the organised labour movement to all corners of the British state, including the House of Lords. The enterprise spirit as the driving force within Britain's social structure of accumulation departed her shores long ago for greener pastures around the globe, especially to the independent and republican United States of America, Thatcher's favourite exemplar in her vision of a Brave New Britain.

To repeat an earlier point, the British state is *semi-capitalist* in character but dismantling the panoply of public sector institutions which have evolved since the second world war is simply scratching the surface of the problem. Even turning the clock back to 1799 by reintroducing the Combination Acts would hardly guarantee the resurgence of virile free enterprise. The majority of the British populace is neither materially nor morally equipped to 'start up on their own' and never has been. As Watkins remarked in objecting to Thatcherism:

> the truth is that we do not want either to work very hard or to become very rich. Both attitudes, singly or in conjunction, are not only defensible but rational. Most people's work is boring and, however hard they do it, they are unlikely to acquire any great wealth thereby. In any case, wealth is often more trouble than it is worth and is no guarantor of personal happiness and physical or mental well-being. Nor, contrary to what the worldly-wise often assert, can these desirable states be purchased for cash on the open market. (*Observer*, 3 March, 1985)

On the other hand, just because the strength of anti-bourgeois forces may be sufficient to negate Thatcherism, this does not imply, of course, that these forces constitute a positive basis for the achievement of socialist transformation. Yet Thatcherism's abandonment of social consensus in principle not only strikes at familiar targets like labour market rigidity but threatens also the stability of the entire British establishment, that is the anachronistic structural formation based upon the Crown-in-Parliament. What Thatcherism ultimately implies, therefore, is a confrontation against structural rigidities evident *at all levels* within the British state, but such a strategy is bound to expose starkly the innate contradiction between the individual as public citizen and the individual as the possessor of private property. At an abstract level, Thatcherism is serving to separate rather than unite the needs of individual freedom as against the realization of individualism in societal form. It is a moot point whether the British establishment is willing to risk further the magnification of this irreconcilable dilemma.

Finally, it is worth reflecting briefly upon Thatcherism's ideological impact and its apparent success 'in constructing a new hegemonic project and mobilising popular support for a right wing solution to the economic and political crisis' (Jessop and others, 1984, p. 32). Whereas fair-minded people may be conscious of the irrationality of Thatcher's ideological platform, resting as it does 'more on revelation than research, more on ideographs than history' (Middlemass, 1983, p. 8) it is clear that a form of cultural counter-revolution constitutes an integral component of the Thatcherite project. A variety of often contradictory individualistic creeds have been utilised to legitimise Thatcher's programme. The simple truths 'of glorified grocery-shop morality and book-keeping' (Lawrence, 1980, p. 154) have furnished an effective form of propaganda to disseminate through the electronic and news-paper tabloid media into the British nuclear family's collective spirit of hope and despair. The reduction of complex human issues into the lowest common denominator of the atomistic individual has been translated into a sophisticated mass-marketing technique.

Taking a lead from the Moral Majority in the United States, the Conservative Party achieved electoral success in 1983 by a down-market exploitation of the unfulfilled material aspirations of the conservative, 'upwardly mobile' segment of the electorate previously regarded as the province of the Left. Aided by the disintegration of the Official Opposition in the wake of the 1979 General Election and the impact of altered electoral boundary-lines, the 'Marketing of Margaret' (see BBC1, 1983) provoked a junk reaction in the British electorate sufficient to provide a continued cloak of decency exterior to the Thatcher regime. Hence, Thatcherism's short-run charismatic success in exploiting the cult of the individual and the myth of personality. The spurious reproduction of individualist myths has thus affected the stream of mass consciousness in much the same way as music industry hype. Repeated often enough, the chapter and verse of free market gobbledygook permeates individual awareness as insidiously as an ephemeral pop song. For all that, the image of undiluted freedom and the existential reality of elective dictatorship has opened a yawning gap between individual initiative and political control which even the most professional of marketing techniques will be hard put to bridge.

In similar vein, conventional endeavours by mainstream economists to criticise the Thatcher strategy—epitomised by the letter of discontent signed by 364 professional economists—have amounted to little more than a proselyte murmur from the gallery. Whereas there are sufficient logically correct grounds for dismissing the ideological basis of Thatcherism as intellectual nonsense and for asserting that Thatcherite policy has exacerbated Britain's economic decline, it has to be admitted that reformist criticism has been wiped off the board. After all, Keynes himself so destroyed the logical basis of free-market economies as to discredit its latest recrudescence on purely *intellectual* grounds. The success of the pharisee reaction in reconstructing the edifice of economic deceit merely questions Keynes' unswerving faith in the supremacy of ideas over the material power of vested interest. Far more applicable to the Thatcherite era is the concept of the concrete jungle where 'the success of particular conceptual machineries is related to the power possessed by those who operate them. He/she who has the bigger stick has the better chance of imposing his/her definitions of reality' (Berger and Luckmann, 1971, p. 126–7). Free-market economics is but a thin ideological veil covering the true nature of the capitalist beast.

CONCLUDING REMARKS

The Thatcherite pursuit of 'responsible' policies of economic adjustment since 1979 has served simply to sharpen the irreconcilable contradiction between the rationalising needs of decentralised capital and the realisation problem for capital-in-general. Put another way, the current crisis is an intensification of the interwar impasse, with an added dimension of inflationary chaos on top of the familiar structural deficiency of over-accumulation. In addition, the increased internationalisation of capital since the second world war has destroyed the possibility of creating the ideal conditions for the realization of capitalism in one country, never mind socialism in the same. The 'popular reality' of privatisation and denationalisation with everyone earning their way on their own merits bringing about 'wealth to the many not just to the few' (Thatcher, *BBC2*, 20 February 1985) is but an article of blind faith in the potency of the capitalist phoenix. Lest anyone doubt the lunacy of 'the miraculous (*sic*) computer of the market', consider the following:

if only the politicians would abolish the costs imposed upon the private sector by regulations and tackle the powers of trade unions to fix labour prices, I *believe* that the market would absorb everyone. (Clarke, *Channel 4*, 21 February 1985; emphasis added)

What could be clearer than that?

Thatcher would benefit from taking a tour around the lowly council estates of the United Kingdom. Take Holmewood in Bradford as an instance. Here, in the long hot summer of 1984, over 250 cases of dysentery among poor whites were reported to the local health official. Or she might care to visit one of the many miner's welfare soup kitchens anywhere in the UK. There she will discover a practical example of the Thatcherite virtues of self-help, discipline, thrift, hard work, responsibility, initiative and the voluntary spirit all working towards the creation of the common good. Then she can ask herself: 'Is Thatcherism consciously inspired by the belief and practice of freedom, disciplined by morality, under a law perceived to be just?'

> Margaret Thatcher knows there is no spiritual peacetime. Life is a constant battle between good and evil in which neutrality serves only Satan. She has restored our faith in ourselves and in an Absolute Standard beyond ourselves.
>
> Elizabeth Cottrell, *The Guardian*,
> 9 October 1984

> O Lord God when thou givest to thy servants to endeavour any great matters, grant us to know that it is not the beginning but the continuing of the same until it be thoroughly finished which yieldeth the true glory.
>
> The Prime Minister,
> 20 February 1985.

> The City of God can never be achieved on Earth; attempts to do so lead us to Hell, rather than Heaven, on earth.
>
> David Dunelm
> 28 February 1985

NOTES

1. For reference, the six poisons identified by Sir Keith Joseph as 'standing' between a society and full employment and rising standards of living' are excessive government spending, high direct taxation, egalitarianism, excessive nationalisation, an anti-enterprise culture and a political trade union movement (quoted in Donaldson, 1985, p. 194).
2. According to strict monetarist principles, increases in the money supply emanate solely from the level of public borrowing derived from the banks so that a rise in the interest rate reflects an admission that private borrowing can also contribute to money supply growth.

Suggestions for Further Reading

In addition to the material collected here, you will find arguments on Britain's decline surveyed extremely well in Andrew Gamble, *Britain in Decline* (Macmillan, 1981), F. Blackaby (ed.), *De-Industrialisation* (Heinemann, 1979), and W. Beckerman (ed.), *Slow Growth in Britain: causes and consequences* (Heinemann, 1980). You might consult too J. Eatwell *Whatever Happened to Britain?* (Duckworth, 1982), and K. Williams *et al.*, *Why are the British bad a manufacturing?* (Routledge & Kegan Paul, 1983). Other relevant texts include R.E. Caves and L.B. Krause (eds.), *Britain's Economic Performance* (Washington, Brookings Institute, 1980), G. Roderick and M. Stephens (eds.), *The British Malaise* (Falmer Press, 1982), R. Dahrendorf *On Britain* (BBC, 1982) and J. Bellini *Rule Britannia* (Cape, 1981). Two important Marxist pieces too large to include here are D. Purdy, 'British capitalism since the war', *Marxism Today* (September and October 1976), and P. Anderson, 'Origins of the present crisis', *New Left Review*, 23, (January–February 1964).

Bibliography

Aaronovitch, S. (1981a), 'The relative decline of the UK', in Aaronovitch *et al.*, 1981.

Aaronovitch, S. (1981b), *The Road from Thatcherism. The Alternative Economic Strategy*, London, Lawrence & Wichart.

Aaronovitch, S., Smith, R., Gardiner, J. and Moore, R., (1981), *The Political Economy of British Capitalism, a Marxist Analysis*, London, McGraw Hill.

Aldcroft, D.H. and Fearon, P. (eds) (1969), *Economic Growth in 20th Century Britain*, London, Macmillan.

Allinson, L. (1978), 'The English cultural movement', *New Society* 16 March.

Anderson, P. (1964), 'Origins of the present crisis', *New Left Review* 23 (January–February).

Ashley, W.J. (1914), *The Economic Organisation of England*, Oxford.

Bank of England (1976), *Bank of England Quarterly Bulletin*, June.

Bank of England (1977), *Bank of England Quarterly Bulletin*, June.

Barnett, C. (1963), *The Swordbearers*, London.

Barnett, C. (1975), 'Obsolescence—and Dr Arnold', *Sunday Telegraph*, 26 January.

Beckerman, W. (1965), *The British Economy in 1975*, Cambridge, The National Institute of Economic and Social Research and Cambridge University Press.

Beckerman, W. (ed.) (1980), *Slow Growth in Britain*, London, Heinemann.

Berger, P. and Luckmann, T. (1971), *The Social Construction of Reality*, London, Allen Lane.

Blackaby, F. (ed.) (1979), *British Economic Policy 1960–74: Demand Management*, Cambridge, Cambridge University Press.

Blackaby, F. (ed.) (1979), *De-industrialisation*, London, National Institute of Economic and Social Research and Heinemann.

Blake, D. and Ormerod, P. (eds.) (1980), *The Economics of Prosperity*, London, Grand McIntyre.

Blank, S. (1977), 'Britain: the problem of pluralistic stagnation', *International Organisation*, vol. 31(4).

Blume, M.E. (1980), 'The financial markets', in Caves and Krause, 1980.

Brown, C.V. and Levin, E. (1974), 'The effects of taxation on overtime: the results of a national survey', *Economic Journal*, December.

Brown, C.J.F. and Sheriff, T.D. (1979), 'De-industrialisation: a background paper', in Blackaby, 1979.

Cambridge Political Economy Group (1974), *Britain's Economic Crisis*, Nottingham, Spokesman.

Caves, R.E. (1980), 'Productivity differences among industries' in Caves and Krause, 1980.

Caves, R.E. and Krause, L.B. (eds.) (1980), *Britain's Economic Performance*, Washington D.C., The Brookings Institution.

Clarke, P. (1985), Diverse Reports, *Channel 4*, London.

Cmnd. 7937 (1980), *Committee to Review the Functioning of Financial Institutions*, Report, London, HMSO.

Coates, D. (1983), 'The character and origin of Britain's economic decline', in Coates and Johnson, *Socialist Strategies* Oxford, Martin Robertson.

Coates, K. (1979), *What Went Wrong*, Nottingham, Spokesman.

Cornwall, J. (1977), *Modern Capitalism, Its Growth and Transformation*, Oxford, Martin Robertson.

Cripps, T.F. and Godley, W.A.H. (1978), 'Control of imports as a means to full employment and the expansion of world trade: the UK's case', *Cambridge Journal of Economics* (2).

Cripps, T.F. and Tarling, R.J. (1973), *Growth in Advanced Capitalist Economies 1950–1970*, Cambridge, Cambridge University Press.

Crouch, C. (ed.) (1979), *State and Economy in Contemporary Capitalism*, London, Croom Helm.

Currie, D. and Smith, R.P. (1981), 'Economic trends and the crisis in the UK economy', in *Socialist Economic Review*, London, Merlin Press.

Dahrendorf, R. (1976), 'Europe—some are more equal', *Listener*, 14 October.

Dicey, A.V. (1963), *Law and Public Opinion in England* (new edition, London, Macmillan).

Donaldson, P. (1985), *A Question of Economics*, London, Penguin.

Drucker, P. (1969), *The Age of Discontinuity*, London.

Eatwell, J. (1982), *Whatever Happened to Britain?*, London, Duckworth and BBC.

Economic Trends, August 1977.

Elbaum, B. and Wilkinson, F. (1979), 'Industrial relations and uneven development', *Cambridge Journal of Economics*, September.

Elson, D., 'Discussion: economic trends and crisis', in D. Currie and R. Smith, 1981.

Feldsten, M.S. and Fleming, J.S. (1971), 'Tax policy, corporate saving and investment behaviour in Britain', *Review of Economic Studies*, October.

Fetherston, Martin, Moore, B. and Rhodes, J. (1977), 'Manufacturing export shares and cost competitiveness of advanced industrial countries', in *Economic Policy Review*, no. 3, Cambridge University, Department of Applied Economics, Cambridge, March, pp. 62–70.

Fores, M. (1971), 'Britain's economic growth and the 1870 watershed', *Lloyds Bank Review*, 99.

Frankel, J. (1975), *British Foreign Policy 1945–1973*, London, Oxford University Press.

Friedman, A.L. (1977), *Industry and Labour*, London, Macmillan.

Friedman, M. (1968), 'The role of monetary policy', *American Economic Review*, vol. LVIII, March.

Gaffikin, F., and Nickson, A. (1985), *Jobs Crisis and the Multinationals: deindustrialisation in the West Midlands*, Birmingham, Birmingham TURC Ltd.

Gamble, A., 1981, *Britain in Decline*, London, Macmillan.

Glyn, A. and Harrison, J. (1980), *The British Economic Disaster*, London, Pluto Press.

Glyn, A. and Sutcliffe, B. (1972), *British Capitalism, Workers and the Profits Squeeze*, London, Penguin Books.

Heclo, H. and Wildavsky, A. (1974), *The Private Government of Public Money*, Berkeley, Univesity of California Press.

Henderson, P.D. (ed.) (1966), *Economic Growth in Britain*, London, Wiedenfeld and Nicolson.

Hobsbawm, E.J. (1968), *Industry and Empire*, New York, Panthton Books.

Hodgson, G. (1981), *Labour at the Crossroads*, London, Martin Robertson.

Holland, S. (1975), *The Socialist Challenge*, London, Quartet Books.

Hoskyns, Sir John (1985), This Week, Next Week, *BBC1*, London.

Jay, P. (1976), *Employment, Inflation and Politics*, IEA.

Jessop, B. *et al.* (1984), 'Authoritarian Populism, Two Nations and Thatcherism', *New Left Review*, 147, London.

Jessop, R. (1980), 'The transformation of the state in post-war Britain', in Scase, 1980.

Joseph, Sir Keith, (1975), 'Is Beckerman among the sociologists?', *New Statesman*, 18 April.

Junankar, P.N. (1970), 'The relationship between investment and spare capacity in the UK 1957–1966', *Economica*, August.

Kaldor, N. (1966), *Causes of the Slow Rate of Growth of the United Kingdom*, Cambridge, Cambridge University Press.

Kaldor, N. (1968), 'Productivity and growth in manufacturing: a reply'. *Economica*, November.

Kaldor, N. (1975), 'Economic growth and the Verdoorn law: a

comment on Mr. Rowthorn's article', *Economic Journal*, December.

Kaldor, N. (1979), 'Comment', in Blackaby, 1979.

Kaldor, N. (1980), 'Monetarism and UK monetary policy', *Cambridge Journal of Economics*, December.

Kay, J. and King, M. (1978), *The British Tax System*, Oxford University Press.

Kern, D. (1978), 'An international comparison of major economic trends', *National Westminster Bank Quarterly Review*, May.

Kilpatrick, A. and Lawson, T. (1980), 'On the nature of industrial decline in the UK', *Cambridge Journal of Economics*, March.

Kindleberger, C. (1964), *Economic Growth in France and Britain 1851–1950*, Cambridge.

King, M.A. (1975), 'The United Kingdom profits crisis: myth or reality?', *Economic Journal*, March.

Krainer, R.E. (1967), 'Resource endowment and the structure of foreign investment', *The Journal of Finance*, March.

Labour Party (1976), *Banking and Finance*, London.

Labour Research (1981), London.

Lawrence, D.H. (1981), *Apocalypse and the writings on Revalation*, Cambridge, Cambridge University Press.

Layard, P.R.G. *et al.* (1971), *Qualified Manpower and Economic Performance*, London.

Lewis, W.A. (1955), *The Theory of Economic Growth*, London.

Lewis, W.A. (1967), *The Deceleration of British Growth 1873–1913* Princeton, NJ. (mimeo).

London CSE Group (1980), *The Alternative Economic Strategy, a Labour Movement Response to the Crisis*, London CSE Books and Labour Co-ordinating Committee.

Longstreth, F. (1979), 'The City, industry and state', in Crouch, 1979.

McClelland, D.C. (1961), *The Achieving Society*, New York.

McCloskey, D. (1970), 'Did Victorian Britain fail?', *Economic History Review*, vol. 213.

McCloskey, D. (ed.) (1971), *Essays on a Mature Economy: Britain since 1840*, London.

Macmillan, H. (1975), 'Oxford remembered', *The Times*, 18 October.

Maddison, A. (1964), *Economic Growth in the West*, London Geroge Allen & Unwin.

Maddison, A. (1977), 'Phases of capitalist development', *Banca Nazionale del Lavore Quarterly Review*, June.

Maddison, A. (1980), 'Western economic performance in the 1970s: a perspective and assessment', *Banca Nazionale del Lavore Quarterly Review*, September.

Mandel, E. (1975), *Late Capitalism*, London, New Left Books.

Marris, P. (1974), *Loss and Change*, New York.

Mathias, P. (1969), *The First Industrial Nation*, London.

Matthews, R. and King, M. (1977), 'The regeneration of manufacturing industry', *Midland Bank Review*.

Middlemass, K. (1983), 'The Supremacy of Party', *New Statesman*, 10 June.

Mizoguchi, T. (1968), 'On the high personal saving ratio in Japan', *Hitotsubachi Journal of Economics*, vol. 8, February.

Myrdal, G. (1968), *Asian Drama*, New York.

Nairn, T. (1977), *The Break Up of Britain*, London, New Left Books.

NEDO (1976), *Cyclical Fluctuations in the UK*, London, HMSO.

NEDO (1977), *International Price Competitiveness, Non-price Factors and Export Performance*, London.

Nobay, A.R. (1970), 'Forecasting manufacturing investment—some preliminary results', *National Institute Economic Review*, May.

OECD (1970), *The Growth of Output 1960–1980*, Paris, OECD.

OECD (1978), *Economic Survey: United Kingdom: 1978*, Paris, March.

Panić, M. (1975), 'Why the UK propensity to import is high', *Lloyds Bank Review*, January.

Panić, M. and Rajan, A.H. (1971), 'Product changes in industrial countries trade 1955–1968', NEDO Monograph no. 2.

Panić, M. and Vernon, K. (1975), 'Major factors behind investment decisions in British manufacturing industry', *Oxford Bulletin of Economics and Statistics*, August.

Payne, P.L. (1978), 'Industrial entrepreneurship and management in Great Britain', in P. Mathias and M. Postan, (eds), Cambridge, Cambridge University Press.

Peck, M.J. (1968),'Science and technology', in R.E. Caves *et al.*, *Britain's Economic Prospects*, Washington, Brookings Institution.

Penn, R. (1978), *Skilled Manual Workers in the Labour Process*, unpublished, Nuffield College.

Phelps-Brown, H. (1977), 'What is the British predicament?', *Three Banks Review*, December.

Pillay, V. (1981), 'The international economic crisis', in *Socialist Economic Review 1981*, Merlin Press, London.

Posner, M. (ed.), (1978), *Demand Management*, Economic Policy Papers 1, National Institute of Economic and Social Research, Heinemann.

Pratten, C.F. (1975), *Labour Productivity Differentials within International Companies*, University of Cambridge, Department of Applied Economics, Occasional Paper 50, Cambridge University Press.

Pratten, C.F. (1977), 'The efficiency of British industry', *Lloyds Bank Review*, January.

Pratten, C.F. and Atkinson, A.G. (1976), 'The use of manpower in British manufacturing', *Department of Employment Gazette*, June.

Purdy, D. (1976), 'British capitalism since the war. Part 1—Origin of the crisis: Part 2—Decline and prospects', *Marxism Today*, September and October.

Purdy, D. (1980), 'The Left's alternative economic strategy', in B.

Hindess *et al.*, *Politics and Power 1*, London, Routledge & Kegan Paul.

Rostow, W.W. (1960), *The Process of Economic Growth*, New York.

Rowthorn, R.E. (1975), 'What remains of Kaldor's law', *Economic Journal*, March.

Rowthorn, R.E. (1975), 'A reply to Lord Kaldor's comment', *Economic Journal*, December.

Rowthorn, R.E. (1980), *Capitalism, Conflict and Inflation, Essays in Political Economy*, London, Lawrence & Wishart.

Rubenstein, W.D. (1977), 'Wealth, élites and the class structure of modern Britain', *Past and Present*, vol. 76.

Saville, J. (1970), 'The development of British industry and foreign competition 1875–1914', *Business History*, vol. 12.

Scase, R. (ed.) (1980), *The State in Western Europe*, London, Croom Helm.

Schumpeter, J. (1978), *Capitalism, Socialism and Democracy*, London, Unwin.

Seebohm, Lord (1975), 'The investment crisis in industry', Ernest Sykes Memorial Lecture.

Shonfield, A. (1965), *Modern Capitalism*, Oxford, Oxford University Press.

Simons, H.C. (1948), 'Some reflections on syndicalism', in *Economic Policy for a Free Society*, Chicago University Press.

Singh, A. (1977), 'UK industry and the world economy: a case of de-industrialization', *Cambridge Journal of Economics*, June.

Smyth, D.J. and Briscoe, G., (1969), 'Investment plans and realizations in UK manufacturing', *Economica*, August.

Currie, D. and Smith, R. (eds.) (1981), *Socialist Economic Review*, London, Merlin Press.

Stafford, G.B. (1981), *The End of Economic Growth?* Oxford, Martin Robertson.

Strange, S. (1971), *Sterling and British Policy*, London, Oxford University Press.

Supple, B. (ed.) (1963), *The Experience of Economic Growth*, New York, Random House.

Thirlwall, A.P. (1980), *Balance of Payments Theory and the United Kingdom Experience*, London, Macmillan.

Thompson, A.W.J. and Hunter, L.C. (1978), 'Great Britain', in J.T. Dunlop and W. Galenson (eds), *Labour in the Twentieth Century*, New York, Academic Press.

Treasury (1984), *Economic Progress Report*, London, HMSO.

TUC (1979), *Employment and Technology*, London, TUC.

Ward, T. (1981), 'The case for an import control strategy in the UK' in *Socialist Economic Review 1981*, London, Merlin Press.

Whiting, A. (1976), 'An international comparison of the instability of economic growth', *Three Banks Review*, March.

Wilson, T. (1969), 'Instability and growth: an international comparison', in Aldcroft and Fearon (1969).

Woodward, V. (1976), *Government Policy and the Structure of the Economy*, Cambridge, DAE (mimeo)

Worsthorne, P. (1977), 'Who's left, What's Right?' *Encounter*, March.

Yaffe, D. (1973), 'The crisis of profitability: critique of the Glyn–Sutcliffe thesis', *New Left Review*, no. 80, July–August.

Younger, K. (1964), *Changing Perspectives in British Foreign Policy*, London, Oxford University Press.

Index of Names

Index of Subjects